GREEKS AND ROMANS ON THE LATIN AMERICAN STAGE

Studies in Classical Reception

Bloomsbury Studies in Classical Reception presents scholarly monographs offering new and innovative research and debate to students and scholars in the reception of Classical Studies. Each volume will explore the appropriation, reconceptualization and recontextualization of various aspects of the Graeco-Roman world and its culture, looking at the impact of the ancient world on modernity. Research will also cover reception within antiquity, the theory and practice of translation, and reception theory.

Also available in the Series:

ALEXANDER THE GREAT IN THE EARLY CHRISTIAN TRADITION: CLASSICAL RECEPTION AND PATRISTIC LITERATURE
Christian Thrue Djurslev

ANCIENT MAGIC AND THE SUPERNATURAL IN THE MODERN VISUAL AND PERFORMING ARTS
edited by Filippo Carlà & Irene Berti

ANCIENT GREEK MYTH IN WORLD FICTION SINCE 1989
edited by Justine McConnell & Edith Hall

ANTIPODEAN ANTIQUITIES
edited by Marguerite Johnson

CLASSICS IN EXTREMIS
edited by Edmund Richardson

FRANKENSTEIN AND ITS CLASSICS
edited by Jesse Weiner, Benjamin Eldon Stevens & Brett M. Rogers

GREEK AND ROMAN CLASSICS IN THE BRITISH STRUGGLE FOR SOCIAL REFORM
edited by Henry Stead & Edith Hall

HOMER'S ILIAD AND THE TROJAN WAR: DIALOGUES ON TRADITION
Jan Haywood & Naoíse Mac Sweeney

IMAGINING XERXES
Emma Bridges

JULIUS CAESAR'S SELF-CREATED IMAGE AND ITS DRAMATIC AFTERLIFE
Miryana Dimitrova

ONCE AND FUTURE ANTIQUITIES IN SCIENCE FICTION AND FANTASY
edited by Brett M. Rogers & Benjamin Eldon Stevens

OVID'S MYTH OF PYGMALION ON SCREEN
Paula James

READING POETRY, WRITING GENRE
edited by Silvio Bär & Emily Hauser

SEX, SYMBOLISTS AND THE GREEK BODY
Richard Warren

THE CODEX FORI MUSSOLINI
Han Lamers and Bettina Reitz-Joosse

THE CLASSICS IN MODERNIST TRANSLATION
edited by Miranda Hickman and Lynn Kozak

THE GENTLE, JEALOUS GOD
Simon Perris

TRANSLATIONS OF GREEK TRAGEDY IN THE WORK OF EZRA POUND
Peter Liebregts

VICTORIAN CLASSICAL BURLESQUES
Laura Monrós-Gaspar

VICTORIAN EPIC BURLESQUES
Rachel Bryant Davies

GREEKS AND ROMANS ON THE LATIN AMERICAN STAGE

Edited by
Rosa Andújar and Konstantinos P. Nikoloutsos

BLOOMSBURY ACADEMIC
LONDON • NEW YORK • OXFORD • NEW DELHI • SYDNEY

BLOOMSBURY ACADEMIC
Bloomsbury Publishing Plc
50 Bedford Square, London, WC1B 3DP, UK
1385 Broadway, New York, NY 10018, USA
29 Earlsfort Terrace, Dublin 2, Ireland

BLOOMSBURY, BLOOMSBURY ACADEMIC and the Diana logo
are trademarks of Bloomsbury Publishing Plc

First published in Great Britain 2020
Paperback edition first published 2021

Copyright © Rosa Andújar, Konstantinos P. Nikoloutsos and Contributors, 2020

Rosa Andújar and Konstantinos P. Nikoloutsos have asserted their right under the Copyright,
Designs and Patents Act, 1988, to be identified as Editors of this work.

For legal purposes the Acknowledgements on p. xiii constitute
an extension of this copyright page.

Cover design: Terry Woodley
Cover image © Hemis / Alamy Stock Photo

All rights reserved. No part of this publication may be reproduced or
transmitted in any form or by any means, electronic or mechanical,
including photocopying, recording, or any information storage or retrieval
system, without prior permission in writing from the publishers.

Bloomsbury Publishing Plc does not have any control over, or responsibility for,
any third-party websites referred to or in this book. All internet addresses given
in this book were correct at the time of going to press. The author and publisher
regret any inconvenience caused if addresses have changed or sites have
ceased to exist, but can accept no responsibility for any such changes.

A catalogue record for this book is available from the British Library.

Library of Congress Cataloging-in-Publication Data
Names: Andu´jar, Rosa, editor. | Nikoloutsos, Konstantinos P., editor.
Title: Greeks and Romans on the Latin American stage / edited by Rosa
Andu´jar, Konstantinos P. Nikoloutsos.
Description: London; New York: Bloomsbury Academic, 2020. | Series: Bloomsbury studies in classical reception |
Selected revised papers presented at a conference, Greeks and Romans on the Latin American stage, in June, 2014,
at the University College, London. | Includes bibliographical references and index. | Summary: "The first comprehensive
treatment in English of the rich and varied afterlife of classical drama across Latin America, this volume explores the
myriad ways in which ancient Greek and Roman texts have been adapted, invoked and re-worked in notable modern
theatrical works across North and South America and the Caribbean, while also paying particular attention to the
national and local context of each play. A comprehensive introduction provides a critical overview of the varying issues
and complexities that arise when studying the afterlife of the European classics in the theatrical stages across this diverse
and vast region. Fourteen chapters, divided into three general geographical sub-regions (Southern Cone, Brazil and the
Caribbean and North America) present a strong connection to an ancient dramatic source text as well as comment
upon important socio-political crises in the modern history of Latin America. The diversity and expertise of the voices in
this volume translate into a multi-ranging approach to the topic that encompasses a variety of theoretical and interdisciplinary
perspectives from classics, Latin American studies and theatre and performance studies"– Provided by publisher.
Identifiers: LCCN 2019039210 (print) | LCCN 2019039211 (ebook) | ISBN 9781350125612 (hardback) |
ISBN 9781350125629 (ebook) | ISBN 9781350125636 (epub)
Subjects: LCSH: Spanish American drama–20th century–History and criticism–Congresses. |
Spanish American drama–Classical influences–Congresses. | Caribbean literature 20th century–History and
criticism–Congresses. | Caribbean literature–Classical influences–Congresses. |
Classical drama–Adaptations–History an criticism–Congresses. | Classical drama–Appreciation–Latin
America–Congresses. | Classical drama–Appreciation–Caribbean Area–Congresses. | Theater–Latin
America–History–20th century–Congresses. | Theater–Caribbean Area–History–20th century–Congresses.
Classification: LCC PQ7082.D7 G74 2020 (print) | LCC PQ7082.D7 (ebook) | DDC 862/.00998–dc23
LC record available at https://lccn.loc.gov/2019039210
LC ebook record available at https://lccn.loc.gov/2019039211

ISBN: HB: 978-1-3501-2561-2
PB: 978-1-3501-9388-8
ePDF: 978-1-3501-2562-9
eBook: 978-1-3501-2563-6

Series: Bloomsbury Studies in Classical Reception

Typeset by RefineCatch Limited, Bungay, Suffolk

To find out more about our authors and books visit
www.bloomsbury.com and sign up for our newsletters.

CONTENTS

List of Illustrations   ix
Notes on Contributors   x
Acknowledgements   xiii

1 Staging the European Classical in 'Latin' America: An Introduction
   Rosa Andújar and Konstantinos P. Nikoloutsos   1

Part I   Southern Cone

2 From Epic to Tragedy: Theatre and Politics in Juan Cruz Varela's
   Dido   *Konstantinos P. Nikoloutsos*   19

3 Leopoldo Marechal's *Antígona Vélez*: Rewriting Greek Tragedy as a
   Foundation Myth in Peronist Argentina   *Brenda López Saiz*   33

4 Juan Radrigán's *Medea Mapuche*: Recreating Euripides' Revenge
   Tragedy in an Indigenous Chilean Context   *Irmtrud König*   47

5 Philoctetes and Medea in Contemporary Chilean Theatre
   Carolina Brncić   59

Part II   Brazil

6 *A God Slept Here* by Guilherme Figueiredo: A Radical Modernist
   Amphitruo from Brazil   *Rodrigo Tadeu Gonçalves*   75

7 Guilherme Figueiredo, Amphitryon and the Widow of Ephesus:
   Linking Plautus and Petronius   *Tiziana Ragno*   89

8 Electra's Turn to the Dark Side: Nelson Rodrigues' *Senhora dos
   Afogados*   *Anastasia Bakogianni*   101

9 Becoming Antigone: The Classics as a Model of Resistance in
   Jorge Andrade's *Pedreira das Almas*   *Seth A. Jeppesen*   115

Part III   The Caribbean and North America

10 Distorting the *Lysistrata* Paradigm in Puerto Rico: Francisco Arriví's
   Club de Solteros   *Rosa Andújar*   131

11 Challenging the Canon in the Dominican Republic: *Lisístrata odia
   la política* by Franklin Domínguez   *Katherine Ford*   145

Contents

12 Aeschylus and the Cuban Counter-Revolution *Jacques A. Bromberg* **157**

13 The Contest between *Créolité* and Classics in Patrick Chamoiseau's Stage Plays *Justine McConnell* **171**

14 Dismantling the Anthropological Machine: Feliks Moriso-Lewa's *Antigòn* and Luis Alfaro's *Electricidad* *Tom Hawkins* **185**

15 Antigone Undead: Tragedy and Biopolitics in Perla de la Rosa's *Antígona: las voces que incendian el desierto* *Jesse Weiner* **199**

Notes 213
Bibliography 257
Index 285

ILLUSTRATIONS

8.1 Nelson Rodrigues' *Senhora dos Afogados*: João Valadares (Eduarda) and Sidneia Simões (Moema). Cia da Farsa Production (2015). Copyright: Alexandre Toledo. 107
8.2 Nelson Rodrigues' *Senhora dos Afogados*: The masked chorus (1954). Still from the original production. Copyright: CEDOC [Centro de Documentação e Informação da Funarte]. 110
15.1 Perla de la Rosa's *Antígona: las voces que incendian el desierto*, Scene 6. Copyright: Guadalupe de la Mora. 204

CONTRIBUTORS

Rosa Andújar is Deputy Director of Liberal Arts and Lecturer in Liberal Arts at King's College London (UK). She has published widely across two distinct but complementary areas: ancient Greek tragedy, with an emphasis on the tragic chorus, and Hellenic classicisms in Latin America. She is one of the editors of *Paths of Song: The Lyric Dimension of Greek Tragedy* (2018). Currently, she is completing two monographs: the first examining the various roles and capabilities of the fifth-century Greek tragic chorus beyond the choral ode, and the second on twentieth-century reimaginings of ancient Greek drama in the Hispanic Caribbean. With Justine McConnell, she is co-editor of the new *Classics and the Postcolonial* series at Routledge.

Anastasia Bakogianni is Lecturer in Classical Studies at Massey University (New Zealand). Her research and publications focus on the reception of Greek tragedy on stage and screen. She is author of *Electra Ancient & Modern: Aspects of the Tragic Heroine's Reception* (2011), editor of *Dialogues with the Past: Classical Reception Theory and Practice* (2013) and co-editor of *War as Spectacle: Ancient and Modern Perspectives on the Display of Armed Conflict* (2015) and *Locating Classical Receptions on Screen: Masks, Echoes, Shadows* (2018).

Carolina Brnčić is Professor in the Department of Literature at the University of Chile (Santiago, Chile). Her research interests and publications focus on modern European theatre, comparative drama and contemporary Chilean theatre. Her most recent book is *Nikos Kazantzakis: Tragedia, teúrgia e imaginación* (2018).

Jacques A. Bromberg is Assistant Professor in the Department of Classics at the University of Pittsburgh (USA). His research focuses chiefly on the intersecting intellectual and literary histories of classical Athens. He is author of numerous articles and book chapters on ancient academic disciplines, the Socratic tradition, the history and philosophy of sport, and Latin American receptions of Greek tragedy. He is a contributor to the *Brill New Jacoby* and the Digital Corpus of Literary Papyri, and he is co-editing the forthcoming *Companion to Aeschylus* for Wiley-Blackwell.

Katherine Ford is Professor of Hispanic Studies in the Department of Foreign Languages and Literatures at East Carolina University (Greenville, USA). Her research interests focus on modern Latin American literature, with an emphasis on theatre and performance of the twentieth century. She is the author of *The Theater of Revisions in the Hispanic Caribbean* (2017) and *Politics and Violence in Cuban and Argentine Theater* (2010).

Rodrigo Tadeu Gonçalves is Professor of Latin Language and Literature in the Department of German, Polish and Classics at the Federal University of Paraná (Curitiba,

Brazil). His research interests include the reception of Roman Comedy, especially Plautus, translation studies and translation as reception. A translator himself, he has published translations of Milton and Ovid, among others, and is currently preparing a full translation of Lucretius' *De Rerum Natura* into Portuguese. His most recent monograph is *Performative Plautus: Sophistics, Metatheatre and Translation* (2015).

Tom Hawkins teaches ancient Greek literature together with its ancient and modern legacies at The Ohio State University (USA). He has published extensively on comedy and iambic poetry, including *Iambic Poetics in the Roman Empire* (2014) and (co-edited with C. W. Marshall) *Athenian Comedy in the Roman Empire* (2015). He is currently working on two monographs, one treating the role of Greek and Roman material in the literary history of Haiti and the other on the role of ugly bodies in ancient Greek literature.

Seth A. Jeppesen is a professor of Classical Studies at Brigham Young University (Provo, Utah, USA). His research focuses on the performance of Greek and Roman theatre, Plautine comedy, Roman religion and the reception of Greek tragedy. Seth has recently published chapters on obscenity in Roman comedy (*Ancient Obscenities*, 2015) and lament in early Roman drama (*The Fall of Cities in the Mediterranean*, 2016).

Irmtrud König is Associate Professor in the Department of Literature at the University of Chile (Santiago, Chile). Her research interests focus on reception and comparative studies, with an emphasis on ancient Greek, European and Latin American literature. Her most recent publications include two book chapters on Aimé Césaire, published in *Memorias del silencio, Literaturas en el Caribe y en Centroamérica* (2010) and *Aimé Césaire desde América Latina: Diálogos con el poeta de la negritud* (2011).

Brenda López Saiz is Assistant Professor in the Department of Literature at the University of Chile (Santiago, Chile). Her research interests focus on ancient Greek literature, particularly tragedy, and its reception in modern times. She has published on Greek tragedy, Greek tragedy's reception in Latin American drama, and the reception of Greek and Latin epics in Latin American literature. Her most recent publications include papers in academic journals, chapters of books and the book *Nación católica y tradición clásica en obras de Leopoldo Marechal* (2016).

Justine Mᶜ Connell is Senior Lecturer in Comparative Literature at King's College London (UK). She is author of *Black Odysseys: The Homeric Odyssey in the African Diaspora since 1939* (2013) and co-editor of four volumes: *Ancient Slavery and Abolition: From Hobbes to Hollywood* (2011); *The Oxford Handbook of Greek Drama in the Americas* (2015); *Ancient Greek Myth and World Fiction since 1989* (2016); and *Epic Performances from the Middle Ages into the Twenty-First Century* (2018).

Konstantinos P. Nikoloutsos is Associate Professor in the Department of Modern and Classical Languages at Saint Joseph's University (Philadelphia, USA). His research interests include Latin elegy, gender and sexuality in Roman antiquity, and the classical tradition. He has published widely on Tibullus and the reception of ancient history and drama on the big screen and the modern stage, respectively. He is the editor of *Reception of Greek and Roman Drama in Latin America* (2012) and *Ancient Greek Women in Film* (2013).

Tiziana Ragno is Assistant Professor of Latin Literature at the University of Foggia (Italy). Her teaching interests include the reception of Latin literature, culture in the Roman-Barbarian age and Roman education. Her research focuses on Petronius' *Satyrica* and the afterlife of Latin authors and themes. Her most recent publication is a chapter on Petronius' *Troiae Halosis* in *Re-wiring the Ancient Novel* (2018).

Jesse Weiner is Assistant Professor of Classics at Hamilton College (USA). He publishes broadly on Greek and Latin literature and its reception, with special interests in monumentality and memory, sexuality and gender, and aesthetics. In public humanities, his work has appeared in *History Today* and *The Atlantic*. He is co-editor of *Frankenstein and Its Classics: The Modern Prometheus from Antiquity to Science Fiction* (2018).

ACKNOWLEDGEMENTS

This volume stems from an international conference with the same title held at University College London in June 2014. It was sponsored by the A. G. Leventis Foundation (UCL Leventis Fund), the Institute of Classical Studies, the Institute of Latin American Studies, the Society for the Promotion of Hellenic Studies, the Society for Latin American Studies, the Classical Association and the Gilbert Murray Trust. The conference, held over three days, featured thirty-one speakers and chairs from eight countries across Europe and North and South America, representing a variety of disciplines, including Classics, Hispanic Literatures, Latin American Studies and Theatre Studies.

Of the twenty-three papers that were presented at the above event, thirteen appear in this volume in reworked and expanded versions. A paper which was not read at the conference is also included. We would like to thank the contributors to this volume for their patience during the peer-review process for publication, as well as the anonymous readers for their generous feedback and helpful comments which much improved this volume. We would also like to thank the Dean of the College of Arts and Sciences at Saint Joseph's University for providing the funds to cover the cost of the index. Additional thanks by contributors can be found in the notes of their respective chapters.

CHAPTER 1
STAGING THE EUROPEAN CLASSICAL IN 'LATIN' AMERICA: AN INTRODUCTION
Rosa Andújar and Konstantinos P. Nikoloutsos

This volume explores the rich and varied afterlife of Greek and Roman tragedies and comedies in Latin America, offering nuanced examinations of notable theatrical adaptations of ancient drama from ten countries across this diverse region. Though scholars have now examined the afterlife of the genre in various continents,[1] and in a variety of colonial and postcolonial contexts,[2] Latin America remains a relatively unexplored territory for scholars of classical reception and drama,[3] despite the fact that Latin American playwrights have repeatedly engaged with their Greek and Roman forebears. Especially in the past few decades, the region has seen a number of pioneering theatrical adaptations of ancient drama that address the turbulence of the twentieth century and the dilemmas of present-day realities. These adaptations, unknown even as titles to many in the Global North, are analysed as a body of literature in English for the first time in the present volume.

Since many of our readers might not be familiar with Latin American material, our introduction is structured in four parts, which, besides explaining the aims and scope of our project, summarizes the particular issues and complexities involved in examining receptions from the region. The first and second sections outline critical issues involved in employing the terms 'Latin American' and 'postcolonial', respectively, labels which, though useful for enabling a study on a large-scale and wider level, nevertheless mask a series of particular problems unique to the region which continue to resonate today. These problems are furthermore compounded in an examination of what is essentially an 'inherited' classical tradition from European colonizers. The third section addresses the specific complexities (and ultimately the impossibility) of developing appropriate models of classical reception for this vast and 'hybrid' region, especially in light of the issues raised in the first two parts. The fourth provides a justification of the volume's specific focus on engagements with ancient drama: we provide not only a brief sketch of the history of drama in the region, but also a summary of the larger themes which have emerged from the specific case studies selected for inclusion in the volume. This introduction should moreover be of use to scholars in Spanish, Portuguese and Latin American Studies Departments. The volume supplements the relatively few studies on the topic conducted by scholars in these fields by emphasizing throughout the complex transhistorical and transnational routes and frameworks for the transmission and understanding of Graeco-Roman texts, myths and ideas in modern Latin America.[4] We believe that this broader picture, which charts both the movement and the use of the 'classical',[5] allows for a better insight of the changing value of these dramatic texts in various local contexts across the region.

'Latin' America?

In this volume we use 'Latin America' to cover the large and diverse area south of the US–Mexico border. The problematic nature of the term, which crucially includes the word *Latin*, must be acknowledged at the outset, given its associations with the long and convoluted histories of European and North American imperialisms in the region. There is currently no scholarly consensus on the term's origins: some historians, for example, argue that the French coined it to justify neo-imperialist interventions, most notably their notorious installation of the Habsburg Emperor Maximilian in Mexico during the 1860s.[6] Others have pointed out its earlier use by Central and South Americans as a rallying point for unity against the rising threat of the United States.[7] Despite a lack of clarity on the precise emergence of 'Latin America' as a concept, what is clear is the term's direct connection to various foreign imperialist missions in the nineteenth century.

The fact that the nineteenth century is the specific setting for the construction of this new regional term adds further complications to its use in a study of engagements with the European classical in the region. This is the century in which various independence and revolutionary movements emerged, movements that not only led to the establishment of the nations which exist today, but also ones which themselves were motivated by notions of Graeco-Roman antiquity.[8] This is also when some of the most visible forms of engagement with European antiquity emerge across the region, as is suggested, for example, in the erection of prominent monuments and statues in a neoclassical style in various cities.[9] In other words, this is the time when these newly independent nations constructed national identities visibly aligned with Europe, which furthermore obfuscated indigenous and African histories.[10] Using the term 'Latin America' in the context of examining classical receptions arguably continues propagating these carefully constructed identities that privilege Europe.

In addition to presenting a whitewashed European picture of the region, its use as a single category might furthermore advance North American interests. In the mid-twentieth century, US federal agencies created the category of 'Hispanic' to represent the various groups with ties to places south of the US–Mexico border, uniting in a broad-brush diverse and distinct peoples.[11] Despite its common and wide usage, it is crucial to recognize that employing this and other panethnic categories effectively advances the wishes of a particular country to lump *all* of its southern neighbours (and the majority of the Western Hemisphere) into one group.

Though we acknowledge the various problems associated with this term, we are retaining it not to endorse it, but precisely because of the problems that we have highlighted above. It also allows discussion on a macro-level, illuminating that the manner in which the region's engagements with Graeco-Roman source texts tends to differ from those of other areas. Though grouped under the term 'Latin American', our volume showcases the wide range of receptions that are possible across this region, ultimately reflecting their intense and varied complexities. Each case study nevertheless provides essential contextual information regarding the national and local context of each play, which in *all* cases is more important than a perceived – and artificial – 'Latin American' context.

Latin America and the postcolonial

Nearly all plays featured in this volume were written, produced and performed across the region after independence from their European colonizers.[12] This, however, does not mean that we are dealing with a 'postcolonial' region. Various scholars have pointed out the limitations and inadequacies of applying this particular term, which initially emerged from studies of former British and French colonies, to Latin America. Most notably, anthropologist J. Klor de Alva declared that the concepts of colonialism and postcolonialism are 'mirages' for the region.[13] His main argument hinges on the fact that the region's complex historical experience and hybrid identities led to relationships with Europe that cannot be reduced to binaries of oppressor (colonizer)/oppressed (colonized), which are typically associated with the colonial condition in places such as India, South Africa and Algeria. Since then there have been several attempts to articulate the region's 'postcoloniality' in more refined theoretical terms that address its unique specificities, such as America's conception as an extension of Europe,[14] the exact time of the postcolonial in the region (Peter Hulme asks, 'Just *when* is postcolonialism?'),[15] and the region's peripheral status.[16]

Previous work examining classical receptions in specifically postcolonial contexts has focused mostly on Asia and Africa, in keeping with the development of postcolonial theory,[17] a large majority of which formed part of the British Empire.[18] In the former British colonies, Graeco-Roman classical texts were typically part of what Goff and Simpson call 'the apparatus of colonialism', often embedded in educational curricula.[19] This means that many postcolonial engagements with the Graeco-Roman Classics in these contexts have been subversive, a case of what Salman Rushdie described as 'the empire writes back with a vengeance'.[20] The long tradition and presence of Graeco-Roman ideas, texts and motifs in these contexts facilitates a general awareness of the cultural capital of the European classical.

In Latin America, the Graeco-Roman Classics were not embedded in the colonial curriculum or experience in the same way. Instead, European antiquity was transmitted and mediated by diverse means, from various Catholic missionaries in the sixteenth and seventeenth centuries to twentieth-century artists undertaking visits to North America and Europe, via nineteenth-century engagements with French and Italian literature around the time of independence from Spain. To consider Latin America a straightforwardly 'postcolonial' region in terms of classical reception would be a mistake, as it requires a new framework which would need to account for multiple and varied transmitters of the classical, which crucially include religion as well as encounters with foreign ideas.

As a result, sub-regional and local histories matter enormously. For this reason, our volume groups case studies across three general areas: (1) Southern Cone, (2) Brazil, and (3) the Caribbean and North America. This division allows us to examine some of the most prominent sub-geographical contexts within Latin America, facilitating the analysis of themes and issues beyond specific national borders. We do not offer a comprehensive survey, which would be impossible in a single volume given the extraordinary diversity of responses to ancient drama across Latin America. Instead, we provide a broad cross-section of notable case studies from ten different countries which suggest specific histories. This division furthermore aims to address the fact that Graeco-Roman legacies throughout Latin America are largely muddled and indirect, in addition to being varied and inconsistent throughout the centuries, depending on the location in question and the European nation by which it was colonized. There is a great deal that we still do not know about how classical texts, motifs and ideas have circulated throughout the short history of the region; part of this uncovering will also involve deep engagement with the way in which these texts have circulated and been understood in the Iberian peninsula since antiquity. Certainly, there will be other intermediaries and 'fuzzy connections', to quote Lorna Hardwick,[21] emerging from this much-needed work. Nevertheless, it is possible to propose some general observations about the ways in which the European Classics circulated across the some of the general blocks that make up 'Latin America', which roughly correspond to our division:

1. In Spanish Latin America, the Graeco-Roman Classics have a fragmentary afterlife, one that is incredibly difficult to piece together. Though the Spanish used the ancient past as a way to frame and justify their conquest of the Americas,[22] and despite the presence of a few neo-Latin epics composed in the New World (which were written by Spanish- or Italian-born Jesuit missionaries rather than any native-born men),[23] Spanish-American colonial classicisms tend to be overwhelmingly Latin, and generally connected to or mediated through the Catholic Church and its various orders (e.g. Jesuits, Franciscans).[24] It was the Catholic Church and not the Spanish crown which invested time and energy in controlling the educational framework of the new colonies (see e.g. the various 'Pontifical' universities established in the colonial period across the region). To reckon with the large-scale reception history of the European classical in the region, one must engage with the complicated history of the Catholic Church and its presence in the 'New World', and especially the vacuum left after the Jesuits (who were the chief producers of classical engagements in the region across the colonial period) were all expelled from the region in the mid-eighteenth century.[25] French literature was also a key disseminator of the Graeco-Roman Classics from the nineteenth century onward, especially as many *criollos* (men of Spanish descent born in the Americas) began to turn to France and French culture, in efforts to achieve independence from Spain.[26] From the nineteenth century onward, contact between Europe and the region increased, with the rise of steam ships, which facilitated travel, resulting in a multiplicity of points of access to European classical and modern literature. The sources and inspirations for twentieth-century engagements likewise multiply, this time exponentially, when we think about the myriad ways in which an author/artist could be exposed to Graeco-Roman material. These later engagements can also have explicit ideological aims, particularly when linked to nation-building processes.[27]

2. Brazil has a separate reception history, given its colonization by the Portuguese,[28] leading to a more sustained engagement.[29] Partly responsible is the continual

contact between Brazil and Portugal from the colonial period onward: not only was the Portuguese royal court transferred to Rio in the early nineteenth century, but also the *first* universities across the country were not established until the 1920s, which meant that further education typically involved a trip to Europe, especially to Coimbra.[30] This is in direct contrast to the various colonial universities that are established in the sixteenth century across the Spanish Americas (e.g. Santo Domingo, Mexico City, Lima, Quito) in which intellectual communities could exist more independently from Spain.[31]

3. The Caribbean presents an entirely different, and even more fragmented, picture, given its various components and colonizers: British, Dutch, French, Spanish, even Danish. In all definitions of 'Latin America', the former British colonies are excluded. Emily Greenwood's seminal *Afro-Greeks* illustrates the distinctiveness of Anglophone Caribbean literary engagements with ancient Greece and Rome; many of the writers under scrutiny such as C. L. R. James and Derek Walcott were themselves the products of a 'colonial school curriculum' established by the British, having studied Latin and ancient history.[32] The general situation in the French islands of Martinique and Guadeloupe – Haiti would naturally be a prominent exception – appears to be the same: in Justine McConnell's discussion of Aimé Césaire, she notes that that he completed his *Cahier d'un retour au pays natal* after he 'finished his training at the École Normale Supérieure in Paris to become a teacher of French, Latin and Greek'.[33] This suggests that there had been an educational system in place in Martinique centred around the teaching of Greek and Latin which would have enabled Césaire to undertake such training abroad in the first place.[34] The educational situation in Cuba, the Dominican Republic and Puerto Rico differed. Instead, intellectuals and playwrights there encounter the European classical through a number of important intermediaries, or even from time spent abroad in North America or Europe.[35] There have been recent attempts to conceptualize the Caribbean as a single region,[36] but when it comes to classical reception, we must still rely on a fragmented view of this intensely diverse region: it matters by whom you were colonized, as classical receptions in Cuba have far more in common with other countries formerly colonized by Spain than its immediate neighbour Jamaica.

What this brief summary reveals is that local histories and contexts matter enormously. For this reason, our aim is not to capture any overarching features. The sub-regional groupings which we have adopted instead allow us to address some of these diverse histories and specificities stemming from the unique postcoloniality of the region.

Latin American receptions beyond hybridity

As intimated above, in this volume we contend that an examination of 'Latin American' receptions allows us to interrogate standard narratives currently in place and specifically those produced by investigations centred on the aftermath of British imperialisms around the world. In other words, the region, which is understood as a site of hybridity, has the potential to upend various assumptions about the manner in which the influence of the European Classics has been understood to operate. Nevertheless, a few words must be said about the perceived 'hybridity' of the region, since this might be naively understood as a static and consistent term.

Latin American cultures are syncretic, i.e. the product of the fusion between European, and/or indigenous, and/or African elements (in some places Asian). The predominant term in these conversations is 'mestizaje', which is always summarized as a process in the *singular*. Indeed, the discussions around mestizaje tend to be essentializing, as if Latin American identities were some type of homogenous hybrid, that is, an always consistently hybrid product. Antonio Cornejo Polar summarizes it best:

> El concepto de mestizaje, pese a su tradición y prestigio es el que falsifica de una manera más drástica la condición de nuestra cultura y literatura. En efecto lo que hace es ofrecer imágenes armónicas de lo que obviamente es desgajado y beligerante, proponiendo figuraciones que en el fondo solo son pertinentes a quienes conviene imaginar nuestras sociedades como tersos y nada conflictivos espacios de convivencia.[37]

> The concept of mestizaje, despite its tradition and prestige, is one which falsifies in the most drastic way the condition of our culture and literature. Effectively what it does is offer harmonious images of what is obviously severed and belligerent, proposing images which ultimately are only pertinent to those for whom it is convenient to imagine our societies as terse spaces of coexistence that are in no way troubled.[38]

In other words, if we wish to invoke this term we must be ready to acknowledge its turbulent history, and particularly the fact that hybridity/mestizaje in the region was, as Boaventura de Sousa Santos reminds us, both a product and 'key feature of Iberian colonialism'.[39] In fact, Santos' seminal *Epistemologies of the South: Justice against Epistemicide* illustrates the manner in which the founding myths of 'Nuestra América' ('Our America', i.e. the pan-Hispanic idealization that emerged in the nineteenth and early twentieth centuries which gave impetus to various revolutionary and nationalistic movements across the region) pivot precisely on the idea of Latin America's mixed roots, which produce a particular type of cultural plasticity that made Latin American civilization 'universal'.[40] Santos' examination enables him to connect Simón Bolívar's proclamations that Latin America was 'a small humankind; a miniature humankind' with José Martí's famous declaration that 'there is no race hatred because there are no races'.[41] He even links this to the Brazilian poet Oswald de Andrade's notions of 'anthropophagy' and 'cannibalism', i.e. the capacity of the Brazilian to devour and digest everything in order to produce a new complex identity.[42] Many of these notions, including Cuban ethnographer Fernando Ortíz's 'transculturation',[43] rest on similar assumptions about the static 'hybridity' that is implicitly construed as the essence of the Latin American.

There are some echoes of this Latin American hybrid (in the singular) end-product in recent classical reception scholarship that includes material from the region. For example, the *Oxford Handbook of Greek Drama in the Americas* introduces 'Omni-American' as a critical term for understanding receptions across the Western Hemisphere:

> The sea journey across the Atlantic broke bodies as much as it made the American experience whole, embodied in black, white, brown, and everything in between. Here there is no black, white, brown, high or low culture: there is only meaning newly generated and regenerated.[44]

The emphasis here, again, is on the 'American *experience*', singular. Other scholars who have treated Latin American engagements with the European classical have proposed more productive models, though these typically stem from a narrower focus emphasizing the afterlife of a particular play, or specific engagements by playwrights. Moira Fradinger's work on Antigones, for example, stresses the manner in which playwrights from Griselda Gambaro to Félix Morrisseau-Leroy 'cannibalize' Sophocles.[45] Here she explicitly takes up Oswald de Andrade's seminal concept of 'anthropophagy'/'cannibalism', mentioned above, and identifies it as a model of reception which allows for complexity and hybridity. More recently, Fradinger has additionally proposed the more nuanced model of 'rumination', as follows: 'to ruminate is to turn over and over something that has already been "ingested" (and not properly digested) physically or mentally.'[46] Like 'cannibalization', this concept supports receptions that are diverse and varied, but with a key difference: it additionally acknowledges the legacy of the European classical as a matter somehow 'internal' to the region. In both these cases, however, Fradinger emphasizes the action of individual playwrights as they engage with a specific mythical figure, Antigone, who has a particular intellectual tradition, and does not account for the larger processes that facilitated the transmission and privileging of European texts and ideas, processes which we furthermore believe are crucial to any examination of classical reception in the region. Shane Butler's 'Deep Classics' model, which takes after the geological concept of 'Deep Time', might be more fruitful for Latin American receptions since it speaks to the presence of 'thickly layered histories',[47] which correspond to our general observations above illustrating the ways in which the European Classics circulated across various contexts. Nonetheless, the strata upon which classical ideas accrete in Latin America throughout the centuries are in no way lineal, and this model does not allow for the many muddled and varied intermediaries highlighted above. Laura Jansen's recent book on Borges' classicisms also notes this problem: in a discussion of the Argentine thinker's conception of 'antiquity' and 'modernity' she acknowledges that these terms 'are parts of a deeply layered history of our culture that must be observed laterally, rather than as a palimpsest from the present "above" to the "past" hidden underneath.'[48]

Our volume, wherever possible, illustrates the various hybridities (plural) at play while interrogating the larger frameworks and motivations that enabled the choice of the classical in the first place. Instead of emphasizing a singular end-product – that is, the mythical 'hybrid' 'Latin American' or 'Omni-American' – we showcase the different ways in which playwrights adapt, cannibalize and reframe European material in various contexts and to different ends. We do not propose a single model of reception, as this would be impossible and counterproductive; instead, our case studies showcase a variety of receptions that correspond to the multiple hybridities across the region.

Why drama?

Of all ancient genres transplanted into Latin American soil, drama is the only one that continues to have a strong presence in modern times. As this volume demonstrates, from the mid-twentieth century, numerous rewritings, translations and (re-)performances have breathed new life into it, illustrating how classical antiquity can still appeal to contemporary audiences. Divided into three general geographical regions, as explained above, and arranged in a chronological manner (oldest to most recent play), the essays in this collection discuss the reception of classical drama across Latin America in a synchronic and diachronic manner, seeking to cast light on two basic questions: (1) how drama is rewritten to engage with concerns and debates of a particular time, and (2) to what extent some of these concerns and debates are transhistoric and transnational, informing the reception of ancient drama in different eras and countries across the region. In this respect, the volume employs, and seeks to illustrate with more and diverse case studies across various sub-regions, Moira Fradinger's 'rumination' theory. As discussed previously, she argues that ancient drama was 'ingested' as a foreign artefact, a colonial legacy, in the early nineteenth century; having ceased to be external to the region's symbolic-digestive system, it returns from within this very system to be re-created in various forms in the twentieth and twenty-first centuries.[49] Building on this concept, the collection seeks to examine how the continuous rumination of the multiple stories and figures of ancient drama intersect with the region's pressing problems and concerns (race, religion, gender, the rights of indigenous peoples). As we sketched out above, we additionally emphasize the motivations and processes which lie behind playwrights' choice to engage with ancient European myths or source texts in order to unsettle bland assumptions and conclusions about the alleged 'universality' of the 'classical'.

The volume does not aim by any means to offer an exhaustive treatment of the subject. There are countries that regrettably are not represented in this book. For example, there is no material from Central America, as traditionally defined by physical geographers: that is, from Guatemala to Panamá.[50] Similarly, we do not feature case studies from the northern part of South America. Mexico is arguably underrepresented in this volume, given recent scholarship which has unearthed the country's long history with European classicisms, from its colonial past as the Viceroyalty of New Spain to the twentieth-century *Ateneo de la Juventud* (Youth Athenaeum).[51] However, we do hope that the kind of analysis offered here will generate interest in receptions that we have not been able to include, or which are not, as in the case of Mexico, presently the focus of ongoing work. Our goal is to present the Anglophone readers with some notable case studies whereby they can witness 'the dialectic of continuity and rupture', to borrow terminology from

Fredric Jameson,⁵² which characterizes the afterlife of ancient drama in Latin America in particular and across the globe in general. The volume thus contributes to the previous scholarship on classical reception in general and of drama in particular in different regions. Most of these studies are organized around case studies. Our volume adopts the same methodological tool. It has a particular aptness for the interrogation of drama's Latin American reception, for it reflects the forms of irreducible local complexity that, as we argue above, must be acknowledged by any attempt to conceptualize this region. To a greater or lesser degree, all the chapters engage in a form of comparative analysis of the ancient source text and its modern reworking prior to assessing the case study within its contemporary context. Case studies that examine rewritings in juxtaposition with the ancient plays by which they are inspired and subsequently situate them in their immediate sociopolitical and artistic environment help us avoid overarching interpretive frames and conclusions. This method of analysis, which is followed by practically every essay in the volume, calls attention to an important parameter in the process of reception: the specificity of the historical moment that prompts and shapes a modern author's interaction with, and creative transformation of, classical material. Reading a modern work both within the textual tradition from which it is derived and in connection with the social and cultural conditions that inform it and to which it responds enriches our critical understanding of not only *what* is reproduced, modified or omitted when antiquity is transplanted into modernity but also, more crucially, *how* and *why*.

Although most essays in this volume focus on post-1950 productions, the afterlife of Graeco-Roman drama in Latin America has a long history that dates back to the colonial times. In the centuries during which the continent was under Iberian rule, the classical tradition, under the aegis of Renaissance Humanism, was frequently invoked in order to propagate the superiority of the imperial power (metropolis) and establish and legitimize its hegemony over its uncivilized and savage subjects (periphery). As Andrew Laird has aptly noted about the importation of the classical tradition into the region and its imposition on artistic/literary production, it is 'a monument that can stand only awkwardly on American soil, simply because European imperialism and elitism first put it there'.⁵³ The classical tradition played such a catalytic role in the process of laying the cultural foundations of the New World that even toponyms were appropriated from the sphere of myth and were used as labels for transatlantic territories before 'America' was officially adopted as the name of the new continent. For example, the sixteenth century Spanish chroniclers Gonzalo Fernández de Oviedo and Francisco López de Gómara identified the New World with names that they had borrowed from classical sources. For Fernández de Oviedo, America was the land of the Hesperides and other utopian places found in Aristotle and Pliny. López de Gómara, on the other hand, argued that the new continent discovered on the other side of the Atlantic was Plato's Atlantis. Girolamo Frascatore, an Italian humanist of the same century from Verona, also made use of the Atlantis myth to explain the origins of native Americans.⁵⁴ Even in modern times, ancient myth continues to inform critical analyses of the power relation between metropolis and colony when it comes to Latin America's largest and most populous country, Brazil. When it is compared to its Spanish-speaking neighbours, Brazil is an anomaly in the continent. Before Brazil gained its independence, the Portuguese Court moved to Rio de Janeiro, a process described by some scholars as a reversal of the main theme in the myth of Cronus devouring his children: 'Brazil absorbed its origins, like some mythological figure who swallows its parents.'[55]

In this historical context, ancient drama played an important role. As Hardwick has compellingly argued about West African classical receptions, drama, especially Greek tragedy, is the dominant genre whereby antiquity migrates and becomes alive again in colonial and post-colonial societies.[56] One reason for the preponderance of drama over other ancient genres is that it already intersected with colonialism and expansion (territorial and cultural) in classical antiquity. As early as the fifth century BCE, Athenian tragedies were performed in Sicily during Aeschylus' visits to Hieron's court; with the campaigns of Alexander the Great in the fourth century BCE, it migrated across an even wider expanse, from the Balkans to Asia, as a symbol of Hellenic culture.[57] Because of its didactic power and ability to reach out to wider audiences than other genres (such as novel, epic, history or philosophy), whose appreciation may require solitary reading and a certain degree of erudition, drama (in the form of either rewriting a tragic script for public performance or dramatizing topics appropriated from the realms of myth and history) was placed, directly or indirectly, at the service of the colonial project in Latin America. Colonizers, seeing themselves as crusaders of the 'superior' European culture across the Atlantic, realized quickly that 'the immense popularity of the theatre made it a powerful tool to educate, as well as entertain, the masses'.[58] Among all ancient cultural practices, it was theatre, in particular tragedy, the loftier and more sublime of the two dramatic genres, that was summoned to make the 'glorious' classical past accessible to people untrained in Greek and Latin and indoctrinate them, shaping their aesthetic sensibilities, ethical principles and political thinking.

Despite classical drama's long presence on the Latin American stage, the history of its reception is not always easily traceable. The region is vast and comprises numerous nations, the theatrical history of which has not been investigated in equal depth and/or detail. Because of their size, population and geopolitical/economic importance, some countries have been the subject of a more systematic study than others. Whereas, for example, the history of Argentine, Brazilian, Cuban and Mexican theatre is better researched and documented, this is not the case with, say, Paraguay or Bolivia. In some cases, we know of titles, but they have come down to us without a date or author's name; plays are lost and irrecoverable, which frustrates any effort to chart the genre's transplantation into Latin American soil in a chronological manner – an enterprise which in any case falls outside the scope of the introduction to this volume. Thus, although it is impossible to say when Graeco-Roman drama embarked on its inaugural transoceanic voyage and where and under what conditions performances first took place, we have enough information to be able to tell how classical drama arrived in some countries of the region and through what routes antiquity was revived on stage.

As far as our sources and existing scholarship allow us to determine, ancient drama is not introduced into Latin America by means of performances or adaptations of ancient Greek or Roman plays, but rather with the dramatization of compelling stories appropriated from the spheres of myth or history in line with the neoclassical pattern. As early as the mid-seventeenth century, Juan de Espinosa Medrano, a native of Cuzco, composed a dramatic recreation of classical myth in Quechua in the form of *auto sacramental* (a one-act play in verse thematically related to the sacrament of the Eucharist and performed in the open air as part of the celebration of Corpus Christi) entitled *El robo de Proserpina y sueño de Endimión* (The Snatching of Proserpina and the Dream of Endymion).[59] Neoclassical tragedy arrives in colonial Peru in the eighteenth century through reworkings of French plays, which did not necessarily draw on ancient plays. Father Francisco del Castillo, for example, wrote a tragedy entitled *Mitrídates, rey del Ponto* (Mithridates, King of Pontus) set in ancient Rome and based on Racine's eponymous play.[60] One of the first neoclassical tragedies written in colonial Mexico is *Al amor de madre no hay afecto que le iguale* [sic] (There Is No Love Like a Mother's Love), penned by Pedro de Silva y Sarmiento in 1764 and based loosely on the *Andromache* of Jean Racine (1667) and that of Apostolo Zeno (1724).[61] Almost a century earlier, Sor (Sister) Juana Inés de la Cruz, celebrated in her lifetime as the 'Tenth Muse' and the 'Mexican Phoenix', wrote an allegorical play entitled *El divino Narciso* (The Divine Narcissus). Published in 1689, this work was a *loa* – a short theatrical piece intended as the prologue to an *auto sacramental* – in which the mythical character of Narcissus symbolizes Jesus Christ. Whereas in this play Sor Juana draws on classical myth for religious purposes, in her long poem *Neptuno alegórico* (Allegorical Neptune) published in 1680 myth is used for political ends, with the sea god serving as a figure for the new viceroy of New Spain.[62]

Examples like these set the stage for drama's reception in Latin America in subsequent centuries and illustrate two major theoretical premises about the intersection of classical texts and colonialism formulated by Hardwick. As she argues, classical texts undergo a double appropriation process: first, they are appropriated to justify the purported cultural superiority of the imperial power,[63] and then re-appropriated to show that the capacity to refigure texts that enjoy canonical status is not confined to colonizers alone.[64] In modern times, the period on which most chapters in this volume are focused, classical texts are (to use an agricultural metaphor) already rooted into the literary soil of the country in question after centuries of colonization; in this case, as Hardwick explains, they are invoked as sources of authority whereby new ideas seek legitimization and new systems are established or contested.[65] As this collection aims to demonstrate, Latin American attitudes to the reception of ancient drama can be understood, figuratively, along the lines of colonialism vs. postcolonialism. On the one hand, the genre's reception can be described as a process similar to colonization. The Greek or Roman source text is appropriated, acculturated, and subsequently exploited by modern writers who place it at the service of their own ideology. Modern authors do not subject themselves to the past, but the past to their goals and agendas. On the other hand, the act of rewriting an ancient play for a Latin American audience resembles a postcolonial enterprise.[66] The ancient text is liberated from the ideological closure imposed upon it through centuries of circulation and migration in the northern hemisphere and is set free to take on new roles, meanings and forms.

Given the recentness of the Americas, the classical tradition can be understood as part of the continental history that is close(r) to the surface of its cultural soil and hence easier to return to whenever Latin American playwrights need to redefine and negotiate the present through the lens of the past. Graeco-Roman drama is part of their literary heritage. This is precisely the point made by the editors of the *Oxford Handbook of the Greek Drama in the Americas*, as they emphasize the ubiquity of Classics in general and drama in particular in the continent as a 'subterranean' element.[67] Classical antiquity is not dead but still alive under the ground, as if it were a material of the black soil with enduring value. Thanks to continuous exploitation through the centuries, it became a solid part of the various layers of the cultural/artistic life in the Americas. Like archaeologists, we classicists, therefore, are called to unearth the ways in which ancient texts have been used and abused in colonial and postcolonial America(s). Barbara Goff has cogently proposed a push-pull model to theorize the (ab)uses of classical texts in (post)colonial contexts.[68] According to her formulation, drama, and the classical tradition in general, operate like a farmer's plough or ship's prow, *pushing* their way through time, marginalizing or even attempting to eradicate local artistic elements. Our volume aims to illustrate that this model is applicable even to contemporary times and to those cases in which ancient drama is used as a means for breaking with long-established theatrical traditions and founding a new national stage. Another way, of course, to look at this appropriation process is, as Goff explains, by visualizing the source text as being *pulled*, uprooted from its ancient context and altered (or transplanted, to use a botanical metaphor) in order to suit the needs of its new habitat by literary/artistic forces that utilize it towards their own ends. This is the case with practically every play examined in this collection.

One of these ends is politics, as noted above with respect to rewritings of ancient drama through a neoclassical lens. The use of drama for political purposes becomes more systematic in the second half of the twentieth century, as the majority of the chapters in this volume illustrate. This rise of classical drama in Latin America should be seen, as Frank Dauster explains, as part of a general explosion of theatrical activity that occurred throughout the region in the 1950s and ensuing decades in terms of both quantity and quality.[69] Fuelled by the Cuban Revolution, this boom is referred to by critics with terms like 'new theatre', 'avant-garde' theatre and 'theatre of [the sociopolitical] crisis'.[70] The many plays produced in this period break bear witness to a 'widespread return to classical myth and drama in an effort to express the complex realities of Spanish America',[71] thus becoming more 'dialectical' – reaching out, that is, to larger, non-elite audiences.[72] This dialectical relationship between rewritings of ancient drama and Latin American realities is either representational or oppositional. Drama is used either to support or to interrogate political systems.

This volume, then, aims to provide the reader with a critical introduction to 'Latin American' theatrical engagement with Greek and Roman drama, via a series of case studies that collectively aim to illuminate both the richness of this engagement and the impossibility of interpreting it within any single dominant paradigm. Part I focuses on the Southern Cone of South America, presenting four chapters on plays from

Argentina and Chile. Konstantinos Nikoloutsos opens the volume with the only nineteenth-century play examined here, Juan Cruz Varela's 1823 *Dido*, the first tragedy anchored in classical myth that was produced in Argentina after independence from Spain (Chapter 2). He explores the historical conditions and cultural politics that generated Varela's engagement with Virgil's seminal epic, arguing *inter alia* that Varela rewrites a Roman myth associated in Spain with monarchy to challenge the hegemony of the colonial dramatic canon. His chapter further illustrates how Varela constructs a heroine who fails in her figurative role as mother of her newly established nation, thus allowing Aeneas to emerge as a symbol for the founding father in post-Independence Argentina. Brenda López Saiz illustrates the role that classical tragedy continues to play at key political junctures in Argentina 125 years later, but to a different end. In examining Leopoldo Marechal's *Antígona Vélez*, she illustrates the manner in which Sophocles' text is recast as a national foundation myth set in the nineteenth century, a historical tale specifically engineered to support Juan Perón's dictatorship and a new Catholic nationalism (Chapter 3). Greek drama, López Saiz shows, intersects with debates (e.g. civilization vs. barbarism, European vs. indigenous cultural heritage) that continue to inform the construction of Argentine national identity more than a century after independence. Chapters 4 and 5 turn to neighbouring Chile on the eve of the twenty-first century, where tragedy is used to illuminate pressing sociopolitical issues. Irmtrud König examines Juan Radrigán's *Medea Mapuche*, which situates Euripides' revenge tragedy among the Mapuche indigenous peoples of Chile in order to raise awareness of their continued marginalized status following the end of Augusto Pinochet's military dictatorship (Chapter 4). König illustrates the manner in which Radrigán reworks Euripides' play while also invoking seminal Chilean texts of the colonial period. She argues that Radrigán blends these two diverse literary traditions to accentuate intersecting and persistent concerns of race, gender social exclusion and discrimination. Carolina Brnčić continues the discussion of the use of Greek drama in the new Chilean democracy by turning to the way in which Greek tragedy enables discussion of historical and traumatic memory on the Chilean stage (Chapter 5). She examines two recent plays which draw on the larger symbolism of Philoctetes and Medea, to showcase the resonating themes of abandonment and social trauma in post-Pinochet Chile: *Filoctetes* by Marcelo Sánchez and *Diarrea* by José Palma Eskenazi. As with the other three chapters in this section, this chapter emphasizes that context is not limited to the present, the immediate years around when the plays were written. Brnčić introduces 'present past' as a concept to refer to the national trauma caused by almost two decades of military rule. She additionally illustrates how the ancient dramatic tradition is enriched though modern popular culture, such as TV reality shows. Read together, these four chapters show that Southern Cone playwrights have invoked Greek and Roman material not only in an impressive range of contexts but also for multiple and varied political and social ends.

Part II casts a critical eye on rewritings of ancient drama in Brazil. As Chapters 6 and 7 demonstrate, these crucially include engagements with Roman comedy. Rodrigo Tadeu Gonçalves examines Guilherme Figueiredo's adaptation of Plautus' *Amphitruo*, *A*

God Slept Here, a play which has been neglected in scholarship (Chapter 6). Through a close reading, Gonçalves accounts for the manner in which Figueiredo's play departs from the Plautine model and discusses its relation to contemporary Brazilian society and theatre, with an emphasis on the metatheatrical impact of Figueredo's alterations for the twentieth century. Tiziana Ragno, in turn, analyses another play by Figueiredo, *A Very Curious Story of the Virtuous Widow of Ephesus*, which likewise draws from Plautus' *Amphitruo*, but also Petronius (Chapter 7). Ragno demonstrates the manner in which this play deviates from the 'Paulista' (i.e. based in São Paulo) theatrical movement of the time, which emphasizes themes related to class and rural struggles. She shows how Figueiredo draws upon ancient motifs and myth to create a more light-hearted farce nevertheless informed by the Brazilian present. Chapters 8 and 9 turn to the complex footprint of Greek tragedy in Brazil, which proves more elusive than that of comedy. In an examination of Brazilian playwright Nelson Rodrigues' *Our Lady of the Drowned*, Anastasia Bakogianni reveals a play that masks, rather than proclaims, the debt it owes to Greek tragedy (Chapter 8). Bakogianni demonstrates that *Our Lady of the Drowned* is a hybrid play, the product of a triangular relationship between European, North American, and national textual traditions, including Electra's appropriation in early twentieth-century pop-psychology. As she emphasizes, Rodrigues' play, based loosely on notions of Electra from across time and various contexts, presents a particular challenge for accounts of classical reception. Seth Jeppesen follows a similar approach, illustrating the existence of antiquity as a 'shadow' behind the plot, in his study of Jorge Andrade's play *Pedreira das Almas*, which contains no explicit reference to its ancient source text, Sophocles' *Antigone* (Chapter 9). Jeppesen illuminates the gradual way in which Andrade equates his protagonist Mariana with Antigone, allowing the audience to witness her as she 'becomes' her Greek forbear. Jeppesen also discusses the manner in which this play became a powerful symbol of resistance in its later reception (like its predecessor) during the military dictatorship of the 1970s. In a region filled with competing and varied notions of Graeco-Roman antiquity, Bakogianni's and Jeppesen's respective explorations of 'masked' receptions on the Brazilian stage are important to consider.

Part III explores the Caribbean and North America. As in the previous section, the chapters examining comic material are presented first, followed by notable theatrical adaptations of Greek tragedy in chronological order. The chapters include case studies from several countries in the Greater Antilles: Puerto Rico (Chapter 10), Dominican Republic (Chapter 11), Cuba (Chapter 12) and Haiti (Chapter 14). A chapter on Martinique rounds up the Caribbean (Chapter 13), whereas North America is represented by case studies examining theatrical adaptations in Mexico (Chapter 15) and among the US Chicanx community (Chapter 14). Though the geographical range of this part contrasts the narrower focus of the previous two parts, the case studies presented here nevertheless expand previous points illuminated in the Southern Cone and Brazil sections. Rosa Andújar explores Puerto Rican playwright Francisco Arriví's *Bachelors Club*, a new farce that reverses and rewrites Aristophanes' *Lysistrata* from the perspective of men (Chapter 10). In discussing the play's departures from the original source text, Andújar draws attention to the manner in which the *Lysistrata* paradigm tends to operate in the modern world, and how Arriví deviates from this. She also considers the play's larger political and social context, examining the implications of a farcical and apolitical comedy loosely inspired by an ancient Greek play at a critical time for both Puerto Rican theatre and politics, when the island adopted commonwealth status in relation to the US. Katherine Ford turns to the afterlife of Aristophanes' *Lysistrata* in the neighbouring Domínican Republic, with Franklin Domínguez' biting *Lysistrata Hates Politics* (Chapter 11). Ford analyses Dominican stereotypes of gender, social class and sexuality that are embedded in this loose adaptation of the ancient comedy. Her analysis accentuates Domínguez' larger motivations in his use of Greek drama, specifically as a way of inserting Dominican theatre and issues (both of which are typically seen as marginal) into a larger established dramatic canon and context. Jacques Bromberg, in turn, examines the controversial loose translation of Aeschylus' *Seven Against Thebes* by Antón Arrufat at the dawn of the Cuban Revolution, a play which was perceived to be an allegory for the Bay of Pigs fiasco, thus causing Arrufat's ostracism from Havana (Chapter 12). Bromberg illustrates Arrufat's additional debt to Euripides' *Phoenician Women*, revealing that the Cuban play is a hybrid text combining various source texts. Turning to Martinique, Justine McConnell explores two plays by Patrick Chamoiseau which embed ancient Greek myth within the small island (Chapter 13). By paying careful attention to the tension between orality and literacy, McConnell illustrates the manner in which both plays reveal Chamoiseau's early ideas about his seminal concept of *créolité* (creoleness), which served as a crucial response for *négritude*. Her analysis thus demonstrates the place that Greek literature held in the development of a Francophone Caribbean literary ideology in the last quarter of the twentieth century. Tom Hawkins pairs Haitian playwright Feliks Moriso-Lewa's adaptation of *Antigone* and US-based Chicanx playwright Luis Alfaro's *Electricidad*, in order to challenge the habit current in Classical Reception Studies of looking at isolated reception case studies clustering around the same tragic plotline or character (Chapter 14). Through Agamben's notion of 'biopolitics', he highlights the manner in which both plays use an established classical canon to accentuate verbal hybridity (with Haitian Creole and Spanglish) and social marginalization (of both Haiti and the Chicanx community in the US). Both plays also crucially challenge current notions of 'Latin America' which typically centre around Spanish-speaking countries south of the US–Mexico border. Jesse Weiner offers a biopolitical reading of Perla de la Rosa's *Antígona*, a rewriting which was set and staged in Juárez, Mexico against the larger backdrop of extreme violence and femicide (Chapter 15). He situates de la Rosa's play, with its motif of symbolic death, within a larger philosophical rich tradition of undead Antigones, while also interrogating the concept of biopolitics as a framework for approaching not only the Antigone myth but also present-day humanitarian crises. His analysis thus expands the theoretical engagement with Giorgio Agamben that was begun by Hawkins in the previous chapter. As this summary reveals, our chapters illustrate a variety of case studies that not only engage with the classical in distinct ways but also correspond to particular moments of crisis and foundational junctures in modern Latin American societies.

PART I
SOUTHERN CONE

CHAPTER 2
FROM EPIC TO TRAGEDY: THEATRE AND POLITICS IN JUAN CRUZ VARELA'S *DIDO*
Konstantinos P. Nikoloutsos

This chapter examines a landmark play from early nineteenth-century Argentina – then called United Provinces of the Río de la Plata – entitled *Dido*. Although not a reworking of a play staged in antiquity, it is the country's first tragedy anchored in classical material and merits attention in this volume for historical reasons. The piece was written in 1823, seven years after the declaration of independence from the Spanish crown, by Juan Cruz Varela (Buenos Aires, 1794 – Montevideo, 1839), the chief representative of neoclassicism in the embryonic state and an ardent translator of Virgil, Horace and Ovid. A dramatic rewriting of Book 4 of the *Aeneid*, *Dido* is set in Carthage and recounts the story of its eponymous queen who becomes hopelessly enamoured with Aeneas and commits suicide when the Trojan hero abandons her to sail to Italy and fulfil his destiny of founding the Latin race. The plot unfolds over the course of 1,733 verses divided, almost proportionally, into three acts with five scenes in each one of them.

The chapter will not engage in a close reading of Varela's tragedy to assess how well it compares to Virgil's epic. Ever since *Dido* was produced, critics have sought to investigate the commonalities and divergences between the ancient source text and its modern reworking in terms of plot development and characterization.[1] The chapter will instead explore the historical conditions and cultural politics that generated Varela's interaction with the *Aeneid* and led to the retelling of Dido's tragic story through a neoclassical filter. The first section will draw on a wide range of sources (press releases, reviews and critical essays) pertaining to the play's production history and reception in an attempt to explain what prompted a young poet, previously unfamiliar with dramatic composition, to cross over domains and enter the tragic universe with a piece inspired not by contemporary reality, but by European antiquity.

In the second section, the focal point shifts from Dido's migration across continents and cultures to her passage across genres and media of representation. The story of the Carthaginian queen undergoes a double adaptation in Varela's play: from epic to tragedy and from the page to the stage. Per one scholar, this transgeneric and transmedial process of rewriting Graeco-Roman texts provides the very basis of neoclassical theatre and is invested with political meaning.[2] To be sure, *Dido*'s political connotations have not gone entirely unobserved in literary criticism. As early as 1876, the essayist and politician Miguel Cané interpreted Varela's Aeneas as a figure for the General Manuel Belgrano, one of the country's *libertadores* (revolutionary military leaders) and creator of the Argentine flag.[3] My inquiry pursues a similar line of argument, asking a set of questions in an effort to address a central paradox in the play. Since the public actors of Argentine independence were all men, why is its protagonist a female and not a male, as is the case with Virgil's epic? If *Dido* is the product of a liminal time period during which Argentina transitions from absolutism to republicanism, a political system that perpetuates the traditional association of men with authority, why does Varela's play project such an unorthodox view of government by portraying a woman in charge of her kingdom and granting her a hegemonic role in the public sphere? What message does this heretic representation convey to Varela's spectators who live in a society in which women are excluded from positions of power?

To answer these questions, my analysis draws on a recent study entitled *South American Independence: Gender, Politics, Text*.[4] Its authors argue that women – especially those defying normative roles and the social stereotype of female submission and domestication – emerge in the imagination of Latin American writers of the first half of the nineteenth century (all of whom are virtually male) as embodiments of the vices of the nation. Such transgressive female figures are in need of male control and discipline, thus legitimizing gender hierarchies and men's claim to leadership and domination.[5] Building on this theoretical framework, the chapter will propose that Varela departs from Spanish treatments of the myth of Dido and instead inscribes his version into the Virgilian tradition to cast his heroine both as a threat to patriarchal order and as a conduit facilitating homosocial bonds between men in the context of nation-building and civic identity.

Margin vs. centre

Dido is the tragedy with which Varela made his debut as a dramatist at the age of twenty-nine, after devoting his early youth to the composition of erotic and patriotic verses. The play was not put on stage when it was first penned. As reported in a communiqué published in the newspaper *El Argos de Buenos Aires*, its premiere took place on 23 July 1823 in the form of a reading by the poet himself at a soirée held at the house of Bernardino Rivadavia. Rivadavia was at the time Minister of Government and Foreign Affairs – the chief minister and actual commander in the short-lived government of the General Martín Rodríguez (1821–4). Varela read (most likely portions of) his play before a small, all-male audience comprising politicians, foreign dignitaries and the intellectual elite of Buenos Aires. Present at *Dido*'s inaugural reading were members of the Literary Society, the Minister of Finance and the Minister Plenipotentiary of the Viceroyalty of Peru, Manuel Blanco Encalada, a *porteño* (a native of the port of Buenos Aires) who would be appointed Chile's first president three years later.

Commenting on the audience's reaction to Varela's oral delivery, the press release extols the dramatic power of the modern reworking vis-à-vis the Latin source text and applauds the debutant playwright for his contribution to the national theatre that Rivadavia sought to establish as part of his cultural reforms:

> [N]osotros no podemos menos que felicitar al autor por esta producción, que es la primera que ha hecho en este género ... [Q]uizá no será temeridad el decir, que el

autor ha emulado en algunos cuadros la elocuencia poética del mismo Virgilio … Es ciertamente por primera vez, que hemos visto en nuestra patria un cuadro que no puede menos que excitar fuertemente la emulación … [N]os lisonjeamos al anunciar, que al leerse la *Dido*, todos simultáneamente dieron su voto de aprobación y reconocimiento al autor por la carrera brillante que ha abierto al teatro nacional …[6]

We cannot but congratulate the author on this production, which is the first he has done in this genre … [P]erhaps it will not be daring to say that in some scenes the author has emulated the poetic eloquence of Virgil himself … It is certainly the first time that we have seen in our country a depiction that cannot but strongly instigate emulation … [W]e are pleased to announce that, once *Dido* was read, they all simultaneously gave their vote of approval and recognition to the author for the brilliant career he has launched at the national theatre …

The encomiastic comments that Varela's unveiling as a dramatist received in the press of his time are, as scholars have pointed out, carefully orchestrated and must be read with caution.[7] A member of the Literary Society formed by a group of distinguished *porteño* intellectuals[8] and a holder of high-rank positions in the government,[9] Varela became a militant writer for the modernization of Buenos Aires advocated by Rivadavia since the rising politician returned to his native city in 1821 to assume the office of the minister after serving as a diplomat for seven years in Great Britain and France. During his residence in Europe, Rivadavia became acquainted with influential philosophers, such as Jeremy Bentham and Destutt de Tracy. He also experienced the Industrial Revolution and the ideas of the Enlightenment, which he was eager to implement upon repatriation. The 'Paris of South America', as it is often called, Buenos Aires was a rather insignificant city in cultural terms when Argentina revolted against Spanish rule in 1810. Although it prospered through trade thanks to its strategic geographical position as a port, enjoying administrative autonomy as the capital of the Viceroyalty of the Río de la Plata (1776–1810), it lacked the artistic vibrancy of interior cities like Córdoba, where theatrical activity is documented as early as 1610 thanks to the interaction of the Jesuit missions with the locals.[10]

Varela used the elegance of his pen to influence the public opinion and sway it in favour of the ambitious programme with which Rivadavia aspired to transform Buenos Aires' physiognomy and convert it from a small town of colonial aesthetics to a paradigm of European architectural sophistication and intellectual brilliance. Latin Americans had looked to Paris as a model of what a modern city should look like since the late seventeenth century, when Louis XIV's kingdom became the leading European power and challenged Spain's dominion. By the early nineteenth century, French was the second language of the *criollo* elite, and the Frenchification of the urban space acquired an anti-colonial character, becoming a symbol of the Europhile identity that was in vogue in the region's newborn nations.[11] The founding of the University of Buenos Aires and the continent's first Museum of Natural Sciences, the ecclesiastical reform, and the construction of large avenues, paved and lighted streets, schools and hospitals are only some of the numerous ways in which Rivadavia aimed to seal the period of his hegemony in Argentine political life.[12]

Varela served as a 'poetic chronicler'[13] of Rivadavia's administration, composing odes that celebrated the minister's vision and achievements. The most characteristic example that illustrates how the young poet placed his art at the service of politics is a poem written in 1822 under the title *Profecía de la grandeza de Buenos Aires* (*Prophecy of the Grandeur of Buenos Aires*). Saturated with mythical names and Graeco-Roman allusions, this poem is essentially 'a panegyrical defense of Rivadavia's proposed water system that all but suggests is that Columbus discovered America so Buenos Aires could have pressurized water'.[14] In exchange for Varela's allegiance, Rivadavia used his political power to promote the poet's work among the city's elite circles, essentially acting as his patron. In this capacity, on 28 July 1823, five days after *Dido*'s inaugural reading, he presided over a second reading of the play. The audience gathered at his salon this time was bigger and included a significant number of upper-class women who, as the author of the communiqué in *El Argos de Buenos Aires* quoted above emphatically notes, burst into tears at the end of the poet's recital, thereby demonstrating their approval of his tragedy.[15]

In recognition of Rivadavia's support, but also in an attempt to enhance the authority of his first engagement with theatre, Varela, following the practice of neoclassical dramatists, dedicated *Dido* to his patron. The dedicatory letter, which prefaces the printed edition and in which the poet expresses his gratitude to Rivadavia for his favourable reaction to his previous literary endeavours, closes with a quotation from the *Eclogues* (8.10):

> [Y]o quisiera que mi temeridad sirviera de estímulo a algunos de nuestros jóvenes privilegiados por la naturaleza; que ejercitarán sus talentos en el drama; y que algún día una musa argentina llegue a merecer que se diga de ella:
> 'SOLA SOPHOCLEO TUA CARMINA DIGNA COTHURNO.'
> Tengo el honor de ser, con el más profundo respeto, Señor, atento servidor.[16]

> My wish is that my boldness served as a stimulus for some of our young men privileged by nature; that they will exercise their talents in drama; and that someday an Argentine Muse will deserve to be said about her:
> 'ONLY YOUR POEMS ARE WORTHY OF THE SOPHOCLEAN COTHURNUS.'
> I have the honour of being, with the most profound respect, an attentive servant, Sir.

Carefully selected from Virgil's bucolic poem and inserted into Varela's text in capital letters to resemble an inscription on a gravestone or monument, the Latin verse is appropriated to bestow self-praise and convey a preoccupation with literary impact and immortality. With this quotation, Varela not only displays his classical erudition to a patron who was also versed in Latin but also elevates himself through comparison to Sophocles and expresses a desire for gaining renown in the present and future.

Printed by the Imprenta de los Niños Expósitos, the oldest press in Buenos Aires annexed by the state with a decree issued by Rivadavia,[17] *Dido* reached the *porteño* market on 24 August 1823 and was made available for purchase at six *reales* per copy,[18] earning the title of the first non-religious work published in post-Independence Argentina.[19] In 1825, the play was added to the repertoire of Coliseo,[20] Buenos Aires' only playhouse at the time. Three years later, *Dido* crossed the Andes and was staged in Chile.[21] A production in Montevideo[22] sealed a series of performances in the Southern Cone that cemented Varela's reputation as 'el autor de la *Dido*' ('the author of *Dido*'), a sobriquet that became almost synonymous with his name in contemporary criticism.[23]

Following *Dido*'s enthusiastic reception, Varela wrote another tragedy based on (this time) Greek myth under the title *Argia*, for which he was extolled in a review published in *El Argos de Buenos Aires* as 'the Sophocles and Racine of our country' ('el Sófocles y el Racine de nuestro país').[24] If *Dido* enacts the moral dichotomy love vs. duty, *Argia* explores a politically charged topic, the clash between tyranny and freedom, by reworking the events that followed the disastrous Argive attack on Thebes and the death of Oedipus' sons at each other's hands. The eponymous heroine of Varela's second engagement with the genre is not Antigone, but a less celebrated figure drawn from Statius' epic *Thebaid* (Book 12) and cast by the Italian playwright Vittorio Alfieri as one of the *dramatis personae* in his 1782 play *Antigone*. Argia, the daughter of the king of Argos, Adrastus, and the widow of Polynices, confronts Creon, demanding the return of her captured son Lysander – named Thersander in ancient sources.

Both tragedies are considered foundational works of Argentine dramaturgy. Although not the first plays penned by a native author, they eclipsed, at least in terms of popular reception,[25] previous attempts made by playwrights, such as Manuel José de Lavardén and Manuel Belgrano, to break away from the Spanish dramatic tradition and establish a national theatre. In describing the artistic landscape from which *Dido* and *Argia* emerged and which they sought to Europeanize (and thus de-vulgarize), Juan María Gutiérrez, the leading literary historian of nineteenth-century Argentina, explains as follows why Varela's tragedies are superior to *Siripo* (1786) and *Molina* (1823), the verse dramas respectively attributed to Lavardén and Belgrano:

> La tragedia clásica nació y murió en las orillas argentinas con el señor don Juan Cruz Varela. [Las] propensiones locales fueron tan poderosas entre nosotros, que las tragedias de que nos ocupamos aparecieron entre dos ensayos del mismo género, cuyos autores habían buscado la inspiración en las entrañas de la sociedad americana, y sólo con el asunto protestaban ya contra la tradición. Cediendo a nuevas necesidades y exigencias, la musa dramática de Lavardén sacó a la escena la pasión inspirada a un salvaje de las márgenes del Paraná por los cristianos atractivos de una mujer europea. Movido por iguales influencias, el joven doctor don Manuel Belgrano daba a luz en 1823 la tragedia en verso y en cinco actos

titulada *Molina*, cuya escena es en Quito y cuya principal heroína es Cora, virgen consagrada al culto del sol y amante sacrílega y clandestina del guerrero español que da título a esta tragedia. Sin embargo, es tanto el poder del estilo en las producciones de arte que *Argia* y *Dido* erguirán siempre la cabeza sobre las dos tragedias mencionadas de Lavardén y Belgrano.[26]

Classical tragedy was born and died on the Argentine shores with Mr. Don Juan Cruz Varela. [The] local propensities were so strong among us that the tragedies [*Argia* and *Dido*] with which we are concerned appeared between two exercises of the same genre, the authors of which had sought inspiration in the guts of American society and protested against tradition only with the subject. Yielding to new needs and demands, the dramatic Muse of Lavardén brought on stage the passion experienced by a savage man from the banks of Paraná for the Christian attractions of a European woman. Moved by similar influences, in 1823 the young doctor Don Manuel Belgrano delivered a tragedy, in verse and five acts, entitled *Molina*. It is set in Quito and its central heroine is Cora, a virgin devoted to the cult of Sun and a sacrilegious and secret lover of the Spanish warrior, who gives his name to this tragedy. However, the power of style in the productions of art is such that *Argia* and *Dido* will always raise their head above the two aforementioned tragedies of Lavardén and Belgrano.

Varela's neoclassicism is symptomatic of a time period during which Argentine theatre reflected the national struggle for independence and political sovereignty by renouncing the thematic conventions of Spanish Golden Age drama, especially the nexus between chivalry, romance and nobility. To the historical call for the creation of an autonomous stage, Lavardén and Belgrano responded with two tragedies grounded in contemporary history. To resonate with their target audience, their plays portrayed the clash between civilization and savagery, Christianity and paganism, conquerors and autochthonous people – dichotomies that diachronically informed the construction of Argentine and Latin American identity. Varela, on the other hand, advocated a different aesthetic vision that sought to move away from the production of plays that depicted ordinary characters situated in provincial, primitive settings and involved in storylines with a local appeal. Against the peripheral trajectory into which his forerunners launched Argentine dramaturgy, Varela proposed a model of versification successfully tested in France and Italy, and drew on the classical past with its celebrated heroes and timeless, familiar stories in an attempt to demonstrate that New World theatre could compete with Europe in erudition and creativity and become a central node in the cultural geography of the West.

Resorting to the Graeco-Roman literary corpus as an alternative source of inspiration does not necessarily mean that Varela's approach to dramatic composition is evocative of his colonial mentality, as Ricardo Rojas maintains in the preliminary note to his 1915 edition of *Dido* and *Argia*.[27] The son of a Galician merchant and a *porteña* upper-class mother, Varela studied Latin and philosophy at the prestigious Colegio de San Carlos, founded by the Jesuits in Buenos Aires in 1661. In 1810, a few months after the Revolution of 25 May, he left for Córdoba to continue his studies at another historic institution, the Colegio de Monserrat, from which he graduated in 1816, the same year in which the Congress of Tucumán endorsed Argentina's independence from Spain. Although in terms of subject matter *Dido* does reflect the poet's classical upbringing acquired through an elitist system, it does not *ipso facto* denote a failure to free himself from the artistic norms of the colonial past. To the contrary, as Hardwick notes about the appropriation of classical material in postcolonial contexts, Varela's engagement with Virgil illustrates that 'the capacity to refigure ancient texts is not confined to colonizers'[28] alone. Far from being a symptom of Varela's adherence to colonial practices, the interaction with Rome's national epic serves both as a counter-model to the dominant Spanish paradigms and to give legitimacy and authority to Argentina's embryonic theatre. Varela set a similar goal for his verse translation of the *Aeneid*. As he explains in a letter published *post mortem*,[29] his aim was to decolonize Virgil's transmission in Latin America and dethrone the monopoly of his translations by peninsular authors, such as Gregorio Hernández de Velazco whose 1557 translation had been considered canonical in the Hispanophone world and is cited in *Don Quixote* by Cervantes, who could not read Latin to this extent.

By privileging the Franco-Italian tradition, Varela demonstrates that a rupture with the canon does not entail a reactive rejection of it as a whole; the periphery/south can still engage in a dialogue with the metropolis/north even after the goal of independence is achieved. The text resulting from this engagement transcends geographical and temporal boundaries, defying the binary opposition between past and present, continuity and change, purity and hybridity. *Dido*, after all, is not fully inscribed within the stylistic conventions of neoclassical tragedy; it displays some of the external characteristics of Spanish Golden Age drama. For example, it departs from the five-act structure of neoclassical tragedies to adhere to the three-act rule articulated by Lope de Vega in his 1609 *Arte nuevo de hacer comedias en este tiempo* (*New Art of Making Comedies in this Age*). It is also composed in the hendecasyllabic metrical form commonly used by Spanish poets in tragedy and epic, the *romance heroico o real* (heroic or royal Romance).

From a historical perspective, Varela's neoclassicism is in line with the basic principles of the *Sociedad del Buen Gusto del Teatro* (Society of Good Taste in the Theatre) founded in Buenos Aires in 1817 to forge an environment in which theatrical production could flourish and proper models of behaviour (such as republican values) could be instilled. The society selected the plays by foreign authors that were to be translated, edited and put on stage in place of Spanish classics. A landmark feat in the history of the Argentine wars of independence contributed to the establishment of this society, giving rise to the desire for a repertoire with a patriotic orientation: the crossing of the Andes by the General José de San Martín (known as *El Libertador*) in January 1817, a deed compared in biographical accounts to the crossings of the Rubicon by Julius Caesar and of the Alps by Hannibal.[30] Although this society practically ceased to exist a year later, its influence on Argentine dramaturgy persisted for at least two decades. Seeing theatre more as an instrument for mass indoctrination and social transformation than as a form of entertainment,[31] the society was established by a group of men who belonged to the political, intellectual and economic elite of Buenos Aires with the goal of laying the foundations for an autonomous stage that, free from the dominion of the Spanish dramatic tradition, would serve as 'an agent for the formation of civic spirit, a forum of opinion, a school of ideas and customs at the service of the American cause' ('un agente de formación del espíritu cívico, una tribuna de opinión, una escuela de ideas y costumbres al servicio de la causa americana').[32] Favouring Racine, Corneille, Voltaire and Alfieri over Calderón and Lope de Vega as the only playwrights worthy of emulation, the society sought to promote the composition of works that in keeping with the national struggle for emancipation from the colonial master celebrated freedom and condemned autocracy. According to the programmatic objectives of the society drafted by one of its principal founders, the colonel and poet Juan Ramon Rojas, domestic output ought to strive to be cast in the eyes of Argentine audiences as 'the wall where fanaticism, anarchy, corruption, and despotism crashed' ('el muro donde vinieron a estrellarse el fanatismo, la anarquía, la corrupción y el despotismo').[33]

Dido is the first neoclassical tragedy written in Buenos Aires following a series of French and Italian dramas produced in translation. Set mostly in Graeco-Roman antiquity, these imports explored patriotic themes, focusing in particular on the rebellion against tyranny and oppression. Some of the titles included Voltaire's *The Death of Caesar*, *The Death of Socrates* and *Orestes*; Racine's *Mithridates*; Alfieri's *Free Rome* and *The Sons of Oedipus*; and Pierre Remy Guéroult's *The Day of Marathon*.[34] Although *Dido* emerged in this post-revolutionary environment, it is not recognized by scholars as a piece that bears a relation to its contemporary sociopolitical reality. This perception dates back to a review published in the *porteño* press a few weeks after the play was printed. After singing Varela's praises for over three pages, the anonymous reviewer closes the text with the following exhortation to the young poet:

> Deseamos que la *Dido* logre en las tablas el mayor aplauso, y que su estimado autor escoja cuanto antes, para segunda pieza, un argumento más dramático y *nacional*, si se puede; o al menos alguno que aluda a nuestra situación y aspiraciones.[35]

> We wish that *Dido* obtains the greatest applause on stage, and that its esteemed author chooses as soon as possible, for the second piece, a more dramatic and national storyline, if possible; or at least one that alludes to our situation and aspirations.

Almost two centuries later, this view still prevails. Shumway, in his astute analysis of Rivadavian Buenos Aires, dismisses Varela's engagement with tragedy, stating: '[U]nlike his patriotic verse, neither play has much to do with Argentina ... National theater based on Virgil and patterned after Corneille? No wonder modern nationalist critics like Rojas consider Varela a symptom of cultural colonialism.'[36] In what follows, I will defend *Dido* against such transparent readings and argue that the appropriation of a seminal story from Roman epic and its conversion into a tragedy are not just an exercise in versification in the neoclassical style; they carry political connotations that intimately link this play to the larger nation-building project.

Dido's homosociality

One of the basic rules of neoclassical tragedy was the unity of time, space and action. The plot had to be set at a particular locale, which was to remain unchanged throughout all the acts, and unfold within a twenty-four-hour period or less. In adhering to this principle, Varela's play takes place at a salon at Dido's palace during the course of a single day. Although his tragedy creates a distance between spectators and the stage in temporal terms by being set in the classical past, it produces a sense of proximity in spatial terms by situating the action at Carthage's very centre of power, the queen's dwelling, identified in the eyes of Varela's audience with Rivadavia's house, where *Dido* was first read. The entire play revolves around one central action: Aeneas' departure from Carthage that leads Dido to take her own life. In rewriting this tragic episode from Virgil's epic, Varela fuses gender and politics. Aeneas' escape from Dido's kingdom is cast as an act of emancipation from the fetters of erotic desire that keeps him emotionally captive and derailed from his mission. By the same token, Dido's suicide is portrayed as an unavoidable result of her enslavement to uncontrolled passion and as self-punishment for her failure to act as a virtuous ruler and civic paradigm of moral fortitude and reason.

When the play opens, Aeneas has already decided to end his affair with Dido and sail to Italy with his comrades, staying true to duty. Setting the stage for the drama, the Trojan chieftain Sergesto reveals that per Aeneas' commands the secret voyage is to take place before dawn and describes the upcoming exodus from the African kingdom as a return to the heroic code of conduct and gender propriety. Carthage, a female-led city, keeps the Trojan warriors in a state of softness and emasculation – or, in Oedipal terms, castrated and reduced to the powerless, passive position of women. The fleet is eager to sail away from a port 'in which time is wasted in soft leisure and feminine flattery without honour and gain' ('en que el tiempo / En ocio muelle y femenil halago / Se pierde sin honor y sin provecho').[37] Aeneas undertakes to restore the masculine ethos among his men by engineering their escape from this gender-bending environment and by setting himself as an example of bravery, toughness, boldness and unity – values that Varela's viewer/reader would recognize as key to the Argentine war of Independence. 'Together with us', Sergesto notes, 'he will embark on the sea, he first will confront danger in serene peace, and we will learn to defy death' ('juntamente con nosotros, / Se lanzará a la mar; él el primero / En paz serena afrontará el peligro, / Y a insultar a la muerte aprenderemos').[38]

Aeneas does not appear on stage until the beginning of Act 2, where he converses with his senior captain Nesteo. When the latter makes the point that if they were not operating under divine dictate Dido's love ought to be reciprocated, Aeneas does not deny that his feelings are genuine. He clarifies, however, that he has control over them: 'My passion is great, but does not blind me' ('Es grande mi pasión, mas no me ciega').[39] Contrary to Aeneas, Dido, in her soliloquy that closes Act 1, confesses that she has completely succumbed to the power of desire described as a fire raging untamed inside her. When she finds out that the man with whom she is infatuated plans to run away from her in secret, she implores her sister Ana: 'Go, fly, call the cruel man: tell him that Dido burns more in her love every minute; tell him that my guts are consumed in a destroying, unquenchable fire and that my entire being... Don't say anything...' ('Ve, vuela, llama al cruel: dile que Dido / Arde más en su amor cada momento; / Dile que se consumen mis entrañas / En destructor inapagable incendio, / Y todo mi ser ... no digas nada ...').[40]

Dido and Aeneas are depicted as polar opposites. While she unashamedly declares her submission to desire, in his first appearance on stage he emerges as a paradigm of moral force and self-mastery. The head of Carthage is identified with weakness, dependence, vulnerability, emotional excess and ambivalence. She thus represents a poor model of leadership. Dido fails to exercise dominion over her passion which has become an obsession, her main preoccupation; she is a ruler lacking self-rule, unable to shift the focus of her attention away from her personal life. By contrast, Aeneas epitomizes strength, moderation, discipline, autonomy and determination. He knows how to keep the private and public spheres apart and harden his heart to avoid the inner torment that Dido experiences. Although, as he admits to Nesteo, he is in love, he does not allow his feelings to cloud his reason and take priority over his duty. The role of nation-builder he is destined to play does not permit the idyll with Dido to flourish and presents the hero with a strict script he is coerced to follow.

Varela's Aeneas is crafted to represent a model of man whose sense of identity depends on journeys and conquests, on exploits performed away from the safety and comfort of the urban space identified as the proper locus of the feminine. The play equates masculinity with mobility and femininity with fixity. Commenting on his portrayal of the Trojan hero, Varela noted: 'In my tragedy, Aeneas is neither unfaithful nor ungrateful: to the contrary, he loves Dido, he loves her as much as he can love her; but, before his love, he obeys the Heavens, the oracles, and his glory, which command him to depart' ('En mi tragedia, Eneas ni es infidente ni ingrato: al contrario, él ama a Dido, la ama cuanto puede amarla; pero, antes que a su amor, obedece al Cielo, a los oráculos, y a su gloria, que le mandan partir').[41] Varela's Aeneas is not a seducer who is about to abandon his helpless victim. The Argentine playwright revives on stage a hero who knows how to suppress his feelings and choose duty over passion, responsibility over pleasure, self-sacrifice over self-interest. In his address to Nesteo, Aeneas accepts his fated path and proclaims: 'The relics of Troy, saved to form a superb nation, must be anchored only in the regions where the Tiber runs and the Latin race reigns. The holy oracle has ordered it' ('Las reliquias de Troya, reservadas / Para formar una nación soberbia, / Deben sólo fijarse en las regiones / Dó el Tíber corre, y el Latino reina: / El oráculo santo lo ha ordenado').[42]

Like his Roman counterpart, Varela's Aeneas emerges as a *pius* (dutiful) man, devoted both to the gods and to his fellow Trojans. As such, he is aligned with one of the basic rules of neoclassical theatre called *bienséance* (propriety, decorum). Since tragedy's protagonists are drawn from the realm of the aristocracy, this principle entailed that they act in a manner suitable for their rank; they must be 'noble both in the social sense and in the moral sense of the word'.[43] Elevated from a simple member of Troy's royal house, with no prospect of reigning at home, to a 'king elected by the Trojans who escaped from the fire of their country' ('Rey elegido por los troyanos que escaparon del incendio de su patria'),[44] Aeneas delivers a speech in which he comes across as a leader who is fully aware of his obligation to bring his comrades to their new home where they can live with dignity and respect: 'never could

Aeneas allow so many heroes, since they have survived the fatal destruction of their country, to be pilgrims in the expanse of the broad earth, beggars for foreign shelters, and slaves to alien law' ('nunca Eneas / Pudiera permitir que tantos héroes / Como han sobrevivido a la funesta / Destrucción de su patria, peregrinos / En la extensión de la anchurosa tierra, / Mendigasen asilos extranjeros, / Y esclavos fuesen de una ley ajena').[45] The affair with Dido caused Aeneas to lose track of his destiny, albeit temporarily. Recalled to duty by means of a divine sign, the hero rises to the occasion again and accepts the honour to lead his men, like another Moses, to the land where their sufferings will come to an end.

Although the departure from Dido's kingdom is said to be a celestial dictate, there is no scene taking place on Olympus, as in Virgil, in which Jupiter orders Mercury to fly down to Carthage and deliver his message to Aeneas. Varela's hero receives a prophecy by means of a dream before the play begins. Similarly, the Argentine playwright does not recreate the scene in which Juno and Venus plot to get him and Dido together in a hunting match in the countryside, thereby providing an opportunity for them to consummate their affair in a cave after a storm. One reason for these departures from the Latin text is that the two episodes would look like subplots and their inclusion in the play would violate the unities of time, space and action. More importantly, Varela keeps the divine and human realms apart to make the actions of his characters more believable. By eradicating the intervention of the gods who are never granted status of *dramatis personae*, as is in ancient drama, but enter the play either collectively (*Dioses*) or in an abstract – more Christian-like – form (*cielo*, the Heavens), Varela adheres to another convention of French neoclassical theatre called *vraisemblance* (variously translated into English as verisimilitude, plausibility or likelihood). This rule concerns the coherence and rationality of plot development. It entailed that all characters and events 'should seem inevitable, the logical outcome of the situation at hand – and at the very least they must not appear out of nowhere or offer inconsistencies that might distract the viewing or reading public from the play's central action'.[46] The inclusion of the gods as overseers and regulators of human fate would undermine the sincerity of Aeneas' motives and diminish his heroism. By reducing the divine element to a prophecy, Varela remains faithful to the General condition described in the Roman text – that Aeneas faces a predicament – and constructs a character who is just as ethical and devout.

To be sure, Aeneas' obedience to celestial powers did not escape notice in the *porteño* press. In a review published in *El Argos de Buenos Aires* on the occasion of *Dido*'s inaugural reading at Rivadavia's house, Varela is criticized for casting Aeneas as an 'instrument to the will of the gods' ('instrumento de la voluntad de los Dioses'),[47] which prompted the poet to defend his choice as follows:

> En nuestros tiempos es muy difícil que un hombre de talento se persuada que lo habla el cielo: pero en los grandes tiempos del paganismo, en que los hombres tropezaban con los Dioses, esto era de otro modo: al menos así lo creemos nosotros. Y si no lo creyéramos ¿veríamos con gusto (por ejemplo) la tragedia que sola basta a inmortalizar a Racine? Agamenón en Áulide consiente en el sacrificio de Ifigenia, porque el Sacerdote Calcas pide esta víctima en nombre del cielo … Si nosotros

estuviéramos persuadidos de que en aquel tiempo Agamenón creía que era tal la voluntad del cielo ¿no diríamos ¡que hombre tan fatuo, tan fanático, tan beato! ¿Como vos llamáis Eneas? ¿Qué mas ha hecho este que aquel? Creer, y nada más; y nosotros creemos que ellos creían; porque a no ser así, no veríamos con tanto placer tantas tragedias, cuya acción se levanta sobre el dicho del oráculo.[48]

In our times it is very difficult for a man of talent to be persuaded that the Heavens talk to him: but in the great times of paganism, when men bumped into the gods, this was otherwise: at least that is what we believe. And if we did not believe it, would we see with pleasure (for example) the tragedy that alone suffices to immortalize Racine? Agamemnon at Aulis agrees to the sacrifice of Iphigenia because the priest Calchas demands this victim in the name of the Heavens ... If we were persuaded that at that time Agamemnon believed that such was the will of the Heavens, would not we say: a man so fatuous, so mad, so blessed! What do you call Aeneas? What more has this one done than that one? Believe, and nothing more; and we believe that they believed; because otherwise, we would not see so many tragedies with such pleasure, whose action rises above the words of the oracle.

Although Varela justifies his choice on the basis of Racine's *Iphigénie*, he disregards one of the basic rules of French neoclassical tragedy by portraying Dido's suicide not offstage, but before the viewers.[49] Contrary to Virgil's poem, Aeneas is a witness of Dido's suicide. The inclusion of this scene at the play's close reinforces his tragedy's political message. Dido liberates herself from the torment of unruly, irrational desire by taking her own life, thereby ceasing to be a threat to hegemonic masculinity and patriarchal order that Aeneas represents. Varela's protagonist is a woman who falls short both as a lover and as a leader. She is blinded by her passion to such an extent that she becomes the agent of her ruin and demise. In her figurative role as mother of her nation – a new kingdom she founds by moving her people from Sidon to Carthage – she fails to emerge as a solid symbol of nurturing, protection, family values and social cohesion. She is not the pillar of her society, for her existence is tied to, and defined in connection with, a man who is a foreigner. She is, therefore, banished by means of her suicide from the nation-building process which becomes a male affair, a man's job. At the play's close, femininity is identified with destruction and masculinity with reconstruction.

This highly polarized construction of gender roles in a play addressed primarily to a male audience, as was the case with its original recital, is in line with Eve Kosofsky Sedgwick's view on homosociality and the 'traffic in women' in British literature. She argues that female figures in male-authored texts serve as conduits for cementing social bonds between men (characters as well as readers) and for perpetuating hierarchies and values traditionally seen as the markers of manhood, such as power, status, wealth, physical prowess and sexual accomplishment.[50] The play's final lines echo this theoretical framework that understands masculinity as a homosocial enactment, a quality displayed by men in front of other men who either identify with or compete against them. When

Aeneas sees Dido lying dead, he turns to Nesteo and asks him what to do. The latter responds: 'depart at once' (*partir al punto*). Camaraderie and solidarity between men are achieved through the eradication of the feminine from the public sphere.

This differentiation between Dido as a weak ruler driven by desire she fails to overcome and Aeneas as a steadfast leader swayed by duty does not carry only moral connotations. The inscription of the first neoclassical tragedy produced in post-Independence Argentina into the Virgilian tradition is a political statement, for Varela turns his back to, and thus liberates himself from, Spanish treatments of the story. With the single exception of the myth's first dramatization written by Juan Cirne in 1536, which follows the *Aeneid* closely, the rest of them – from Gabriel Lobo Lasso de la Vega's adaptation composed most likely in 1547 to that by Guillén de Castro that was published sometime between 1613 and 1616 – all draw on the Roman historian Justin of the second or third century AD. In Justin's version (18.4–6), Dido never encounters Aeneas and commits suicide to rescue herself from the sexual advances of the Numidian King Iarbas, in a desperate attempt to remain faithful to her deceased husband Sychaeus. As Lida de Malkiel explains, the reason why Justin's version persists in Spain well into the seventeenth century, unlike in the rest of the European continent, is that the Spanish ecclesiastical tradition relied on his account to celebrate the Carthaginian queen as a paradigm of chastity, marital fidelity and widowhood.[51]

Justin presents a 'Dido remarkable for many reasons, fortitude, leadership, vision, and craft among them'.[52] Seeking to break away from Dido's peninsular reception as a *univira*, a woman with a high sense of morality who is bound to the memory of one man, Varela draws on Virgil to depict a monarch that succumbs to desire to such a degree that she becomes mad, self-destructive, and completely out of control. She might be a respected widow-leader in one strand of the literary tradition, but in Varela's tragedy she comes out as a travesty of these qualities that are attributed to her elsewhere. From the perspective of the republican viewer/reader to whom Varela's play is addressed, Dido could be interpreted as a figure for imperial Spain. This association is not without a historical parallel: the one who financed the 1492 voyage of Christopher Columbus to the New World was Queen Isabel I, who ruled with an iron fist and was compared to Dido and Cleopatra in Spanish literature, especially after the Castilian victory over the Portuguese forces in western Africa.[53] By undertaking to lead his men away from Dido's kingdom and thus rescue them from submission to foreign law, Aeneas symbolizes, in the eyes of his viewers/readers, the father figure or patriarch in charge of the neonate republic's breaking with the administrative and institutional dependencies of the colonial past. Varela's *Dido* metaphorizes an idea prevalent in Latin American fiction and art of the (post-)Independence era. The Mother Nation, identified with the European metropolitan power, is demonized, rejected and replaced by the myth of the male founder who becomes a symbol of continental liberation, unity and progress. The Latin American imaginary space is 'filled by the ubiquitous figure of the military-uniformed soldier-statesman, famously celebrated in iconography and literature'.[54]

The Trojan War marks the end of an era and beginning of a new one. Aeneas sails to Italy destined to found Rome. The wars of 1810–18 mark the beginning of a new era for the region of Río de la Plata: the transition from monarchy to republic. Aeneas who will marry the daughter of the king of the Latins, Lavinia, visualizes a new Troy, just as Rivadavia who married Juana del Pino, daughter of the penultimate Viceroy of Río de la Plata, lays the foundations for a new state. Three years after the *Dido*'s first reading, Rivadavia will be appointed as the first President of the United Provinces, albeit for a short period of time (8 February 1826–27 June 1827), after which he goes into exile. Interestingly, Dido appears for the first time on the Spanish stage in 1536, the year Buenos Aires was founded by the conquistador Pedro de Mendoza.[55] The 1823 rewriting of Rome's foundational myth is very appropriate in a county called (albeit unofficially at the time) Argentina, a derivative of the Latin *argentum* (silver).[56] A year earlier, the patriotic celebrations of 25 May 1822, following the example of the civic festivities staged in Paris in the years after the French Revolution, featured, *inter alia*, invocations to Roman deities, including an exaltation of the image of Jupiter.[57] Within this context of classical appropriations, drawing from Rome's national epic does not come as a surprise. Virgil,[58] like Horace and Ovid whom Varela also translated into Spanish, represents the Augustan Age, an era of rebirth and prosperity after decades of civil wars and political instability in the Italian peninsula. Likewise, with Rivadavia as the chief minister Buenos Aires is modernized to such a degree that sympathetic contemporary historians will label the period of his administration *la feliz experiencia* (The Happy Experience).

CHAPTER 3
LEOPOLDO MARECHAL'S *ANTÍGONA VÉLEZ*: REWRITING GREEK TRAGEDY AS A FOUNDATION MYTH IN PERONIST ARGENTINA

Brenda López Saiz

This chapter examines *Antígona Vélez*, a reworking of Sophocles' *Antigone* written by the Argentine author Leopoldo Marechal and staged in 1951 as part of the Peronist cultural agenda, amidst extreme socio-political unrest in Argentina. Exploring the relation between two works – text A: ancient source; text B: modern reception – entails, as Jauss proposes, an examination of the questions raised in the Greek play and how they are related to its context, or else 'historical horizon', in order to understand why the source text is still relevant in another historical moment.[1] At the same time, to understand fully why aspects of the source work are still important, it is necessary to consider some of the parameters of the reception process, which include, as Lorna Hardwick notes, 'the routes by which a text has moved and the cultural focus which shaped or filtered the ways in which the text was regarded'.[2] Building on this theoretical framework, I argue that *Antígona Vélez* appropriates the plot and some of the central questions of the *Antigone* in order to cast Sophocles' text as a national foundation myth from both a Catholic and a nationalist point of view, thereby aiming at the ideological legitimation of the Peronist government and movement.

This paper suggests two reasons for Marechal's choice to draw on the *Antigone*. First, the problematic relationship, explored in Sophocles' play, between individual and the state and between the human and divine spheres; both inform Peronist ideology and Marechal's political and religious views. These are revisited in *Antígona Vélez*, albeit from a different angle. Second, in this reworking the ancient tale is retold through a Catholic and nationalist filter, with classical antiquity being perceived as part of a common legacy supposedly shared by countries which witnessed fascism and nationalist ideologies in the 1930s and 1940s. This ideological context is necessary in order to evaluate Marechal's rewriting.

The chapter additionally argues that an appreciation of Marechal's play requires an examination of its Argentine political and cultural context. The immediate context of the play is the end of Juan Domingo Perón's first presidential term (1946–52), a time of intense socio-political polarization, during which Perón and the opposition parties campaigned for the presidential elections of November of 1951. Perón became president in 1946, advocating the defence of the nation and the interests of the working class. During his first term, he passed reforms that resulted in his concentrated power and aimed at the establishment of a corporative state. This authoritarian regime, based on a charismatic leader who championed 'the emancipation of Argentine people from oligarchic and imperial domination' ('la emancipación del pueblo argentino de la dominación oligárquica e imperialista'),[3] divided Argentine society and politics into the loyal followers of Peronism and their radical critics. As sociologist Carlos Altamirano points out: 'the emergence of Peronism divided Argentine politics of the twentieth century into two ... an antagonistic dichotomy with lasting consequences for the national public life' ('el surgimiento del peronismo dividió en dos la política argentina del siglo XX ... una dicotomía antagónica de largas consecuencias en la vida pública nacional').[4] *Antígona Vélez*, informed by the Peronist cultural agenda, is part of this specific moment in Argentine history.

But context is, in temporal and cultural terms, a much broader concept and does not necessarily refer only to events that occurred during or immediately before the year of the play's production. As historians Loris Zanatta and David Rock note, Peronism is part of a political and social process that goes back to the 1930s.[5] They argue that there is a close relationship between the basic principles of this movement and the Catholic-nationalist ideology which developed during that decade. Contrary to other historians who focus on the social impact of Peronism and overlook or deny its conservative and even fascist traits, Zanatta and Rock are concerned with its evolution. During the 1930s, Catholic nationalism propagated an essentialist and authoritarian view of the nation, with Catholicism and Spanish legacy as its central components. As will be further discussed in the first part of the chapter, Peronism retains these basic tenets and incorporated them into the advocacy of social justice and national unity as its core elements.

The chapter also argues that context includes the author's previous works. *Antígona Vélez* should be viewed as part of the mythic image of the nation developed by Marechal since the 1930s in *Poemas Australes* (*Southern Poems*) and his famous novel *Adán Buenosayres* (*Adam Buenosayres*). The first version of this image, formulated in *Southern Poems* in 1937, establishes the themes and the literary motifs that were used again in the novel and particularly in *Antígona Vélez*. My reading, therefore, differs significantly from previous scholarship that overlooks the author's earlier work. Additionally, although some scholars consider the play's immediate political context, they do so briefly and without exploring the ideological dimensions of both the play and Peronism, thereby failing to notice the play's religious and political conservative traits.[6] To elaborate these ideas, the first part of the paper focuses on the political and cultural beliefs and processes involved in the creation of a national myth in Marechal's work. The second part presents the characteristics of the mythic image of the nation created by Marechal and analyses *Antígona Vélez* to show how and why this image is central to understanding Marechal's reworking of the *Antigone*.

Catholic nationalism, Peronism and myths of the nation

Antígona Vélez was staged during the last year of Perón's first presidential term. Before being elected president for the first time in 1946, he had participated in the military-nationalist regime that came to power through a *coup d'état* in 1943 and which had strong ties with Catholic nationalist groups and ideas in the 1930s. During his participation in that regime, Perón became one of the strongest political figures and the most popular one, as a result of his work as Secretary of Labour, which led to a remarkable improvement in workers' rights. By 1945, when the dictatorship was forced by the opposition to call presidential elections, Perón was one of the candidates, representing both the continuity of the regime and the hope of the popular groups which demanded improvement of economic and social conditions. Despite a harsh campaign directed against him by most political parties, including socialists and communists, Perón was elected President receiving 54 per cent of the votes. His first three years, between 1946 and 1948, were marked by huge economic success, while higher social mobility and increased welfare granted him the support of the majority of the working class.[7] At the same time, however, the first Peronist government carried out reforms that resulted in the concentration of political power to such a degree that by 1949 a ferocious political opposition had arisen, dividing the country into two extremes: Peronists and anti-Peronists.

During the same period of time, i.e. the 1930s and 1940s, Marechal's career ran almost parallel to the establishment of Catholic Nationalism and Peronism. Since 1931, he participated in the *Cursos de Cultura Católica* ('Courses on Catholic Culture'), an institution dedicated to the study of Catholic thought. It relied on the Church's support since its foundation in 1922 and acquired ecclesiastical status the same year Marechal joined it. As Zanatta notes, the *Cursos* played a fundamental role in the development of Catholic Nationalism, since they were both the physical and political space where the various active nationalist groups gathered, and the intellectual centre of elaboration of Catholic nationalist ideology, with an influence even on the army.[8] The complex and close interaction between the Catholic Church, the various nationalist groups and the army resulted in the spread of nationalism during that period and eventually in the *coup d'état* of 1943. This ideological and political alliance is evident in the participation of many members of the *Cursos de Cultura Católica* in the military government, especially in cultural offices, including Marechal, who was appointed President of the General Board of Schools in the Province of Santa Fe. In 1946, he took part in Perón's campaign, and after the latter's election he contributed actively to the formation and spread of Peronism through his political and literary writings, as well as through his work at the Department of Artistic Instruction.

In 1951, the year of *Antígona Vélez*'s premiere, Perón was campaigning for re-election amidst a violent political and social climate. In this context, culture was an important medium of propaganda, with which the government tried to claim the country's defence and equate the opposition's actions to its destruction. *Antígona Vélez* was part of that agenda: it was commissioned by the director of the Cervantes National Theatre – the most important official theatre – where it was staged in May, under the direction of the famous artist and committed Peronist Enrique Santos Discépolo.[9] However, the play is significantly different from the dominant theatrical trend of the period, comprising mainly 'nativist plays' and 'sainetes', i.e. popular dramatic genres with explicit didactic contents that exhibit the polarity between the 'people-fatherland' (pueblo-patria) and oligarchy-anti-fatherland (oligarquía-antipatria).[10] Instead, *Antígona Vélez* reworks a Greek tragedy in order to represent a metaphysical and religious view of individual and collective existence, which in turn is expressed through a symbolic dramatic discourse and structure, whose religious and political content is far from explicit.

These symbolic traits are a fundamental feature of the mythical image of the nation that Marechal began to develop in *Poemas Australes* more than a decade before he wrote *Antígona Vélez*. This mythical image is informed by the religious and nationalist ideas of the 1930s, but at the same time both the project of creating a nation's myth and the concept of nation underlying it – shared by Catholic Nationalism and afterwards by Peronism – are strongly related to social and political developments which took place years before, during the celebration of the declaration of Independence in 1910. At a time marked by radical social transformation itself caused by rapid modernization, urbanization and massive European immigration, a group of intellectuals subsequently called 'cultural nationalists' reacted, considering these changes as 'foreign elements' and responsible for the 'loss' of the nation. As Jane Delaney explains, the cultural nationalists' concern about the loss of the nation springs from a Romantic concept of nationhood that sees the nation as a unique natural entity, possessing a timeless essence or kernel from which it derives its particular and unique features as well as its 'cultural mission'.[11] For all cultural nationalists, despite the strong political differences among them, the essence of the Argentine nation is a 'spiritual quality' associated with Catholicism, Spanish roots and the countryside. In their view, this essence is threatened by the materialism brought by the modern city, immigration, cosmopolitanism, capitalism and positivist philosophy – all of which were perceived as the outcome of the liberal governments that ruled the country since the second half of the nineteenth century. According to historian Elías José Palti, this essentialist definition of the nation goes alongside a process of 'deconstruction of national history', substituting a historical causal relationship between present and past – dominant during the nineteenth century – with an 'irrational' vision of the past, which since the Centennial comes to conform to the requirements of the present.[12] For Palti, from that period onwards, the historical definition of the nation is replaced by the creation of 'foundation myths' and the historical discourse yields to the literary one.

The concern about the loss and corruption of the nation expressed by the cultural-nationalists and the necessity of creating national myths intensified during the 1930s, a time of political crisis in Argentina that several historians consider as a crisis of the whole liberal political system and the parties that had governed the country since the second half of the nineteenth century.[13] The aforementioned nationalist-conservative and anti-democratic political groups that emerged from this crisis, in alliance with leaders from the Church and the army, developed an ideology that blamed the 'foreign' liberal system for corrupting the nation and demanded the establishment of a 'new order' that would serve as an alternative to liberal democracy. This form of nationalism viewed Catholicism as the nation's essence and conceived the nation as a hierarchical and harmonious entity based on divine law and Christian morals, according to which every individual contributes to the unity of the social body by occupying his/her particular place in it and by obeying authority. This concept excludes conflict and division from the nation and condemns liberal democracy and even politics as a whole, considering them as the cause of disorder. This idea of a 'Catholic nation' also involved a renewed appreciation of Argentina's Spanish roots and, through them, of its inclusion into what was considered as the 'Greek and Latin Christian civilization', whose continuity was guaranteed by countries that 'opposed' the liberal and communist 'heresy', i.e. Italy, Portugal and Spain, 'Latin' countries governed by fascist regimes seen as 'relatives' by Catholic nationalists.

Many of these ideas fuelled Peronism, which preserved the basic tenets of the nationalist ideology while it also redefined part of it. As Zanatta, Sigal and Verón explain, Peronism conceives the nation, similarly to the Catholic-nationalist view, as an essential and un-political entity, which in turn implies the exclusion of any opposition and the condemnation of the political sphere as a realm of division and conflict.[14] Under this ideology, Peronism and the Peronist government present themselves as the incarnation of the national essence and not as a political movement. However, while Catholic Nationalism regards the Catholic religion as the kernel of the nation, Peronism emphasizes the idea of 'unity' as the nation's most essential quality and Catholicism as a fundamental attribute. At the same time, as Verón and Sigal suggest, Peronist discourse associates the government with the 'process of national construction', a process conceived of as the fulfilment of the nation, whose temporality is mythical and cyclical, in that it is constituted by the repetition of 'strong moments' – that is, the moments as the nation unfolds.[15] According to Peronist discourse, therefore, the opposition to the regime is an opposition to the country, to the fatherland (patria): an anti-Peronist is an *antipatria*. At the same time, both current political adversaries and previous liberal governments are excluded from the 'time of the national construction' and relegated to the historical time of corruption and destruction of the nation. In this manner, Peronist discourse and ideology identify with the mythical vision of the nation developed by the cultural nationalism and, as Palti notes, transform it into a 'mass ideology' and a strong social power.[16]

In the 1930s, when Catholic Nationalism proposed a 'new order' but did not have a concrete political project, Marechal created a set of poetic scenes in the *Poemas Australes*, which together form a timeless view of the nation's essence. In 1951, the situation was quite different: two successive governments championed the Catholic and nationalist ideas, presenting their political activity as part of a 'revolution' whose aim was the 'recovery' of the nation. Marechal had worked at cultural institutions of both governments, committing himself actively to the Peronist cause. At that moment, he saw the conflict of Greek drama as the best medium whereby to express the necessity of defending the threatened nation's essence and recast the plot of an ancient tragedy as a foundation myth. In that context, as we will see, *Antigone* is appropriated as a re-elaboration of central moral, religious and political problems involved in its conflict in order to legitimate the Peronist government. At the same time, Marechal's creative reception responds to the Catholic-nationalist desire of incorporating Argentina into the 'Graeco-Latin Christian civilization' to which it supposedly belongs, redefining it as a leading nation in the advancement of (metaphysical and political) 'truth' on earth.[17]

Antigone as a foundation myth

Antígona Vélez situates its dramatic action in the Argentine pampa during the time of the 'conquest of the desert' – the military campaign carried out in the late nineteenth century against the indigenous population of Patagonia and parts of the 'región pampeana'. Marechal replaces Thebes with the ranch owned by the Vélez family called *La Postrera* ('The last one'). The play, thus, takes advantage both of a central image of Argentine culture (the pampa) and of a fundamental episode of Argentine history. In this setting, the dramatic conflict unfolds in ways similar to Sophocles' tragedy: two brothers, Martín and Ignacio Vélez, have died fighting against each other – Martín defending his land, Ignacio attacking it with the pampa Indians. The authority in charge, Facundo Galván – the foreman who became head of the ranch after the master's death – deprives the traitor's corpse of funeral rites, but one of Ignacio's sisters, Antígona Vélez, infringes the prohibition and as a result, she faces punishment. As in the Greek play, the action starts immediately after the decree's promulgation; as the plot unfolds we see the confrontation between the two figures and the consequences of their actions. This apparent similarity, however, fades away when we pay closer attention to the way the dramatic conflict develops. As opposed to the Greek tragedy, where the conflict takes place inside Thebes, involving a clash of values, obligations and interests within the society, *Antígona Vélez* establishes a spatial and semantic opposition between the internal space of the ranch *La Postrera*, represented on stage, and the external space of the pampa inhabited by the indigenous people. Although that space and its inhabitants do not appear on stage, they are constantly referred to in the speeches of the characters, since the attack on that world of 'savagery' threatens the inhabitants of the ranch throughout the dramatic action. This way, while the Greek source text develops only one sequence of actions and events and presents the Argive attack against Thebes as an antecedent to the conflict, *Antígona Vélez* includes a parallel sequence of actions and events around the anticipated attack.[18]

In this spatial and semantic opposition, the world of *La Postrera* includes elements and ideas of the mythical image of the nation already introduced in *Poemas Australes* and reworked in *Adán Buenosayres*. In both works, the pampa or the south – a well-known image in Argentine literature and often metonymy for the nation – is presented as a timeless and archetypal world whose features relate to St. Augustine's conceptions of human existence: there, human beings face their fallen condition, undertaking the pilgrimage to God's realm.[19] The different scenes and images presented in both works show a series of features and acts through which southern men and women acknowledge suffering as a consequence of sin and indispensable part of human existence. Thus, they turn hard work and life into an act of penance and *caritas* – that is, love for God and for creatures and earthly things insofar as they are created by him, a virtue that puts the soul in movement back to God and to the place in the divine order that human beings abandoned as a consequence of the sin. In this rural-metaphysical place, the dependence on nature is described as a form of integration into the divine order, through which the temporal succession of earthly life partakes of unity and eternity. The endless and scarcely populated plain of the pampa, where the gaze 'flies from horizon to horizon' ('vuela de horizonte a horizonte'),[20] becomes the place where truth is neatly and unavoidably manifest. This proximity of men and women to God is repeatedly illustrated in their silence and in their attitude when they face death, which is experienced as the unavoidable step to the possibility of eternal life. In this mythical image of the nation, two actions particularly express *caritas* and combine a religious metaphysical idea of order, emanating from Augustinian thought, with the authoritarian and hierarchical ideas of nationalism and Peronism: men of the pampa conform to the divine order where man is superior to other earthly creatures but subordinated to God, by fulfilling the divine command of the Genesis: 'let man rule over the fish of the sea and the birds of the air, over the livestock, over all the earth, and over all the creatures that move along the ground.'[21] This act of ruling is presented as man's mastery over livestock and wild animals, and that act, in turn, is a manifestation of *caritas*, since it appraises the creatures, assigning them the place they hold in the divine order. While the acceptance of the domestic animal's submissiveness is presented as an act deprived of violence, the taming of the wild horse is depicted as an action accomplished by force and domination over a chaotic and overwhelming nature, necessary to integrate it into order, which is also presented as a state of harmony. By means of this figure, order and harmony are associated with hierarchy and domination, and the use of violence for its establishment is legitimized as a necessary act of *caritas*.

In *Antígona Vélez*, the world of *La Postrera* is portrayed by means of the same elements and symbols of the southern world of *Poemas Australes* and *Adán Buenosayres*. The vast pampa under the sky, the hard-working men and women, the horses and horse tamers, silence and death are all its main components. In the first act, the interior and exterior spaces are metonymically depicted through the features attributed to both brothers and their deaths: Martín Vélez, who died like his father 'killing infidels with his sabre' ('murió sableando a los infieles'), was killed by a spear on his side, 'like Jesus Christ' ('como Cristo Jesús').[22] Like the southern men in *Poemas Australes* and *Adán Buenosayres*, he receives the epithet 'the one who did not talk', and is described in the following terms by a young woman: 'He was like a tree. Strong, right and mute. But he provided shade' ('era como un árbol; fuerte, derecho y mudo. Pero daba sombra').[23] Martín is thus portrayed as a *miles Christi*, whose austerity symbolizes his knowledge of the true sense of earthly life. Accordingly, after his death he is repeatedly said to lie 'over a pine table, wrapped in clean sheets' ('sobre una mesa de pino, envuelto en una sábana limpia'), 'among his four righteous candles' ('entre sus cuatro velas honradas'),[24] with light symbolizing the spirit and its qualities associated with this man who lived having God and eternal life as his goal. Cleanness symbolizes the overcoming of the material dimension and sin already accomplished by Martín during his life.

By contrast, Ignacio Vélez 'went over to the Indians, he, a born Christian!' ('se pasó a los indios, ¡él, un cristiano de sangre!').[25] His epithet is 'the party guy' ('el fiestero').[26] After his death, his body lies outside, 'alone and naked, there, in the tainted water' ('solo y desnudo, allá, en el agua podrida'),[27] 'thrown in the darkness' ('tirado en la negrura'),[28] where the 'visitors with beak and talons were coming through the air, to the smell of Ignacio Vélez and his dead flesh' ('los invitados de pico y garra ya se venían por el aire, al olor de Ignacio Vélez y su carne difunta').[29] The emphasis on darkness, filth and decomposition acts as a reminder of the sin and evil associated with the primacy of the material dimension in his life and the world to which he adhered; his idea(l)s collapse the moment the deceptive pleasure of the senses gives way to the reality of the material existence symbolized by the corruptibility and disintegration of the body.[30]

Another feature of 'southern men' used in *Antígona Vélez* is the figure of the horse tamer. Men of *La Postrera*, born to 'ride a stallion and handle a spear' ('jinetear un potro y manejar una lanza'),[31] are all experienced horse tamers. However, their main struggle does not involve dominating the wilderness, as it is the case in previous works, but defending their land against the 'barbarian' dwellers of the pampas who surround it – not only in the present but, as Facundo Galván states many times, in the name of a future world redeemed of the sufferings they themselves have to endure: 'That is what we are here for, to bleed and weep. Do you understand? ... And what else could we do? One day, men will live on this hill, who do not bleed and women who did not learn to weep' ('Para eso estamos aquí, para sangrar y llorar. ¿Entienden? ... ¿Y qué más podríamos hacer nosotros? Algún día, en esta loma, vivirán hombres que no sangran y mujeres que no aprendieron a llorar').[32]

As noted above, Ignacio is depicted as an example of a man who surrenders to sin and who, by resting his love on earthly things and allowing his body to command the soul, 'sinks to the level of the beasts, and, indeed, in his ferocity and malice towards other men often sinks below the level of the animals', as Herbert Deane puts it about the Augustinian concept of *cupiditas*.[33] This concept informs the construction of interior and exterior space. While the men of *La Postrera* work to return men and wild creatures to their place in the divine order, the 'others' who live outside yield to the material world and, while besieging the ranch during the night, without lighting a fire and standing in the darkness, *eat* their horses raw, an action which explicitly shows the violation of the divine order and hierarchy. If we bear in mind that in Christian and particularly Augustinian philosophy evil is a privation of goodness, and that the goodness of creatures manifests itself through the place each creature holds in God's creation, just as we saw earlier, the external world of *La Postrera* turns out to be one extremely deprived of goodness. In this respect, the men of the ranch fight against a corrupt world not only to defend their land, but also in order to bring goodness to the human world. The opposition between the two worlds implies a transcendental fight between good and evil, in other words, between life and death, soul and body, order and corruption. The fight against evil waged by the people whose mission in life is 'bleeding and weeping' ('sangrar y llorar') – a phrase constantly repeated[34] – for the sake of future women and men, who will live in a world free of suffering, is cast as an act leading to the future salvation of the community. The play, therefore, presents a messianic vision of a future community free of 'evil', whose expectation implies fighting and suffering. Significantly, the representation of this future community, in whose name evil is faced and endured, excludes conflict from its interior and places it outside, associating it with the threatening outer world that must be dominated.

At the same time, this metaphysical confrontation is situated in the historical context of the conquest of the desert, which is an important episode in the process of 'national construction' carried out in the second half of the nineteenth century. However, in line with the nationalists' mythical view of the past, this episode is not only deprived of its historical dimension, but also of its political association with the liberal governments that accomplished it.[35] The historical event is thus de-historicized and inserted into the mythical time of the nation, with the fight against evil cast as an essential act of the nation's fulfilment. Simultaneously, the play associates this fight with a central image of the liberal national project, the construction of the nation as a fight between civilization and barbarism, but re-semanticizes it from a religious and metaphysical point of view. In this way, *Antígona Vélez* appropriates the past for the needs of the present that seeks to 'reflect and represent itself symbolically through it' ('reflejarse y representarse simbólicamente a través de él').[36]

A past event, which has become a mythical moment of the 'non-historical and timeless process of the nation's construction' ('tiempo a-histórico de construcción de la patria'),[37] symbolically represents and legitimates the present, which seeks itself to become one of those moments. As a result, the fight between Peronism and the political opposition becomes a new version of the fight against evil, where the 'Indian attacks' ('indiada de los malones') stands for the 'antipatria' and must be fought for the defence and constitution of the nation. At the same time, the image of the conquest of the desert as a fight against 'barbarie' invests this new version of the fight waged by Peronism with the same attributes, incorporating it into the civilizing crusade of the nation's construction, now redefined as an attempt to establish the transcendental order on earth. The appropriation of that image makes full sense if we consider the vision of Peronism as a new episode of barbarism spread by the political opposition since 1945.[38] In response, Peronism will try to detach itself from that association, establishing continuity with the 'civilizing project' of Sarmiento through different discursive and symbolical strategies, and associating the (other) political parties with barbarism, as this example of one of Peron's speeches clearly shows:

> En el orden político, los partidos se han combatido con encono, unos a otros, en tal forma, que en determinados momentos han parecido tribus salvajes que se disputaban su propio sustento.[39]
>
> In the political order, parties have fought each other with ill-will, in such a way that in certain moments they seemed savage tribes disputing their own living.

By means of the mythical appropriation of the historical past, *Antígona Vélez* can be considered as part of the symbolic strategies of Peronism that attribute the condition of barbarian to the 'antipatria' opponents.[40]

Returning now to the plot's development, the actions of Antígona, her brothers and Facundo (Creon) are part of that central opposition: Ignacio Vélez dies and is punished because of his participation in a siege whose final struck will occur only at the end of the play. Antígona's opposition to the leader is refashioned as an opposition to the one who not only defends *La Postrera* against the constant threat of the world of disorder and evil that surrounds it, but also as the one who defends the seed of the future community free of evil. Consequently, Antígona's opposition to Facundo is neither the main conflict of the play nor her principal action. On the one hand, we do not find here two opposed positions about the hierarchy of social values and obligations, as in Sophocles, where the priority given by Antigone to the obligations prescribed by family/blood relationship ties and founded on traditional religious *nomima* clashes with the ruler's edict based on the hierarchical predominance of civic bonds and interests – a moral and political stance which in Creon's (erroneous) view necessarily expresses and coincides with the divine judgement. Instead, in the confrontation between Antígona and Facundo, an encounter that takes place in the second act of the play, she mainly objects to the legitimacy of his authority. On the other hand, the funeral rite becomes the most important act of Antígona, whose execution is dramatically prepared and anticipated since the beginning of the play. Its narration by Antígona *herself* is located exactly at the middle of the dramatic action, *after* Antígona's and Facundo's debate. This happens because her action entails her going into the dangerous external space, where her brother's corpse lies. This action is then refashioned as an intense spiritual experience of suffering, which in Christian views constitutes the soul's experience of evil.

In *Adán Buenosayres*, the protagonist Adán defines the saint as the perfect imitator of God in the order of redemption,[41] i.e. the saints take part in Christ's redemptive love and sacrifice, making men's suffering his own, and loving them as Christ loved them. In the climactic moment of the spiritual experience which constitutes the focus of the plot, Adán thinks of exemplary figures who can guide him in his ordeal. Two of them are figures of the Catholic Church: the Blessed philosopher and mystic Ramón Llull, and Santa Rosa de Lima, famous for the obsessive practice of mortification of the flesh. Surprisingly, the third figure who accompanies these saintly models is Antigone, whose action is redefined as a victory of the spirit over the flesh, a gesture which appropriates the Greek character and includes it in the Catholic Christianity's hosts:

> La carne corruptible no soporta el asco de su propia disolución. Pero el alma no tiene olfato: ¡venerable Antígona, disputando a cuervos y hombres el cadáver de su hermano, cumpliendo el rito fúnebre, a medianoche, solita su alma entre la polvareda y el hedor con que la carne grita su derrota![42]

> The corruptible flesh does not bear the nausea of its own dissolution. But the soul has no smell: Venerable Antigone, competing against raven and men for the corpse of her brother, carrying out the funeral rite, at midnight, her soul alone among the dust cloud and the stench with which the flesh screams its own defeat!

The main features of this Catholic Antigone, presented in the novel published three years before, are dramatically developed in *Antígona Vélez*. In the play, like Christ and the saints, Antígona suffers and faces the evil that surrounds her dead brother who, by lying outside in abandonment, is totally deprived of the possibility of redemption through love. When she narrates her action of burying her brother in a dialogue with Lisandro (Haemon's role) and the women and men of *La Postrera* – which stand for the chorus –

she describes it as an experience of 'loss' and 'recovering of the soul', signalling through this Paulinian vocabulary the risk involved in the confrontation with the radical and definitive lack of goodness, which her soul overcomes:

Lisandro (*Consternado*) ¡Antígona! ¡Sola y de noche! ¡Y con la furia del sur alrededor!

Antígona (*Dirá su relato con absoluta naturalidad*) Se levantaba la luna. Los perros me acompañaron hasta la Puerta Grande.

Mujeres ¡Tu alma sola!

Hombres ¡Y el miedo afuera!

Mujeres ¿Qué alma tuviste?

Antígona Mi alma no la sentía en mí: estaba fuera, junto al Otro, en el barro. Se me había ido, y salí a buscarla. En la Puerta Grande los perros me lamían las manos …

Antígona ¡Era fácil! Porque yo había encontrado mi alma junto a la pena de Ignacio Vélez. La recogí entonces y me puse a cavar: los pájaros volvían como enloquecidos; se descolgaban sobre mí con sus picos gritones; y yo los hacía caer a golpes de pala. Creía estar en un sueño donde yo cavaba la tumba de Ignacio, lo escondía bajo tierra y le ponía flores de cardo negro. Yo estaba soñando. Y al despertar vi que todo se había cumplido. Mi alma se desbordó entonces y me vino un golpe de risa.[43]

Lisandro (*with dismay*) Antígona! Alone and during the night! With the fury of the south around her!

Antígona (*She will tell her account with absolute easiness*) The moon was rising. The dogs came along up to the Great Gate.

Women Your soul alone!

Men And fear outside!

Mujeres What soul did you have?

Antígona My soul, I didn't feel it inside me: it was outside, by the Other, in the mud. I had lost it, and I went out seeking it. By the Great Gate the dogs licked my hands … It was easy! Because I had found my soul overwhelmed by sorrow for Ignacio Vélez. I picked it up then and started digging: the birds came back as if they were driven mad; they hung above me with their screaming beaks; and I made them fall with shovels. I thought I was in a dream in which I dug Ignacio's grave, hid it under the earth, and put black thistle flowers on it. I was dreaming. And on awakening I saw that everything had been fulfilled. My soul burst then and I started to laugh.

At the same time this experience reveals to her the truth and justice of Facundo's fight, eliciting from her the recognition of her former misjudgement, exposed in the preceding act. Then, the funeral rite is not the rebelling act which, once accomplished, prompts the irreconcilable conflict, as in the *Antigone*; conversely, it is the transcendental experience which solves the conflict, confirming the right of the ruler's decision. After her mystic experience of recognition, Antígona accepts the necessity of submitting to Facundo's authority, and faces her death as a necessary part of the transcendental fight and mission conducted by him:[44]

> **Antígona** El sur es amargo, porque no da flores todavía. Eso es lo que aprendió hace mucho el hombre que hoy me condena. Yo lo supe anoche, cuando buscaba una flor para la tumba de Ignacio Vélez y solo hallé las espinas de un cardo negro ... El hombre que hoy me condena es duro porque tiene razón. Él quiere ganar este desierto para las novilladas gordas y los trigos maduros; para que el hombre y la mujer, un día, puedan dormir aquí sus noches enteras; para que los niños jueguen sin sobresalto en la llanura. ¡Y eso es cubrir de flores el desierto![45]

> **Antígona** The south is bitter, because it has not produced flowers yet. That is what the man that condemns me today learnt long ago. I came to know it yesterday, when I was searching for a flower for Ignacio Vélez's grave and only found the thorns of a black thistle ... The man that condemns me today is harsh because he is right. He wants to gain this desert for the fat cattle and the ripe wheat; so that man and woman, one day, can sleep here their whole nights; so that children play in the plain without startling. And that entails covering the desert with flowers!

In this way, Antígona's sacrifice joins the fight against evil waged by the men of *La Postrera* as part of the foundational actions of the future community.[46] At the same time, like Christ, Antígona faces evil, and from it she retrieves goodness. Thanks to her redemptive love, the 'other' is not totally defeated, but receives the possibility of redemption, which includes it symbolically into the community.

Antígona's actions, however, do not finish with her sacrifice: her experience of evil is followed and complemented by an intense experience of goodness. The play reworks the frustrated marriage between Antigone and Haemon and Antigone's marriage with death, and dedicates the fourth act to the love scene between Antígona and Lisandro, Facundo's son and skilled horse tamer. After facing death and suffering, Antigone experiences life and joy, a complementary opposition which is emphasized by images of light. In this scene, both figures remember and narrate the moment of love's emergence, which significantly occurred while Antígona watched Lisandro taming a horse for the first time: both past and present scenes occur during midday under the sun, 'with so much sun above' ('¡Y con tanto sol arriba!', Antígona), 'so much light above and beneath' ('¡tanta luz arriba y abajo!', Lisandro).[47] The domination of the horse mingles with the erotic emotions which both felt for the first time and which are also openly acknowledged for the first time in the dramatic present. Like her former transcendental experience, this one is cast as an initiation: the experience of love yields a new comprehension about her encounter with death and evil. After it, Antígona recognizes the creative force of love as a necessary act for the sake of a future community.

The transcendental connotation of the love scene is reinforced and clearly marked by the religious imagery attached to it. In the notes of the script, Antígona and Lisandro are cast as the first couple of the biblical image:

> Explanada en la loma: tierra desnuda, cielo desnudo. En el centro, un ombú de raíces viboreantes y copa desarbolada. Lisandro, a la derecha del ombú, y Antígona Vélez, a la izquierda, los dos inmóviles, darán la impresión de una estampa bíblica: la pareja primera junto al árbol primero.[48]

> Flat area on the hill: bare land, bare sky. In the centre, an ombú with serpentine roots and leafless toptree. Lisandro, on the right side of the ombú, and Antígona Vélez on the left, both motionless will give the impression of a biblical image: the first couple by the first tree.

Unlike the biblical first couple, who abandoned paradise because of sin, this couple live in a present heavily defined by the consequences of the fall. Consequently, their love cannot but be marked by suffering and death: while the narrative of the 'falling in love' scene presents love and desire mingled with pain, at the end of the play the union of both lovers can realize only in death.

At the same time, while the acts of the biblical couple distanced men of paradise and God, the death of these lovers is presented as an act that leads women and men back to God through love. As in Sophocles' tragedy, they also die together, this time killed by the same 'Indian' spear, as they ride out of *La Postrera* facing the sunset. This couple, however, is not the corrupted manifestation of the union between *thanatos* and *eros*; on the contrary, they overcome dead, becoming the foundational couple of the future community free of evil:[49]

> **Don Facundo** (*Arrancándose a su contemplación, dice a los Hombres*) Hombres, cavarán dos tumbas, aquí mismo, donde reposan ya. Si bien se mira, están casados.
>
> **Mujeres** ¿Casados?
>
> **Don Facundo** (Doliente y a la vez altivo) Eso dije.
>
> **Hombre 1°** (*A Don Facundo*) Señor, estos dos novios que ahora duermen aquí, no le darán nietos.
>
> **Don Facundo** ¡Me los darán!
>
> **Hombre 1°** ¿Cuáles?
>
> **Don Facundo** Todos los hombres y mujeres que, algún día, cosecharán en esta pampa el fruto de tanta sangre.[50]

Don Facundo (*Coming back from contemplation, says to the Men*) Men, you will dig two graves, here, where they already rest. As a matter of fact, they are married.

Women Married?

Don Facundo (*Grieving and at the same time lofty*) That is what I said.

1st Man (*To don Facundo*) Sir, this couple, now sleeping here, won't give you grandchildren.

Don Facundo They will!

1st Man Which ones?

Don Facundo All men and women who, one day, will harvest in this pampa the fruit of so much blood.

The reworking of Sophocles' play in *Antígona Vélez* serves to restate some of the central problems posed by the Greek tragedy: the relation between individual and community and between the private and public spheres; the bonds and obligations associated with them and the potential conflicts arising from their interaction; the relation between human world and actions and a metaphysical divine realm which transcends it. Through the representation of a mythical moment of the nation's construction, the play legitimizes the 'sacrifice' of the individuals for the sake of the community by means of a metaphysical and religious basis, casting it as part of a redemptive fight against evil, whose final moment lies in the messianic fulfilment of the nation. This way, the play contributes to the Peronist's 'construction of the nation' towards its final goal: the 'union' of all Argentine people in 'love',[51] in whose name violence and domination are presented as legitimate actions. At the same time, the reworking of the *Antigone* Christianizes the Greek play, seeking to integrate the ancient tradition into the 'universal truth' of Christendom, and to reincorporate the Argentine 'Latin culture' into the 'Graeco-Latin Christian tradition' to which, in Marechal's view, it belongs.

CHAPTER 4
JUAN RADRIGÁN'S *MEDEA MAPUCHE*: RECREATING EURIPIDES' REVENGE TRAGEDY IN AN INDIGENOUS CHILEAN CONTEXT
Irmtrud König

> . . . la historia nos cuenta que hubo un tiempo en que sus habitantes originarios fueron libres y felices, pero no hay prueba de ello. De lo que sí existen pruebas, es que de pronto sobrevinieron trescientos años de lucha por aquello que más les pertenecía: la tierra y libertad.
>
> Juan Radrigán

> . . . history teaches us that there was a time when its original inhabitants were free and happy, but there is no evidence for that. Evidence does exist of the three hundred years of struggle that suddenly fell upon them to defend what was most rightfully theirs: land and freedom.[1]

> Chile se fundó sobre la ruina de la sociedad indígena del sur. Sobre una masacre.[2]
>
> José Bengoa

> Chile was founded on the ruins of the southern indigenous society. On a massacre.

Next to Antigone, Medea is probably the most frequently adapted figure of Greek drama in Latin America. Her disturbing complexity has given rise to a number of productive versions, many of which, whether serious or parodic, and more or less faithful to the Greek model, stand for social, racial or gender demands in the region.[3] This chapter is concerned with Juan Radrigán's *Medea Mapuche* (2000), which reworks the Medea plot within a specifically Chilean indigenous environment, as suggested by its title. Based explicitly on Euripides' *Medea*, this rewriting of the Greek tragedy recaptures, with unsettling rawness, the figure of the wife who murders her children out of revenge, purposely against the backdrop of the ethnic, cultural and historical context of the Mapuche. This indigenous group still inhabits Chilean territory today despite genocide and persistent ostracism since the Spanish occupation in the sixteenth century.[4] With this adaptation, Radrigán joins a number of other earlier Latin American rewritings of Medea, which are set in the context of indigenous issues, such as Mexican Jesús Sotelo Inclán's *Malitzin, Medea americana* (1957) and Argentine David Cureses' *La frontera* (1960).

In this chapter, I consider Radrigán's motivations for relocating this prominent figure from ancient Corinth to a local and marginal Mapuche setting. Certainly, there are no definitive answers to such questions, but the fact that both female protagonists come from oral cultures is, in my view, a key element that provides insight to the issues discussed in this play. This chapter, therefore, explores the manner in which the personal characteristics that the Mapuche protagonist shares with the Greek Medea – in particular, an unhinged thirst for revenge – can be traced back to a cultural context of oral tradition whose norms and values have been breached, especially the custom of oath-breaking. Given that revenge is the central motif which results in murder – in this case a most disturbing kind as it entails wreaking vengeance through the killing of one's own children – I argue that *Medea Mapuche* should be considered a modern and 'local' drama in the tradition of the ancient Greek subgenre of revenge tragedy,[5] against the specific background of the invasion of Mapuche territories and their continued struggle for physical, cultural and territorial survival. Furthermore, the essay illustrates how these issues can help comprehend the rewriting of this Greek tragedy in the context of the Mapuche people's tough realities within contemporary Chilean society.

The political and cultural setting of the play

Medea Mapuche premiered in Santiago de Chile in 2000, a decade after the country initiated its democratic reconstruction, following nearly seventeen years of military dictatorship (1973–89). The play's author, Juan Radrigán (1937–2016), had already been featured on the national theatrical stage since 1979, some years after the military coup. Despite the regime's severe restrictions on the freedom of speech, Radrigán created an initial cycle of intense theatrical production, staging about fifteen plays during this period,[6] which, briefly summarized, can be characterized by their realism in local settings, and protagonists who survive in extremely precarious economic and social conditions caused by their displacement and marginalization by an authoritarian power.[7] This initial cycle of plays soon earned the author national and international recognition and came to an end around 1990, when Chile began its return to democracy.[8]

In the early 1990s, a period heavily marked by the end of the dictatorship and the beginning of the often ambiguous process of democratic 'transition', Radrigán commenced a new cycle in his dramatic production. This cycle was far more engaged with issues concerning the country's democratic reconstruction as well as the intellectual and moral challenges inherent in this period's confrontation with its immediate past and present.[9] Hence, Radrigán forms part of a group of authors who, from different perspectives, set forth to reflect on memory and its dramatic elaboration. However, he does not participate in the iconoclastic and postmodern theatrical poetics of his peers, especially evident in the young authors that emerged in the local theatrical scene.

Medea Mapuche forms part of the dramatic production in this new cycle. Its subject addresses a reality traditionally ignored by Chilean society: the disturbing life conditions of the Mapuche people who have been ostracized and discriminated against by the Chilean state since its foundation and who were harshly repressed during the dictatorship. Radrigán's *Medea* poses central questions about this situation, which to date remain unresolved in Chilean society. This is briefly the political and cultural context, indispensable for understanding Radrigán's updating of the myth in the Mapuche universe.

In regard to the formal dramatic aspects of the play, *Medea Mapuche* constitutes a short text whose plot develops in just one act, parcelled into units or frames marked by the entrance and exit of characters. Though none of the characters is named after those in Euripides' tragedy, the intertextual relations are explicitly emphasized throughout the text, since, aside from the title and subtitle's direct reference,[10] both the plot and the dialogue frequently quote or paraphrase Euripides' *Medea*.[11] Although the text is primarily written in Spanish, there are passages in Mapudungun, the language of Mapuche people, probably suggesting that the on-stage representation is also meant for a Mapuche audience.

The most obvious comparable elements between the Greek model and its Chilean rewriting are, with slight variations, the play's three central characters: Kütral, her husband Licán and the *lonco* (chief in the Mapuche language) Lemunao, who is Licán's father, all of whom find their Greek counterparts in Medea, Jason and Creon, respectively. As in the source text, the characters who clash with one another belong to different communities. While Medea comes from what the Greeks considered a barbarian and remote region of the then-known world, in Radrigán's version Kütral is of *lafkenche* origin (i.e. she comes from the coast). Adhering to an exogamic Mapuche custom, she integrates herself into her husband's community in the Andean region of southern Chile. Both husband and wife are descendants of the prestigious families of *loncos* and *ulmenes* (chiefs or patriarchs in Mapuche communities), just as Medea and Jason belong to royal dynasties. Although Kütral has not killed in her past – unlike Medea who has killed in order to aid Jason – her 'heart is a well of guilt' ('su corazón es un pozo de culpas')[12] and nostalgia for her old surroundings, as a result of having married the warrior Licán against her brothers' will. Finally, in both stories the dramatic conflict is instigated by an act of betrayal and oath-breaking, unleashing revenge by means of infanticide.

As in the story of Medea, Kütral's past is renewed in the dramatic present through the dialogue between Lemunao and Maitú, whose role is similar to that of Medea's nurse. The reference to a Mapuche context is constructed through a variety of elements, including the use of language; the symbolic meaning of several names (Kütral, for example, means 'fire'); the nostalgia for a 'blue land' (ancestral homeland); the good harvest ceremony addressed to Mapuche divinities such as Ngenechen, Wenu Fücha and Wenu Kushe; constant references to *lonkos*, *ulmenes* and *winkas*;[13] the presence of *werkenes* (messengers); and finally the invocation of Anchimallen and Witranalwue, here spirits of vengeance. In this context, the dominating presence of the *winka* is heavily felt on a daily basis: speaking in Mapudungun is prohibited, and even the barest expression of rebellion is met with zero tolerance. However, this subjugation is only a façade; a result of strategic aims settled by the Elderly Council, 'the *winkas* are victorious, but only until the arrival of winter, when the rivers rise and they are unable to manoeuvre ... Then ... the struggle will begin again' ('los winkas son vencedores, pero sólo hasta la llegada del invierno, cuando los ríos estén crecidos y ellos no puedan maniobrar ... entonces ... comenzar[á] ... de nuevo la lucha').[14]

Kütral, thus, is no foreigner and anything but a 'barbarous outsider' in her new community. However, she has violated her family duties and loyalty out of love for the warrior Licán, just as Medea betrays her family out of love for the leader of the Argonauts. Both protagonists, therefore, share the fundamental premise that unites them in an act of betrayal and provides the central motif of the tragic conflict and its ill-fated consequences. In the Greek tragedy, Jason betrays Medea by marrying the daughter of the king of Corinth, an act that outrages the solemn and godly protected oath that in Medea's eyes legitimized their marital engagement,[15] in exchange for her help in seizing the Golden Fleece back in Colchis. As Anne Burnett has observed, Jason is 'a man of injustice', a man who, aside from his opportunistic motives, is persistently mentioned by the Chorus and even by Medea as an 'impious oath-breaker'.[16] Therefore, what is questioned is not only the act of sexual infidelity but also, first and foremost, the infringement of the oath, deemed unbreakable by Zeus and Themis, 'the enforcers of oaths'.[17] In other words, their alliance introduces a customary and divinely protected code in Medea's cultural environment, which remained valid in Euripides' society.[18]

In Radrigán's play, we do not know if a comparable oath legitimizes the matrimonial relationship between Licán and Kütral. However, we are told that when Licán arrives in Kütral's community for 'matters of war' ('asuntos de guerra')[19] against the *winkas*, she joined him, captivated by his courage and beauty. So, it seems, they became a 'married' couple by means of Mapuche customary elopement, mutually consented,[20] and this engagement was never violated by Licán in the play. Consequently, Kütral's outrage is not motivated by erotic or matrimonial infidelity. Considering the contextual circumstances, the major difference to the Greek tragedy, as we will see below, rests in the fact that revenge results from an infringement of the Mapuche warrior code of ancestral customary law, provoking a profound feeling of betrayal in Kütral's heart. The motives that unleash her vengeance can only be fully understood in light of Mapuche history, whose major events Radrigán incorporates throughout his text in order to generate the contextual background for the conflict between Kütral and her family-in-law.

Radrigán's play may be read along the historical background given by fictional and non-fictional 'con-textual' references, which construct a dramatic discourse that merges different periods of Mapuche history, surpassing the limited and somewhat undefined frames that constitute the play's fictional timeline. Specifically, the timeline includes the Spanish invasion of southern Mapuche territories met with prolonged resistance through the 'Arauco War' between the sixteenth and eighteenth centuries,[21] as well as the so-called 'Pacification of Araucanía', also known as the 'Death War', undertaken by the Chilean army at the beginning of the nineteenth century.[22] The most obvious references to the Arauco War emphasize the torture of Mapuche prisoners at the hands of Spanish soldiers. Scattered throughout the text, these references include torture by means of 'burning, severing hands, tongues and ears' ('quemar, cortar manos, lenguas y orejas'),[23] forcing Licán's family to witness his 'horrible death' ('atroz muerte')[24] probably by impalement,[25] by threats to destroy the entire community, female violation and 'dogging' (intentional attacks by dogs), among others. These practices are documented in various sources, such as the sixteenth century epic poem *La Araucana* written by Alonso de Ercilla, a Spanish soldier who participated in the war to conquer Arauco.[26] Though a subject of the Spanish Crown, as a direct witness, his explicit intention was to offer a 'real history' of the events of war.[27] In Chile, since Independence, this poem has been considered a foundational text for the nation on account of (among other reasons) its description of the war and its recognition of the tough and valiant resistance of the Araucan people. Their most distinguished warriors, Galvarino, Caupolicán and Lautaro, are portrayed with exceptional, almost mythical characteristics. Ercilla's epic provides descriptions of how the Spanish executed the warrior Galvarino, first by cutting off both his hands (Canto XXII) and later hanging him (Canto XXVI), as well as Caupolicán's execution by impalement, described in Canto XXXIV. Other testimonies of monstrous punishments can be found in letters sent to the Spanish Crown. For example, the *conquistador* Pedro de Valdivia wrote to Emperor Charles V about how he 'tormented' Indians to obtain information.[28] Likewise, the Dominican priest Fray Gil González de San Nicolás, first defender of the indigenous population in Chile, wrote to the royal authorities of the Consejo de Indias in the year 1559 explicitly condemning how Indians were 'dogged, hung, their arms, feet, noses, countless fingers cut off, and after cutting off their thumbs or other members, were packed into the Governor's carriage' ('los aperrearon, ahorcaron muchos, cortaron brazos, pies, narices, dedos sin número, y después de haberles cortado los pulgares o otros miembros los cargaban con el carruaje del Gobernardor').[29]

With this context in mind, it is worth looking at one of Kütral's most telling lines: 'I have always chosen to clutch the spear a hundred times rather than give birth once' ('¡Siempre preferí empuñar cien veces la lanza que parir una sola!'),[30] which recalls Medea's famous line, 'I would rather stand three times with a shield in battle than give birth once' (ὡς τρὶς ἂν παρ' ἀσπίδα / στῆναι θέλοιμ' ἂν μᾶλλον ἢ τεκεῖν ἅπαξ, 250–1).[31] Radrigán likely uses this phrase to allude to the female figure of Janequeo, a warrior and Mapuche military strategist, known as a *toqui*, still alive today in the collective imaginary, in the Mapuche community as well as in the Chilean society. Janequeo is a legendary figure – Guevara includes her in his Mapuche history with the title 'The legend of the warrior women' ('La leyenda de las mujeres guerreras')[32] – and relates perfectly to Kütral's militant nature, a feature that is underlined by the paraphrased quotation taken from Euripides.[33]

On the other hand, when Radrigán's text mentions, on different occasions, the act of 'burning', it refers not only to the burning of people but also to the systematic burning of Mapuche crops and homes. This practice, intended to defeat the Mapuche through hunger and fear, was common from the time of the invasion until recently as part of the 'pacification' and 'colonization' implemented during the nineteenth and twentieth centuries. There are also indirect references to the usurpation of indigenous lands, today occupied by large *haciendas* and lumber companies.[34] This practice has confined the

Mapuche people to reduced territories, proving to be severely detrimental to a population who had prospered from livestock for centuries.[35] Today, the Mapuche survive literally 'enclosed' on small plots of land that can barely sustain them; their lives are characterized by sacrifice and poverty.

Among some other references in Radrigán's text to practices dating back to colonial times,[36] there is reference to the prohibition of the Mapuche language, Mapudungun,[37] a measure of forced assimilation first employed by the Spanish conquistadores, and later, during the Republic – for example, in public schools – in order to integrate, by all means possible, the indigenous population into a Western-centric 'civilization'.[38] Since the foundation of the Republic, José Bengoa writes, 'the need for "integration", for "assimilation"... will preside over all the politics of the Chilean State' ('la necesidad de "integración", de "asimilación"... presidirá todas las políticas del Estado chileno').[39]

The conflict between Kütral and her family-in-law is intimately linked to the historical background briefly reviewed above. This conflict unravels once Kütral receives word that her husband Licán – whom she believed was absent at war – has been taken prisoner for 'parleying' with the *winkas*, a mission ordered by his father and which he fulfilled unarmed. Upon discovering the nature of the encounter, Kütral:

> ¿A parlamentar? ¿Un guerrero? Nuestros ojos sólo sirven para ver las infernales matanzas que hacen los winkas, nuestros oidos solo escuchan decir que despedazar a un mapuche no es despedazar a un ser humano, ¿y ustedes hablan de parlamentar?... ¿Acaso Licán no los ha visto arrancar las criaturas de las tetas de sus madres y estrellarlos contra las peñas? ¿No los ha visto quemar, cortar manos, lenguas y orejas?... Buenos guerreros teníamos en el tiempo antiguo, ya no, ya no luchan. La contestación que dan es la sumisión, el parlamento. ¡Infeliz raza que se extingue, cómo fue que llegaste a esto![40]

> Parleying? A warrior? Our eyes only serve to see the hellish massacres committed by the winkas; our eyes only hear that dissecting a Mapuche is not the same as dissecting a human being. And you speak of parleying?... Has Licán not seen them strip babies from their mothers' teats and hurl them against rocks? Has he not seen them burn, cut hands, tongues and ears?... We used to have good warriors in ancient times, but not anymore, they do not fight anymore. The response they give is submission and parley. Miserable race falling into extinction, how is it that you've come to this!

And she adds, referring to *lonco* Lemunao: 'Was it he? Did he dishonour his own son? I would've never expected this from an Ulmen! He'll pay a high price for this miserable deed!' ('Fue él? ¿Deshonró a su propio hijo? ¡Jamás lo hubiera esperado de un Ulmen! ¡Caro pagará esta miserable acción!').[41] Learning that Licán was captured without offering resistance not only causes Kütral's profound grief and anger, which highlight the motives of her infanticide, but also summarizes the historical density which the author lays upon her. Through Kütral, Radrigán installs, on the present-day stage, the heroic struggle and resistance of the Mapuche people since the Spanish invasion – a resistance that has ultimately been vanquished since the War of Pacification started by the Chilean state after Independence.

'Parleys' were essentially 'Peace Accords' between Mapuche *loncos* and Spanish authorities, dating back to the mid-seventeenth century. The Parley of Quilín, carried out in 1640, was the first documented procedure of this type, which sought to establish Mapuche obedience to the King in exchange for their freedom from exhausting labour on Spanish *haciendas* and mines; it also gave them the right to live where they pleased, without confining them to reduced territories.[42] Despite frequent violations of this treaty on both sides, successive parleys consolidated stable borders between two 'nations' on the basis of permanently recognizing Araucan peoples as vassals to the Spanish Crown, a measure ratified in the last parleys held in the eighteenth century.

However, when the stability of the border drastically changed with Independence, the Mapuche suffered a definitive military defeat in November of 1881.[43] Since then, as Chilean Congressman Francisco Huenchumilla has stated, the Mapuche have been subject to constant 'reductionism, a combination of conquest and colonialism, with abusive and eradicating procedures, ... humiliation and discrimination that has left them with a pessimistic outlook on life, full of mistrust and lacking confidence in the "huincas", represented by the State and Chilean society' ('reduccionismo, mezcla de conquista y colonización, con procedimientos de abusos y atropellos ... humillaciones y discriminaciones que [los] dejarán con una visión pesimista de la vida, llena de desconfianzas y de falta de credibilidad en los "huincas" representados por el Estado y la sociedad chilena').[44] These events are crucial in order to understand Kütral's reaction. For her, the fact that Licán 'parleyed' with the *winkas* means he gave up the struggle, hence he '*betrayed his race*'[45] ('ha traicionado a su raza'),[46] a betrayal that includes herself. Therefore, subsequent events such as the 'Pacification of Araucanía', as well as the violence and degrading treatment by the Chilean state regarding basic rights, can only ensure a road to 'death', symbolically represented in the text by Licán, who is imprisoned and executed for parleying. This symbolic death – physically and in terms of submission and cultural assimilation into Western civilization – is projected onto the present of the dramatic enunciation, which represents the author's voice.

In 1989, a few years before Radrigán began working on *Medea Mapuche*, the so-called 'Accords of Nueva Imperial'[47] took place with the participation of practically all the indigenous organizations in Chile, resembling, to some extent, the old Parleys between the Mapuche and the Spanish crown. On this occasion, Patricio Aylwin (future President of Chile, 1990–4), solemnly promised to 'draft a new Indigenous Law and present a Constitutional reform that recognized indigenous populations as valid participants in national institutionalism ... Indigenous organizations, in return, promised to abide by democracy' ('dictar una nueva Ley Indígena y presentar una reforma a la Constitución que reconociera a los pueblos indígenas como actores válidos en la institucionalidad nacional ... Las organizaciones indígenas, por su parte, se comprometían con la democracia').[48] Though President Aylwin kept his promise and presented the legal project in 1993, the law 'remains inactive in Congress since those years' ('duerme en el Congreso desde esos años'), as Bengoa states.[49]

Departures from Euripides' *Medea*, or why Kütral becomes 'Medea'

What was discussed above is the political setting in which Radrigán situates his reworking of Euripides' tragedy. My discussion aimed to provide the necessary background information with which to appreciate Kütral's character, as well as the play's grim outcome. However, we should emphasize that the play does not idealize Mapuche people; rather it attempts to recover the memory of their tragic historical past in order to highlight, but not to justify, the protagonist's outrage and grievance, just as Euripides' Medea demands vengeance on account of past events that occurred before the couple's arrival at Corinth. In this perspective, Kütral emerges with the same complexity and ambivalence as her Greek model. Haughty and proud, she is described from the viewpoint of her opponents with expressions that recall Euripides' text. She is said to be notable for her 'cruel nature, and ... the dark vigour of her passions' ('índole cruel, y ... negro ímpetu de sus pasiones');[50] her 'heart ... [that] cries out and swears' ('su corazón ... clama y jura');[51] her defiant attitudes, as she claims 'no one shall laugh at my pain'[52] ('nadie se reirá de mis dolores').[53] Such characterizations, among others, point to Radrigán's intention to draw a parallel between both protagonists. Another example of this intended assimilation can be found in Kütral's monologue, which recalls Medea's famous monologue in which she bids farewell to her children.[54] Kütral borrows Medea's words, but utters them in a different order, adjusting them to her existential situation. In Radrigán's reworking, the murders of both Lemunao and her sons do not occur on stage, nor are they narrated in the same way they are in Euripides. Rather, her monologue serves this dramatic function; in addition to expressing the internal conflict of the protagonist, it also anticipates these unfortunate deeds, which will take place in the subsequent episodes.

At the end, like Medea, Kütral escapes punishment for her awful murders, but without the *deus ex machina* with which Euripides' tragedy ends. Radrigán's final scene surpasses Medea's cruelty in the ancient text: Kütral manages to visit Licán before his execution and confronts him, telling him she has killed 'our' children and poisoned his father, therefore multiplying his imminent suffering. Her final words to Licán sum up the bitter toll of a defeat in which she is clearly included: 'what should have been does not exist; we only have what we have: you wait for death amongst horrible pains; I go free and avenged. Nothing more to add' ('lo que debiera ser, no existe, existe lo que es: esperas la muerte en medio de horrendos dolores; yo salgo libre y vengada. Nada más hay que agregar').[55] She has fulfilled her revenge and will not have to witness her husband's ignominious torture. Her freedom, however, is a freedom without any future.

With reference to Euripides, H. T. Lehmann remarked that impunity from terrible deeds, as are Medea's, can be understood as an implicit but deliberate option to withhold any kind of judgement of the characters.[56] This option allows the author the dramatic depiction of contradictions and injustices of his time, and the exploration, as in this case, of the extremes of the human soul, which, in the words of Gilbert Murray referring to Medea, is capable of 'enormous revenges ... when suffer[ing] enormous wrong'.[57] This assessment can also apply to the case of *Medea Mapuche* and justifies a possible interpretation from the viewpoint of a distinctive trait in Greek tragedy: to question reality through its construction as problematic. As J. P. Vernant, *inter alios*, has noted, many Athenian tragedies do not accurately reflect contemporary reality; rather they reveal problems and examine reality by staging legendary heroic models.[58] In some plays, this combination renders as tragic subjects whose actions may establish a critical view of the present. In the case of Euripides' Medea, she suffers from Jason's abandonment in circumstances of extreme legal and family vulnerability, as a woman and foreigner stigmatized by her poor reputation, aspects that the author carefully takes the trouble to establish. But the real cause of her shocking revenge comes from Jason's violation of his oath, on account of which she promised love and support to such an extreme that she ended up incriminating herself, even against her own family. Considering this referential background, the motif of revenge in Radrigán's play calls for a more complex interpretation, embedded within the 'sous-text' of Mapuche history: the strategies of survival that Lemunao and Licán employ by 'parleying' become problematic through the figure of Kütral, who feels betrayed, in this case, not by the union with another 'woman,' but rather by the union with 'death'. Her suffering is not the result of infidelity, but of the tragic contradictions she confronts amidst war and the resistance to invaders and oppressors (*winkas*). It is the Chorus' role to bring these contradictions to light:

> **Coro** ¡Infeliz mujer! ¡Ay, cuántos serán tus dolores, cuántos tus antagonismos! ¡Haber venido de tan lejos para que la vida te fuerce ver morir a tu esposo en vergonzoso cautiverio! ¡Qué humillación, qué ultraje para ti, soberbia hija de Ulmenes! . . . ¡Como soportarás la vida si aceptas la ofensa! ¡Y cómo podrías soportarla si no la aceptas, y por tu causa mueren todos los que te acogieron! ¡En peligrosa borrasca, oh, Kütral, te han lanzado los dioses![59]

> **Chorus** Unhappy woman! Oh, how many your pains will be, how many your antagonisms! Having come from so far, and life forces you to witness your husband's death while in shameful captivity! What humiliation! What insult for you, proud daughter of Ulmenes! How will you live your life if you accept the offence! And how will you live if you do not accept it, and your actions cause the death of all those who took you in! The gods have thrown you, oh Kütral, into a dangerous squall!

In Radrigán's play, the brief but significant involvement of the Chorus – as in the *parodos* of Euripides' *Medea*[60] – aims to display or summarize the complex origins of the play's conflict, as well as its political, cultural and ideological complexities. The Chorus makes clear that Kütral's revenge does not originate only from the betrayal of a personal oath, as is the case with Medea,[61] but from the situation that forces her to choose between subjugation in order to save her community and rebellion in order to honour her ancestors who resisted Spanish siege for centuries. Although a strategic choice, the 'parley' causes Licán's 'shameful captivity' and impending execution, constituting for Kütral a historic betrayal against her race and a personal betrayal against herself, and these motivate her revenge. However, whereas in Euripides betrayal pertains to the private sphere – although it points to the moral corruption of Corinthian society through Jason's opportunism and Creon's complicity[62] – in Radrigán it acquires broader connotations and implies the survival of an entire society from the moment of invasion and conquest up until the present.

In both plays, oath-breaking violates a moral code prevailing in both societies through the customary use of oral tradition. In the Mapuche case, their practices and beliefs are governed by the customary law of *Ad Mapu*,[63] which necessitates, as the historian of Mapuche traditions Tomás Guevara has noted, a strict moral adherence to their ancestors' commandments lest they attract the ill-will of spirits.[64] It is within the framework of this moral code that we have to assess – following the words of the chronicler Gómez de Vidaurre – cases as 'high treason' punishable by death under the *toqui*'s discretion; these cases referred to as 'high treason' ('traición a la patria'), adds Guevara, were reserved for chiefs who colluded with Spaniards, either forming alliances with them or allowing them to build forts and churches on Mapuche land.[65] Considering the premise of this code, which remains valid among many Mapuche, it is possible to understand Kütral's actions. 'Parleying' for her means that Licán (and his father) infringed ancestral laws and, although they did so for strategic reasons, they also surrendered to the enemy's Western logic.

To that effect, it is worth reviewing the contextual premises implied in taking an oath within a cultural space determined by its oral tradition. With respect to the ancient Greek world, Anne Burnett offers a reflection that casts light on this problem:

> Oaths in their world were no mere human conveniences . . . they were absolutely necessary to society, but more than that, they were divinely ordained and magically protected. Oaths stood like the primeval pillar that supports the sky, a link that could at the same time hold off a possibly angry weight . . . The broken oath, like the drop of kin blood, brought an erinys into being (Hes. *Erg.* 804) and the demon was not to be appeased until the wrongdoer had been made to suffer. Such beliefs persisted even in classical times, and Euripides makes them a part of the explicit instruction of the *Medea*, for we are told that violation of an oath is an act that outrages the great Olympian divinities, Themis and Father Zeus (169–70; cf. 158, 161, 207); it is considered to be an example of *hubris* (1366) that alienates all of the gods (1391–92; cf.493) and creates an *erinys* (1260).[66]

More than supposing that Radrigán engages in an explicit intertextual relationship with Euripides with respect to this point, the latent parallelism is undeniable as far as both plays invoke a 'moral', whose legitimacy is based on oral culture. As Burnett states, Jason's crime lies in having 'replaced his sacred alliance with another that is more ordinary but also, now the old dangers are past, more to his advantage'.[67] In Kütral's perspective, Licán and his father have infringed an ancestral oath (an act applicable to all war-time alliances under *Ad Mapu* law); in other words, they insulted the authority of the ancestors by initiating a parley with the *winka* enemies. Kütral takes her stand under the protection of the gods or spirits of her ancestral mythology; and the Witranalwues spirits, who respond to her beckoning and order her to kill her children, are vengeful and bloodthirsty beings, comparable to the Erinyes in Greek mythology.

That said, it is necessary to reiterate that Kütral, though without outstanding features related to witchcraft, murder and exile, is rendered a more complex and problematic character in several aspects, beyond the aforementioned temperamental attributes that connect her to Medea. Licán is not Jason's exact counterpart, neither in moral terms nor in what Kütral regards as an act of infidelity akin to the performance of the Argonaut. Rather, it is Kütral who fails to understand and accept the strategic reasons that force Lemunao and Licán to feign submission in order to confront an unequal and ruthless war. She confuses strategy with cowardice and is unable to subdue her pride in order to protect life in her new community. Along this same line, Radrigán modifies the end of the play: although Licán insults Kütral, in nearly the same language as that used by Jason, upon discovering that she has murdered their children and his father, there are relevant changes in the final passages of the scene. Instead of the *deus ex machina* that safeguards Medea against any judicial sentencing, Radrigán focuses on a triumphant Kütral who has negotiated her freedom with the oppressor, a freedom that nonetheless can only be solitary and void of future. What remains in the end – and this is what prevails in the spectator's vision – is the picture of a Mapuche warrior shamefully imprisoned and waiting for a dreadful execution by the foreign invader who invited him to parley. This ending – open and ambiguous, as in *Medea* – sums up a desolate conviction that accounts for a world profoundly unhinged by a military-political and human conflict, whose protagonists, as those in the Greek tragedy, are neither absolutely guilty nor innocent.

Conclusion

Radrigán began working on his *Medea Mapuche* when Chile initiated the 'transition' towards the reconstruction of a democracy following the end of the dictatorship. The texts he wrote during that period are profoundly marked by his concern to take on the pressing ideological and aesthetic issues of the post-dictatorial phase in his dramatic work. As is evident in several of his non-literary texts, for Radrigán in order to revive democracy, the horror of recent history must first be recognized and established in memory:

> Como habitante de este mundo, en todo momento me ha parecido de suma importancia humana, saber por qué lloran los muertos, y que es eso lo que me ha llevado a escudriñar en los vivos; posiblemente sea esa filuda inquietud la que haya hecho dolorosa mi dramaturgia, pero no veo culpa en ello . . .[68]

> As an inhabitant of this world, at all times it has seemed to me of uppermost human importance to know why the dead cry, and this has led me to examine the living; this sharp concern may possibly be the reason why my theatre is so painful but I don't see any fault in that . . .

This question of 'uppermost human importance' has been undertaken very slowly and ambiguously by large Chilean social sectors and Chilean institutions, especially in the immediate post-dictatorial period.

Although at first glance *Medea Mapuche* does not seem to allude explicitly to post-dictatorship problems, it clearly fits into this general context. First of all, by situating the myth of Medea in a Mapuche context, Radrigán seeks to recover the history and memory – forgotten memory, as José Bengoa would say[69] – of Chile's original inhabitants. Furthermore, he draws attention to a nation formerly admired by poets and several chroniclers, which has resisted unjust and humiliating treatment for more than three centuries and managed to survive, against all odds, until the present day. In this sense, the use of classical myth is not just an artistic device. Quite the contrary, by establishing a connection between classical myths and unresolved ethnic problems, the author appropriates traditional forms with a profound critical stance that displays and dignifies these issues in a contemporary setting, issues that Chilean authorities and the society in general have systematically neglected and ignored.

On the other hand, by rewriting a situation so close to the Greek tragedy, Radrigán proposes – if we can say so – a *mestizo* version that synthesizes an European myth with an indigenous story.[70] In a society such as Chile's, where most people choose to identify with their Euro-Western roots more so than with their mestizo and indigenous ancestors (biological and cultural), this proposal can be interpreted as a provocation. Nevertheless, it can also be understood as the moral appeal to a country placing efforts into restoring democracy to first recognize its ethnic and social pluriculturalism and admit responsibility for the ethnic ostracism at the heart of its community[71] – unavoidable when realizing a more just and inclusive society.

Finally, in confronting new problems, Radrigán also explores new forms of poetic expression, different from the realist sensibilities of his first dramatic pieces, as, for example, plots and themes taken from the mythic tradition. While his *Medea Mapuche* appropriates the myth of Medea, it is in this case – as we have stated – a very close rewriting of Euripides' version. Not only the title and subtitle but also the protagonist's and essential plot structures, as well as the quotes textually taken or paraphrased from Euripides' text, provide good reasons to understand that the Greek tragedy is part of the enunciation in the Mapuche version of Medea.[72] Euripides is in this way summoned by the Chilean author to warn the twenty-first-century spectator of the 'enormous revenges' that can result, as Murray says, from the 'suffering of enormous wrong'.[73] Probably, too, to project a tragic sense of the centuries-old struggle for survival of the Mapuche people, and that all efforts to restore democracy will be useless if the society does not also deal with this flagrant 'wound of Chile'.[74]

CHAPTER 5
PHILOCTETES AND MEDEA IN CONTEMPORARY CHILEAN THEATRE
Carolina Brncić

This chapter examines two Chilean plays from the 2000s: *Filoctetes, la herida y el arco* (*Philoctetes: The Wound and the Bow*, 2004), a rewriting of Sophocles' *Philoctetes* by Marcelo Sánchez, and *Diarrea* (2002), an adaptation of Euripides' *Medea* by José Palma. Using style very different from each other's on account of their generational gap – the first more serious, cynical and sceptical; the second more parodic and idiosyncratic – the two playwrights choose Philoctetes and Medea to discuss loneliness and exclusion in a present heavily informed by the past. Written at the turn of the new millennium, both plays offer an account of the political and social trauma in the years after the collapse of the dictatorship, when Chile transitioned to democracy. While Sánchez focuses on Philoctetes' wound that never heals and thereby becomes an indelible memory of 'those days' carrying political connotations, Palma transforms Euripides' vengeful Medea into a pathetic victim of society and particularly of the economic and cultural imperatives.

As in other countries that have suffered a dictatorship, memory has been a constant theme in Chilean literature and particularly in theatre over the last forty years. Already during the time of Augusto Pinochet's dictatorship, theatre adopted a political stance of criticism and resistance, which was prohibited in other spheres of popular culture, such as publishing, film and television. During these two decades, theatre was the voice that discretely pronounced the name of hidden and silenced horror.[1] With the transition to democracy and the dictator Pinochet still commanding the military, political discourse was dominated by the advocacy for 'justice to the extent possible' ('justicia en la medida de lo posible'). Victims of the regime were recognized in official reports that sought resolution endorsed by the new popular slogan 'Never again' ('Nunca más').[2] With this premise, along with consolidating the image of a new Chile under the wings of economic growth and social transformation, the country progressively attempted to overcome the trauma of its dark past. The decade of the 1990s, with its opening towards the globalized world, began to deal with the pain and aftermath of profound repercussions in Chilean society.

In his *Chile, Anatomía de un mito* (*Chile, Anatomy of a Myth*) the sociologist Tomás Moulián makes a clear diagnosis: in his view, the 'democracy of agreements' achieved in the 1990s is characterized by a triad that defines the new paths through which Chilean society sought to transition: consensus, laundering-forgetting and consumerism.[3] The political agreements of transition made between civilians and the military are chronicled in the consensus as a superior stage of oblivion, which seeks to silence the past, homogenizing differences under the logic of consumerism that allows to accelerate and reinvent the identity of a 'new Chile'.[4] Confronted with this new imperative of oblivion promoted by mass media, artistic expression in general and post-dictatorship theatre in particular continue to concentrate on unresolved issues of memory and social inequality through different poetics and languages.[5]

The dichotomy between memory and oblivion becomes a leitmotif in post-dictatorial theatre, mirroring counter-official discourses that arise from different sectors and groups, such as the Group of the Relatives of the Disappeared Detainees (Agrupación de Familiares de Detenidos Desaparecidos, AFDD), who coined the slogan 'neither forgiving nor forgetting' ('ni perdón ni olvido'). This slogan, frequently used even today, emerged in opposition to the official politics of reconciliation and the failure to resolve numerous cases of victims of the dictatorship.

Elizabeth Jelin, in *Los trabajos de la memoria*, establishes an inseparable relationship between memory and oblivion, demonstrating how the first is a field of action and reaction against the second: 'the space of memory is a space of political struggle, and not infrequently is the struggle conceived in terms of a struggle "against oblivion": remember in order not to repeat' ('El espacio de la memoria es un espacio de lucha política, y no pocas veces esta lucha es concebida en términos de la lucha "contra el olvido": recordar para no repetir').[6] She goes on to add that there are 'the "narrative memories", those that can find or construct the senses of the past, the wounds of memory more than the wounded memories that have so much difficulty in constituting their meaning and piecing together their narrative' ('Las "memorias narrativas", las que pueden encontrar o construir los sentidos del pasado, las heridas de la memoria más que las memorias heridas que tantas dificultades tienen en constituir su sentido y armar su narrativa').[7] These views are important for this essay and can help explain how the playwrights of the 2000s delve into memory, what name(s) they give it and what meaning they seek to reconstruct under those names. For, according to the Chilean philosopher Sergio Rojas, writing is inscribed as a process of recomposing a fragile and contextual subjectivity in relation to memory.[8]

When it comes to theatrical production during the 1990s, dramatic texts often serve as vehicles of the political and ideological positions of many established authors who experienced the dictatorship as adults – an experience that had a profound impact on their artistic expression. On the other hand, the dramas that inaugurate the new millennium are written by a younger generation of authors who, for the most part, were born under the first years of Pinochet's regime, but grew up in democracy. This distance from direct trauma and the military coup partially determines a new way in which these authors view past and present, as well as drama and theatrical activity.[9] The majority of these playwrights – often actors and directors in their own productions – seek to express their consciousness about the mission and place of theatre in society. This explains why many of their plays employ self-reflexivity as a means of thinking about reality. Self-reflexivity becomes a common trope and emerges as an alternative discourse articulated in, from, and as theatre. I understand dramatic reflexivity as an underlying structure of the play that reveals its condition of artifice through metadramatic and metatheatrical strategies. The object of these strategies is drama itself, and its goal is to achieve a critical-reflective distance that allows us to think about the conditions and forms in which dramatical fiction is produced and, simultaneously, on how empirical reality is sustained and elaborated on fiction.[10]

In this context, we can identify a shift towards constructing a poetics that critically poses itself against current reality, through a highly elaborated dramatic discourse that fuses serious speech register (nurtured by dramatic tradition) with colloquial register, including pop culture, publicity, mass media and others. Within this search for new textualities, the plots of ancient Greek tragedy have been very useful. From 2000 onwards, Oedipus, Antigone and Medea, among other characters, have been revived (some of them repeatedly) on the Chilean stage.[11] Greek tragedies have been appropriated reflexively, that is, tragic plots are reworked because of their capacity to serve as discourses that critically position themselves against the so-called official discourses.

My goal in the analysis of *Filoctetes, la herida y el arco* and *Diarrea* is threefold: first, I will focus on the relation between the ancient source text and its modern reworking and will discuss the departures of the latter in terms of plot, as well as the use of self-reference and self-consciousness as reflexive strategies in an attempt to demonstrate the bonds between the Chilean rewriting and the Greek hypotexts; second, I will investigate the ways in which contemporary reality informs the reworking and how the ancient plot is informed by modern popular culture; and third, I will look at how the two plays under consideration address the issue of memory.

Filoctetes (la herida y el arco)

Philoctetes is one of Sophocles' tragedies that has not received much attention in Latin-America.[12] For this reason, Sánchez starts with a brief explanatory note about the name of the play and the character.[13] The note reads:

> Filoctetes es referido por la *Ilíada* como uno de los guerreros que iban en la expedición contra Troya, pero que fue despojado del mando de sus naves y abandonado en la isla de Lemnos, ya que los demás guerreros no podían soportar el hedor que provenía desde él por una herida que le hizo una serpiente. Sin embargo, un oráculo predijo que sólo sus armas podrían vencer a Troya.[14]

> Philoctetes is referred to in the *Iliad* as one of the warriors who went on the expedition against Troy, but who was stripped of command of his ships and abandoned on the island of Lemnos, since the rest of the warriors could not stand the stench that came from him on account from a wound caused by a serpent. However, an oracle predicted that only his weapons could defeat Troy.[15]

A reason for the vagueness of this note may be Sánchez's willingness to distance himself from the Greek source text and rewrite the Philoctetes story by taking liberties, obliterating some aspects that have been important in other reworkings of the tragedy while, at the same time, focusing on a particular motif: the stench of the character. In this respect, the Chilean reworking echoes other adaptations of the last few decades, mostly European ones, which, as Schein points out, emphasize the hero's 'physical pain and psychological suffering, contrasts and conflicts between innocence and experience, ends and means, and individual inclinations and the needs and demands of society',[16] among other traits of his.

My analysis of Sánchez's play will focus on four such attributes: the binary wound/smell, the binary suffering/loneliness, the opposition between authenticity/masking and the deployment of language as a manipulative weapon and unmasking arrow. The wound is the visual manifestation of difference. The permanent suppuration and the pestilent smell that it exudes are the living memory of a human body and downgraded individual, an indelible mark that establishes a distance between the present and the past. On a symbolic level, it is a marker of difference, one that distinguishes an individual from the community. This mark is the very reason for Philoctetes' isolation and loneliness, which already in Sophocles are torturous for the character, as they amplify his physical suffering, becoming both psychological and social. If the experience of pain is non-transferable, the suppurating wound becomes a bodily image that represents the putrefaction of the self with respect to the others. As Edith Hall points about suffering in the *Philoctetes*, 'the play examines in close detail how an individual's acute suffering deforms his everyday life and his relationships with his or her community. It also shows how very differently individuals respond to the suffering of others'.[17] It is precisely the indifferent or utilitarian responses to this non-transferable experience that Sophocles highlights when he turns his attention to Philoctetes' treatment by Odysseus and Neoptolemus.[18]

To the issue of suffering raised in Sophocles' tragedy, we should also add the problem of language.[19] The polarity between the uncivilized and animalistic language of Philoctetes when he is overwhelmed by pain and the rhetoric used by Odysseus accounts for the gap between two ways of living: isolated, alien to society, on the one hand, and useful and depending on it, on the other. The exercise of *logos*, fundamental for Greek tragedy and all the civic practices of fifth-century BCE Athens, seems to be the touchstone and one of the central features in Sánchez's play. The Chilean author recovers the manipulative character of the Greek Philoctetes and transforms his dramatic figure into a wordsmith.

The action begins with the dialogue between Ignacio, a TV producer, and his assistant; both are distressed about the potential bankruptcy of the television channel and the loss of their material privileges, should they fail to increase the ratings. They resolve to call Filoctetes, the most successful 'storyteller' ('contador de historias').[20] He is self-exiled on a beach on account of the foul smell emanating from a wound on his leg and a 'story' of the past that is not specified. The writer spends his days on a sunlounger, drinking alcohol and guarding the ancient weapons of a hero when he receives their call. He is the only one who can prevent disaster and raise the television ratings. And so, it happens. Filoctetes arrives at the production company, impudently exhibits his stinking smell and ensures success by writing the script for a series. He then returns to the beach and burns in a bonfire the weapons that he formerly guarded (a few unrecognizable flags, a bow, shovels and some books). After a while, Ignacio disembarks on the beach. He has come for his weapons; he wants to recover something from the past. Filoctetes indifferently points to the ashes of the weapons. The play closes with Filoctetes' final speech addressed to the spectators, while on stage two images fuse: a giant promotional poster of a Caribbean beach and Filoctetes' beach.

Four features define the character of Filoctetes in this play: his exile, his wound, its odour and his skill with words. All four are present in the original Greek tragedy, but are recreated here with a new meaning. Like the Sophoclean archer, Filoctetes finds himself abandoned on a beach, but his separation from society is cast as self-exile on account of his foul odour. At first, it seems his wound is not attributed to a concrete origin. It can be a racial condition, a nationality, a street or school condition. He states, 'one does not choose anything, one is chosen and tries to play the role as best as possible' ('uno no elige nada, uno es elegido y trata de representar el papel lo mejor posible').[21]

This apparent indeterminacy is deceiving. Filoctetes' affirmation must be read as an index of his self-awareness as a role within and for fiction. As he admits, he did not choose his wound and its odour springs from his condition as a figure embedded in a dramatic tradition. Although at the *dénouement* he states that he was bitten by a snake and was abandoned by his comrades,[22] just as in the ancient Greek play, the self-perception of each character is different. Sophocles presents an emotionally wounded and resentful figure, in permanent mourning because the infamy of his exile was, according to Odysseus, a sacrifice for the sake of the community.[23] In the Chilean play, as the action unfolds, it becomes clear that his self-exile is a mechanism of defence and preservation. His odour is the ability to distance himself from society and protect the hero's weapons in the solitude of a beach.

Filoctetes' exile allows him to preserve the authenticity of his ideas symbolized by his body's revolting stench. There is an important variant in Sánchez's reworking. This play replaces the physical pain caused by the wound in Sophocles with the smell as a differentiating feature. The stench becomes a personal marker, a kind of halo that protects and separates the character from society. In fact, the character permanently alludes to his smell and his ability to tell stories, as if they were the same condition: 'the worse I smell, the better my work' ('ya que mientras peor huelo, mejor es mi trabajo');[24] 'I'm disgusting to the noses, but loved when telling stories' ('Soy repugnante a las narices, pero amado al contar historias');[25] 'Also, I smell bad and I know my place' ('Además, huelo mal y sé cual es mi lugar');[26] 'But I'll live among you like a pariah persecuted by my bad smell and its good habits' ('Pero viviré entre ustedes como un paria perseguido por mi mal olor, y sus buenas costumbres');[27] 'I'll stop smelling rotten if it isn't a success, and we all know that my smell isn't negotiable' ('Dejaré de oler a podrido si no es un éxito. Y todos sabemos que mi olor no es negociable').[28]

Such pungent smells starkly contrast with the superficiality and concealment of the *Hugo Boss* cologne worn by the television producer Ignacio, the counterpart to Odysseus. The contrast between odour and cologne carries important connotations. Cologne implies not only grooming but also a certain economic and social status. Perfume can also serve as a mask of bodily odours.²⁹ This contrast shows how the old brother-in-arms undergoes a transformation. Ignacio is *the* hero who has erased his friendship with Filoctetes. In the past, both were combatants in a war, and the battle they waged ended with the advent of the dictatorship. That is the 'untold story', suppressed by some of the heroes who were integrated after the triumph into a new system as officials, masked in their artificial smell. Ignacio has obliterated his identity by becoming a successful television producer, an aspect symbolically illustrated by his cologne, which marks his new status and role in society.³⁰ In a contextual reference, the concealment becomes a parody of former leftist militants, today part of the Chilean 'Caviar left', locally known as 'Red Set'. By contrast, Filoctetes' smell *is* the wound, the living memory of the past that society tries to erase or at least mask. As Ignacio himself maintains: 'not a single word about his smell. Understood? We must make him understand that we don't care at all' ('Ni una sola palabra sobre su olor. ¿Entendido? Debemos darle a entender que no nos importa en absoluto').³¹ Ignacio's opportunism exhibited with total cynicism, recalls the attitude and deception that Odysseus deploys throughout Sophocles' play in order to obtain Philoctetes' bow. In Sánchez's play, this aspect emphasizes the 'de-memorialization' suffered by Chilean society on its way to progress, success, and overcoming the past and recent history. However, this forgetful career is hampered by all those marks and traces that attract (unpleasantly for some) the memory of the wound. As Filoctetes indicates:

> La herida seguirá aquí, abierta, supurante, dolorosa, hedionda sin remedio y aunque los que se vean obligados a pasar a mi lado habrán aprendido a disimular, yo todavía seguiré sintiendo el penetrante olor del pus y las historias revoloteando en mi cabeza.³²

> The wound will remain here, open, festering, painful, stinking without remedy and, although those who are forced to pass by my side will have learned to pretend, I'll still feel the penetrating smell of pus and the stories fluttering in my head.

Filoctetes is the past. His pestilence that nobody wants to smell is the memory of *that* story, but at the same time his stories are the weapons to challenge the present. This aspect parallels Sophocles in the sense that the victory over Troy is accomplished once the archer and his bow are reintegrated into the Achaean army. In Sánchez, Filoctetes' skill and weapon are his language. He is the best storyteller, the best soap opera screenwriter, able to transform dramatic stories into contemporary successes with a mass appeal. He has gained acclaim in academia, the sphere of criticism and show business. He is master of dramatic strategies and sensationalism, reinventing tales in which grand narratives give way to daily situations. Filoctetes' self-portrayal in the role of a writer is full of cynicism. He is a dream builder who, as part of the system, keeps his wound in order to be able to go to exile. His wound can be interpreted as the place of enunciation, from which the contemporary dramatic discourse is articulated. As he states, 'my wound that doesn't close speaks to me every day and is the cause of my stories' ('mi herida que no cierra, me habla todos los días y es la causa de mis historias').³³

This place of enunciation is partly that of the fictional Filoctetes and partly that of the playwright Marcelo Sánchez. In this sense, the dramatic character's cynicism highlights Sánchez's scepticism about his own profession: a dramaturgy that vehemently attempts to reposition great tales by reflexively revealing a discourse that mirrors other discourses – that is, the literary reference to Sophocles and the cultural references to national history and memory, as well as the act of writing.

Once Filoctetes has triumphed, he returns to his beach to leave the hero's weapons – flags, shovels, a bow and some books – as a way of preserving the past. Several months after the soap opera's ephemeral success, Ignacio returns to the beach to retrieve the weapons as a way of reinventing himself and recovering something of what these objects once were and meant during his youth. However, Filoctetes, wishing to discover a 'reality without words' ('una realidad sin palabras'),[34] has already burned the weapons including the old and filthy manuscripts.

A deeper comparative analysis could reveal many other ways in which Sánchez transforms Sophocles' text. However, given the limitations of this chapter, and based on what we earlier reviewed about Chilean theatre, I would like to explore briefly the reflexive dimension of the play. *Filoctetes* is not reflexive because it reconstructs an ancient tragedy, rather because it employs a dramatic figure and a dramatic plot that display themselves as dramatic discourse. By positioning itself as dramatic discourse that interacts with Sophocles' dramatic plot, Sánchez's play exhibits itself as a reflexive discourse against the dramatic tradition and as critical discourse against the contextual reality. Filoctetes' self-awareness of his own character within the dramatic tradition is explicitly displayed when he states, 'I only played my role' ('¡Yo sólo hice mi papel!').[35] However, a subtler instantiation of this characteristic deserves attention. Given the outcome of Sophocles' text, it is clear that the victory over Troy will be obtained upon retrieving the archer. In this modern rewriting, we could apparently consider as Filoctetes' victory his success in terms of television ratings. But, on a reflexive level, Filoctetes' metadramatic self-consciousness is exhibited once the character pronounces his final words:

> Era un héroe, tenía mi nave, mis armas, mis hombres, pero una serpiente me hirió y la herida nunca más cerró. La pestilencia llevó a mis compañeros a dejarme abandonado en una playa. Lo que no sabían es que sólo mi arco puede derrotar a la ciudad amurallada. La fábula de la herida y el arco. Mi propia historia, mi tragedia y mi final feliz.[36]

> I was a hero. I had my ship, my weapons, my men, but a serpent wounded me and the wound never healed. The stench led my comrades to leave me abandoned on a beach. What they did not know was that only my bow can defeat the walled city. The story of the wound and the bow. My own history, my tragedy, and my happy ending.

We can perhaps attempt to read this walled city, this new Troy, as the Chilean unconscious that has deployed different tricks to disguise a lurking past, an unhealed wound.

Undoubtedly, such devices are the fruit of both political discourse and that of publicity and television, which, far from displaying what we really are and have been, mask reality with odours and images that are transversal, globalized and supposedly real. On the level of fiction, Filoctetes' return to civilization with his storytelling language only reinforces this imaginary construct, elaborated from other types of language, until it becomes part of the official consumer culture. However, Filoctetes' final speech, which no longer forms part of the fictional level, exhibits the dramatic fiction as discourse, showing the reflexive and critical nature of the play. The dramatic language on theatre, like a bow and arrow, parodies trivial dramatic language from television, defying the invisible barriers that outline our vision of reality. It presents language as a construct of illusions and, in contrast, as a means to reconstruct memory and identity. As Carlos Ossa states about the relationship between language, writing, memory and the Chilean Transition: 'Narrating is to provide a place for the undone, to join with used words and stupefied fragile memories, retaining the pieces banished by the language of agreements' ('Narrar es proveer de sitio para lo deshecho, hilvanar con palabras usadas y estupefactas memorias frágiles, retener los pedazos desterrados por la lengua de los acuerdos').[37]

Helenus' prophecy, which underlies Sophocles' dramatic action, is replaced in Sánchez's play by Filoctetes' self-ironic commentary.[38] At the *dénouement* he states: 'The story of the wound and the bow. My own history, my tragedy, and my happy ending. Cheers!' ('La fábula de la herida y el arco. Mi propia historia, mi tragedia y mi final feliz. ¡Salud!').[39] In these lines, Sánchez refers to the act of writing. On a fictional level, 'my tragedy, and my happy ending' is Filoctetes' final determination: to abandon the system and return to the beach, self-exiled without words. On a reflexive level, 'my tragedy, and my happy ending' is Sánchez's text that adopts a critical and reflexive stance against literary tradition, expressed in terms of modification and difference in relation to Sophocles' text, just as different dramatic versions of a myth were elaborated in ancient Greece. Likewise, this text resonates in the context of unresolved issues of memory and forgetting in Chilean society. By employing a discourse that dramatically declares its fictional condition in order to criticize cultural discourses that seek evasion, the play displays theatre as a space for reflection. Meditation on the current reality and his bond with the historical past, a reflection on the relationship between ancient and modern 'histories' and the actuality of Greek plots and myths.

Diarrea

Written by José Palma Eskenazi,[40] *Diarrea* is a free adaptation of *Medea*. It borrows only the name of Euripides' protagonist and the theme of abandonment from the ancient play. *Diarrea* enjoyed great popularity: it was selected for inclusion in the Eighth National Dramaturgy exhibition (2002) and for two years was produced in the capital and other cities. In 2003, it was staged by La Desgracia Company with Alejandro Cid playing the role of Medea Marisol. This version toured the country and received praise by journalists for the incorporation of transvestism and kitsch scenery.[41]

Although the play appropriates Greek themes and includes multiple allusions to pop culture (international and Chilean), it does not offer its viewers a story with a structured plot development and clearly delineated characters. It portrays, almost as in a snapshot, a sordid reality framed upon the themes of abandonment, violence and loneliness. The play shows Medea Marisol Cuevas, a middle-class woman who has been abandoned by her partner, owner of a motel, being reunited with her two children, Michael and Jackson, over dinner on New Year's Eve. Included in the plot are her neighbour Don Mario and his daughter Teresa, a domestic employee with a mental disability. The dinner concludes with fireworks in the background as Medea disgorges the drugs she ingested in an attempt to commit suicide. In the midst of her delirium, she recalls her desertion by her partner nine years earlier. Pretending to go and buy bread, Miguel Pérez Tapia, a Michael Jackson impersonator, abandons her. The recollection ends, and the play returns to the present time: dawn on New Year's. Now it is Don Mario, Teresa and the children who desert Medea. The first takes refuge at a hospice because he has AIDS, the second escapes with the Mormon who raped her years earlier and, finally, her sons, Michael and Jackson, who leave to buy bread, imitating the departure of Miguel (Jasón).

The protagonist, Medea Marisol Cuevas, is haunted by her name before the action begins. The proper name is a legacy and symbolic burden that establishes a *de facto* plot and recalls the character's tragedy. Medea acknowledges that her strange name can be attributed to one of the few books her mother kept at home. Although she refers to it as 'the story of a novel written by what's his name … *Euripicus*' ('un cuento que escribió cómo se llamaba … ¡eurípico!'), she is aware that it is a Greek story.[42]

What is highlighted throughout the play is this self-consciousness of Medea as a character whose name determines two important aspects of her personality: abandonment and motherhood. Through her speech and actions, she seems to re-enact an action already plotted in advance. As she later states: 'what is destiny, if the story of our lives could be changed, I'd forget my name and I wouldn't have to …' ('lo que es el destino, si se pudiera cambiar la historia de nuestras vidas, me olvidaría de mi nombre y no tendría que …').[43]

It is not without significance that the only memory of Miguel Pérez she has is that of the day of her abandonment, shown parodically in the nickname she gave him (Miguel Jasón), because that is 'the way Michael Jackson is said in Spanish' ('como … se dice Michael Jackson en castellano').[44] By giving him this nickname, she ironically assigns to him the role of Jason in Euripides' text and parodically anticipates the double desertion, from him and from her children. Thus, the play parodies Euripides' Medea's infanticide, subverting the label attached to the character on the list of *dramatis personae*: 'Medea Marisol Cuevas: the bad mother of Chile' ('la mala madre de Chile').[45] Medea Marisol organizes her destiny as a character, rewriting Euripides' plot and redefining abandonment as the central motif of the story in a parodic way. As opposed to the triumphant exit of her Greek counterpart in Euripides' play, Palma's Medea remains immersed in the most complete solitude when all those who form part of her earlier life abandon her: Teresa, the nursemaid, leaves in search of a new life; Don Mario, moves out of his home, seeking therapy for his disease; and, finally, her own sons leave.

The text provides ample evidence as to why the allusion to 'tragedy' can be understood in this parodic manner. In the first scene, when Medea is on the telephone with a client, she refers to herself, her tragedy and the spectacle of her life as follows:

> Bueno lo que si debis tener claro es que soy la protagonista de mi propia historia. Como si se hiciera una película con mi vida filmada en todo momento menos el baño que me da vergüenza, un show real, el fascinante mundo, the diarreal world, con la actuación estelar de mi, Teresa, Michael, Jackson y Don Mario.... Esos son los personajes de mi vida actual, cualquier otro que aparezca lo hará bajo su exclusiva responsabilidad y con la única condición que yo siga siendo la superestrella, a propósito niños, por favor no repitan en sus casas lo que las superestrellas hacemos con meses de ensayos y ahora no se relajen en sus asientos porque esto comienza a ponerse macabro. MI TRAGEDIA ES LA TRAGEDIA DE MI VIDA Y TODAS LAS VIDAS TIENEN SU ESPECTÁCULO.[46]

> Anyway what you have to understand is that I'm the protagonist in my own story. As if they made a movie of my life filmed at every minute except for the bathroom 'cause that makes me embarrassed, a real show, the fascinating world, the diarrhoeal world, with the stellar performance by myself, Teresa, Michael, Jackson, and Don Mario.... Those are the characters in my current life, anyone else who appears will do so taking full responsibility for their actions and with the sole condition that I remain the superstar, and by the way, kids, please don't try at home what we superstars do with months of rehearsal and now don't relax in your seats 'cause this is starting to get morbid. MY TRAGEDY IS THE TRAGEDY OF MY LIFE AND ALL LIVES HAVE THEIR SPECTACLE.

This quote emphasizes Medea's state as a theatrical character whose existence differs from real life people. There are clear allusions to the differences between theatre and life, as well as between film or television (reality TV shows) and life. (Note the wordplay between 'the real world' and this staging of the tragedy of her life as a spectacle, parodied in 'diarrhoeal world'.) Whereas in Sánchez's *Filoctetes* the acknowledgement of the fictitious nature of the protagonist is included in the epilogue, already separated from the action, Palma's character emphasizes this condition from the beginning. This presentation strengthens Medea's fictional identity and highlights her origins so that the spectator can easily recognize the hypotext and establish the difference between it and what is enacted on stage. Whereas in Sánchez's play the title suggests a horizon of expectations stemming from the Greek source text, *Diarrea* only stimulates our morbid curiosity. From this moment on, the play inscribes itself in three different types of discourses. First, the theatrical practice of self-reference illustrated in the notion of 'spectacle' that the protagonist declares will unfold on stage: the tragedy of her life; second, the literary tradition, in that it draws on Euripides' play; and third, contemporary cultural and Chilean references inserted in the text in a fragmented mode.

As M. L. Hurtado has observed of other post-millennium authors who rewrite classic texts, they emphasize social decomposition, the reduction of the human by globalization, consumerism, that leads to the spectacularization of life.[47] In *Diarrea*, spectacularization is illustrated not only through the self-reflexive condition of the play and its protagonist, but also in the language, in the fragmentation and the hyper-saturation of overlapping discourses from different origins. The world depicted by Palma is one of desertion, rejection and ejection, a condition already suggested in the title. The definition *diarrhoea* as 'a frequent and copious discharge of abnormally liquid faeces'[48] is first and foremost displayed in the language of the play, characterized by the lack of punctuation, its incorrect syntax and lexicon, as well as the inclusion of colloquial speech called *flaite*, a sociolect contaminated by the vulgar emptiness in publicity and religious discourses.[49] Such language exposes the draining of meaning and persistence of isolated phrases and images that are mechanically repeated and memorized in the collective unconscious, primarily from language used in television, advertisements, pop music, culture and even Mormon religious discourse. Language becomes incapable of communicating; words lose their significance and become mere phonetic sequences that convey, semantically and syntactically, a morbid sexual content – as is the case, for example, with the various insinuations to feminine and gastric fluids throughout the play. The fluidity and incontinence transform the text into an outpour of violent verbal images that beat and insult one another. Hence, this linguistic violence mirrors the inability of language to create emotional connections, reproducing the violence and abandonment experienced by the characters. For instance, an excerpt of Medea's monologue:

> ay me duele, tanto dolor, aquí adentro es como si tuviera algo ¿qué es lo que tengo?, no tengo nada amasticulosis, estreñimientos, retención de líquido, hemorroides te parece poco Medea, que el deterioro y la enfermedad te sorprendan cagada de la risa en el baño (...) dios! ¿Por qué te llevaste a mi hombre? y me dejaste con esta herida, como una herida con una tremenda herida de mujer ... uno de estos días se me hace la costra con lo que me chorreo de ti, con lo que de mí me desangro, y me muero aquí tirada en el suelo, bailo.[50]

> Oh it hurts, so much pain, here inside me, it's like I have something, what is it? There's nothing wrong with me, just amasticulosis, constipation, water retention, hemorrhoids, isn't that enough, Medea? That the deterioration and the illness catch you off guard, laughing in the bathroom (...) God! Why did you take my man away? And you left me with this wound, like a wound, with a woman's terrible wound ... one of these days your cum's gonna ooze out of me and with my bleeding it's gonna scab, and I'm gonna die right here on the floor, I dance.

The play also draws on social clichés that reveal class and racial problems. For example, *Diarrea* parodies a well-known commercial from the 1980s and 1990s, the *manjar Colún*, a caramelized, condensed type of milk produced by the national dairy company Colún.

In the commercial, the mother distributes equal portions to all her children.[51] In the play, one child is blonde and the other is dark-skinned:

> **Jackson** Mi mamá me da manjar común, me da panqueques con manjar común, me da tortas con manjar común y me da me da empolvados con manjar común.
>
> **Michael** A mí también si somos hermanos.[52]
>
> **Jackson** My mom gives me regular *manjar*, she gives me pancakes with regular *manjar*, she gives me cakes with regular *manjar*, and she gives me cookies with regular *manjar*.
>
> **Michael** Mine does too – we're brothers.

In the commercial, the wordplay lies in *Colún/común* (common). In the play, however, the parody lies in that *común* has become common and regular, that is, really cheap. In addition, the play portrays the boys as not being equal in Medea's eyes. Michael is the favourite child because of his white skin, while Jackson is dark-skinned. Both are sons from different fathers who abandoned them when they were babies. This situation parodies some of the lyrics of *Black or White*, Michael Jackson' song, as well as the process of skin whitening he underwent. The positive valuation of white skin as contrasted with dark skin – Chile has a *mestizo* population, product of its indigenous population, Spanish colonization and European immigration – emphasizes cultural racism and classism. This is further reinforced by another quote, where the blonde and white members of the upper class also end up consuming most of the products. So, Medea wants to dye her hair blonde:

> Pa ponerme a la pinta no me atrevo, en todos los anuncios y en los paraderos, yogures pa los hijos de los rubios colchones pa que los rubios duerman, mayonesa, maquillajes, cosméticos pa las rubias esto esto y lo otro, y que queda pa una señor ¡todos vestidos iguales por la vida! ¡nooo! Imagínese a toda la gente rubia y viviendo en el barrio alto, si no se puede con tanta igualdad no nos conviene.[53]
>
> I don't know if I could become a blonde, on every billboard, at every bus stop, yogurt for blonde kids, mattresses for blondes to sleep on, mayonnaise, makeup, cosmetics for blondes, this this and that, and what's left for a woman, everyone dressed the same their whole lives! Nooo! Think of all those blonde people living in upper neighborhoods, you can't live with so much equality, it doesn't benefit us.

In a society that privileges white skin, not everyone is the same, like the children in the commercial or like the politically correct lyrics of Michael Jackson's *Black or White*: 'It don't matter if you're black or white.'

Diarrea also denounces social alienation caused by consumerism. The emptiness and the fragmentation of discourses coming from retail, advertising, religion and literature denounce another type of social/personal 'wound': marginalization and emotional abandonment. In this play, marginalization is portrayed as a consequence of desertion and oblivion, most evidently displayed in the speech register of each character. Furthermore, if we pay close attention to each character's own depiction, it is safe to assume that they belong to the middle class. They own a plasma TV and microwave, symbols of their economic status that, nonetheless, betray the shell of cultural exclusion and abandonment in which they live. Medea understands these material goods as symbols of her socio-economic position, which is also emphasized by the reference to her neighbours whose house was demolished because they failed to make monthly payments on a major department store credit card, probably used to purchase the same or similar goods.

The abandonment develops into a violent feeling that leaves a lasting mark on Medea. This aspect is reinforced in the lack of genuine emotional bonds, substituted by virtual erotic encounters on the telephone. This same situation of violence and desertion characterizes Medea's domestic worker. Teresa, a personification of vulnerability, has been sexually abused repeatedly: first by her father, then by Medea's children in successive rapes, and later by four Mormon missionaries, 'the brothers'. The last rape results in the birth of a daughter who is taken away by the state child protection agency on the basis of Teresa's perceived inability to raise children. Absolutely no one escapes violence and abandonment in this play, even Medea's sons, Michael and Jackson, who are cast as ostracized, drug-addicted teenagers with no education or job experience. *Diarrea* violently denounces social marginalization and individual loneliness through parody, in a language that spectacularizes segmentation and paradoxically incontinence and deprivation.

'Chile is not that pretty'

Both plays are structured around the motif of abandonment that entails forgetting and (as a result) remaining silenced. Clearly, the perspective of enunciation in Sánchez and Palma is different. This can be partially explained by the fact that the two dramatists belong to different generations. Palma is older by twenty years and experienced the dictatorship when he was young. This age difference results in a more serious tone in the first play and a more parodic in the second. However, the two perspectives converge in the play's treatment of reality. Sánchez focuses on the silencing of history and the past, on failing to remember an identity that is necessary to recover one's self vis-à-vis the alienation and homogenization of individuals promoted in modern society. Mass media discourse is the paradigm for dissolving identity markers, for silencing individual and collective histories, opting instead for globalization. In an interview, Sánchez stated that his theatre displays 'intimate situations, with pain' ('situaciones íntimas, con dolor') in a society which is 'not that pretty' ('Chile no es tan lindo').[54]

'Chile is not that pretty' is the bitter observation that the joy promised with the return to democracy did not come. The horrors of the past survive in the social wound that generated a democracy of consensus and reconciliation that, as the plays suggest, is not such. While some concealed and changed their identities, forgetting the past, supplanting ideals for social success, to others social transformation, identified with the acquisition of material goods, did not deliver that well-being either. Although the emphasis and tone are different in each rewriting, Philoctetes and Medea are the victims of the Chilean historical process. Both appear as the embodiment of abandonment, forgetfulness and loneliness. If the smell of Filoctetes' wound is the sign that something is rotten in Chile, the emotional abandonment of all the characters in *Diarrea* reveals the social fractures under the ephemeral brilliance of the fireworks. The success or joy, artificial in both plays, is only a flash that hides the loneliness and (self) marginalization of individuals within the social system, reflecting and parodying the process of the Chilean Transition.

PART II
BRAZIL

CHAPTER 6
A GOD SLEPT HERE BY GUILHERME FIGUEIREDO: A RADICAL MODERNIST *AMPHITRUO* FROM BRAZIL

Rodrigo Tadeu Gonçalves

This chapter examines *Um Deus Dormiu lá em Casa* (*A God Slept Here*), one of the most innovative rewritings of Plautus' *Amphitruo* penned by Brazilian author Guilherme de Oliveira Figueiredo (b. 1915, Campinas – d. 1997, Rio de Janeiro). *A God Slept Here* premiered at Teatro Copacabana on 13 December 1949 in a prominent production, a year after Figueiredo's debut as a playwright with *Lady Godiva*.[1] My goal in this chapter is to identify the departures of Figueiredo's play from the Plautine model and discuss its relation to contemporary Brazilian society and theatre. Since there is almost no scholarly work on Figueiredo's reworking, even in Portuguese, this chapter builds on my previous work on the play and conducts a closer comparative analysis not offered before.[2]

Figueiredo's play is generally excluded from comprehensive studies of the reception of Plautus' *Amphitruo*,[3] with the exception of Bertini who considers it 'the most revolutionary of all re-elaborations of the *Amphitruo* theme',[4] noting that:

> I commediografi del '900 ... alterano deliberatamente i dati del mito, operando un progressivo ribaltamento delle parti, che raggiunge il suo culmine proprio in Figueiredo. Se il vero Giove di Molière e di Kleist desidera essere amato come amante e non ci riesce, il falso Giove di Figueiredo ci riesce, ma non lo desidera; se Giraudoux ha rovesciato l'ottica di Alcmena, perché ella è informata in precedenza della visita di Giove, Figueiredo ha rovesciato l'ottica di tutti i personaggi, che finiscono per assumere un atteggiamento speculare, o meglio antitetico, rispetto ai loro rispettivi archetipi.[5]

> Comic writers of the twentieth century ... deliberately change the facts of myth, performing a progressive reversal of the parts, which reaches its proper climax in Figueiredo. If the real Jupiter of Molière and Kleist wishes to be loved as a lover and does not succeed, the false Jove of Figueiredo does, but without wanting to; if Giraudoux has inverted Alcmena's viewpoint because she is informed in advance of Jove's visit, Figueiredo inverts the viewpoint of the all characters, who end up assuming a specular, or rather antithetic, attitude with respect to their respective archetypes.

Whereas better-known reworkings of *Amphitruo* by playwrights from the Northern hemisphere, such as Camões, Molière, Dryden, Kleist and Giraudoux, sometimes downplay the specific kind of metatheatre found in the Roman source text,[6] Figueiredo was the first author to eliminate the presence of the gods as characters in favour of a major metatheatrical outcome. In this rewriting, it is two mortals who play two gods who play the two mortals, as I discuss below.

Even in Brazilian scholarship, studies of Figueiredo's play are meagre;[7] its author is equally neglected. Some important Brazilian theatre critics mention him briefly, usually in positive terms, but tend to exclude him from serious approaches, because they consider him a playwright who wrote for the masses.[8] Some histories of Brazilian theatre only cite his critical work on seminal authors such as Nelson Rodrigues, the originator of modern theatre in Brazil.[9] This chapter seeks to offer a corrective to this critical neglect by discussing basic dramatic aspects of *Um Deus Dormiu lá em Casa*, situating it in the context of Figueiredo's own theatrical criticism published as a series of eight dialogues under the title *Xanthias: Dialogues on Dramatic Creation*,[10] where the Brazilian author lends his voice to Dionysus conversing with his slave Xanthias (a spin-off of Aristophanes' *The Frogs*). This collection is an important document, for in those dialogues Figueiredo discusses the play under examination here, casting light on his view on the ancient theatrical tradition in a conscious attempt to use it in order to appeal to larger audiences not necessarily familiar with it. Among other pivotal topics, the author discusses theatre in general and his models, as well as some specifics of performances and productions.

In order to understand how *Um Deus Dormiu lá em Casa* can be analysed in the context of classical reception, it is necessary to present some biographical information on Figueiredo, as well as on twentieth-century Brazilian political and social history, since the élites in Brazil were the only portion of the population that had access to European cultural heritage through education and literacy. Figueiredo's father, the general Euclides Figueiredo, opposed Getúlio Vargas' dictatorial urges and was one of the leading members of the Constitutionalist Revolution in 1932 against the *coup d'état* of 1930, thanks to which Vargas assumed power, thus ending the Old Republic and ruling without constitutional rights. The revolution defeated, General Figueiredo was imprisoned and then exiled. In 1937, with another *coup d'état*, Getúlio Vargas shut down the Congress and inaugurated the so-called New State, which was to last until 1945. In 1946 a new period, called re-democratization, saw another constitution, the resurgence of political parties, and the end of censorship. This politically unstable period would last until the military coup of 1964, which deposed the left-wing president João Goulart, paving the way for a long military dictatorship that lasted until 1984. The last president of this regime was Guilherme Figueiredo's brother, João Figueiredo.

Guilherme Figueiredo, son of a general and a devout Catholic mother, also took part in the Revolution of 1932 with his father, at the age of seventeen. His duties as a messenger included carrying a gun, with which he might have killed a man, according to his memoirs.[11] After his father's defeat and exile, he enrolled in the military school along with the sons of other oppositionist military leaders and, as he confesses, started to feel an urge to write literature, in a clear departure from Christianity and military service.[12] He then went on to law school and began working as a journalist. He enjoyed a lengthy career, until he resigned the day on which his brother became president, for political and ideological reasons. This contextual information is important for us to understand the nature of his works, for they might seem too subtle or alienated politically if considered out of context without connection to his opposition to violence and support of the idea of freedom, which derive from specific life experiences.

Figueiredo wrote and staged other plays which are adaptations of classical works, such as his retelling of *Satyricon*'s Milesian tale of the widow of Ephesus (*Sat.* 110.3–113.1) entitled *A muito curiosa história da Matrona de Éfeso* (The Very Curious History of the Widow of Ephesus), first staged in 1958;[13] his retelling of Socrates' trial in *Os fantasmas* (The Ghosts), first staged in 1958 as well; *Greve Geral* (General Strike) based on Aristophanes' *Lysistrata* (1949); and his critically acclaimed version of the Life of Aesop, an ode to liberty, entitled *A raposa e as uvas* (The Fox and the Grapes).[14] This choice of models seems to result from topics he usually treated, i.e. human emotions (ambition, jealousy, love) and other general themes (poverty, freedom, injustice and war). However, his approach to these subjects was usually comic, although serious topics never cease to appear, albeit hidden in the shadows of the plots and characters. Nonetheless, *A God Slept Here* stands out for its unique treatment of the plot of its model. Its most striking trait is the total absence of the gods as characters. In Plautus, the bulk of the plot is shared by Jupiter and Mercury, who pretend to be Amphitryon and his slave Sosia in order for the Olympian god to enjoy yet another love story with a beautiful mortal (Alcmene); this incidentally gives Hercules a divine ascent. By contrast, in Figueiredo's reworking, the general Amphitryon is possessed by jealousy resulting from a prophecy by Tiresias (absent in Plautus' play) who foresaw that a man would sleep in his house the night at which he was supposed to go to war against the Teleboans. He thus decides to leave briefly with his slave Sosia only to return immediately, both disguised as Jupiter and Mercury pretending to be Amphitryon and Sosia. Amphitryon's main attributes (his impiety, lack of rhetorical skill, cowardice and especially jealousy) are all Figueiredo's departures. Alcmene also receives a radically new treatment. A pious woman, she constantly complains about her husband's social faux pas, while also being coquettish, almost craving to be possessed by a different, more powerful man, or even a god. Amphitryon's homecoming, then, can be seen as a self-fulfilling prophecy, a motif inserted in the plot probably via *contaminatio* with Sophocles' *Oedipus King*: not only are Tiresias and Creon mentioned in the play; a herald called Demagogós also starts the play with a long review of Thebes' terrible fate after Oedipus deciphered the Sphynx's riddle.[15] This results in a brilliant use of metatheatre culminating in an aporetic ending, in which the general's farce forces him to choose between being a war deserter and a cuckold.

In what follows, I offer a thorough analysis of the play in three sections which highlight some critical repercussions produced by Figueiredo's exclusion of the gods. The first section briefly presents the overall structure of the play, discussing the ways in which the double layer of metatheatre (characters disguised as gods disguised as themselves) creates interesting comic effects through slips of the tongue and false starts; as the situation gets more complicated (especially in Act II), it generates multiple attempts by 'Jupiter-Amphitryon' to leave the role and put an end to the farce, all interpreted by Alcmene as attempts to reinforce the role of the god. In the next section, I discuss the radical reinterpretation of the roles of husband and wife, the former in a lowered, stooge-like manner, and the latter in a complex new portrayal of Alcmene as a mid-twentieth-century urban woman, self-aware and liberated. In the final section I argue that, by removing the gods altogether, Figueiredo casts new light on the possibilities of the myth itself. There are no gods, but the only possible solution to the *aporia* at the end of the play is a *deus ex machina*: Amphitryon has to acknowledge, before the angry mob which comes to kill Alcmene for being unfaithful, that it was Jupiter that visited his house, thus *creating* the myth.

The double layer of metatheatre

The plot has a rather straightforward structure: the four main characters, Amphitryon, Alcmene, their slave Sosia and his wife, Tessala (also a slave), re-enact the basic outline of the myth of Amphitryon modelled on Plautus and possibly other playwrights whom Figueiredo admired.[16] The setting is the interior of Amphitryon's house; all interactions with the people of Thebes take place through a balcony window. The first striking feature is the absence of the gods – to which I will return later. On several different occasions, Figueiredo explains the origin of his stripped-down version of Plautus: in the preface to 1970 edition, he recalls the birth of the idea of writing the play while teaching a theatre class in which he explained theatrical spectacle as the 'degradation of a ritual' ('degradação de um rito'): '[i]n the ritual performance, the gods are present; in their gradual degradation, they are mixed with demigods and humans. Finally, there are only humans' ('No ofício ritual os deuses estão presentes; na sua gradual degradação, misturam-se aos semideuses, e aos homens. Finalmente, ficam só estes').[17] His view on Greek theatre is not scientifically sustained. He speaks from the perspective of a theatre historian and critic, writing at a time when classical scholarship did not circulate widely or as easily as it does nowadays in Brazil. He even makes basic mistakes while talking about Roman theatre, misspelling names of authors, plays, genres and cities. Nevertheless, he places his version at the end of a long line of modern *Amphitruones*, admitting his fascination with the idea of re-narrating the myth without gods.[18] In a long passage from *Xanthias*, he discusses many possible variations of the myth, some of which are even variations of his own retelling:

> Tome por exemplo o mito de Anfitrião, um dos mais consumidos no teatro. Você pode usar a história tal como a conta Hesíodo, tal como em Plauto: o general Anfitrião parte para a guerra; Júpiter, enamorado de sua esposa, desce ao lar do general, sob a forma do marido; da união adúltera e sagrada nascerá Hércules. Você pode imaginar que Júpiter não existe, que o general tem ciúmes da mulher e resolve ele próprio voltar para espioná-la; ela, crente, toma-o pelo deus, entrega-se ... Outro entrecho: a mulher não crê nos deuses, Anfitrião decide voltar para simular o deus e convertê-la, já o profeta da cidade anunciou que Júpiter viria seduzi-la. Anfitrião volta, mas Júpiter também vem. Que série de incidentes se pode fazer partindo daí! Outro: Alcmena teve uma aventura, está grávida, e não

pode explicá-lo ao esposo impotente; quando este parte para a guerra, ela engendra a história da vinda de Júpiter, fazendo com que o amante a visite vestido nas roupas do general...[19]

Take, for example, the myth of Amphitryon, one of the most consumed in theatre. You could use his story as Hesiod tells it, or as Plautus does: the general goes to war; Jupiter, in love with his wife, goes down to his house in the form of the husband; from the sacred adultery Hercules is born. You can imagine that Jupiter does not exist, that the general is jealous of his wife and decides to return to spy on her; she, a believer, takes him for the god, gives herself to him ... Another development: the wife does not believe in the gods, Amphitryon decides to come back and pretend to be the god and try to convert her, and the prophet had announced that Jupiter would come to seduce her. Amphitryon comes, and so does Jupiter. What a series of incidents one could derive from that! Another one: Alcmene had an affair, she is pregnant, and cannot explain it to her impotent husband; when he leaves for war, she devises the story of the coming of Jupiter, making the lover to come visit her in her husband's clothes...

The absence of the gods as characters creates a double layer of metatheatre: as the two male characters decide to play the gods playing themselves, they create a play similar in structure to Plautus' but with fewer characters, as they have to double themselves by virtually creating the gods through a *coup de théâtre*. After a jealous Amphitryon devises the plan, a good deal of negotiation and decision-making takes place onstage between him and Sosia. The same elements present in the Plautine *ludificatio* are also deployed here, including decisions about the 'plot' made by an internal 'director'; comments about props and costumes; the rehearsal; the debate on the nature of their representation; and the ensuing difficulties of sustaining the role within the role.[20] Some examples can be seen in the following passages, placed at the end of Act I, after the presentation of the main complications in which the characters' traits and predicaments (the prophecy by Tiresias, Amphitryon's jealousy about what he believes to be king Creon's interest in Alcmene, etc.) are staged:

> **Anfitrião** É isto! Os dois! Você de Mercúrio, eu de Júpiter. Corre ao depósito. Há lá, entre umas coisas velhas, algumas que se aproveitam. Traga o raio de ferro dourado que serviu para a última dionisíaca. E o manto. Há na cozinha uns pombos que Alcmena vai sacrificar... Torce o pescoço de um pombo e corta-lhe as asas, para amarrar nos teus pés. E arranja um casco para a cabeça.[21]

> **Amphitryon** [That's it! Both!] You as Mercury – I as Jupiter. Run to the storehouse. There are some old costume bits we can use. Bring the [golden iron beam used at the last Dionysian festival] – and a robe. There are some doves in the kitchen that Alcmene plans for a sacrifice... [Twist the neck], [c]lip off the wings of a dove for your feet and tie [th]em to your ankles. And find a helmet for your head.[22]

This first passage introduces the negotiation of props and costume. These are simple metatheatrical jokes that stimulate a first level of comic effect.[23] He then expands the level of metatheatre:

> **Anfitrião** ... daqui por diante não és escravo, nem eu sou senhor. Sabes bem teu papel.
>
> **Sósia** Sei, senhor.
>
> **Anfitrião** Então mostre maior majestade. Um deus não anda trêmulo e encurvado como você está. Faça como eu. (*Assume um ar estupendo, altivo e sereno.*) Que tal?[24]
>
> **Amphitryon** From now on, you are not a slave[, nor I am your master]. Do you know your part?
>
> **Sosia** Yes, master.
>
> **Amphitryon** Then show some majesty. A god never trembles [or bends like you are]. Behave as I do ... (*He assumes a [stupendous], lordly [and serene] bearing.*) How's that look?[25]

Moving beyond the simple humour of the previous passage, the master and the slave start discussing the role of gods and the proper way of playing such roles. The first answer provided by Sosia already exemplifies the motif of the slip of the tongue used throughout the farce. Additionally, the comment on the divinity of the gods and their possible fear when walking among mortals illustrates Figueiredo's constant critique of religiosity, evidence of the de-sacralization that generated the play in the first place.

The follow-up to this theme shows us Figueiredo's ability to use metatheatre at a deeper level. Following in the footsteps of his Plautine model, he starts joking with simple allusions to costumes and props, then delving deep into a metatheatrical self-conscious dialogue:

> **Sósia** O que eu quero dizer é que, se tens de representar o papel de Júpiter no papel de Anfitrião, não deves fazer o papel de Anfitrião no papel de Júpiter. Do mesmo modo, se sou Sósia fazendo o papel de Mercúrio no papel de Sósia ... É este o problema do teatro grego, senhor. Os deuses são irrepresentáveis.[26]
>
> **Sosia** I'm trying to tell you to behave like Jupiter behaving like Amphitryon – not like Amphitryon behaving like Jupiter. Just like me. Now I'm Sosia behaving like Mercury behaving like Sosia ... That's the problem of the Greek theatre. How can a God be played like themselves – because nobody knows what they're like.[27]

These witticisms stem from Figueiredo's daring choice to remove the gods from the play altogether. Thus, he is able to make meta-literary comments associating immortality with mortal actors capable of occupying a divine position no longer available in a desacralized world. Although used as a joke here, Dionysus in *Xanthias* claims that the main reason for writing a play is the 'fear of death that resolves itself in the yearning for immortality ... you believe that this is the way of fixing the world, making it crumble, divulge your ideas, your faith, your despair, your certainties, your doubts' ('essa espécie de medo da morte que se resolve em ânsia de imortalidade ... julga ser esse o meio de consertar o mundo, desmoroná-lo, divulgar suas ideias, a sua fé, o seu desespero, as suas certezas, as suas dúvidas').[28] Moreover, this passage can be seen as the closing of a kind of comic rhetorical tricolon, a crescendo which is able to please a diverse public, from the simple jokes about props to the sophisticated metatheatrical and metaliterary nature of the third passage. Figueiredo thus emulates Plautus, who was able to please an audience of varying levels of sophistication,[29] with simple gags for slow-witted members of the audience to highly complex meta-poetic discussions, such as Mercury's prologue in *Amphitruo*.[30]

After this dialogue, Act I ends and the second one stages the farce. Amphitryon-Jupiter and Sosia-Mercury enter. Throughout Amphitryon's funny attempts to preserve his honour, the audience oscillates between two possibilities: either Alcmene realizes he is really acting or she really believes in the visitation of Jupiter himself. Figueiredo keeps us in the dark until the end of the play. To prevent any kind of possible confusion brought about by the prophecy, the women trade bedrooms. When the men enter and find the wrong women, a scene with typical Plautine elements follows, with *lapsus linguae* and the carnivalization[31] of slave and master roles.[32]

Later on, a striking instance of metatheatre and irony occurs, when Alcmene tries to adapt the prophecy to the baffling current situation:

Anfitrião Era ... Creonte?

Alcmena Não, Senhor.

Anfitrião (*esquecido de que é deus*) Com certeza você vai dizer que era eu! ...

Alcmena (*tábua de salvação*) Éreis vós, Senhor! Vós! A profecia dizia 'um homem' – e sois vós em forma humana, igual ao meu marido!

Anfitrião (*quase consigo mesmo*) É verdade, não é que esse raio dessa profecia se cumpriu mesmo?[33]

Amphitryon Was it ... Creon?

Alcmena No, Sire.

Amphitryon (*forgetting he is a god*) You're surely going to say it was I! ...

Alc (*profits from his idea*) It was you, Sire! You! The prophecy said 'a man' – and it's you in human form, just like my husband!

Amphitryon (*almost to himself*) It's true, this damn prophecy has just been fulfilled![34]

This initiates a series of attempts by Amphitryon to abandon his role as god in disguise, followed by the cunning refusal of Alcmene who insists that his attempts to deny his divinity are part of the disguise, e.g.:

> **Anfitrião** Suponhamos que eu seja Anfitrião. Que eu seja o teu marido. E te visse, agora, de braços estendidos para outro ...
>
> **Alcmena** Não pode ser. Meu marido está na guerra.
>
> **Anfitrião** Alcmena! Eu sou o teu marido! Em carne e osso!
>
> **Alcmena** Não tens necessidade dessa mentira para obter-me. Meu marido está na guerra. Crês que ele abandonaria a batalha para voltar para casa? És um deus estranho. Não conheces os homens.[35]
>
> **Amphitryon** [Let us] suppose [that I am Amphitryon, that] I'm your husband ...And now I see you with your arms extended to another ...
>
> **Alcmene** [It cannot be.] My husband is at the battle ...
>
> **Amphitryon** But Alcmene – I am Amphitryon in the flesh!
>
> **Alcmene** You needn't lie to [get] me ... Besides my husband is at the battle, I tell you. Do you think he would flee the battlefield to crouch in the arms of his wife? ...You are a funny God. You don't understand us humans at all.[36]

To sum up, metatheatre in the play is a tripartite concept: first, the politically incorrect tradition of jokes about marriage in Roman comedy; second, the intertextual play on Jupiter's reputation as a naughty and mischievous god; and third, other rewritings of *Amphitruo*, such as Antônio José da Silva's and Giraudoux's (and, for a contemporary reader/audience member, Jean-Pierre Giraudoux's and Alfonso Sastre's) receptions of Plautus, which intensify the jokes about marriage, since in those plays Juno takes on important roles in dismantling the logic of male preponderance.

The reinterpretation of the roles of husband and wife

The irony and humour in Amphitryon's characterization are illustrated early on in the play. On several occasions following his initial appearance, he is depicted as a brave soldier with a limited capacity for public speaking and absolutely no belief in the gods, coupled with a lack of respect for sacred matters. In the excerpt below, Alcmene describes her husband in a funny manner. The passage exemplifies another characteristic quality of Figueiredo's play: his frequent deployment of allusion and intertextual connections with other genres, literary trends, authors and works:[37]

> **Alcmena** Nunca, nem mesmo nas grandes datas, como hoje, aniversário de nosso casamento, consegui levá-lo ao templo. Durante as libações, manda

reservar a melhor parte do carneiro, a que se oferece aos deuses, para comer com
cebolas. E nos concursos trágicos, ronca como um javali, e só acorda na hora do
vinho e da comédia.[38]

Alcmene Never . . . – not even on [big] feast days, [like today, the anniversary of
our wedding], can I coax him to the temple. During solemn sacrifices, he orders
them to save him the best [part of the] meat [offered to the gods] to eat with
onions. He roars with laughter during tragedies in the theatre. [He only wakes up
at the time of wine and comedy].[39]

This depiction is not consonant with the usually tragic nature of Amphitryon in the Plautine hypotext and most receptions, such as the extreme example of Georg Kaiser's *Zweimal Amphitryon* (first staged in 1943),[40] in which his military character is recast as a brave, arrogant, stubborn personality (he is usually portrayed as a character who is willing to kill the impostor and take matters in his own hands). Here jealousy and intellectual inability are more important traits for his characterization. This could be read as a sign of Figueiredo's distaste for military life and war, and his preference for freedom. The ludicrous and cowardly nature of his Amphitryon is a major departure from other modern receptions.[41]

Another twist in the tradition of Plautus' *Amphitryon* is found in the construction of the character of Alcmene. She is pious and coquettish at the same time. Alcmene, thus, is both a reproduction of the Plautine model in her virtuous respect for the gods and a reflection of modern Brazilian women, representing the sexually and socially liberated woman of the newly democratic country.[42] In the first act, she confesses to Tessala the sexual interest that King Creon supposedly displays for her. We as audience know that Creon is in fact interested in Tessala, but it is Alcmene's pride and pleasure in thinking she is desired by noble men that leads Amphitryon to come up with his plan to stay home instead of leading the army against the enemy. Although he knows how important his position as a general appointed by the king is, after Sosia tells him about the prophecy, his insecurity drives him to pursue the course of action that will create the major complication of the plot and the bizarre reworking of the myth.

As an example of this new characterization of the couple, during the confusion generated by the arrival of the men and the trading of rooms, Alcmene coquettishly makes sexual advances on Mercury-Sosia. After all, if Jupiter-Amphitryon does not want her because he tries to avoid her betrayal of him with himself, another god might. After some confusion resulting from this action, Alcmene manages to lead Amphitryon to bed. Having asked him about which of his usual forms the 'god' would appear in to love her – as a shower of gold, a swan or bull – she convinces him to love her as 'a man' ('homem'),[43] ending the second act.

The third and last act of the play begins the next morning, when Tessala tries to convince Alcmene that the gods disguised as men in the previous night were nothing but men disguised as gods disguised as men. Alcmene starts to doubt, but her lines never solve the riddle for the audience: did she figure out the farce from the beginning? Act 3 then presents the problematic results of the illusion attempted by the male characters and the negotiation between the couples: if in Act 2 Alcmene sometimes suggests that she is aware of the fact that Jupiter is actually Amphitryon, her first dialogue with Tessala in Act 3 leaves the audience in the dark about that, which could be interpreted as a nice *coup de théâtre* by Figueiredo (since the riddle will not be solved in the play).

That morning is also the morning of the announcement of victory by the Thebans. Amphitryon returns after taking King Pterelas' head on a spike to Creon. He then grimly describes his rage at the moment when he entered Pterelas' tent and the king begged for mercy as a supplicant. The narration shifts mood and genre, oscillating between tragic and epic. The passage below is a clear stance against war and violence, and Amphitryon breaks down because he feels he was forced to kill a man out of jealousy and emotional instability:

> Se tivesses visto, Alcmena ... Não existe glória, não existe nada ... No fim da batalha, avancei até onde me pareceu ser a tenda do rei Teleboano. Abri o pano com a espada e entrei. Ele estava diante do altar, e erguia uma taça cheia de sangue, gemendo uma prece, invocando Júpiter, Marte e Minerva. Quando me viu, a taça rolou das mãos. Com os olhos abertos, perguntou: 'Tu és Anfitrião?' Depois falou: 'Perdi a batalha, herói. Poupe-me. Serei teu escravo, minha mulher será tua escrava, meus filhos serão teus escravos. Mas poupe-me a vida! É à tua generosidade de vencedor que eu suplico.' Ainda era possível dar-lhe fuga, mandá-lo embora, mostrar a loucura que cometera ao cercar uma cidade como Tebas com um bando de maltrapilhos. Quis dar-lhe fuga, eu te juro que quis dar-lhe fuga. Mandei que ele se levantasse. O pobre velho tremia, e me olhava com uns olhos onde havia carinho e gratidão. Eu perguntei: 'De que serve a vida sem glória, Ptérelas? De que te serve a vida como escravo?' ... E a sua boca ainda se movia quando lhe cortei a cabeça. Seus olhos ficaram me olhando, como se estivesse por trás de uma máscara trágica. Espetei a cabeça na lança e voltei para Tebas. Ao passar, os soldados davam-me vivas. Dirigi-me para a praça do palácio, onde o povo se aglomerou. Creonte veio ao pórtico. Enfiei a lança no chão, de modo que os olhos de Ptérelas ficassem fixando os olhos de Creonte. Sem dizer uma palavra, corri para cá.[44]

> You should have been there, Alcmene. There's no glory, there's nothing. Near the end of the battle I advanced [as far as it seemed] to [be] the tent of the Teleboan king. I opened the tent with my sword and the king was there, kneeling before an altar [raising a cup full of blood] and praying to Jupiter. Then he saw me and pled with me. 'You are Amphitryon? Spare me. [I lost the battle, hero!] I will be your slave – my wife and son too – but spare us. [It is your generosity as conqueror I appeal to].' There was time – time to let him go, to watch him run. I wanted to let him escape. I swear it. I made him stand up. The pitiful creature trembled, gazed at me with grateful cow eyes. I asked 'What good is life without honor? How will you, a king, live as a slave?!' ... His lips were still moving when I cut off his head. His eyes were fixed on mine like a tragic mask. I don't know why I did it. I was going to

let him go. Then suddenly – (*walks up and down*) – Then – then I speared his head and returned to Thebes with the cheers echoing in my head. I went to the palace where there were great crowds. Creon came out on the balcony and I drove the spear in the ground so that the dead eyes of Pterelas fixed themselves on those of the king. Then I ran away – here – to escape the crowds.[45]

Here we can detect the stream of consciousness revealing the motivation behind Amphitryon's brutality: the same jealousy of Creon that made him devise his profane farce has also turned him into an impious victor and murderer. The figure of the old man Creon looms around the event being recalled as the sole motivation for his vainglorious acts of war. Many literary allusions can be found in the passage: Aeneas' frequent killing of supplicants (cf. especially the killing of Turnus in *Aen.* 12.950–2) and the obvious allusion to tragedy in the comparison of the terror on Pterelas' face with a tragic mask, a strong pathetic image. This culminates in the question of whether she was faithful. The obvious answer would be no, but the other man was himself. The infidelity took place, and yet it did not. For Figueiredo, the question is *to be AND not to be*, a bizarre sophistic quandary.

Amphitryon Zero

It can be argued that jealousy is the main theme of Figueiredo's reworking, which is certainly an innovation in the theatrical tradition of this play: the myth is thus a theatrical invention caused by the jealous impulses of an insecure mortal warrior. The final conflict of the play will be the impossibility of coming to terms with the growing rumours of Alcmene's infidelity and Amphitryon's acclaim as the saviour of the people of Thebes. The rumours of marital infidelity finally prevail over honour gained at war, and an angry mob rushes to the house to demand explanations and to lay claim to the life of the adulteress.

In a twisted 'recognition' scene, Alcmene attempts to maintain her 'chastity' before the people, accepting imminent death by stoning, while Amphitryon is paralysed; it takes some time until he settles the matter with a doubtful display of courage. To prevent her stoning, he is forced to accept before everyone that his wife was visited by Jupiter, thus losing the honour of his victory. Figueiredo ends the play by making Amphitryon *become* the god he so comically failed to become throughout the plot. This Brazilian version of Amphitryon is insecure, mortal, modern and human.

Thus, together with jealousy, the central theme of the play is metatheatre. But instead of being a theatrical device, metatheatre is thematized and explored as never before in the tradition of the rewritings of Plautus: it is actually the central device of the play. For Slater, Plautus' play is all about the nature of the theatre, because the gods play a farce in a self-aware manner; it is 'theatrically self-conscious theatre, theatre which is aware of its own nature as a medium and capable of exploiting its own conventions and devices for comic and occasionally pathetic effect'.[46] But Figueiredo's play, as a rewriting of this kind of metatheatre, amplifies it and generates a funny and sophisticated comedy that represents a definitive turning point in this particular hypertextual chain. In the absence of gods, the male characters create the farce and the plot according to the pattern of *ludificatio*, which multiplies the levels of interpretation. On one level, we have actors 'imitating' humans (one of lower rank and another of higher rank), which is followed by a second level of imitation, on which they pretend to be gods (here maintaining but also inverting the Plautine tradition, at which level one would be humans playing gods). This second level is already explored in some of Plautus' plays, where characters (level one) imitate and (re)-enact more deeply into the metatheatrical play, 'creating' new characters (as is the case of the sycophant in *Mostellaria* or Simia in *Pseudolus*). However, what is more interesting and probably unique in Figueiredo's play is that we have a third level of imitation: characters (level one) imitating gods (level two) imitate themselves (level three), and sometimes even fluctuate between levels two and three (when Jupiter-Amphitryon apparently gives up the farce attempting to return to being Amphitryon).[47] This seemingly chaotic theatrical experience is managed superbly by a playwright who is deeply aware of the possibilities of self-conscious theatre. His characters alternate between the various levels through hesitations, forged inability, real inability, *lapsus linguae*, desperate attempts to escape the self-created illusion and the final (and comically unintended) consolidation of the theatrical lie. Apart from the birth of Hercules, omitted in Figueiredo's play, what we have is a performative translation of Plautus' *Amphitryon*, a cunning etiological play which postulates the myth as a result of the metatheatrical function. The gods do not need to exist, but their existence will have to be enforced by the conclusion of the theatrical action.

In *Xanthias*, Figueiredo also reveals an important point of view on reception of ancient material that may be unfamiliar to modern audiences; as Dionysus tells Xanthias: 'the story you are going to turn into theatre maybe has the advantage of not being known to the spectator today as any passage from mythology was known by the Greeks' ('A história que você vai teatralizar talvez leve a vantagem de não ser tão conhecida do espectador de hoje quanto qualquer trecho da mitologia o era dos gregos').[48] This explains, albeit in part, his fresh new start in the chain of the myth of Amphitryon, an advantage for a modern author who wishes to *make it anew*. His choice of an ancient subject matter can also be understood as a denial to invent national theatre, i.e. he refused to use Brazilian themes and folklore. In some passages of *Xanthias*, Figueiredo claims that Brazilian folklore lacks the psychological depth to be turned into universal theatrical plays.[49] For him, the only universal folklore is Graeco-Roman mythology, a subject matter that can be used in radically new ways while preserving its universal nature, even though this seems to contradict the earlier statement.[50] By eliminating the gods, Figueiredo rewrites the story in a more humanized way, with a focus on the themes of jealousy, marriage, adultery, avoiding the gods' potentially alien nature for a modern audience.

As discussed above, military life and religion shaped Figueiredo as a writer and a playwright, leading him to express a neo-humanist and universalist view in his plays strongly influenced by Greek mythology. His works featuring classical subject discuss peace and freedom at the dawn of modernist theatre in Brazil, after the Second World War and before the military dictatorship. As Figueiredo himself notes:

> A verdade é que essa greguice serviu para encaminhar fora do país um pensamento nosso, como a de Giraudoux (*excusez du peu*, de novo ...) serviu de veículo para um pensamento francês. No meu caso, acredito que as mensagens são a da Paz e da Liberdade... Essas mensagens, inteligíveis aqui como na Europa, nas Américas, na Ásia e na África, no mundo das sociedades abertas e fechadas, fizeram viajar duas modestas criações teatrais brasileiras.[51]

> The truth is that this Greekness served to convey abroad a thought of our own, just like Giraudoux's (excusez un peu, again ...) served as a vehicle for a French thought. In my case, I believe that the messages are those of Peace and Freedom... These messages, intelligible here as in Europe, in the Americas, in Asia and in Africa, in the world of open and closed societies, made two modest Brazilian creations travel.

By degrading and desacralizing the ritual, the myth is (re)created. If Giraudoux could say his Amphitryon was number 38, Figueiredo can say his is *Amphitryon Zero*.[52]

CHAPTER 7
GUILHERME FIGUEIREDO, AMPHITRYON AND THE WIDOW OF EPHESUS: LINKING PLAUTUS AND PETRONIUS
Tiziana Ragno

Quae petam Alcmene loca?

[Sen.] *Herc. Oet.* 1796

'Chaque Théâtre a sa Matrone d'Éphèse' ('Every theatre has its own Widow of Ephesus'):[1] this is the comment made in 1733 by Maupoint about the numerous theatrical adaptations of the tale of the Widow of Ephesus narrated by Petronius in his *Satyrica* (111–12).[2] Despite its original prosaic form, most modern rewritings of this story are dramas. In the twentieth century, especially in the years before and during the Second World War,[3] several European playwrights offered testament to the theatrical potentials of this tale.[4]

Outside Europe, one such reworking is *A Very Curious Story of the Virtuous Widow of Ephesus* (*A Muito Curiosa História da Virtuosa Matrona de Éfeso*) written by the Brazilian playwright Guilherme Figueiredo.[5] After its first performance at São Paulo's Teatro Brasileiro de Comédia (director: Alberto D'Aversa) on 5 March 1958, this comedy was staged a few more times, four of which by the Grupo Giz-en-Scène that produced dramatic readings of the piece in 1991, 1998, 2006 and 2007.[6]

Inscribed into the twentieth-century genre of Brazilian urbane and literary comedy, this play (as with others written by Figueiredo) is distant – in terms of subject but not in temporal terms – from the 'Paulista theatrical movement',[7] which is dominated by the theme of class struggle, rural or regional settings, and realistic aesthetics. On the contrary, Figueiredo's plays consist mostly of amusing parables[8] in which serious ideological messages (e.g. support to peace) are lightened by good-natured humour and mitigated by means of tasteful aphorisms, sophisticated quotations, and courteous *jeux d'esprit*. In addition to *A Very Curious Story of the Virtuous Widow of Ephesus*,[9] Figueiredo analogously reworks other ancient Roman material for a Brazilian audience in *A God Slept Here* (*Um deus dormiu lá em casa*, 1949), which was inspired by Plautus' *Amphitryon*.[10] In both plays, Figueiredo draws upon ancient themes and myth considered to be a symbolic 'code', as the author declares:

> O único folclore que atingiu a condição de universalidade no mundo ocidental é a mitologia greco-romana. Por isso ela se impõe a muitos autores, de diversos países e épocas. É mais densa de significações, de intenções, de possibilidades poéticas – e logrou a posição de uma espécie de código e vocabulário teatral.[11]

> In the Western world, Greek and Roman mythology is the only universal folklore. This is the reason why it has been developed by many authors throughout different areas of the world, over the centuries. It is so rich in meaningfulness, thought, poetic potential that it can be assumed to be a sort of theatrical code and vocabulary.[12]

Regarded as a language particularly suitable for deployment within the 'game of literature', myth seems to bond well with a ludic approach to writing. Assuming that contemporary European models (especially Jean Giraudoux)[13] could have acted as paradigms for this approach to theatre, Figueiredo's contribution is another important link in antiquity's modern chain of receptions.

In this chapter, I aim to investigate Figueiredo's rewriting of the Widow of Ephesus in relation to its main source (Petronius) and to Figueiredo's treatment of the myth of Amphitryon, which I will also read in light of its ancient source text, Plautus. While a comparative overview of the Plautine source and its adaptation by Figueiredo has already received some degree of scholarly attention, no analysis of Figueiredo's drama of the Widow of Ephesus has ever been produced, neither in the light of the Petronian source nor in terms of its obvious similarities with Plautus' *Amphitryon* and Figueiredo's version. Additionally, the chapter will explore the historical context of the two plays and look at the ways in which the revival of the classical past is informed by the Brazilian present.

Figueiredo's Widow of Ephesus as a Petronian adaptation

In *Xântias: Eight Dialogues about the Theatrical Creation* (*Xântias: oito diálogos sôbre a criação dramática*),[14] Figueiredo wrote that it was his reading of Petronius' Widow of Ephesus at the age of sixteen that prompted him to consider the possibility of adapting this subject for the theatre.[15] Although also aware of the 1946 rewriting entitled *A Phoenix Too Frequent* by English playwright Christopher Fry,[16] he chose to disassociate himself from Fry's sophisticated approach, thereby aiming at a truly comic version.

Figueiredo moves away from the Latin source text in a variety of ways, e.g. by adding new scenes or characters, and this license was one of the methods by which he combined the two classical sources, Plautus and Petronius. Among the additional figures, the lord of Olympus stands out: infatuated with the soon-to-be-widow, Jupiter disguised himself first as a cultured prophet and then as a soldier with whom the widow would admit adultery. Employed as a framework within which the main intrigue is embedded, this secondary plot echoes not only the literary (ancient or modern) tradition about Jupiter's amorous affairs with mortal women but also the Amphitryon myth.

Indeed, there are several commonalities between Figueiredo's rewriting of Plautus' *Amphitruo* and his adaptation of Petronius' tale (e.g. the prophecy motive; the narrative impasse produced by the risk of capital punishment for desertion; the falsehood as a stratagem to escape the dishonour possibly produced by a military sentence). *A Very Curious Story of the Virtuous Widow of Ephesus* also features common topics with previous rewritings of the Amphitryon theme[17] that were likely familiar to Figueiredo (e.g. those of Molière and Giraudoux, where Jupiter aspired to enjoy human feelings).[18] Moreover, in *A God Slept Here*, it is the protagonist Amphitryon himself who explicitly evokes the Petronian tale suggesting an analogy between his wife and her supposed double, the allegedly chaste (then unchaste) widow of Ephesus:

Alcmena Você não confia em mim?

Anfitrião Confio. Desconfio mas é dêles. Um guarda do cemitério de Éfeso seduziu uma das mais respeitáveis matronas, que estava velando o cadavér do marido . . . Chega o momento em que . . . Você está me entendendo? É maior do que as nossas fôrças.[19]

Alcmene Don't you trust me?

Amphitryon I trust you. But I suspect them. A guard of the cemetery in Ephesus seduced one of the most respectable matrons, who was watching over her husband's corpse . . . There comes a time when . . . Do you understand me? We can't resist.

Departures from the Latin source occur not only in the framework of the comedy *A Very Curious Story of the Virtuous Widow of Ephesus*, but also in its main plot where Petronius' text seems to have been reworked in light of modern perspectives. For instance, a political stance is applied to the ancient subject possibly prompted by Figueiredo's family background: his father was Colonel Euclides Figueiredo, a leading fighter for the 1932 Paulista Revolt,[20] while his brother was the soon-to-be President João Baptista de Oliveira Figueiredo, a military president from 1979 to 1985.[21] This modern aspect pervades the entire piece in the form of an underlying controversy against nationalism, autocratic power and false priggishness, typical of politicians who behave appallingly but exhibit an honourable public image of themselves or compel citizens to be upright and 'virtuous'.

Recognizable in Jupiter disguised as a fortune-teller (Eromante) is the author's voice that debunks the 'Mystique of Virtue' preached in Ephesus (a prototype of the Ethical State *ante litteram*). Power, Jupiter declares, is truly grounded not in people's genuine attachment to moral principles, but in their fear of brutal cruelties ordered by the State.[22] The characters, exploited to introduce this new perspective, are the Archon and the thief Partenocleptus (a telling name, because of his stealing the goddess' sculpture from Ephesus' temple). This was one of the crucified men whose execution had been the reason that, in line with the ancient tale, the soldier was working as a guard, so that he accidentally came across the widow and her maid in the cemetery where the crosses were located. Figueiredo actually expands this narrative frame, giving voice to roles that originally appeared as minor characters. Thus, the formerly anonymous thief's relatives, featuring in Petronius (*Sat*. 112.5), receive new life here as the *personae* of Necron and Clepsia (the condemned man's brother-in-law and mother respectively) who also act in a more concrete form for Petronius' indistinguishable *populus*.[23] Moreover, they occasionally make cruel jokes about the paradoxical gap between the poor classes, forced by starvation to become robbers, and the ruling classes, who stole the right of people to be given food:[24] an element which, in a light-hearted manner, once again displays Figueiredo's intention to reveal brutalities carried out by the State.

From the same perspective, Petronius' *magistratus*, who tries to dissuade the widow from committing suicide, and the ambiguous *imperator provinciae*, who orders the crucifixion (*Sat.* 111.3 and 5), merge to form one articulate figure – the abovementioned Archon – who stands for the bad politics flooding Ephesus. The bright idea to set the drama during an electoral campaign amplifies the image of the Archon as a corrupt man: like a *caudilho* (a military and political leader, a warlord), the Archon avails himself of spurious appeals to patriotism ('mística da pátria', 'Mystique of Nation'), claiming the security of the entire city to be his own personal triumph.[25]

In fact, the role of Ephesus as an allegory for a modern country is supported by contemporary history. Four years after the suicide of President Getúlio Vargas (1954), Brazil was able to see, with some detachment, the tragic experience of the nationalist, corporative, fascist, right-wing authoritarian regime known as *Estado Novo* (1937–45).[26] At that time, the country prepared to face an equally challenging period in its history under Juscelino Kubitschek (1956–61), before the so-called dictatorship of the *guerrillas* (1964–85), which would follow immediately after the presidential terms of Janio Quadros and João Goulart (1961–4).[27] Moreover, in 1958, when the play was first performed, the country was shortly to be put through tremendous hardship caused by economic problems, such as high levels of both inflation and national debt. This contemporary history informs Figueiredo's comedy, when, for example, it parodies the increase of the price of essential goods (bread, wine and prostitutes, the latter comically portrayed as being as much a priority as the former).[28]

Figueiredo himself theorized the use of the classical past as an allegory for the present as follows:

> Ah, como está atual a minha Grécia! ... uma e outra peça – assim como *A Muito Curiosa História da Virtuosa Matrona de Éfeso* ... – são, pelo tratamento do assunto, pela intençao do conteúdo, pela linguagem, peças brasileiras, tanto quanto a Grécia seria francesa com Racine, alemã com Goethe, inglêsa com Shakespeare.[29]

> How modern my Greece is! ... Both pieces [*scil. The Fox and the Grapes* and *A God Slept Here*] – as well as *A Very Curious story of the Virtuous Widow of Ephesus* – are Brazilian pieces because of the treatment of their subject, the intention of their content, language: similarly, Greece would be French with Racine, German with Goethe, English with Shakespeare.

The politicization of the Widow of Ephesus theme does not necessarily lie in adding new content to the original plot but also in renewed emphasis given to certain elements taken from Petronius, such as the theme of role model, which occurs throughout Figueiredo's comedy as a connecting principle for the community of Ephesus. In this respect, if the conviction of Partenocleptus signifies a rebuke as an 'example' for everybody,[30] an analogous pattern characterizes the representation of Cynthia, the widow of Ephesus. When she appears on stage, she introduces herself as the perfect example of virtue,[31] stating that she aims to die as an 'example' and, in short, follow a dogma which implies that everyone has to set a good 'example' without exception or insubordination.[32] Indeed, in Petronius the widow is described as 'the one true ... **example** of chastity and love' ('solum illud ... verum pudicitiae amorisque **exemplum**': *Sat*. 111.5). Converting the ancient theme into a political principle, Figueiredo extends a quality, originally conceived of as an extraordinary trait of the protagonist,[33] to the entire community.

Although rewritten in line with Petronius' text, the mourning scenario also highlights Figueiredo's goal to alter the ancient model, which was inspired by epic and tragic patterns,[34] and to introduce political elements. Indeed, converted into a 'National Tragedy',[35] even grief and its aberrant displays – e.g. the suicide – seem to have a social value, whereas in ancient Rome excessive mourning was forbidden by law and already by the Twelve Tables.[36] Thus, seen as socially unacceptable in ancient times (and, on this basis, ironically reproduced by Petronius), in the present extreme mournfulness is, paradoxically, regarded as an expression of 'Public Virtue' symbolized by the matron of Ephesus – in life or in death.

Petronius's text is explicitly quoted by the soldier when he talks to the widow. The sentinel eruditely recalls Virgil's intertext which appears in the ancient tale when the humble maid resorts to hexameters from the *Aeneid* that would actually convince the widow to change her mind.[37] Indeed, in the *Satyrica* the hazardous comparison between the widow of Ephesus and Dido (to whom the incitement to love had been addressed in Virgil) turns out to be persuasive;[38] otherwise, in Figueiredo's adaptation, where Virgil's two quotations are deferred and nearly deprived of its parenetic purpose, the device of citation turns into an artificial citation, thereby creating an impression of estrangement: in fact, treated as a sort of *ipse dixit*, the two hypotexts (Virgil and Petronius) appear distant and long gone.

In this context, Figueiredo's correction of Virgil's first quotation is worth noting. Petronius had actually recalled Virgil with a variation that has long been debated by scholars: instead of the original *curare*, Petronius employs *sentire*. This substitution of words has been traced back to different reasons: either a copyist's error[39] or a conscious revision,[40] perhaps triggered by the epicurean-materialistic vision typical of a strand in Virgil's reception.[41] Regardless of such theories, a sort of philological attitude seems to be exhibited here by Figueiredo, who employs 'ter cura' almost in order to rectify Petronius' text (*sentire*) and recall Virgil's original expression (*curare*) somewhat more closely. Nevertheless, the restoration of Virgil's text is clearly deceptive, being possibly prompted by a pure assonance ('**ter cura**' ~ *curare*) and conceivably intended to be a joke, since the Brazilian phrase 'ter cura' (to have possibilities of healing) is certainly not pertaining to the Latin *curare* (to take care of something or somebody).

In short, reduced to isolated sentences to be quoted in a narcissistic (albeit faithful) manner, broken into pieces and displayed on stage, classical literature – or, in general, literature[42] – becomes nothing but a 'tool' used by its rewriter (that is Guilherme Figueiredo, 'escritor literário')[43] who takes advantage of literary tradition, combining sources and intertwining them.

Figueiredo's Widow of Ephesus as a case of *contaminatio*

Figueiredo's portrayal of the task of the soldier in a comic manner in *A Very Curious Story of the Virtuous Widow of Ephesus* deserves analysis. The overzealous watchman fulfils his duty with ludicrous fervour; just like the overstated chastity of the widow of Ephesus, his fervour is a prelude to the contrary (desertion). Both the scene with the sentinel who mistakes someone for somebody else[44] and the motive of the desertion caused by love are not unattested in Figueiredo's work; both themes have already been elaborated in *A God Slept Here*. In this last play, a witty scene is performed three times by two watchmen charged with overseeing military operations, who misunderstand what they see or hear.[45] Therefore, if in the reworking of the tale of the widow of Ephesus the soldier is mistaken when he believes he sees what does not actually exist (he wrongly charges most people with an attempted theft of cadavers), in the play devoted to Amphitryon the sentinels are mistaken when they do not recognize what actually exists. The subversion of truth will be the main issue in the epilogue of both comedies, where the charge of desertion is parallel to the theme of adultery.

In *A God Slept Here*, the theme of war is key, as is in Giraudoux's *Amphitryon 38*.[46] This topic provides the Brazilian playwright with a further opportunity to rewrite the ancient plot from a political perspective. Indeed, it is peace, Figueiredo himself states, that is the universal message in this comedy, where an unbelievable shift of Amphitryon occurs in the end: he labels himself as a cuckold and does not attempt to pass as a cowardly deserter.[47] Amphitryon's vicissitudes in Figueiredo's rewriting are remarkable: in this adaptation it is not Jupiter that disguises himself as Amphitryon, but Amphitryon that introduces himself as a double of the lord of Olympus, despite the fact that he keeps his own human features. In fact, jealousy prompts the general to subject his wife to a test of faithfulness in the hope that, even if Jupiter-as-Amphitryon visits her and reveals himself as a god, she will not fall into the temptation to betray her husband. On the contrary, even though (or as) she is aware of her guest's allegedly divine identity, the coquettish Alcmena is very keen on committing adultery with him. This dishonours Amphitryon, either (on the side of falsehood) because he is deceived or (on the side of truth) because of his desertion: in fact, the man actually commits that, in order to put his wife to the test.

The motif of desertion provides good grounds for comparison between Figueiredo and Plautus,[48] because the characters display a controversial attitude towards war. In the Brazilian rewriting, mainly in the farewell scene (when the true Amphitryon is greeting his wife), Alcmena proves herself to be somewhat self-contradictory: she declares herself to be against the male ideology of violence, but she finally regards glory as the highest kind of self-actualization for a man and, in turn, for his wife.[49] In this respect, the Brazilian rewriting seems to follow Plautus' comedy. In the source text (499–550), Alcmena complains about the conduct of her husband; as in the episode between Hector and Andromache in the *Iliad* (6.390–493), his leaving home reduces her to tears. Yet, in her *canticum* she praises *virtus* (648–9, 652–3) as 'the cornerstone of Rome's traditional ideology',[50] which combines in itself all the qualities of an ideal *civis Romanus*.[51]

Plautus' influence is also prevalent in Sosia's characterization. In the Latin comedy, he exhibits the typical attitude of a fearful person: this refers not only to the usual fear of his master (*metus erilis*: especially in 293–5 and 334–7) but also to the fear that prompts him to run away from the battlefield, while others fight intensely (*pugnabant maxume ~ fugiebam maxume*, 199). From the perspective of a good Roman soldier – which Sosia was not – proper behaviour stipulated that he remained at his assigned post at whatever cost, even if that meant losing his life: in Plautus, Sosia delivers a panegyric on this type of expected behaviour in a *canticum* whose epic tone contrasts with the cowardliness of the speaker (especially in 238–41).[52] Sosia's fear of war is also reproduced in Figueiredo's text, where the slave declares himself to be in favour of desertion, mostly by trivial good sense.[53]

These similarities between ancient and modern text are enriched with innovations which involve other characters: this is another sign of an astute strategy to reread the source, combining analogies and novelties, and to encourage the audience to recognize parallels or appreciate fresh elements. In the Roman text, Amphitryon as a soldier respects the legal-institutional protocols of his own office (*praefectus legionibus*). Before going to battle, he plays a diplomatic role in line with the ritual made by the Fetials, who claim the right to regain looted goods and start a war, if enemies arrogantly refuse (203–17).[54] Moreover, following the renowned duties of 'subduing the proud' and 'sparing the submissive' (Verg. *Aen.* 6.853; but see also Cato *pro Rhod. fr.* 163 Malc.), Amphitryon demonstrates that he is merciful towards suppliants (256–7). Plautus' *imperator* is also respectful towards religious obligations pertaining to his position, thus offering vows to Jupiter (229–30) and securing victory not only 'through the strength and courage of ... soldiers', but also 'under the command and auspices of ... Amphitryon' (191–2).[55]

On the contrary, Figueiredo's character is impious. He rejects any delay in military action[56] and is not merciful to his suppliant Pterelaous, the king of Teleboans killed also in Plautus. Plautus' Amphitryon slays his enemy in accordance with an ancient ritual that sanctioned the general to strip off the rich spoils from the corpse of an opposing chief killed in a single combat (252 and 415).[57] By contrast, Figueiredo's Amphitryon is deaf to his enemy's pleas, thereby decapitating him (a likely legacy of Plautus' verb *obtruncare*?),[58] either aiming to show off or, more probably, being provoked by jealousy.[59]

As for the theme of desertion, Figueiredo's Amphitryon himself first wants to reject any mark of pusillanimity on his reputation,[60] but then he does not hesitate to desert his duty in order to join Alcmena. From this perspective, this character does not display heroic traits; instead, he borrows some characteristics of the false Amphitryon from the ancient comedy.

In Plautus, it is Jupiter disguised as Amphitryon who admits abandoning the legion (523), despite being aware of the responsibilities of a general holding the supreme command, that is, to remain with the army (504–5). Here two choices are contrasted: either to honour the military and public duties or to honour the conjugal and private duties (527–8). As opposed to the Latin source text, this choice is not to be made by Amphitryon in the finale of the story readapted by Figueiredo,[61] where 'a hypocritical safety before society' ('uma salvação hipócrita diante da sociedade')[62] is offered as a third option.

In terms of dramatic structure, the happy ending is what illustrates more than any other elements the similarity between Figueiredo's two comedies. In both, falsehood prevails and the theme of desertion appears to be connected to that of adultery, two crimes Amphitryon (or the soldier) and Alcmena (or Cynthia, the widow of Ephesus) are accused of, respectively. The Theban general as well as the sentinel run the risk of being condemned to death and must make a choice between two evils: either admit their desertion or suffer (or commit) another dishonour. Indeed, if Amphitryon does not admit his desertion, he must admit he was betrayed by his wife; likewise, if the soldier does not admit his desertion, he must admit he was guilty of insulting a public officer (this wrongdoing, in reality, had been committed by a false soldier who happened to be there).[63] Not unexpectedly, the two men choose the lesser evil, telling a lie.

Whereas the situation of the two male characters is quite similar, that of the female characters appears to be symmetrically opposite. Indeed, for both Amphitryon and the soldier, the desertion implies that the military duties are subordinated to their private interests, in particular, to their sexual delights enjoyed with his own wife (in the case of Amphitryon) or with a lover (in the case of the guard). However, as far as Alcmena is concerned, the admission of the desertion – that is the truth – would mean to acknowledge her untarnished conjugal reputation; as for the widow of Ephesus, to admit the truth would result in the complete reversal of her celebrity as a chaste matron. As falsehood prevails, the relationship between the two women appears to be similar yet different. In the end, even though Alcmena has actually spent the night with her husband, she has to simulate being unfaithful and admit she spent the night with an outstanding partner, Jupiter. Contrariwise, Cynthia pretends to remain respectful towards her dead husband, although she has an affair with an unknown and seemingly humble man.

In spite of this reversal, the destiny of both wives will finally be revealed to be analogous, and their former fame as virtuous matrons will be restored. The widow of Ephesus will assert her Virtue and, then, her reputation as 'the most virtuous of the women of Ephesus' ('a mais virtuosa das damas de Éfeso')[64] in accordance with Petronius' manifesto: 'a certain married woman in Ephesus of such famous ... chastity' ('matrona quaedam Ephesi tam notae ... pudicitiae': *Sat.* 111.1). As for Alcmena, she will be proclaimed 'the purest woman in Thebes' ('a mais pura das mulheres de Tebas')[65] in agreement with Plautus' line: 'the absolutely best of all in Thebes' ('omnium Thebis ... unam ... optumam': *Amph.* 677). Indeed, in the finale of Figueiredo's comedies, the supposedly divine and extraordinary identity of Jupiter as alleged adulterer (in the case of Alcmena), as well as the triumph of deception (ensured by Jupiter himself being the adulterer and disguised in the case of the widow of Ephesus), guarantee an elevated reputation for the two women.

Figueiredo, therefore, commits an act of *contaminatio*, as these mutual correspondences between the two plots illustrate. I further argue that what might have prompted Figueiredo to consider the two ancient sources (Plautus and Petronius) as connectable is the role of the female protagonists who represent the trajectory of chastity turned into adultery.[66] Being essential in Petronius, this theme also stood out in Plautus' text, where Amphitryon repeatedly accuses his wife of committing *probrum*, *stuprum* and *dedecus* (e.g. 882–3); all three charges originated from the guilt of the *impudicitia* which was much more dishonourable for a woman whose virtue had always been the subject of rumour in all Thebes (678).⁶⁷

Figueiredo develops this link and furthermore eliminates the discrepancy between the two women, making Alcmena aware of her alleged adultery with Jupiter. If the matron of Ephesus finally reveals herself as unchaste (as in the original tale), Alcmena actually turns out to be faithful towards her husband (because she does not actually meet Jupiter) in spite of having the desire to (and that is despite the fact that she declares quite late that she had previously become aware of the trick of Amphitryon and had gone along with it, only to punish her husband for his jealousy).⁶⁸ Thus, Alcmena would have willingly been adulterous, if she had had the opportunity to do so. In Figueiredo, therefore, she seems to somewhat share the wrongdoing with which the widow of Ephesus has always been associated.

The combination of the two stories is further amplified by an unprecedented prequel inserted in the plot of the widow of Ephesus, which refers to the efforts of Jupiter to test the most chaste woman in Ephesus in the hope – which is the case – that she would become unchaste. On the contrary, in *A God Slept Here*, since no god is involved in it, it is Amphitryon who tests his wife in the hope – which is unfortunately not the case – of proving her alleged virtue.⁶⁹

It is also worth mentioning that just as in *A God Slept Here* the absence of Jupiter and Mercury is the main departure from Plautus,⁷⁰ so, too, in *A Very Curious Story of the Virtuous Widow of Ephesus* the inclusion of Jupiter and his daughter Diana (disguised as the maid Sofia) represents the main addition to Petronius' plot. In both comedies, although conversely, the theme of female unfaithfulness (or, that is, to say human weakness) intertwines with divine motives – in other words, with the issue of free will and that of the superhuman power of influencing the choices of human beings.

In *A Very Curious Story of the Virtuous Widow of Ephesus*, as previously mentioned, Jupiter forms first the double of a fortune-teller and then that of a soldier. These disguises recall elements already developed by Figueiredo himself with respect to Amphitryon. In particular, as a fortune-teller, Jupiter generally plays a satirical 'counter-melody' against the moralistic approach that pervades Ephesus. For example, he predicts the punishment of the model-couple, the matron of Ephesus, Cynthia, and her husband, Endymion.⁷¹ Indeed, the former will surrender to the soldier's seduction and the latter will be likewise seduced by Diana in the last part of comedy.

An analogous prophecy of adultery is also at play at the beginning of *A God Slept Here*, where the prophet Tiresias predicts that on the following night a man will visit Amphitryon's house, while the master of the house is away.⁷² This alone prompts the jealous general to form his own double, not only to test his wife's faithfulness, but also to allow the oracle to be fulfilled in an acceptable manner. The role of Tiresias is not actually unattested in the myth of Amphitryon, as the Portuguese António José da Silva had made him a character in his comedy, *Amphitrião* (1736), which was most certainly known by Figueiredo.⁷³ Also in a strand of the ancient tradition, Tiresias is mentioned as the man who solves the enigma of the double, revealing the intrigue to Amphitryon.⁷⁴

A similar epilogue seemed to be thinly veiled also in Plautus, where Amphitryon (after Bromia briefly tells him about the relationship between Jupiter and Alcmena) wants to ask Tiresias what he should do (1128–9). But Jupiter's epiphany makes the recourse to the soothsayer worthless (Jupiter clarifies that, being a god, he is able to report the past and to predict the future much better than any other fortune-teller, 1132–4). The prophetic qualities give Figueiredo's Jupiter no longer a sort of special pre-eminence over the common fortune-tellers (as in Plautus), but rather evidence of his impotence. Indeed, he admits that the gods cannot alter and influence reality, but only predict it – just as with ordinary soothsayers.[75]

The ineptitude of the gods before destiny impacts the relationship between mortals and deities. In fact, the former are mistaken for being masters of their own destiny and the latter can only foresee this without the possibility of changing it. If the former live in a state of incertitude (which is a privilege granted to them), the latter are forced to face the truth. Finally, if the former enjoy the right to hope, the latter lack this right because of a lack of uncertainty.[76] Moreover, Jupiter makes reference to his love for Cynthia and his desire to have an affair with her preferably without any recourse to his extra powers and enchanting abilities,[77] but as himself (or as who he would be, if he were a man).

As is well-known, this issue has continued throughout the history of the reception of the theme of Amphitryon. Molière[78] (and then Giraudoux)[79] had firstly developed the crisis of Jupiter, who aspires to be loved not as a magic double of Amphitryon but as himself. Figueiredo's Amphitryon, playing the role of Jupiter, pretends to be envious towards men who are considered happier than gods, because of their brief but passionate pleasures that depend on the certainty of death. And he once again says that he would like to love Alcmena as a man and not as a god.[80]

In *A Very Curious Story of the Virtuous Widow of Ephesus*, Figueiredo appears to fulfil the aspirations elsewhere expressed by Jupiter: the widow of Ephesus loves the god as if he were a man and his disguise is not even necessary to carry out adultery. Jupiter introduces himself in the guise of an anonymous man, who is unknown to Cynthia; moreover, the metamorphosis does not imply any kind of double, because the originals (the real fortune-teller or the real sentinel) do not appear on stage. Thus, even if the Brazilian playwright restores the abilities of Jupiter as capable of assuming many disguises (*versipellis*) and being an adulterer (*moechus*),[81] he actually defuses the double-motive and its dramatic or existential consequences (e.g. the perturbing trouble before the loss of identity; the misunderstandings arising from the co-existence of two identical beings on stage). Converted into a mere camouflage, the disguise appears rather to be used by Jupiter as a device to have relationships with humankind. Furthermore, he does not actually employ any means that were not already familiar to the mortals: pleasure of food, pleasure of sex, *joie de vivre*. He provokes and tests human enjoyment granted to himself (as a man) and to everybody because of a kind of universal compulsion. Diana has an analogous destiny; her chastity – like the *pudicitia* of Cynthia, her priestess – soon yields to love: at the end of the play, the goddess 'steals' the body of Endymion (Cynthia's husband) away from the cross and arranges it again in the tomb, where his sleep of death turns into a sleep of love (in passing, Figueiredo brings forth another sort of *contaminatio*, inserting into his elaborate pastiche-drama also the reference to the myth of Diana and Endymion).

Conclusion

What does Figueiredo aim to demonstrate through his rewriting of the tale of the Widow of Ephesus? By eradicating the sublime (almost super-human) ethics embodied in the political authority of the State, the Brazilian playwright illustrates weakness as the most typical human characteristic. By constructing a sort of 'twilight of the gods', he makes any difference between mortals and deities disappear, for the gods introduce themselves to show that nobody can aim for Virtue (or any 'categorical imperative'). In short, Figueiredo adds Jupiter as a character only to confirm the message conveyed, nine years before, in his innovative Amphitryon-without-gods. *A Muito Curiosa História da Virtuosa Matrona de Éfeso* has to be considered not as a palinode, but rather as evidence (under the divine guise) of ideas already elaborated in *Um deus dormiu lá em casa* (under the human guise).

No divine entity can influence the actions of human beings or affect their nature. As the author has stated, '*A Very Curious Story of the Virtuous Widow of Ephesus* [is] a comedy about the ephemeral quality of the immortality of love.'[82] In the fictitious reality that theatre can create, gods, by not being able to alter anything on earth, can merely imitate humanity not only in *changing* themselves by means of certain disguises, but also by feeling *unchangeable* emotions that are all too human.

CHAPTER 8
ELECTRA'S TURN TO THE DARK SIDE: NELSON RODRIGUES' *SENHORA DOS AFOGADOS*
Anastasia Bakogianni

O que caracteriza uma peça trágica é, justamente, o poder de criar a vida e não imitá-la. Isso a que se chama *vida* é o que se representa no palco e não o que vivemos cá fora.

Nelson Rodrigues

What is characteristic of a tragic play is precisely the power of creating life and not imitating it. This that we call *life* is what is performed on stage, and not what we live out here.[1]

Who has the authority to proclaim a connection to an ancient model/source text(s)? Is it the artist, the audience or critics? And how can those of us working in classical reception engage in a meaningful way with more 'indirect' receptions where the exact nature of the connection is far from clear, implicit, and can even be contested?[2] My aim in this chapter is to argue for the existence of 'deep'[3] thematic and structural connections between *Senhora dos Afogados* (*Our Lady of the Drowned*, 1947), a play by Brazilian playwright Nelson Falcão Rodrigues (1912–80), and the portrayal of Electra in Greek tragedy. This is not a simple case of an ancient source (text A) being received in a modern rewriting (text B), but a complex and dynamic nexus of dramatic texts engaged in a multi-directional conversation. With this case study, we cannot point to a direct line of descent. Instead, we deal with a bricolage of both ancient and later sources, including receptions of other receptions.[4] Rodrigues' play, thus, exemplifies the challenges of engaging in a meaningful way with such 'masked' receptions,[5] where a connection has to be carefully unpacked and defended.

I am by no means the first scholar to propose the existence of a connection between Rodrigues' plays and Greek tragedy. The Brazilian theatre critic and scholar Sábato Magaldi (1927–2016)[6] was the first to propose the division of Rodrigues' oeuvre into 'psychological', 'mythic' and 'Carioca' tragedies.[7] In Magaldi's schema, *Senhora dos Afogados* together with the *Family Album* (1945) and *Dorotéia* (1950) form what he termed Rodrigues' 'mythic' cycle modelled on ancient Greek tragedies.[8] Magaldi convincingly argued that these three dramas explore the dark underbelly of mythical archetypes,[9] and this view has become widely accepted among theatre practitioners.[10] What is less clear is the precise nature of Rodrigues' connection to Greek tragedy. In focusing on *Senhora dos Afogados*, this chapter argues for the benefits of comparing this twentieth-century Brazilian play to the fifth-century BCE tragic versions of Electra. Before proceeding further, however, I wish to note that *Senhora dos Afogados* is first and foremost a Brazilian play that masks rather than proclaims any debt it owes to Greek tragedy or, more generally, to a diffuse notion of the myth of Electra. The connections I am proposing are without a doubt hard to pin down, distorted and unstable. But it is precisely these kinds of challenging instances of classical reception that can help us push back the boundaries of our field and fully engage with the richness of the reception process itself.

Drawing on developments in adaptation studies and comparative literature,[11] I wish to propose a bidirectional model of reception that does not inherently seek to valorize a 'classical' source(s). Rather than comparing Rodrigues' *Senhora dos Afogados* to the ancient tragic texts that feature Electra with the narrow aim of highlighting how Rodrigues' play 'succeeds' or 'fails' to reflect an ancient 'original(s)', I wish to dispense altogether with such a hierarchical and reductive model. Instead, I propose adopting the post-structuralist option of juxtaposition, according to which our texts co-exist on the same level rather than in relationships of priority and dominance. Thinking in terms of what is 'added' by bringing these texts into dialogue rather than focusing on their perceived impurities has a number of advantages. Comparing texts from different time periods and cultures in such a way can help us begin the process of breaking down the boundaries between text, reception and interpretative communities, and thus to destabilize canonical and Euro-centric views of the Classics.

In comparing *Senhora dos Afogados* with the ancient tragic plays featuring Electra, what emerges is how distinctive Rodrigues' drama is. Whatever elements he might have creatively 'borrowed' from both ancient and modern sources, he proceeded to submerge them fully into his own very idiosyncratic dramatic vision. This is clearly demonstrated in his choice of the name Moema Drummond for his heroine.[12] In Brazilian literature, Moema is best known as a character in *Caramuru: Poema Épico do Descobrimento da Bahia*, an eighteenth-century neoclassical epic poem by Frei Santa Rita Durão considered to be a foundational narrative of Brazil's colonization. In the poem, she is a native woman who drowns by swimming after the ship of her Portuguese lover. In *Senhora dos Afogados*, Rodrigues subverts Moema's association with the sea by having his heroine drown her sisters and incite her brother to commit suicide by walking into the sea. In so doing, he decolonizes a story from classical antiquity, disseminated in Latin America by the colonial powers. His Moema is not just a mourner who prays for vengeance, as Electra does in Greek tragedy, but a callous murderess in her own right operating within a specifically Brazilian social milieu. She is without a doubt the villain of Rodrigues' bleak tragedy of revenge. In Electra's rich and varied reception history,[13] Rodrigues' antiheroine stands out because she has well and truly turned to the dark side.[14] The Brazilian playwright offers audiences and scholars a particularly striking Latin American 'masked' reception of the ancient Greek tragic heroine that demands further critical attention.[15]

A nexus of receptions, ancient and modern

Nelson Rodrigues does not provide his readers/spectators with explicit authorial guidance. Thus, we cannot rely on intentionality to propose a connection between his drama and the ancient dramas featuring Electra.[16] It is up to us as scholars, readers and spectators to forge (or not) such connections based on more impressionistic processes of reception.[17] However, by examining more closely some of the ancient and later receptions at the heart of the proposed nexus of texts, we can activate connections that enrich both our understanding of Rodrigues' play and of the classical plays. I propose to begin my investigation not with the ancient texts, but with an important intermediary source text, an American twentieth-century reception of the story of Electra by the Irish-American playwright Eugene O'Neill (1888–1953).[18] Rodrigues' understanding of Electra was shaped by his encounter with O'Neill's trilogy *Mourning Becomes Electra* (1931).[19] This reception is closer to Rodrigues' play both in chronological and geographical terms; it mediates and shapes *Senhora dos Afogados*' dialogue with the classical story.

Unlike Rodrigues' 'masked' reception, O'Neill proudly proclaimed his connection to his ancient models in the title of his trilogy. In his work diary, he even referred to his three plays (*Homecoming*, *The Hunted* and *The Haunted*) as the 'Yankee Electra', thus explicitly drawing attention to his act of appropriation and inviting comparison with the ancient dramas featuring Electra, in particular Aeschylus' *Oresteia*.[20] One key element of *Mourning Becomes Electra* that did spark a creative response in Rodrigues is O'Neill's psychoanalytical reading of the story of Electra – or, to be more precise, the pop-psychology version of this emerging science.[21] In O'Neill's reception of Greek tragedy, the ancient concept of *moira* (fate/destiny) is replaced by deep-seated psychological drives that make the outcome of the story a foregone conclusion. Rodrigues shares O'Neill's interest in psychological motivation and his characters are driven even more forcibly by intense psychological urges.

The portrayal of the lead heroines in O'Neill and Rodrigues testifies to this strong thematic connection between *Mourning Becomes Electra* and *Senhora dos Afogados*. In *Homecoming*, O'Neill's version of Electra, whom he named Lavinia, tells her mother Christine:

> I hate you! You steal even Father's love from me again! You stole all love from me when I was born! Oh, mother! Why have you done this to me? What harm had I done you? Father, how can you love that shameless harlot? I can't bear it! I won't! . . .[22]

O'Neill foregrounds Lavinia's internalization of the Electra complex coined by Carl Jung in 1913.[23] Like her ancient counterparts, Lavinia rejects her mother in favour of her father, but O'Neill takes this a step further. Lavinia develops an unhealthy attachment to her father and a corresponding sexual jealousy for her mother. Rodrigues builds on this foundation, but takes it a step further. Compare Lavinia's speech with Moema's explanation why she drowned her two sisters, Clarinha and Dora, in the sea:[24]

> Tiraram todo o amor que
> eu teria de ti. Receberam as carícias que eu
> não tive . . . Elas descalçavam e acariciavam

os teus pés ... E eu, não! Era preciso que dei-
xassem este mundo ....[25]

They took all the love I should've had from you. They got all the caresses I never got. They would take off your shoes at night and caress your feet. Not I! They had to leave this world.[26]

Rodrigues emphasizes, even more strongly than O'Neill, the character's aberrant sexuality. Deep-seated desires underpin the motivation of O'Neill's and Rodrigues' heroines, and provide an explanation for their criminal behaviour and their 'tragic' ends (tragic in the modern sense of the word, meaning ending in catastrophe). Lavinia ends up destroying her family and atones by imprisoning herself in the Mannon mansion.[27] Moema's plotting and cruelty are also ruinous for her family and end up costing the heroine her own sanity.

In the long history of Electra's *metamorphoses*, two main trends stand out; her near identification with the act of mourning and her desire for revenge.[28] In O'Neill, both are evident, but the emphasis is on vengeance. In Rodrigues, Moema eschews the role of mourner entirely, except in outward appearance.[29] The Brazilian playwright thus boldly jettisons one strand of Electra's reception, that of a mourner, in order to emphasize her desire for vengeance, taking it to extreme lengths. Unlike Lavinia and some of her ancient counterparts, Moema displays no regrets or remorse; hence, she is punished by the loss of her reflection. She cannot see herself in mirrors. This loss symbolizes a rapture of the self. There is no redemption or hope for the future for Rodrigues' anti-heroine and his play ends, as in O'Neill, with the destruction of the family and the self-destruction of the Electra figure. O'Neill's American Gothic becomes Brazilian Grotesque in Rodrigues.

Let us now turn to an examination of the connections between Rodrigues' play and the ancient treatments of the myth: Aeschylus' *Choephori*, Sophocles' and Euripides' *Electra* plays, and the latter's *Orestes*. Scholars working on Rodrigues have already identified the link between *Senhora dos Afogados* and Aeschylus' seminal trilogy.[30] The status of Aeschylus' trilogy as a foundational dramatic text in the Western canon[31] has led scholars to undervalue the debt that Rodrigues owes to Sophocles' and Euripides' dramas. Another reason for the emphasis placed on the Aeschylean connection is O'Neill's marketing of his trilogy as an American version of the *Oresteia*, although, as with Rodrigues, a strong case can be made for Sophoclean and even Euripidean elements. Rather than privileging one connection over the other two, I will explore Rodrigues' relationship with all three ancient Greek tragedians, in particular the complex dialogue between these ancient plays and their reception in *Senhora dos Afogados*.

What is so striking about Rodrigues' anti-heroine is how she is gradually revealed as a murderess. In Greek tragedy, Electra remains largely an observer, although at times she comes tantalizingly close to taking direct action. In Aeschylus' *Choephori*, she is initially reluctant even to pray for vengeance (122), but in the *kommos*, she openly supports her father's cause even though it involves matricide (394–9). In Sophocles' *Electra*, she is prepared to make the attempt herself when she believes Orestes to be dead (954–7,

1019–20), and in Euripides' *Electra*, her hand is on Orestes' sword when he kills Clytemnestra (1224–6). That is actually the closest she comes to acting out her desire for vengeance in fifth-century BCE Athenian drama. Rodrigues' Moema, on the other hand, has gone over to the dark side before Rodrigues' play even opens. She is consumed by her desire to become the only woman in her father's life. Misael Drummond, the Agamemnon figure, only dies at the very end of the play.[32] It is through her interactions with her father that the full extent of Moema's obsession and its tragic consequences are gradually revealed. Unlike Euripides' tragic heroine, or O'Neill's Lavinia, Rodrigues' Moema never expresses any remorse or guilt for her crimes, nor does she hesitate like Electra in Aeschylus' *Choephori*. Moema is ruthless in her pursuit of her goals, but also less honest than Sophocles' heroine, who openly admits to her mother that she knows all too well that she behaves badly (616–21). Sophocles' Electra blames her mother's bad example for her own unseemly behaviour, but in Rodrigues, Moema goes much further than her mother ever does.

Juxtaposing Rodrigues' drama and the ancient tragedies featuring Electra allows us to activate connections in terms not only of shared commonalities but also of distinctive differences. This process also offers the opportunity to reassess the uniqueness and subtlety of each ancient dramatist's portrayal of the tragic heroine and reflect on her transplantation in Brazilian soil. Rodrigues' distorting lens throws into even sharper relief the peculiarities of our ancient dramatic versions of Electra. *Senhora dos Afogados* is more than just the sum of Electra's treatment in Western literature, ancient and modern. It is a bold, creative new work, featuring a fascinating and complex central character.

The turn to the dark side

In his theatrical oeuvre, Rodrigues displays a keen awareness of the impact of spectacle, dramatic reversals and shocking revelations on the audience. His *Senhora dos Afogados* demonstrates his mastery of these dramatic techniques. The shock value of his characters' revelations in the play is a well-thought out strategy he artfully employs to keep his audiences engrossed and guessing what comes next. In *Senhora dos Afogados*, the Brazilian dramatist focuses closely on the dark side of familial bonds and portrays an inward-looking incestuous sexuality that destroys his characters. A case in point is Moema's incestuous love for her father. It is these aberrant feelings that lead her to commit a series of terrible crimes. In a radical departure from the classical model, Rodrigues' Misael is still alive when the play begins, thus allowing the audience to witness, first-hand, the father-daughter relationship and their interactions on stage. Like her ancient counterparts, Moema rejects her mother in favour of her father. As Eduarda acknowledges in Rodrigues' play: 'My daughter doesn't like me, or I her ... Each wishes for the death of the other' ('Minha filha não gosta de mim, nem eu dela ... Cada uma deseja a morte da outra', 273). Moema mirrors her ancient counterpart's desire for matricide, most closely resembling the Sophoclean heroine, who feels no compunction for desiring her mother's death, which she views as a just punishment for Clytemnestra's involvement in the murder of Agamemnon. Sophocles' Electra actually encourages her brother to 'Strike with redoubled force, if you have the strength' ('παῖσον, εἰ σθένεις, διπλῆν', 1416). Moema's manipulation of both her brother and her father, however, means that she is more directly involved in the family's criminal history. Her vengeance is not motivated by any crime her mother has committed – her father after all still lives – but by her own dark desires. She deliberately drives her mother towards self-destruction and takes great pleasure in her father's punishment of Eduarda's adultery. She labels her mother a 'Prostituta!' ('Prostitute!', 276) and celebrates her death by putting on a white dress,[33] the first time she wears lighter-coloured clothes, according to the stage directions.[34] Moema changes out of her black clothes only when she thinks she has won her heart's desire and become the only woman in her father's life. Her white dress, thus, becomes an outward symbol of her incestuous love for her father. Her mother's death opens up a world of possibilities for Moema, the incestuous daughter who hopes to replace her mother in her father's affections.

In *Senhora dos Afogados*, Misael dies cradled in the arms of his daughter, just as she celebrates her triumph. In this scene, Moema becomes both daughter and mother to her father. His death, it could be argued, is the direct result of Moema's revelations about what she has done and her secret feelings for him. Finally, having eliminated all her rivals, she is the only woman in his life, as was her expressed desire throughout the play. Her incestuous love for her father is the deep-seated motive that leads her to murder her sisters, as she reveals to her father. Rodrigues, thus, has his Electra take on the executioner's role in the sacrifice of her sisters, raising the spectre of the sacrifice of Iphigenia, a key element of the ancient story of the cycle of violence under which the House of Atreus labours – described briefly by the chorus in *Agamemnon* and dramatized by Euripides in his *Iphigenia at Aulis*. In *Senhora dos Afogados*, it is Moema rather than her father who kills her sisters on the altar of her perverted love. Moema, thus, becomes a malevolent force that destroys everything in its path.

In performance, Moema's aberrant sexuality can be further emphasized. Cláudia Tatinge Nascimento, who directed the US premier of *Senhora dos Afogados* for the Theatre Department of Wesleyan University (2002),[35] argues that Rodrigues' plays do not require explicit portrayals of sex and violence on stage.[36] The Wesleyan production relied largely on suggestion rather than graphic representation. In the Cia da Farsa production (Belo Horizonte, 2015), however, Moema's sexuality was given greater prominence. In a key scene, Eduarda and Misael sleep on the marital bed, a focal point in the production, while Moema bathes in the nude in a hipbath. Her pose was reminiscent of a modern bathing Aphrodite, which lent the scene an erotic charge. She provocatively sank into the hipbath and proceeded to wash herself ostentatiously in full view of the audience. She, thereby, put her nude body on display deliberately, while throwing glances at the audience in a knowing manner. This Moema is more of a coquette than in Rodrigues' text and did not confine herself to black clothes, choosing instead very feminine dresses. In the first scene, she shared with the Misael character this version of Moema caresses his feet, thus fulfilling on stage the desire to share this intimacy with her father that she expresses later on in the play. As the performance progressed, she acted increasingly affectionately and flirtatiously towards her father. In another key scene, Moema also forced her brother Paulo to watch Eduarda and the fiancé have sex on stage as a means of stirring up his jealousy. This allowed her to manipulate her brother into murdering her fiancé. Most crucially, in the Cia da Farsa production Sidneia Simões, the actress playing Moema, was the only real woman; all the other female parts were played by men, and this was a deliberate choice on the part of the director João Valadares, who himself took up the role of Eduarda (Figure 8.1). This directorial decision left Moema as the only biologically female woman on stage surrounded by female cross-dressing simulacra.

In this production, Moema's sexuality and sexual jealousy become the main focus of attention and the means by which her criminal behaviour is explained to the audience. According to Simões, Moema is mad, totally mad.[37] But she also argues that Rodrigues' portrayal is true to life. In her day job as a journalist reporting on the criminal justice system, she has encountered a number of mad, bad and dangerous-to-know women. This interpretation of Rodrigues' anti-heroine, however, suppresses some of the darker aspects of her portrayal, specifically her cruelty and evil, which are precisely the traits that make her such a powerful dramatic persona in *Senhora dos Afogados*. As is the case

Figure 8.1 Nelson Rodrigues' *Senhora dos Afogados*: João Valadares (Eduarda) and Sidneia Simões (Moema). Cia da Farsa Production (2015). Copyright: Alexandre Toledo.

with modern Electras on stage, directors and performers shy away from plumbing the darkest depths of the character,[38] perhaps because they fear that if these were revealed, audiences will be unable to connect with the tragic heroine in performance. Focusing on Moema's madness and her aberrant sexuality in effect softens Rodrigues much darker portrayal; as a result, the play loses much of its dark fascination. Rodrigues' Moema is an extreme character, one of world theatre's truly evil anti-heroines, a cold and calculating manipulator and murderess without any redeeming qualities.

Ironically, it is the daughter who draws the neighbours' attention to her mother's deviation from the Drummond model of how a good wife behaves. Drummond women are repressed and faithful, but Eduarda is emotional and ultimately decides to cast off social strictures by choosing love over duty. Her husband punishes her adultery with Moema's fiancé by the amputation of her hands.[39] The precise nature of the punishment originates in a suggestion put forward by Moema: 'Why don't you punish her hands? . . . The hands are the guiltiest in love. They sin more. They caress . . . They run over the body' ('E por que não a castigas nas mãos? . . . As mãos são mais culpadas no amor . . . Pecam mais . . . Acariciam . . . Correm no corpo', 259–60).[40] Moema's obsession with hands arises out of the fact that they are the only body part in which she resembles her mother. This is mentioned in the opening stage directions. Later in the play, her brother Paulo explicitly draws attention to this resemblance, as she urges him to give in to the call of the sea.[41] In the Cia da Farsa production, this is illustrated much earlier in a scene where Paulo mistakes Moema for Eduarda when she embraces him from behind; all he can see of her is her hands. Moema not only takes advantage of this fact; she also wishes to excise them symbolically by destroying the original, her mother's hands, of which hers are the copy. Hands are a key feature of Rodrigues' play and can be further highlighted in performance.[42] This emphasis on the importance of hands in drama, which commit the actions that move the plot forward, invites us to reflect on their key function in Euripides' *Electra*, where the heroine joins her hand to that of her brother on the sword Orestes uses to murder their mother. In ancient Greek 'αὐτόχειρ', a compound word whose second half is the word for 'hand', can refer to 'one who kills himself or one of his kin' in other words a 'murderer' or 'homicide', which perfectly describes the situation of the siblings in Euripides' play, but also more generally that of Orestes in classical drama and mythology. After all, he killed his mother with his own hand.

In Rodrigues' play, mother and daughter also reflect each other's movements and gestures.[43] This disturbing mimicry, coupled with Moema's lack of reflection, suggests that the daughter is her mother's simulacrum, a false copy whose psychological make-up lacks some essential element of what it means to be human. Her perverted love for her father and the extreme lengths to which she goes in order to become the only woman in his life reveal a deep-seated longing for completion, for a way to become whole. But Moema's journey towards becoming a fully realized human being involves excising her own mother and several members of her nuclear family, so that she can become the sole focus of her father's attention. Rodrigues, thus, takes the psychoanalytical interpretation of the ancient story of Electra to its extreme outcome.

Rodrigues' play enters into a dialogue not only with the ancient dramatic versions of Electra but also with other ancient Greek plays. For example, there is an *anagnorisis* (recognition) scene, but instead of the heroine's recognition of the identity of her brother Orestes – so crucial in the ancient dramas featuring Electra – in Rodrigues the fiancé reveals himself to be the illegitimate son of Misael.[44] This revelation suggests that he has assumed the role of Hippolytus.[45] But this Brazilian Hippolytus actively pursues his father's wife rather than rejecting women in general and Phaedra's incestuous passion in particular. In Rodrigues, the rejected son's revenge for the murder of his own mother is explicitly sexual in nature. The location of that earlier murder is also significant, and a further spur to the son. It was on the marriage bed shared by Misael and Eduarda later that day that he murdered the fiancé's mother, a prostitute, nineteen years before the action of the play begins.

The other main male character, Paulo, the Orestes figure, is portrayed as weak and effeminate; he also displays clear Oedipal urges towards his mother.[46] In this respect, he resembles O'Neill's Orestes character, Orin Mannon. It is Paulo's jealousy of the fiancé and of his own father that makes him susceptible to Moema's manipulation and leads him to destroy himself by walking into the sea. O'Neill's Orin also commits suicide because he is unable to face the consequences of his involvement in the murder of Adam Brant, also motivated by sexual jealousy, and of its impact on his mother who commits suicide as a direct result of the death of her lover. In *Senhora dos Afogados*, since the father figure still lives, it behoves him to exact vengeance on his adulterous wife. Rodrigues' focus on the family, thus, both echoes and departs from ancient plotlines and develops further themes explored by O'Neill. The incestuous trend towards endogamy in the Drummond family is taken to extremes by Rodrigues and leads inexorably to the utter destruction of all its members.

This growing list of disasters is overseen by the ghosts of the family,[47] who like their ancient counterparts, weigh down the family and cut off all avenues of escape. In Greek tragedy, the House of Atreus is trapped in a vicious cycle of revenge and blood pollution. The answer is sometimes supplied by the gods, as in Aeschylus' *Eumenides*, where the goddess Athena intervenes and declares Orestes innocent of the crime of matricide. At the end of Euripides' *Electra*, the Dioscuri help to guide Orestes and Electra towards a solution, albeit dramatically unsatisfactory. In Rodrigues, however, there is no escape, sin is followed by punishment and there is not even a glimmer of redemption.[48]

Rodrigues' play is one of revelations and dark secrets exposed. Misael's crime is strongly foreshadowed, but Moema's murder of her sisters is unexpected and shocking, potentially making her one of the darkest versions of Electra, if not *the* darkest, I have encountered in my work on the tragic heroine's reception in the modern world. In his oeuvre, Rodrigues subverts the picture card, tourist view of Brazil as a land of sun, beaches and fun to reveal its dark underbelly.[49] Rodrigues created a world populated by awful characters, who behave amorally. They are only capable of a corrupt form of love that destroys rather than nourishes. The Rio de Janeiro of the Drummonds is a place full of terrible secrets, adultery, incestuous love and murder hidden under a veneer of respectability.

The chorus in Rodrigues

In terms of the reception of ancient theatrical practices, a distinctive feature of *Senhora dos Afogados* is the presence of a chorus.⁵⁰ Rodrigues, however, went further, amplifying the effect and significance of his chorus, by creating two distinct choruses.⁵¹ The first chorus comprises the Drummonds' neighbours, who witness and contribute to the disintegration of the family. The second is a chorus of prostitutes, who lament the murder of their colleague nineteen years ago. It is this crime, the murder of a woman that lies at the heart of the cycle of violence in Rodrigues' drama. But it is another woman, Moema, the daughter of the murderer, who eventually destroys him with her obsessive love.

Rodrigues also appropriates the ancient Athenian theatrical practice of using masks and uses it metatheatrically to comment on the hypocrisy of bourgeoisie life. Addressing a male member of the chorus of neighbours, Eduarda says: 'But that isn't your face, that's your mask. Put on your real face' ('Mas este não é o teu rosto – é tua mascara. Põe teu verdadeiro rosto', 211), which according to the stage directions turns out to be a 'máscara hedionda' (hideous mask). The veneer of politeness exhibited at first by this chorus turns out to be nothing but an act. The Drummond family attempt to put on a show for their neighbours, but ultimately the hollowness of their pretence is revealed, as is their neighbours' true nature. In fact, there are strong indications in Rodrigues' dramatic text that this chorus of neighbours is one of his surrealistic touches.⁵² They could exist only in the minds of the troubled Drummond family. In the 1954 production of the play, the true nature of this symbolic chorus was revealed on stage (Figure 8.2). Whatever the case might be, the mixed chorus of male and female neighbours are certainly not there to

Figure 8.2 Nelson Rodrigues' *Senhora dos Afogados*: The masked chorus (1954). Still from the original production. Copyright: CEDOC [Centro de Documentação e Informação da Funarte].

support the family, as the female choruses of Aeschylus, Sophocles and Euripides do. Their envy secretly makes them revel in the misfortunes that beset the family.

By contrast, the chorus of prostitutes come across as more down-to-earth, honest and capable of real empathy, thus further undermining preconceived ideas of social order and class. In this respect, *Senhora dos Afogados* picks up on themes explored in Rodrigues' Carioca tragedies.[53] In these modern tragedies of life in the city of Rio de Janeiro, Rodrigues portrayed the lower middle-class, a subject never before represented on the Brazilian stage. As the choruses in *Senhora dos Afogados* reveal, however, it is counterproductive to try to subdivide too strictly his theatrical output of seventeen plays into the categories of mythical, psychological and social dramas.[54] Elements of all three of these preoccupations surface throughout Rodrigues' oeuvre and his plays resist easy categorization. Rodrigues, like Euripides, was a playwright who delighted in innovation. His plays gleefully break traditional genre boundaries, but do so always in the service of the story.

Rodrigues' use of the chorus demonstrates that he shares the ancient Greek tragedians' keen awareness of the dramatic impact of spectacle, violence (even when reported, as in Greek theatre), and reversals of fortune. *Senhora dos Afogados* shocks and disturbs with its violent spectacle. The Drummond family undergoes a kind of *sparagmos*, utterly destroying itself over the course of the play. The revelations about Moema's and Misael's criminal actions lead to even more violence being performed/reported, thus bringing the house of Drummond crashing down in a modern saga of a family's tragic destiny. In Rodrigues' case, we should stress spectators' responses in particular, since his *Senhora dos Afogados* derives much of its power in performance from this visual spectacle and the shock effect of its revelations on the audience.

Sadly, Nelson Rodrigues' highly creative contribution to the history of the reception of Electra is not particularly well-known or explored in detail in Anglophone scholarship. His plays rarely make an appearance in the repertoire of British and North American theatre companies, and this has impeded recognition of their contribution to world theatre among non-Portuguese-speaking audiences. When they are staged, his plays tend to be produced by smaller companies and university theatre departments. In Britain, StoneCrabs, a fringe theatre company based in South London, was the first to bring Rodrigues' dramas to the British stage.[55] There is not even an established English translation of the title of Rodrigues' *Senhora dos Afogados*.[56] Rodrigues' play received its premier in the United States at Wesleyan University (2002), as discussed above. This all-too-brief performance history of *Senhora dos Afogados* illustrates the marginalization of Rodrigues' oeuvre in Anglophone theatre, despite his importance in Brazilian theatre. In these performance contexts, audiences are more likely to be familiar with the ancient sources about the story of Electra than with Rodrigues' play. Even in Brazil, *Senhora dos Afogados* is rarely performed today, exposing an underlying anxiety that the dark anti-heroine at its heart will prove too much for audiences.[57]

In classical reception theory, the reader/audience is construed as central to the very process of reception and is the means by which we can test the state of our relationship with the classical past. Audiences unfamiliar with the ancient dramas featuring Electra or the story of Orestes' revenge will not be in a position to make these connections while watching Rodrigues drama, unless, of course, it was explicitly pointed out to them in the programme notes. But even in the case of knowledgeable audience members, familiar with the classics in general and the story of Electra in particular, *Senhora does Afogados* still surprises, because it subverts the expectations of both knowledgeable and non-knowledgeable audiences.

Conclusion

We have no way of determining with any degree of certainty how familiar Nelson Rodrigues actually was with the dramatic texts of Aeschylus, Sophocles and Euripides. As early as 1951, Fonseco Pimental condemned Rodrigues for taking liberties with Greek drama and argued against any real connection between the two.[58] Greek tragedy was known but not performed on the Brazilian stage until much later in the twentieth century.[59] O'Neill's *Mourning Becomes Electra*, therefore, acts as a key connecting stepping-stone that forms a bridge between the ancient dramas on Electra and Rodrigues' *Senhora dos Afogados*.[60] Angela Leite-Lopes argues in favour of a connection, but stresses that the two dramatists recover the ancient story in different ways and what Rodrigues offers us is an 'extremely original' version of the story of Electra that combines elements from both myth and the Greek tragedies in which Electra features, but ultimately offers audiences a creative response rather than an adaptation of a model(s).[61]

In this chapter, I have touched on only some of the possible classical connections. These juxtapositions darken even further Rodrigues' play by connecting it to the archetypical story of the destruction of the House of Atreus. However, even if Rodrigues did have the ancient Electra in mind when creating his Moema, he was not at all concerned with 'fidelity' and one can certainly appreciate his play on its own merits without being aware of any classical connections. But juxtaposing his drama with the ancient tragedies about Electra only serves to increase our appreciation of the richness and complexity of *Senhora dos Afogados*. As Charles Martindale has argued, the ancient model(s) and its reception can 'mutually illuminate each other, suggesting interpretive possibilities without closing discussion down'.[62] In this chapter, I argue for the value of throwing 'masked' receptions into the mix because they, too, enrich our appreciation of all the dramatic texts brought into dynamic inter-action within our nexus.

In terms of the history of Electra's reception, Rodrigues' drama reflects an important shift. After centuries in which Electra's passionate voice demanding vengeance was silenced, it was heard once again in the twentieth century, and it resonated particularly strongly in the performative arts.[63] It is the intensity of Electra's passion that made her such a memorable character in fifth-century BCE tragedy. Her darker side makes her stand out even in a genre that is famous for its portrayal of 'bad' women, including of course that of her own mother Clytemnestra. In her twentieth-century manifestations, these traits were once again allowed full expression. A large part of the reason for this change in attitude was the popularity of Freud's psychoanalytical theories that made Electra's extremism understandable again – indeed, one could even say fashionable.

Rodrigues' *Senhora dos Afogados* has the potential to take this interpretation of the myth of Electra to its very limits and beyond.

Rodrigues believed in the important role, played in society by 'the theatre of the unpleasant'. In the *Flower of Obsession*, Rodrigues said:

> In my texts, desire is sad, pleasure is tragic and crime is hell itself. The spectator goes home terrified by all his sins, past, present and future.[64]

On account of Rodrigues' obsession with the exploration of the darkest reaches of the human heart, Brazilian censors were so disturbed by *Senhora dos Afogados* that the play was banned and not put on stage until 1954.[65] The play's troubled performance history demonstrates that Rodrigues' heroine challenged contemporary ideas and values. The classical elements in this play require the active participation of the reader/spectator in order for the connections to be made. By drawing attention to these connections, I hope to aid in the project of unpicking the strands of the irreverent conversation that I believe the Brazilian playwright enjoys with classical drama. In the twentieth and twenty-first centuries, the Graeco-Roman classics have gradually won a significant position in global culture, moving beyond their position as a Western cultural product as this edited collection aptly demonstrates by drawing attention to the less-well explored topic of the reception of Greek and Roman drama on the Latin American stage. Classical antiquity has become a global meeting place where a multi-lingual and multicultural dialogue can take place. Rodrigues' *Senhora dos Afogados* deserves to take its rightful place on this global platform.

CHAPTER 9
BECOMING ANTIGONE: THE CLASSICS AS A MODEL OF RESISTANCE IN JORGE ANDRADE'S *PEDREIRA DAS ALMAS*

Seth A. Jeppesen

Você não acha que os mitos que iluminam a experiência humana são sempre os mesmos, apenas revivendo em formas diferentes?

Don't you think that the myths that illuminate human experience are always the same ones, just coming back to life in different forms?[1]

In his book *Raízes do Brasil* (Roots of Brazil), Sérgio Buarque de Holanda argues that a recognition of the antipathy between the family and the state, as represented by Antigone and Creon in Sophocles' *Antigone*, is fundamental to understanding the political and social upheavals that occurred in Brazil in the early twentieth century. The country underwent the twin processes of urbanization and industrialization, changes that witnessed the old social order, based primarily on ties of kinship, yield to institutions governed not by mutual obligation and affection, but by abstract principles.[2] This world of transition that Buarque de Holanda describes is the world in which the dramatist Jorge Andrade grew up; this world forms the core of his dramatic work.[3]

Andrade would eventually express this theme of family versus the state in what many have considered his most important play, *Pedreira das Almas* (Quarry of Souls), first published and performed in 1958.[4] Andrade makes no explicit reference to Sophocles' *Antigone* in the play, but the connection between *Pedreira das Almas* and *Antigone* was noted as early as the essays of Anatol Rosenfeld and Lourival Gomes Machado that accompany the 1970 edition of the play in the collection *Marta, a Árvore e o Relógio*.[5] Since then, a number of scholars have discussed this connection, often just in passing. These mentions emphasize either the theme of the unburied body,[6] the identification of Mariana with Antigone,[7] the motif of personal rights versus the unbridled power of the state[8] or the general processes of intertextuality.[9] None of these works, however, explains adequately the gradual way in which Andrade equates Mariana with Antigone throughout the play, thus allowing the audience to witness Mariana's choice to assume the intractable stance of her Grecian predecessor. This process of becoming is also reflected in the performance history of the play, principally in the 1958 debut of the play and in the 1977 production at the Teatro Alfredo Mesquita. Over time, *Pedreira das Almas* became, like Antigone, a symbol of resistance, this time to the abuses of the military dictatorship of the 1970s. Furthermore, the playwright himself, in his interviews and memoirs, eventually became like Antigone in his conscious acceptance of the responsibility to fight against violence and repression wherever he saw it.

Pedreira das Almas: The historical setting of the play

Pedreira das Almas, Andrade's second play, was written in 1957 and debuted at the Teatro Brasileiro de Comédia in 1958 to mixed reviews.[10] Andrade subsequently revised the play twice, once for publication in 1960 and again for inclusion in his cycle of plays entitled *Marta, a Árvore, e o Relógio*, which was printed in 1970.[11] This collection arranges Andrade's ten major plays into a cyclical narrative about the origins of modern Brazil, from the colonial *bandeirantes* to the life of the author. *Pedreira das Almas* comes second in this work, as it is set during the liberalist revolt of 1842 in the early decades of independence from Portugal.

Though *Pedreira das Almas* owes much to *Antigone*, it is not a direct derivative of the Sophoclean play; it has a unique plot populated by characters that often resemble the Greek ones, but are ultimately distinct from them.[12] Of the relationship between the two plays, Fernanda Maddaluno states: '*Antigone* . . . no longer has meaning in and of itself: it becomes privileged material in a new construction, assimilated and transformed by the intertextual process' ('Antígona . . . já não significa por conta própria: torna-se material privilegiado de uma nova construção, assimilado e transformado pelo processo intertextual').[13]

The town in which the play is set (and which gives the play its name), Pedreira das Almas, does not actually exist, but is clearly a fictional doublet for the actual town of São Tomé das Letras, perched in the mountains of Minas Gerais.[14] The most important link between the two towns is the grotto of São Tomé, which gives the actual town its name and provides a hiding place for the fugitive Gabriel in the play.[15] Other places mentioned in the play, such as Baependi and Bela Cruz, are actual locations and Andrade alludes to historical events that took place at them, such as the fall of Baependi to government forces in 1842 and a massacre at the Fazenda Bela Cruz in 1833, thus anchoring his fictional town within the historical landscape of Minas Gerais.[16]

Andrade also sets the play during an actual uprising in 1842 in the provinces of São Paulo and Minas Gerais that threatened to expand into an all-out civil war. The impetus for this insurrection was a movement at the level of the national government called the *Regresso*, which aimed to counteract the liberalism of the early years of independence and centralize power under the national government at the expense of regional autonomy.[17] By early 1842, the effects of this policy became evident in the provinces, where power to prosecute crime was taken from the justices of the peace (*juizes de paz*) and given to police delegates (*delegados de polícia*) who were appointed at the national level. In the play, Vasconcelos, who resembles Sophocles' Creon, is one such *delegado de polícia*, who has arrived from the capital with a body of troops to restore order.[18] Vasconcelos' name in the play appears to be inspired by Bernardo Pereira de Vasconcelos, a leader of the *Regresso* movement and one of the premier lawmakers of his day.[19] The Polyneices character, Martiniano, is also reminiscent of José Martiniano de Alencar, a leading nativist and senator from Ceará.[20] Andrade marshals these historical details in his effort to present a cyclical view of Brazilian history and link the conflicts of the past with the tragedies of the present.

Mariana becoming Antigone

From the beginning of Andrade's play, there are hints about the connection between *Pedreira das Almas* and *Antigone*, but it is only in the second act that the similarities in the plot and the relationship of the various characters to their Sophoclean counterparts become evident. In the first act, the characters feel out different options for themselves, which makes their decisions in the second act all the more meaningful because the audience sees other choices they could have made.

As with Sophocles' *Antigone*, *Pedreira das Almas* begins with an expository dialogue between two female characters: Mariana, the eventual Antigone character, and her friend and confidante Clara, who stands in the place of Ismene in the opening scene.[21] The dialogue between the two informs the audience of the physical and temporal setting of the action, as well as of the allegiances of the various characters. Mariana is waiting for her fiancé Gabriel (Haemon), a ringleader of the liberal rebellion whom she expects to return shortly from the battle in the valley below. She is also waiting for her younger brother Martiniano, who followed Gabriel into the conflict despite his mother Urbana's wishes. When Gabriel arrives, he informs Mariana that the rebels have been defeated and that Martiniano has been taken captive, yet he assures her that since her brother only followed orders, he will be released shortly.[22] Gabriel knows that the government-backed army is looking to arrest him as a ringleader of the rebellion, so he plans to marry Mariana immediately and leave the city for the fertile lands of São Paulo with any who will follow.

When Mariana's mother Urbana enters, she remains impassive as she hears of the defeat of the rebel force, since she has refused to say her son's name since he disobeyed her and left for the war. Instead of addressing the situation at hand, she discusses with the priest, Father Gonçalo, her plans for expanding the town cemetery by bringing soil up from the valley, since there is no longer room for any more burials due to the rocky landscape.[23] This mundane task has become more urgent, since Gabriel's father is on his deathbed and will be buried in the last available plot. This detail becomes important later in understanding Vasconcelos' decision to forbid Martiniano's burial, because it would have required people to leave the town.

When Urbana and Mariana finally encounter each another, Mariana asks for her mother's blessing in her marriage to Gabriel, which Urbana refuses to give. The two then engage in a debate about the nature of laws (*leis*), rights (*direitos*) and justice (*justiça*) that is reminiscent of Antigone's *agon* with Creon (441–525), except without the gender polarity. Urbana expresses sentiments similar to Creon's such as 'The government should be respected. It is not with insurrections that errors are corrected' ('O Govêrno deve ser respeitado. Não é com desordens que se corrigem erros') and 'Everyone knows my respect for the law, for order' ('É conhecido de todos o meu respeito à lei, à ordem').[24] Mariana in turn echoes Antigone by remarking: 'Injustice is everyone's business' ('Injustiça diz respeito a todos') and 'I am defending my right' ('Defendo um direito meu').[25] Urbana is also very similar to Creon in the connection that the two make between obedience to the law and a sense of belonging within the physical boundaries of

117

the city.²⁶ Creon in his opening speech says: 'And whoever thinks that his friend is greater than / his fatherland, I say this man is from nowhere' ('καὶ μείζον' ὅστις ἀντὶ τῆς αὑτοῦ πάτρας / φίλον νομίζει, τοῦτον οὐδαμοῦ λέγω', 182–3). Urbana echoes this sentiment when she says: 'People like you who are empty of memories, do not have a place anywhere' ('Os homens vazios de recordações, como sois vós, não têm lugar em parte alguma'),²⁷ thus aligning her more with the pro-government absolutist party in the context of the revolt of 1842.

In spite of this initial resemblance of Urbana and Mariana to Creon and Antigone, the similarity is reversed when one looks at their opinions on how to treat the dead. Mariana dreams of leaving a town made up only of rocks, paving stones and tombs,²⁸ while Urbana is fiercely loyal to the dead, to the point of telling the priest: 'If it is a sin to honour and love my ancestors, the city, and the deeds of my parents, then I will not live except in sin!' ('Se fôr pecado honrar e amar os antepassados, a cidade, e os feitos de meus pais ... não poderei viver a não ser em pecado!').²⁹ When it comes to their devotion toward Martiniano before his death, Urbana refuses to speak his name and Mariana is willing to leave the town with Gabriel, even though she knows her brother has been captured and may need her help.³⁰ This distribution among the characters of themes from *Antigone* concerning laws, justice and respect for the dead opens up possibilities for each, making their choices more meaningful in the end. In Sophocles' play, we do not see the moment in which Antigone decides that it is worth sacrificing her own life to bury her brother. In *Pedreira das Almas*, however, Mariana initially expresses antipathy towards her connection to her dead ancestors and ambivalence toward her brother's situation, which makes her choice to become Antigone all the more meaningful because the audience can see a different path that she could have chosen.³¹

An additional piece of evidence that supports the intertextual relationship described so far is the theme of proper care for the dead, which is an issue from the opening of the play. Before Urbana's entrance, the townspeople, who act as a chorus, enter from the church and begin a debate about whether it is best to stay in the city that is full of their dead ancestors but harbours little hope for future prosperity, or follow Gabriel to a new land of promise. The following lines represent the various opinions of the women of the town:

Graciana Deus castiga quem abandona seus mortos ...

Clara E passaremos o resto da vida guardando cemitérios?

Elisaura Cemitérios onde repousam teus antepassados!

Genoveva Se for necessário, arrancaremos essas lajes e os levaremos!

Graciana Isso é uma ofensa a Deus!³²

Graciana God punishes those who abandon their dead ...

Clara So should we pass the rest of our lives tending cemeteries?

Elisaura Cemeteries where your dead ancestors rest!

Genoveva If necessary, we would tear up these gravestones and take our ancestors with us!

Graciana That is an offence against God!

This scene not only emphasizes the theme of proper treatment of the dead, but also multiplies the female characters from Sophocles' source text.³³

Three days later at the funeral of Gabriel's father, Vasconcelos arrives with the army, throwing the city into panic, while Mariana sends Gabriel to hide in the grotto of São Tomé. Urbana sees Gabriel enter the grotto and finally has a chance to exact revenge on him by revealing his whereabouts.³⁴ Vasconcelos enters, bringing Martiniano with him, and tells the citizens that if they do not hand over Gabriel, he will hold Martiniano responsible for Gabriel's crimes.³⁵ As Dona Urbana wavers between the love of her son and loyalty to her daughter, Martiniano breaks free and is shot dead by one of the soldiers.³⁶ Upon seeing her son die, Urbana decides not to succumb to the violence of Vasconcelos and refuses to reveal Gabriel's hiding place. Vasconcelos, in turn, refuses to let anyone leave the city, which means Martiniano's corpse cannot be taken to the valley for burial, nor can soil be brought up to provide a proper covering for the corpse, until Gabriel is captured.³⁷ When *Pedreira* was revived in 1977, this scene would have had resonance with the practices of the dictatorship in the way that government agents frequently tortured family members in front of each other for maximum leverage. The official report compiled by the Archdiocese of São Paulo says the following about this practice: 'The objective of torture was to bring about the victim's moral destruction by breaking down emotional ties based on kinship.'³⁸ The report includes accounts of parents threatened with the torture of their children and siblings forced to witness the torture of each other, which is essentially what happens in this scene from *Pedreira*. In the 1970s, in response to the brutality of the military regime, torture increasingly became one of the themes of Andrade's writing, as is evinced in *Labirinto* and *Milagre na Cela*.³⁹

The death of her brother is the impetus that Mariana needs to take on the persona of Antigone in earnest. She squares off against Vasconcelos in a discussion about which laws are most important: divine or civic.⁴⁰ Vasconcelos expresses his intention to hold the entire town responsible for the insurrection, maintaining that 'The law is clear and it will be respected and obeyed' ('a lei é clara e será respeitada e cumprida'). Mariana bursts out in response, 'Laws! Laws! Neither I nor the people of Pedreira das Almas will accept your laws!' ('Leis! Leis! Não aceito nem o povo de Pedreira das Almas acetará suas leis!').⁴¹ In the 1960 edition of the play, Mariana's similarity to Antigone is even more pronounced, since Mariana's line reads: 'Laws! Laws! Neither I nor the people of Pedreira das Almas will accept other laws besides those of God!' ('Leis! Leis! Não aceito nem o povo de Pedreira das Almas acetará outras leis além das de Deus!').⁴² Here Mariana sounds much like Sophocles' Antigone in her famous encounter with Creon at lines 449–55, which reads:

Κρ. καὶ δῆτ' ἐτόλμας τούσδ' ὑπερβαίνειν νόμους;

Αν. οὐ γάρ τί μοι Ζεὺς ἦν ὁ κηρύξας τάδε,

οὐδ' ἡ ξύνοικος τῶν κάτω θεῶν Δίκη
τοιούσδ' ἐν ἀνθρώποισιν ὥρισεν νόμους,
οὐδὲ σθένειν τοσοῦτον ᾠόμην τὰ σὰ
κηρύγμαθ' ὥστ' ἄγραπτα κἀσφαλῆ θεῶν
νόμιμα δύνασθαι θνητά γ' ὄνθ' ὑπερδραμεῖν.

Creon And indeed you dared to transgress these laws?
Antigone Yes, for it was not Zeus who announced them to me,
Nor did Justice who dwells with the gods below
mark out such laws for mankind. Nor did I believe that
a man such as you, being mortal was strong enough
in his decrees to be able to override
the unwritten and firm laws of the gods.

Vasconcelos' identification with Creon becomes even more obvious when Padre Gonçalo appeals to divine regulations and asks that they be allowed either to take the body to the valley for burial or to get soil from the valley with which to bury the boy, to which Vasconcelos responds:

Vasconcelos Não permitirei nem uma coisa nem outra. Não posso facilitar meios para a fuga de um homem, que é um dos responsáveis pela desordem que lavra na Província.

Gonçalo É um ato de caridade cristã que vossa mercê não pode negar.

Vasconcelos Tanto posso que impedirei.

Gonçalo Senhor! É uma impiedade deixar um corpo sem sepultura. É uma offensa aos mortos![43]

Vasconcelos I will permit neither the one nor the other. I cannot facilitate the escape of a man who is one of those responsible for the disorder which has taken place in the Province.

Gonçalo It is an act of Christian charity which your mercy cannot deny.

Vasconcelos I can and I will impede it!

Gonçalo Sir! It is an act of impiety to leave a body without burial. It is an offence to the dead!

Vasconcelos refuses to modify his orders and Urbana, Mariana and the townswomen begin mourning as they take Martiniano's body into the church.[44]

In the second act, a group of soldiers talks about the stench of the rotting corpse that is filling the town and their own superstitions about leaving a body unburied, fearing not only the punishments of God but also the visitation of Martiniano's wandering spirit.[45]

All of the men have been deported from the city to prevent an uprising and a curfew is in effect to keep the women at home until Gabriel is found. Sophocles' scene of Antigone disobeying orders and being caught by the soldiers is multiplied in Andrade's version, as four groups of three townswomen each are caught breaking curfew in order to beg Vasconcelos to allow the burial of Martiniano.[46] The women then imagine they see the ghost of Martiniano wandering in the cemetery, which unnerves the soldiers and causes Vasconcelos to demand that Mariana come out of the church and tell him where Gabriel is, otherwise she will face Gabriel's punishment in his place.[47] At this point, the audience finds out about the death of Urbana, when Mariana tells Vasconcelos that he can find Gabriel by entering the church, thus forcing him to see the results of his unjust orders.[48] Vasconcelos, like Creon, sees the error of his ways, though too late, and tells Mariana that he will report to his superiors that Gabriel died in the fighting.[49] He leaves and allows the people of Pedreira to prepare for the burial of the mother and son. The play closes a few days later, when Mariana chooses to stay behind in the city rather than go to São Paulo with Gabriel, because now it is her dead who reside in Pedreira and she cannot abandon them. Thus, Mariana commits an act of ersatz suicide by remaining behind alone in the church at the end of the play, thus making her transformation into Antigone complete.[50]

The equation between Mariana and Antigone, as described here, is confirmed in Jorge Andrade's autobiographical novel *Labirinto*, which provides a key to interpreting much of the material in Andrade's plays. The novel is rife with allusions to Graeco-Roman mythology; some are simple references to characters from myth, such as an ancestor labelled as a *Hécuba lavadeira* (washerwoman Hecuba), while others are more complex, like his allusion to Virgil's account of Aeneas' journey to the underworld.[51] Andrade equates the characters of *Pedreira das Almas* with characters from *Antigone*,[52] thus confirming the similarities noted by various scholars. At this point, Andrade is remembering the image of his teenage friend Paulo immediately after he committed suicide. Jorge had apparently made a pact with him that they would drink poison together and escape an oppressive world. Of this moment, Andrade states:

> Tudo o vento leva, só não leva a saudade, o remorso do pacto traído, prendendo-me para sempre, sígno da morte. Explicação primeira dos meus Martinianos expostos. Conhecimento de Polinice! A voz de Mariana, enfrentando o Creonte imperial, ergue-se na paisagem baiana ensolorada.[53]

> Of all that the wind takes away, it just doesn't take away the longing, the remorse for the betrayed agreement, forever taking hold of me, the symbol of death. The first explanation of my Martinianos left unburied. The knowledge of Polyneices! The voice of Mariana confronting an imperial Creon lifts itself from the sunbaked landscape of Bahia.

In case the connection were not sufficiently clear, Andrade then follows this passage with a direct quote from Mariana's speech to Vasconcelos in the second act of the play,[54] though only a savvy reader will catch this, since Andrade includes no quotation marks or explicit citations to the play.[55] Though he does not mention Antigone by name in this passage, he does so in a number of other passages in the novel, for example, when he calls his aunt an *Antígone cabocla* (mestiza Antigone) on account of her participation in the Revolution of 1932.[56] He also connects this moment to *Pedreira das Almas* by comparing the older matrons involved in the revolution to Urbana in the play, even quoting one of her lines in the process.[57] Thus, in *Labirinto*, Andrade himself confirms the connections that critics had previously noted between *Pedreira das Almas* and *Antigone*.

One major difference between *Antigone* and *Pedreira das Almas* is that in Andrade's play, there is a way in which the body of the dead brother can be buried, but it involves the town sacrificing its hopes for the future and accepting subordination to the central government. What is more, in *Pedreira das Almas* it is Urbana, not Mariana, who symbolically buries Martiniano, by taking him into the church and throwing her own body over his. This image mirrors the death of Haemon in Sophocles' play, when he falls on the lifeless body of Antigone. Yet what we see in Andrade's version is an embrace of the mother grieving for her son, rather than the final unification of the lovers in death.[58]

Although Urbana's act is here identified as a symbolic burial, it is important to note that, unlike in *Antigone*, the body is not actually buried – it remains exposed. In fact, the ultimate result of Urbana's symbolic burial is that there end up being two unburied bodies, one of the mother and one of the son. This inversion from the Sophoclean original is thematically important for both the play and for Andrade's overall dramatic programme.[59] For Andrade, the image of the exposed corpse, which first appears in his texts in *Pedreira das Almas*, becomes symbolic of the need to expose the abuses of the past in order to heal the present.[60] In *Labirinto*, Andrade compares the fate of Polyneices in *Antigone* to the execution of rebels during the *Revolta dos Alfaiates* (Revolt of the Tailors) in Bahia in 1798. After discussing how the dismembered bodies of the criminals were spread throughout the province, he explains that the colonial government did this to keep the population in line. Andrade argues, however, that such actions only make the people more resistant to unjust rule: 'They tried to plant in the Bahians a fear of the revolution, but what planted itself instead was a dread of despotism' ('Procura se plantar nos baianos o temor pela revolta, mas na verdade o que se planta é o horror ao despotismo').[61] The exposed bodies in this case ultimately had a positive effect on the people of Bahia by helping them fight against despotism. Andrade sums up the concept by drawing attention to the difference between the contemporary situation and the plot of Sophocles' *Antigone*: 'The times are different: the important thing is not burying the bodies to benefit the gods but benefiting the living by leaving the bodies exposed' ('Os tempos são outros: não é enterrar que importa, servindo aos deuses; mas servir aos vivos ficando expostos').[62]

The exposed bodies in *Pedreira das Almas* function in much the same way as the exposed bodies in Bahia, as can be seen in the way in which the crisis is resolved at the end of the play. When Vasconcelos and Mariana finally encounter each other again in the second act, after Martiniano has been dead for three days, Mariana calls on Vasconcelos to witness what his unjust orders have done, saying:

Gabriel é a única saída dêste túmulo imenso que seu Govêrno fêz de Pedreira das Almas ... Chame seus soldados e entre na igreja! Prove a êles que não teme os mortos. Que pode encarar seus crimes. Governos como o seu, senhor, só executam leis ímpias, mas com braços subordinados ou mãos escravas. Não presenciam nunca a verdadeira imagem de suas vítimas. Se o senhor entrar ... verá a que ficou reduzida a Província sob sua justiça.[63]

Gabriel is the only exit from this immense tomb which your Government has made out of Pedreira das Almas. Call your soldiers and enter the church! Prove to them that you do not fear the dead – that you can bear to look at your crimes. Governments such as yours, sir, only execute unjust laws, but they do it by the arms of subordinates or with enslaved hands. They never witness the true sight of their victims. If you, sir, enter [the church] ... you will see what the Province has been reduced to under your justice.

When Vasconcelos and the soldiers finally do enter the church and see Urbana's corpse draped over that of her son, it is not a fear of disobedience but rather a dread of despotism that seizes them. The soldiers desert their posts and Vasconcelos agrees to leave the town and report that Gabriel died in the fighting. Within the play, the dead bodies left exposed prove to be efficacious for the living who remain in Pedreira das Almas, freeing them from repression.[64]

Pedreira das Almas as a symbol of resistance

Realmente, o problema fundamental de Pedreira [das Almas] *é a resistência.*

In reality, the fundamental problem of *Pedreira [das Almas]* is resistance.[65]

In the world outside of the play, Andrade's programme of exposing the abuses of the past in order to comment on the present allowed the play to become a symbol of resistance to the military dictatorship nearly twenty years after the play first premiered. Absolutist rule by the Brazilian military began with the coup of 1964, which ousted left-wing President João Goulart and put an end to a popular movement that many on the right feared would become a communist revolution.[66] The level of control of the military government over the populace slowly increased until it reached its peak with the decree of Institutional Act no. 5 in 1968, which officially disbanded the national congress and allowed for the systematic imprisonment, torture and disappearance of Brazilian citizens in the name of national security.[67] This situation persisted until the presidency of General João Figueiredo, who passed an amnesty act in 1979, though some abuse still continued until the end of the dictatorship in 1985.[68]

It was in this climate of harsh repression that the themes of *Pedreira das Almas* finally made sense to Brazilian audiences.[69] After having experienced the military dictatorship for six years, Andrade revised the play in 1970 for inclusion in the collection *Marta, a*

Árvore e o Relógio. Andrade would later affirm that the play was not ready at the time of its premiere in 1958:

> Quando subiu à cena em 1958, comemorando o décimo aniversário do TBC, eu senti durante os espetáculos, e depois lendo as críticas e avaliando as reações da platéia, que ela ainda não estava terminada. Então retomei a peça e trabalhei muito ... Mas a remontagem me satisfez inteiramente. A peça estava lá, viva, e contava o que se estava passando nas ruas de São Paulo. Era um grito de liberdade contra a opressão, contra tudo o que cai sobre o homem.[70]

> When it went up on stage in 1958, commemorating the tenth anniversary of TBC, I felt during the show, and afterwards while reading the reviews and evaluating the reactions of the audience, that the play was not yet complete. And so, I took up the play again and I worked a lot ... But the restaging of it satisfied me completely. The play was there, alive, and it told what was happening on the streets of São Paulo. It was a shout of liberty against oppression, against everything that befalls humans.

The restaging to which Andrade refers here is the 1977 production of the 1970 revision of *Pedreira das Almas*. This production ran from 20 May to 7 August 1977 and served as the inaugural production of the Teatro Alfredo Mesquita in São Paulo.[71]

Andrade was not the only one who saw the relationship between the previously written play and what was currently unfolding on the streets of São Paulo. The following review appeared in the *Folha de São Paulo* on 8 June 1977. The title of the piece itself says much about how this subsequent production of the play was viewed: 'Pedreira no Momento Certo' (*Pedreira* at the Right Moment).

> Não há mais condições para se ver o drama de Urbana, Gabriel e Mariana apenas como um belíssimo trabalho artístico. Porque em cada um desses personagens e no povo fictício de Pedreira podem ser reconhecidos problemas e aspirações do aqui e agora brasileiro.[72]

> It is no longer possible to see the drama of Urbana, Gabriel and Mariana merely as a very beautiful work of art, because in each one of these characters and in the fictitious people of Pedreira one can recognize the problems and aspirations of Brazilians here and now.

In the phrase beginning 'It is no longer possible ...', the author suggests that this is how the characters were viewed in 1958, simply as personalities in a beautiful work of art. In the political climate in Brazil in 1977, however, one could not help but make a connection between the present and the events depicted in the play. To put a finer point on it, the same reviewer goes on to say:

> Parece bastante clara a atualidade de *Pedreira das Almas*, sua adequação ao momento, em que estudantes saem às ruas e políticos liberais falam na Assembléia Constituinte.[73]

The topicality of *Pedreira das Almas* is extremely clear, as is its suitability to this moment in which students are running out into the streets and liberal politicians are speaking out in the Constitutional Assembly.

Similar sentiments were also expressed by theatre critic and professor Clóvis Garcia in his article, 'Em texto já antigo, a presença do real' ('The presence of reality in a text that is already old'):

> A peça se revela com uma surpreendente atualidade, não somente na divergência entre os conservadores e os inovadores, conflito de todas as épocas mas mais acentuado nos tempos difíceis que vivemos, como também, ao tratar da revolução liberal de 1842 coloca o problema do autoritarismo, que se considera capaz de julgar o que é bom para o povo, frente às necessidades, anseios, à realidade enfim da população, o que é uma problemática dos nossos dias.[74]

> The play reveals itself with a surprising topicality, not only in the divergence between the conservatives and the innovators, a conflict from every time period but more accentuated in the difficult times in which we live, but also, in dealing with the liberal revolution of 1842, the play places the problem of authoritarianism, which considers itself capable of judging what is good for the people, face to face with the necessities, anxieties, and ultimately the reality of the population, which is also a problem in our days.

This game of social commentary through the theatre was not without its dangers for Andrade and those involved in the production. Many plays and other works of art and literature were censored during this time, including Andrade's play written in 1977, *Milagre na Cela*.[75] Although the government allowed the theatrical production of *Pedreira das Almas* to proceed in 1977, it did put a stop to Andrade's television adaptation of the same play, which would have reached a national audience.[76] During this dangerous time, censorship of one's text was not the only issue at stake. In 1972, José Celso, the founder and director of Teatro Oficina was imprisoned for a month and tortured, undergoing what he described as a process of 'cultural assassination' for himself and his theatre.[77]

The censorship and persecution against the theatre during the dictatorship made Andrade's method of using specific historical details to make universal commentaries on the human condition all the more effective. Andrade could say that he was not writing about the dictatorship per se, but about any situation in which human liberties were being infringed upon. When asked in an interview about the topicality of the 1977 production of *Pedreira das Almas*, Andrade responded:

> Nós não vivemos em democracia, mas o sentido de Pedreira, além de particular, é, sobretudo, universal. Pois eu sempre me pergunto em que parte do mundo o homem que deseja ser livre não está sendo torturado ou perseguido. Em que lugar ele não está sofrendo por suas próprias idéias.[78]

> We do not live in a democracy, but the meaning of *Pedreira*, besides the particular, is overall universal. For I always ask myself, in what part of the world is the man who desires to be free not being tortured or persecuted. In what part is he not suffering for his own ideas.

Andrade even saw Sophoclean tragedy as a model for how to make drama universal rather than partisan. The key for him was in creating characters that were living and believable. He says:

> No momento em que Antígona gritou contra opressão, há dois mil anos, ela gritou como personagem viva. Ficou dois mil anos no palco – e vai continuar. Não importa se os autores pertenciam, na época, a tal ou tal partido político. Eram dramaturgos, grandes poetas que registraram o homem no tempo e no espaço.[79]

> In the moment that Antigone shouted against oppression, some 2,000 years ago, she shouted as a real live character. She's been on the stage for two thousand years – and she will continue to be. It doesn't matter if the authors aligned themselves, at the time, with one political party or another. They were playwrights, great poets, and they recorded man in his time and space.

In addition to illustrating Andrade's view of Antigone as a universal character, this quote also reveals to us that, for Andrade, the voice of Antigone was a shout against oppression, language nearly identical to the description he gave of *Pedreira das Almas* when he said that the play in 1977 became 'a shout of liberty against oppression' ('um grito de liberdade contra a opressão').[80] Some of Andrade's works were censored, but he managed to escape imprisonment and continue his fight. In June of 1977, he is reported to have said: 'There is no censorship that can put an end to the Brazilian man. No one is able to erase history. Sooner or later, it comes to the surface' ('Não há Censura que acabe com o homem brasileiro. Ninguém pode apagar a história. Uma hora ou outra ela vem à tona').[81] Through the process of restaging the play in 1977, *Pedreira das Almas* assumed the identity of a *mulata, paulista, brasileira* Antigone, decrying the injustices of the military regime in spite of the potential for grave consequences.

Conclusion – Andrade as Antigone

Sinto que vou lutar sempre contra a violência!

I feel that I will always fight against violence![82]

The reception of the 1977 production of *Pedreira das Almas* fits in with what Andrade increasingly saw as his responsibility to society as an author living in troubled times. In his autobiographical writings, Andrade saw himself as one who uses art to fight against violence and despotism. He expresses this impulse by equating himself with Antigone and endeavouring to variously expose or bury the corpses that haunt him.[83] At one point, he imagines Antigone turning into a seven-year-old version of himself, the age he was when his grandfather lost the family *fazenda*, while in another passage, he equates himself with two of the Antigone-like characters in his plays, Mariana in *Pedreira das Almas* and Marta in *As Confrarias*, saying: 'When Marta and Mariana try to bury their exposed corpses, is it not me trying to bury my dead?' ('Quando Marta e Mariana tentam enterrar o corpo exposto, não sou eu querendo enterrar meus mortos?').[84] It would be through his theatre that Andrade was truly able to assume the identity of Antigone, since theatre was one of the most effective fronts for resistance against the dictatorship in the 1960s and 1970s. During this period, Jorge Andrade transformed himself and his work to become an integral part of this resistance, as evinced by the 1977 production of *Pedreira das Almas* discussed above.[85]

In *Labirinto*, Andrade includes a quote from an interview with the Brazilian novelist Érico Veríssimo, who spoke of the writer's responsibility to his time period in the following terms:

> Sempre achei que o menos que um escritor pode fazer, numa época de violência e injustiças como a nossa, é acender a sua lâmpada, fazer luz sobre a realidade de seu mundo, evitando que sobre ele caia a escuridão, propícia aos ladrões e aos assassinos. Segurar a lâmpada, a despeito da náusea e do resto. Se não tivermos uma lâmpada elétrica, acendamos o nosso toco de vela ou, em último caso, risquemos fósforos repetidamente, como um sinal que não desertamos nosso posto.[86]

> I always thought that the least an author can do in a period of violence and injustices like ours is to light his lamp, create a light over the reality of his world, making sure that the darkness conducive to thieves and murderers does not fall over it. Hold the lamp, in spite of the nausea and all the rest. If, perhaps, we do not have an electric lamp, let us light the wick of a candle, or, in the last resort, let us strike matches, over and over again, as a sign that we have not deserted our post.

When Andrade first wrote *Pedreira das Almas* in 1957, he could not have anticipated that this play would become part of the light that he as an author would hold up against the military regime in the 1970s. Nevertheless, in his character of Mariana, who through the course of the play becomes Antigone, he created a symbol that, like Sophocles' Antigone, was able to transcend the immediate context of its creation and stand as an emblem of resistance. Like Mariana, the play *Pedreira das Almas* and the playwright Jorge Andrade were both able to assume the unyielding role of Antigone by means of the 1977 production of the play. The way in which Andrade employed specific historical details from Brazil's distant past in order to present what he viewed as universal truths allowed the production to avoid censorship while still commenting on the ills of the current regime. In the play, Dona Urbana pronounces: 'You can't cut off the past. It follows us wherever we go' ('Não se pode cortar o passado. Êle nos acompanha para onde vamos').[87] Andrade embraced the past in *Pedreira das Almas* and, like the exposed corpses of Martiniano and Urbana that proved to be the salvation of the people of Pedreira, he turned the past into a tool to fight for a better Brazil in the present.

PART III
THE CARIBBEAN AND NORTH AMERICA

CHAPTER 10
DISTORTING THE *LYSISTRATA* PARADIGM IN PUERTO RICO: FRANCISCO ARRIVÍ'S *CLUB DE SOLTEROS*
Rosa Andújar

This chapter examines a novel and frequently neglected adaptation of Aristophanes' *Lysistrata*, *Club de Solteros* (*Bachelor's Club*, written in 1951, performed in 1953) by Francisco Arriví (b. 1915, Santurce – d. 2007, San Juan), one of the founding fathers of Puerto Rican national theatre. This play has long been excluded from accounts of classical drama in Latin America,[1] and even from studies of Arriví's theatre, where it is glossed over in favour of more weighty (i.e. non-comic) drama, such as *Vejigantes* (*Masks*), which directly tackles racial prejudice.[2] Despite the fact that the play itself engages with the Aristophanic play, and that Arriví himself openly admits to the connection in his writings,[3] it is also ignored in accounts of modern adaptations of *Lysistrata*. On the surface, *Club de Solteros* appears to be a simple reversal of the famous Greek comedy: a group of men vow to achieve their political aims through a general ban on sex. In modern adaptations, Lysistrata espouses a variety of social and political causes, which she accomplishes directly through a sex strike (such as the struggle for women's equality, the Russian Revolution, or even the gang wars in the South Side of Chicago).[4] By contrast, Arriví inverts this modern Lysistrata paradigm in order to explore an absurd concept that is explicitly divorced from a larger political framework – in this case a club of ascetic men which is suitably led by Dr Hipólito (Dr Hippolytus). In *Club de Solteros*, the playwright stages an extreme version of Aristophanes' *Lysistrata*: an adaptation centred on a sex strike by men, who aim through their abstinence to end the tyrannical rule of the female race, in an imaginary world (specifically, an imaginary country called Burundanga, 'A Big Ol' Mess')[5] in which women rule through marriage. Arriví furthermore develops this explicitly apolitical comedy at a critical juncture in both 1950s Puerto Rican theatre and politics, when the national theatre scene was emerging and the island adopted commonwealth status in relation to the USA.

The chapter has three parts: I first discuss both the play's original departures from the modern *Lysistrata* 'formula', that is, the manner in which adaptations and reworkings of the ancient play tend to operate in modernity, as well as its many points of convergence with Aristophanes' source text. I argue that this unique combination of changes and similarities forces us to rethink the manner in which the Lysistrata paradigm typically operates in the modern world. Secondly, I discuss the fact that Arriví rewrote and continued to engage with his own novel interpretation of Aristophanes' play in every single decade of his career: the *Club de Solteros* was itself a radically rewritten expansion of a 1940 one-act high school sketch with the same title, though without any classical elements. After writing the new classically inflected play under scrutiny in this chapter (staged in 1953), Arriví continued to tinker with this material, developing a series of sequels for *Bachelors' Club*: in 1966, he produced the farce *Cóctel de Don Nadie* (*Cocktail of Mr. Nobody*), and in 1972 the musical comedy *Solteros 72* (*Bachelors 72*). I contend that Arriví's continual practice of adapting and recasting *Club de Solteros* allows us to reflect on the Aristophanic practice of διασκευάζειν, that is, rewriting and redrafting the same dramatic material (as in *Clouds* and *Wealth*), and the suitability of this practice in the modern world. Finally, I end with a consideration of the larger political and social context in which this play was conceived. In particular, I consider the implications of composing a farcical and expressly depoliticized comedy at a time when stages across the island were filled with 'Puerto Rican' plays which attempted to capture addressing the nation's complex socio-political realities. Despite being a loose and 'flipped' adaptation of *Lysistrata*, *Club de Solteros* provides a unique opportunity to study the multiple ways in which ancient comedy and its associated practices can be invoked to varied ends in modernity.

Adapting *Lysistrata* in the modern world

Despite the thematic focus on men, Arriví's *Club de Solteros*, demonstrates a profound engagement with Aristophanes and in particular with the notion of a gynaeocracy that is imposed on society, which is found throughout his women plays. In a similar fashion to *Lysistrata* and *Assemblywomen*, which stage the intrusion of women into the most public of Athenian spaces, *Club de Solteros* stages a female intrusion into the only remaining private male space in an imaginary country, Burundanga, dominated by women. Like its Athenian predecessors, the play's comic core rests on a series of stereotypes about the licentiousness of women and the ease with which men succumb to sex. In various scenes, the secretary of the Bachelor's club, Ricardín, has to be physically restrained from kissing the mannequin of a woman; in another, a young man who is happily engaged is forcibly brought into the club and submitted to a special cold water treatment. A recurring joke throughout Arriví's play centres around an elderly widower, Don Pepón, who, though he professes a deep commitment to the celibate cause, cannot literally resist the flirtations of Ello, a woman disguised as a man who takes every opportunity to flaunt her very real femininity. These examples not only offer a new twist on key scenes in Aristophanes such as those in *Lysistrata* in which Myrrhine teases and easily takes advantage of her visibly aroused husband Cinesias (865–951), but they also stress how effective the general notion of a sex strike is for generating humour in both the modern and ancient contexts.

The structure of *Club de Solteros* is also indebted to the ancient text: the second act, which is the centre of the three-act play, consists of an elaborate *agōn* between the two opposing leaders of men and women, Dr Hipólito and Lucila. Their lengthy and passionate arguments are reminiscent of those between the choruses of old men and

Distorting the *Lysistrata* Paradigm in Puerto Rico

women that are found in the place of the *parabasis* in Aristophanes' *Lysistrata* (614–705). Furthermore, Lucila, like Lysistrata, is not defined by a relationship with a man in the same manner as her counterparts: throughout the play she is cold and methodical, and utterly in charge of the female offensive. Unlike Lysistrata, she is married; however, as the following excerpt from the long *agōn* demonstrates, Lucila is shown to possess complete control and power over her husband, Afrodito:

Hipólito ¡Señora! Le habla al animal superior de la madre naturaleza.

Lucila Querrá decir al más fácil de domesticar. ¿Verdad, Afro?

Afrodito ¡Sí!

Hipólito ¡Scram los dos! Y perdone la mogolla de idiomas. Puro Burundanga.

Lucila ¡Abusa usted del sexo débil!

Hipólito ¿Débil?

Lucila (*Imponiéndose calma*) ¡Afro!

Afrodito ¡Sí!

Lucila ¿Somos o no somos débiles las mujeres?

Afrodito ¡Debilísimas!

Hipólito (*Mordiendo las palabras con un brote de ira contenido*) ¡Serpiente! Haga el favor de esfumarse junto con ese monigote que arrastró hasta aquí. De veras que provoca nauseas ese olor a hombre deteriorado, a conciencia momificada, a pantalones sin inquilino.

Lucila (*Acercándose a Hipólito*) ¿Una rabietita?

Hipólito (*Recomponiéndose*) Ya le gustaría.

Lucila (*Tirándole de la barba dulcemente*) Sansón perdió su melena. Usted perderá su barba. (*Tirando de sus bigotes.*) Y estos manubrios también.

Hipólito ¡Suéltelos!

Lucila Si me ruega después de nuestro triunfo, quizás le permitamos manubrios.[6]

Hipólito Madam! You are speaking to mother nature's superior animal.

Lucila You mean to say the easiest to domesticate. Right, Afro?

Afrodito Yes!

Hipólito Scram you two! And forgive the jumble of languages. Pure Burundanga.

Lucila You are abusing the weaker sex!

Hipólito Weak?

Lucila (*with an enforced calm*) Afro!

Afrodito Yes!

Lucila Are women weak or not?

Afrodito The weakest!

Hipólito (*Biting his words with a contained bout of anger*) Serpent! Do me a favour and vamoose with this puppet whom you dragged here. Truly it makes me gag that smell of deteriorated man, of a mummified conscience, of tenantless trousers.

Lucila (*coming closer to Hipólito*) A little tantrum?

Hipólito (*composing himself*) You would love that.

Lucila (*softly tugging his beard*) Samson lost his locks. You will lose your beard. (*Tugging his moustache*). And this handlebar as well.

Hipólito Let go!

Lucila If you beg me after our triumph, we might allow handlebar moustaches.[7]

Here, Afrodito only speaks in single words, and always at the prompting of his wife. Besides demonstrating Lucila as the puppeteer of her husband, this excerpt also underlines the palpable taint of misogyny that runs throughout the play. In this passage, not only can Hipólito barely contain his hatred of women (which can be evidenced through his matter-of-fact statement that men are the superior animal), but also he has a visceral reaction to the emasculated man, Afrodito, whom he describes as a 'deteriorated man, of a mummified conscience' and 'tenantless trousers', as can be seen above. In fact Hipólito declares that his entire campaign and establishment of the Bachelors' club is motivated 'to liberate [emasculated men] by psychoanalysis and other ultramodern methods' ('para librar por psicoanálisis y otros métodos ultramodernos').[8] Afrodito typifies the sort of man Hipólito aims to liberate, as can be seen by the explicit and precise stage directions:

Afrodito contará treinta y cinco años. El cuido de Lucila lo ha engordado porcinamente. Carga un bebé y varios paquetes. Complementan el fárrago del perfecto doméstico unos globos de colores flotando a tres pies sobre un sombrerito lo más mono.

Afrodito is around thirty-five. Lucila's care has fattened him up like a pig. He carries a baby and various parcels. To round out the strange image of the perfect domestic there are also a few coloured balloons floating about three feet over the cutest little hat.[9]

This is in direct contrast to his wife Lucila:

Lucila exhala tendencias futuristas. Vive tan segura de su hombre que llega a ser desafiante. Luce recorte hombruno, gafas contra el sol, camisa con corbata y slacks.

Lucila exhibits futuristic tendencies. She is so sure of her man that she is defiant. She has a mannish haircut, sunglasses, a shirt with a tie and slacks.[10]

In this manner, Arriví paints a clear picture of the emasculated man, who is continually juxtaposed to his domineering wife throughout the play.

Aristophanes' three women-focused plays, *Lysistrata*, *Women at the Thesmophoria* and *Assemblywomen*, frequently portray men as effeminate and emasculated. Given the context of Athens' military losses after Sicily in the Peloponnesian War, the 411 BCE women-centred plays, *Lysistrata* and *Women at the Thesmophoria*, arguably stage a prevailing sense of impotence and masculine anxiety, though in the comfortable confines of the comic stage. This anxiety informs the depiction of the many examples of feminized and cross-dressing men in Aristophanes' plays: besides the ubiquitous and much-ridiculed Cleisthenes, we may think of the magistrate (Proboulos) in the *Lysistrata* who is given a woman's veil (530–8),[11] or Praxagora's husband in *Assemblywomen* who is forced to wear his wife's dress while relieving himself since she has stolen his clothes in order to attend the assembly (311–47), or, even more radically, the young man who is forced to have sex with an older woman at the end of that same play in a blatant subversion of marital norms (976–1111).[12] Likewise, a prominent scene in *Women at the Thesmophoria* involves Euripides' kinsman having his genitals singed on stage and dressing as a woman in order to infiltrate the women's rituals (213–65); this is the same kinsman who in an earlier scene could not stop commenting on the tragic poet Agathon's flagrant effeminacy (97–8 and 130–45).[13] In a similar fashion, Arriví continually singles out Afrodito's emasculation throughout *Club de Solteros*, and in particular the power of Lucila over him, in order to embody the fear which both led to the formation of the club and which ultimately drives the absurd play, arguably in the same manner that it drives Aristophanes' 'women on top' plays.

Arriví additionally weaves other important classical strands into *Club de Solteros*, many of which are related to Hippolytus as a mythical character. The various descriptions of Dr Hipólito emphasize a certain savagery and a hirsuteness that correspond to a mythical figure connected to nature and the outdoors.[14] Arriví's protagonist also praises the goddess Diana: 'Long live Diana the huntress!' ('Viva Diana cazadora!').[15] Though he likens Dr Hipólito to other figures, such as Juan de Tirso (i.e. Don Juan), Orpheus, Zeus, and is even explicitly called by various characters 'Prometeo Segundo' (Second Prometheus),[16] Arriví at times directly invokes Euripides' *Hippolytus*, particularly when Dr Hipólito delivers in the opening of the second act a violent anti-woman speech which bears a striking similar function to the speech delivered by his namesake in Euripides' tragedy.[17] The only critic who has written on this play focuses on the sheer misogyny of the speech, taking it as a farcical condemnation of the machismo characteristic of Latin

American and Puerto Rican culture of the time.[18] The classical elements that are clearly present are overlooked. *Club de Solteros* was itself a significantly rewritten expansion of a 1940 one-act high school sketch centred on a men's club also bearing the title *Club de Solteros*. The sketch's protagonist, however, was called Don Osvaldo; a decade later, Arriví's more fully elaborated three-act play *Club de Solteros*, the play under scrutiny in this chapter, was led instead by Dr Hipólito. This change, as well as the presence of these other prominent classical elements, is most likely the result of Arriví's time at Columbia University in New York City, where he spent the 1948–9 academic year thanks to a scholarship from the Rockefeller Foundation. At Columbia, Arriví took courses in Greek drama, perhaps encountering plays such as *Hippolytus* and *Lysistrata* for the first time.[19] His time there most likely inspired the decision to inject classical elements into what had previously been a high school sketch comedy. Given the specific change from Don Osvaldo to Dr Hipólito, it is more profitable to equate the general undercurrent in Dr Hipólito's speech to that in the famous *rhesis* found in Euripides' *Hippolytus* (616–68), which similarly emphasizes the evil of women, specifically the theme of woman as a plague unto man.[20] This is a sentiment that Dr Hipólito voices directly at other points in the play: 'Woman ... is a plague ... a bubonic plague' ('La mujer ... Es una plaga ... una peste bubonica').[21]

Other more direct invocations to Euripides are likewise present. Arriví's women are portrayed with a threatening air of maenads, who describe their attack on the Bachelor's club as a 'hunt': for example, Lucila at one point describes how hunting men excites her,[22] and in another prominent scene she discusses with Ello 'fishing' for the men.[23] Despite his mythical connections with the outdoors, Arriví's Hipólito is stuck inside the Club for the entirety of the play and the women must hunt and lure him out. In another scene, this connection to Euripides' *Bacchae* is made more explicit: when Lucila finally surrounds the house, she issues the following instructions: 'Women ... surround the house in a Dionysiac state ... Here. You will hunt the secretary' ('Las mujeres ... cercan la casa en actitud dionisíaca ... Toma. Tú cazarás al secretario').[24] I would like to suggest that through the invocation of Euripidean features, namely Hippolytus' misogyny and also other echoes of the *Bacchae*, Arriví forcefully puts misogyny front and centre into his adaptation of Aristophanes' *Lysistrata*. By additionally invoking Euripides, who is ever-present in Aristophanes' female-dominated plays, Arriví also gives a playful nod to the ancient comic tradition of paratragedy.

In Aristophanes' play, Lysistrata's conspiracy consists of two plots. The first is a conjugal and panhellenic strike staged by young wives from the warring cities of Athens and Sparta and their allies and designed to force their warrior husbands to lay down their arms and come home. The second is the occupation of the Acropolis and its treasuries by the older wives of Athens, so that the politicians will no longer be able to finance the war. In many ways this is a fantastic and convoluted plot that is characteristic of Aristophanes' 'heroic' plays, such as *Acharnians*, *Peace* and *Birds*, in which a hero or heroine representing a class of citizens who feel frustrated or victimized by the operations of contemporary Athens, by means of a far-fetched scheme, manages to evade or alter the situation of which she or he initially complains, effecting a triumph of wish-fulfilment over reality.[25]

The notion of a sex strike in the ancient world would have been equally absurd on two grounds: firstly, Ancient Greek men, particularly Athenians, had recourse to a variety of outlets for sexual pleasure outside the home, and secondly, if the men were all away fighting in the war, the notion of a sex strike waged at home would be simply ridiculous. As Paul Cartledge points outs, the plot of the play 'depends for its success on a prodigious suspension of disbelief on the part of the audience'.[26] Yet, despite the fact that a real sex strike would have been preposterous in ancient Athens, the modern world has been fascinated with the idea and particularly its perceived effectiveness. From François-Benoît Hoffman's *Lysistrate* in post-Revolutionary France (1801–2) to Spike Lee's *Chi-Raq* (2015), modern adaptations of the play have focused on the idea of the sex-strike as an effective means of resolving male conflicts and problems. As David Stuttard helpfully summarizes: 'readers, directors and audience are readily seduced by the play's attractive packaging (the "make love not war" theme), see it as surprisingly modern, and, as a result, too easily overlook the social and political context in which it was written.'[27] This 'make love not war' slogan was the very same one adopted by Ellen McLaughlin in her 2003 Lysistrata project, a global protest against the then imminent American invasion of Iraq. This project, called a 'Theatrical Act of Dissent', coordinated 1,000 parallel readings from Aristophanes' play in more than fifty-nine countries and every single state in the US, in which over 300,000 people participated.[28] In other words, in the modern world *Lysistrata* is the standard model for modern female political activism and in particular pacifism, a reading that challenges the content of the ancient play.

Scholars have recently acknowledged the discrepancies between these modern wilful misinterpretations and the realities of the ancient play. Martin Revermann calls this modern glib tendency to see the *Lysistrata* as an ancient feminist and pacifist play a 'productive misreading'.[29] Helen Morales, however, takes the condemnation further: in an article in which she discusses Aristophanes' *Lysistrata* as the 'go-to trope for any women's activism involving the withdrawal of sex'.[30] Particularly when it is employed to describe a recent example in contemporary Liberian politics, she declares it an 'irresponsible use of the classical, in which an ancient text is deployed in a manner that trivializes the modern political debate and silences modern political agents. It is not so much an abuse of antiquity, an abuse of modernity.'[31] Adding to this productive discussion on the manner in which Lysistrata tends to operate in the modern world, I propose that another crucial result of what Revermann calls a 'productive misreading' and Morales terms 'irresponsible use of the classical' is the manner in which the aggressiveness and agency of the women are over-emphasized to the exclusion of the men, the intended passive recipients of the sex strike. Wholly focused on the aggressive actions of the protesting women which will immediately produce the desired result, the modern Lysistrata paradigm is thus fundamentally uninterested in any nuanced dynamics between men and women, unlike the ancient play which crucially features a chorus divided by gender while performing various versions of both masculinity and femininity.

In this manner, Arriví's *Club de Solteros* significantly deviates from this modern Lysistrata paradigm. By placing men at the centre of the sex strike, Arriví refocuses the absurdity and the misogyny of the ancient, features that are often lost or de-emphasized in modern adaptations which are lured by the false idea of the *Lysistrata* as a proto-feminist play. In Aristophanes' play, the withdrawal of sex by wives is not the most effective tool despite what we moderns may insist; it is rather the occupation of the older women of the Acropolis (and the subsequent blockade of funds) that allows the women to triumph over the men. Arriví's play reminds us that we moderns have lost sight of the many absurdities of the source text, as we insist on perpetuating an erroneous and modern myth of an activist Lysistrata.

Comic rewritings in the modern world

Arriví's play illuminates our understanding of Aristophanes in another important way. *Club de Solteros*, as I mentioned above, was the significantly rewritten and expanded version of an earlier one-act sketch about a male club featuring protagonist Don Osvaldo, directed by Arriví and staged by his drama students at Ponce High School on 13 June 1940; this sketch lacked the various defining classical elements examined in the previous section, including the *Lysistrata* flipped framework.[32] In addition, the fully elaborated play, now in three acts and performed in Teatro Tapia on 18 March 1953,[33] itself produced two further sequels:

1964 *Cóctel de Don Nadie* (billed as an inverted version of *Club de Solteros*)[34]
1972 *Solteros 72* (musical comedy)[35]

The 1953 *Club de Solteros* thus initiates a chain of receptions centred on this unusual spin on Aristophanes' *Lysistrata*, all of which are carried out by the same author. All three plays were performed in San Juan at the famous Teatro Tapia in Old San Juan (with a seating capacity of 600), but they were also published as texts. These three plays testify to the fact that Arriví *re-adapted* the same comic material across various decades.[36] However, this self-reflexive return to comedy is curiously left unremarked in scholarship, particularly for an author who is typically known for his more serious drama.

In ancient Greek drama, the concept of reworking the same material is not a foreign one. Of course, scholars of ancient Greek theatre emphasize that Athenian dramatists composed their plays for a single performance at a unique event, a festival competition under the auspices of the god Dionysus. To rewrite or reboot a particular Greek comedy (a practice called διασκευή), however, was not uncommon in the classical period, and there are various examples of comic poets rewriting their plots.[37] Aristophanes, in particular, is famous for revising particular plays, the most famous example being *Clouds*.[38] The *hypotheses* (summaries of the plot of ancient plays) written by Alexandrian scholars indicate that the *Clouds* that survives today is itself an unperformed revision of an earlier failed performed version:

Clouds Hypothesis A6:

αἱ πρῶται Νεφέλαι ἐδιδάχθησαν ἐν ἄστει ἐπὶ ἄρχοντος Ἰσάρχου, ὅτε Κρατῖνος μὲν ἐνίκα Πυτίνῃ, Ἀμειψίας δὲ Κόννῳ. διόπερ Ἀριστοφάνης ἀπορριφθεὶς παραλόγως ᾠήθη δεῖν ἀναδιδάξας τὰς Νεφέλας τὰς δευτέρας καταμέμφεσθαι τὸ θέατρον. ἀτυχῶν δὲ πολὺ μᾶλλον καὶ ἐν τοῖς ἔπειτα οὐκέτι τὴν διασκευὴν εἰσήγαγεν. αἱ δὲ δεύτερα Νεφέλαι ἐπὶ Ἀμεινίου ἄρχοντος.

The first *Clouds* was produced at the City Dionysia in the archonship of Isarchus [424/3 BCE], when Cratinus won with *Wineflask*, and Ameipsias [came second] with *Konnos*. For this reason, Aristophanes, being irrationally rejected, thought it necessary to produce the second *Clouds* and rebuke the theatre public. But his luck was even worse with this and he did not thereafter produce the revised version. The second *Clouds* belongs to the archonship of Ameinias [422].[39]

and *Clouds* Hypothesis A7:

τοῦτο ταὐτόν ἐστι τῷ προτέρῳ. διεσκεύασται δὲ ἐπὶ μέρους ὡς ἂν δὴ ἀναδιδάξαι μὲν αὐτὸ τοῦ ποιητοῦ προθυμηθέντος, οὐκέτι δὲ τοῦτο δι' ἥνποτε αἰτίαν ποιήσαντος. καθόλου μὲν οὖν σχεδὸν παρὰ πᾶν μέρος γεγενημένη διόρθωσις· τὰ μὲν γὰρ περιῄρηται, τὰ δὲ παραπέπλεκται, καὶ ἐν τῇ τάξει καὶ ἐν τῇ τῶν προσώπων διαλλαγῇ μετεσχημάτισται. ἃ δὲ ὁλοσχερῆ τῆς διασκευῆς τοιαῦτα ὄντα τετύχηκεν· αὐτίκα ἡ παράβασις τοῦ χοροῦ ἤμειπται, καὶ ὅπου ὁ δίκαιος λόγος πρὸς τὸν ἄδικον λαλεῖ, καὶ τελευταῖον ὅπου καίεται ἡ διατριβὴ Σωκράτους.

This play is the same as the first but has been revised in details, as if the poet wanted to produce it again but, for some reason or other, never did so. Taking the play as a whole, the revision affects virtually every part, with some material removed, new material worked in, and changes made in arrangement and in the characters' exchanges. And some material as it now stands belongs entirely to the revised version: thus the *parabasis* of the chorus (518–62) has been replaced, and where Right Logos chatters to Wrong (889–948), and finally where Socrates' school is burned (1476–1511).

Though only one of these hypotheses describes in some detail what Aristophanes reworked in the missing first version of *Clouds*, these summaries, if taken as accurate, offer us a small insight into the comic process in Athens.[40] The two excerpts contain the verbs ἀναδιδάσκω and διασκευάζω, which illustrate that revision and re-editing were a significant part of that tradition: the prepositions ἀνα and δια transform the verbs διδάσκω ('to teach') and σκευάζω ('to make ready, prepare') into 're-teach or teach better' and 'to prepare thoroughly', producing the standard terms for a reproduction or a second edition. These terms appear again in testimonies about other Old comic plays which also apparently circulated in two separate versions: these include Aristophanes' *Women at the Thesmophoria*, *Wealth*, *Peace* and the lost *Aeolosicon*, but also Diocles' *Thyestes*, Magnes' *Dionysus* and Eupolis' *Autolycus*.

Accounts of the double performance tradition for all these plays is our best evidence for the apparently widespread ancient practice of διασκευάζειν, to revise and re-edit.[41] This practice is one of the features that differentiates Greek comedy from tragedy which tended to alter the same mythical material (such as the *Electra* plays) but never truly revisit or rewrite the same play, at least not by the same author.[42] That Arriví himself engaged in such deliberate and continual redrafting activities can be seen as yet another important – and perhaps unintended – engagement with Aristophanes and Old Comedy. These multiple attempts at *Club de Solteros* moreover inspired another subsequent Puerto Rican adaptation by Antonio García del Toro, *Guerra menos Guerra igual a Sexo* (War minus War equals Sex), a play which also premiered in San Juan's Teatro Tapia on 29 June 1977, only five years after *Solteros 72*. Crucially García del Toro's adaptation consciously returns to the hypertext of Aristophanes' *Lysistrata*: when it is finally published in 1985, the text is accompanied with the author's own translation of the Aristophanic play (produced by consulting Italian and Spanish translations).[43] In this manner Arriví's multiple attempts at *Club de Solteros* have an important impact in Puerto Rico, giving rise to a rich chain of receptions specifically related to *Lysistrata*.

Club de Solteros and Puerto Rican drama

Besides being a clever inverted reading of the Aristophanic source text, how else might we understand Arriví's novel play? In this final section, I end with a brief exploration of the context in which the play was written in order to propose that the play, despite its comic and absurd content, had profound implications in the larger context of 1950s Puerto Rico. Like its ancient forebear, which exposes the anxieties of the citizen male during the tumultuous second half of the Peloponnesian War, Arriví's comedy reveals various important concerns – both theatrical and political – about Puerto Rico.

Modern theatre in Puerto Rico was born in the late 1930s in response to a series of calls for a specifically 'Puerto Rican' Theatre. In 1938, the Ateneo Puertorriqueño instituted the first drama competition (Certamen de drama) in order to promote works by Puerto Rican authors who tackled specifically Puerto Rican subject matters. A year later, the intellectual Emilio Belaval published an influential manifesto entitled 'What a Puerto Rican Theatre Might Be' ('Lo que podría ser un teatro puertorriqueño'). Belaval proposed a social theatre centred on the Puerto Rican, which would capture and address the realities of Puerto Rico:[44]

> Algun día de estos tendremos que unirnos para crear un gran teatro nuestro, donde todo nos pertenezca: el tema, el actor, los motivos decorativos, las ideas, la estética.

> One of these days we will have to unite in order to create our own great theatre, where everything belongs to us: the theme, the actor, the decorations, the ideas, the aesthetic.[45]

Some might argue that this is in keeping with other trends in Latin American theatre in the period: Lyday and Woodyard highlight the period between 1928 and 1943 as one of the most important for modern Latin American drama, years during which a 'new consciousness of and concern for theater developed in almost all the countries with a significant literary tradition'.⁴⁶ In the specific case of Puerto Rico, however, Belaval's appeal must be understood not as a general theatrical call for freedom from the European models that dominated most Latin American theatre traditions in the early twentieth century, but rather as a specifically political call against the increasing cultural usurpation by the United States which Puerto Rico has faced since 1899, following the Spanish-American War, when it effectively became an American colony. Francisco Arriví was one of the first dramatists to heed Belaval's call; along with Manuel Méndez Ballester and René Marqués, he formed the trinity of the crucial 'Generation of the 30s' (Generación de los 30), which was responsible for founding the various dramatic societies which led to modern Puerto Rican national theatre. As Arriví himself recognizes, the main achievement of his generation was 'the creation of a canon of a repertoire of plays set in the Puerto Rican world' ('la creación de un repertorio de obras ambientadas en el mundo puertorriqueño') which 'revealed the soul of its people on stage' ('revelar el alma de su pueblo en la escena').⁴⁷

Arriví is otherwise known for his visibly Puerto Rican 'social' theatre, for plays that directly address contemporary problems on the island, such as the acclaimed 1959 *Vejigantes* (*Masks*), which tackles racial prejudice, or the 1957 *Sirena* (*Mermaid*), in which a young woman undergoes plastic surgery in order to appear white to her North American boyfriend. Among such plays, *Club de Solteros*, which is billed as a farce, tends to be ignored,⁴⁸ but I would like to suggest that this play (one of Arriví's earliest), with its unique focus on women, is a watershed moment for the staging of Puerto Rican women, just as *Lysistrata* was for the Athenian comic stage in 411.⁴⁹ Where Aristophanes creates a play centred on empowered women and the battle between the sexes, he creates the opportunity for female characters to speak on the comic stage. In Athens, this of course meant actors in drag, but in 1950s Puerto Rico, the act of adapting a play like the *Lysistrata* automatically translated into more prominent roles for female actors. In fact, despite the thematic focus on men, *Club de Solteros* divides its main roles almost equally among male and female actors, at a time when plays featured few leading female roles.⁵⁰ In addition to creating more theatrical opportunities for women, the play also changed the manner in which women were represented on the Puerto Rican theatrical stage. As *San Juan Daily Star* columnist Clementine Rabassa wrote in an article contemporaneous with the play's first performance:

> Arriví correctly regards the strength and independence of the Puerto Rican woman as qualities that antedate any neo-colonial influence. In the manner of Robert Graves, the brilliant classicist and poet, Arriví transcends the contemporary condition of the female character to return to her imposing stature in Greek and Roman mythology where she often stood defying the powers that attempted to violate her or challenging those who sought her subjugation.⁵¹

By making Aristophanes speak to the times, Arriví thus creates more complex roles for women in theatre. But why Aristophanes? And perhaps more importantly, how does an engagement with Aristophanes correspond to creating a specifically 'Puerto Rican' Theatre? Despite Belaval's call for a national Puerto Rican theatre, the staging of 'Puerto Rican' plays was controversial and even banned in the theatre at the University of Puerto Rico, one of the largest on the island,[52] in the fraught period from 1944 and 1956, i.e. in the period immediately before and after the formal adoption of Puerto Rico as a US commonwealth (*Estado Libre Asociado*, literally: 'Associated Free State').[53] This was a period marked by political tension and even violence: on 30 October 1950 the nationalist insurrection sparked various police shootouts across the island, as Puerto Rican nationalists unsuccessfully attacked not only the Fortaleza in San Juan, where governor Luis Muñoz Marín (who benefited from US support) lived, but also Blair House in Washington DC, the temporary residence in which President Harry Truman was based.[54] In all these cases, the Puerto Rican nationalists were stopped and killed, but their capture led to massive arrests of other suspected Puerto Rican nationalists. None of these men was given a trial, as any sentiments in favour of Puerto Rican independence were immediately criminalized.[55] On 1 March 1954, four Puerto Ricans shouting 'Viva Puerto Rico' fired shots at the US Congress while it was in session, wounding five congressmen, again in an attempt to raise awareness of Puerto Rico's right to independence. This of course led to further suppression of Puerto Rican nationalism.[56]

In this context, it is therefore no surprise that *Club de Solteros* (written in 1951 and performed in 1953) is explicitly and eerily apolitical; there is no war nor an overarching political agenda, and moreover the play is set in the imaginary location of 'Burundanga' ('A Big Ol' Mess'), a country that is neighbours with 'Mojiganga' ('Farce'). This also helps explains the frequent explicit announcements of the play's absurdity and non-serious nature: for example, 'the action explodes in the principal room of the Bachelor's Club, an institution even more absurd than a dream of Pinocchio' ('La acción explota en la sala principal del Club de Solteros, institución más absurda que un sueño de Pinocho').[57]

Yet even in this comedy, there are arguably hints of a general anti-American undercurrent that directly speaks to the unique experience of Puerto Rico: for example, characters swear by 'the word of Washington' ('palabra washintoniana')[58] and self-consciously use Spanglish, e.g. 'Scram you two! And excuse the mess of languages. Pure Burundanga' ('Scram los dos! Y perdone la mogolla de idiomas. Puro Burundanga').[59] In one scene, Dr Hipólito scathingly suggests to Ello who boasts of her impending wealth that she 'buy a bank on Wall Street and employ gigolos' ('Compre un banco en Wall Street y emplee gigolos').[60] The references to Burundanga, the imaginary locale for the setting of the play, arguably describe place with a Puerto Rican or, at the very least, a Caribbean stamp: when Ello is trying to tempt Don Pepón to sleep with her she asks him where they might flee, and he responds that they will travel to Mojiganga, which 'like Burundanga, is the lap of luxury for any tourist idiot' ('al igual que Burundanga, es una Jaujita para cualquier turistoide').[61] At a time when many North Americans flocked to visit Cuba and Puerto Rico for leisure, such a comment possessed a significant resonance.

In the ancient Greek world, Old Comedy was 'political', staging, within the context of a public civic festival, serious and often controversial matters related to realities of life in the Athenian *polis*. One of the most debated aspects of Aristophanes' works is how reliable these plays, filled with coarse content and lewd jokes, were as a guide to fifth-century Athens, and to understanding Athenian life at the time.[62] I would like to end by suggesting that *Club de Solteros* – in addition to being an interesting study of how one might adapt Aristophanes imaginatively, bringing to the fore neglected aspects of the ancient text – also offers us an opportunity to consider the complex relationship between comedy and politics in the ancient and modern worlds. Specifically, it allows us to consider whether Aristophanic comedies can continue to address fraught political situations in modernity, such as Puerto Rico's unique and ambiguous status with relation to the United States. In Arriví's creative reworking of *Lysistrata*, references to the island's political reality as a territory of the United States can only be described as muted jabs; nevertheless, their subtle nature does not lessen or remove their keen edge.

CHAPTER 11
CHALLENGING THE CANON IN THE DOMINICAN REPUBLIC: *LISÍSTRATA ODIA LA POLÍTICA* BY FRANKLIN DOMÍNGUEZ

Katherine Ford

Lysistrata is a figure that holds the attention of the public eye given the heady combination of sex and war. Despite this, as critics, we tend to understand less what space she occupies in the theatre of the Caribbean and even less in that of the Dominican Republic given the lack of reflection that this nation receives in literary and drama studies.[1] This chapter brings needed critical attention to the role of ancient Greek comedy in Dominican theatre of the twentieth century through Franklin Domínguez's 1981 play *Lisístrata odia la política: obra teatral en tres actos inspirada en un tema de Aristófanes* [*Lysistrata Hates Politics: A Theatrical Work in Three Acts Inspired by a Topic by Aristophanes*][2] in an attempt to remedy the lacuna in scholarship around Domínguez and this play. Through a return to the plots of ancient Greek drama, Franklin Domínguez (b. 1931), considered perhaps the most important playwright from the Dominican Republic – he was awarded the Premio Nacional de Literatura in 2003 – constructs his own Dominican definition of theatre. Theatre, in particular that written by Dominican authors and looking at Dominican issues, begins to take on a more important presence within the cultural identity of the nation in the 1980s. Domínguez's *Lisístrata*, coming at the beginning of this period, will have a pivotal role in this transformation. Prior to this point, theatre – both the theatre groups that formed in connection to physical theatres and the theatre community that emerged from these – did not receive institutional and governmental support and so did not have the ability to fund productions. Theatre was more commercial and presented topics that were more international. The decade of the 1980s marked a time of tremendous growth in the production of theatre and also in the topics and types of productions. Collaborations across national borders increased in a way that inspired the theatre community to understand Dominicanness through the stage, regardless of the topic and origin of the play in question.

Lisístrata odia la política, for which Domínguez won the prestigious Premio Nacional de Teatro Cristóbal de Llerena, allows him to insert Dominican theatre into a global canon of theatre and, conversely, question the validity of this canon. That is, Domínguez both validates his own and his nation's neglected theatre while interrogating their traditional exclusion by examining the very construction of a global canon. For Latin American studies (my own field of study), this push to widen definitions within the Western canon is what is most thought-provoking about this play, though I would venture to say this is of utmost importance to classicists as well. With *Lisístrata odia la política*, Domínguez challenges the ideas of who is included within the Western canon and forces the reader–spectator to rethink definitions of identity. Ironically, like the source text, he does this within the parameters of these definitions, which is precisely why he is effective.

This challenge to traditional definitions begins with the very genre of theatre that Franklin Domínguez chooses. Whereas many rewritings of ancient Greek theatre return to tragedy, this Dominican playwright chooses the comedy of *Lysistrata*. Comedy holds an important place in theatre in that it uses laughter to provoke reflection and criticism from the reader–spectator. Comedy uses the mask of laughter to question and chip away at its object. This indirectness can afford it an effectiveness in that the sceptical or distrustful reader–spectator can be lured to the comedian's way of thinking through a laughter that breaks down the hero. As seen in ancient Greek theatre, comedy often perceives its 'hero' differently than tragedy, using laughter to degrade the character.[3] In *Lisístrata*, the obvious object of the play's laughter is politics and politicians, namely the men and their insistence on involving themselves in politics. The women's solution – withholding sex until the men pay more attention to them – however, is just as comical as they gradually resemble the men by creating their own war-like atmosphere. The exploitation of stereotypes provokes much of the laughter in the two versions, originating in Aristophanes' version where the men engage in war and the women worry about the home front. Through the examination of the construction of stereotypes of gender, social class and sexuality, this essay demonstrates that Domínguez's *Lisístrata* undermines and questions its immediate community within Santo Domingo and the Dominican Republic, but also the wider community of the Caribbean, Latin America and the Americas, and even global theatre. It is through the exploitation of these very divisions that the play becomes funny and poignantly comments on the social situations in which it is written. For Domínguez, this exchange is exactly what makes the play a success in that, like the challenging of the theatrical canon, these stereotypes are mostly turned upside down and show another way in which the play dismantles its object of study and interrogation, although, in the tradition of *Lysistrata*, these stereotypes are not always destroyed.[4]

How does moving Lysistrata from ancient Greece to a Caribbean setting in the twentieth century change the story? More importantly, why does this playwright (among others) return again and again to ancient Greek myths to convey their perspectives and how does this return enrich or detract from their arguments? Thanks to definitions from eighteenth- and nineteenth-century Europe, ancient Greek drama is perceived as holding the keys to the essential issues that occupy our interest. Through a return to some of these myths, then, Hispanic Caribbean theatre attempts to understand its own surrounding context within the established canon of the West.[5] Using classical theatre offers an historical exploration of universal themes, connecting these playwrights with an accepted tradition. The use of Greek comedy transforms the local interests into global concerns typical of all communities. We often see that playwrights use Greek drama in moments of political or social crisis, though we also understand that the return to the archive of Greek theatre helps to legitimize one's own work and tradition.[6] Borrowing from the ancients, however, is also a subversion of the original since a Dominican playwright challenges what is included in and excluded from the Western canon, a tradition that, for the most part, has not acknowledged him. In this way, the modern text similarly challenges the ancient canon that it wishes to expand by interrogating its place and evaluation of others, a similar claim to what Andújar and Nikoloutsos assert in their respective studies of the Cuban plays *Electra Garrigó* and *Medea in the Mirror*.[7] Additionally, as Isabelle Torrance underlines in her analysis of the Cuban play *Seven Against Thebes*, 'the way in which a play is received, reinvented, rewritten, and reinterpreted for a new generation can be important for our appreciation of the original.'[8] Thus, renovating the ancient text gives it new life in a modern context that will renew its relevancy in the twentieth century. Both the ancient and the modern text benefit from this borrowing, since the latter is legitimized while the former is archived in an innovative context.

While the classical tradition from which Domínguez borrows is widely accepted as part of a 'well-rounded education', the theatre of Latin America or the Dominican Republic is much less familiar to audiences outside the respective national borders, and even sometimes within them given that the audience may be more familiar with performances of Shakespeare or Beckett than those of their home-grown talent. Despite the historical and geographical richness that the Island nation offers, the Dominican Republic has largely been ignored in literary and theatre studies and even in Latin American Studies. While Dominican theatre is not well known outside of its borders, even within the island, it suffers from a lack of attention, something that is common to many Latin American countries where major theatre houses will more often stage European plays than home-grown talent. That said, there is a strong tradition of dialogue between some Spanish-speaking countries in the Americas that can be seen particularly in Buenos Aires, Havana and Mexico City, as well as other smaller centres (such as Enrique Buenaventura's Cali).[9] Dominican theatre, outside national borders (and sometimes even within them), is practically unknown, although Domínguez is perhaps the most well-known playwright in the country because of his topics, abilities and the awards that he has won. Despite his undeniable importance in the theatre community, Domínguez has not been well-studied and his *Lisístrata odia a la política* is even less studied than his other works. It is clear that this lack is a result of the general dearth of attention and understanding that Dominican theatre has outside of the country in both Anglo-American academic circles and those dedicated to Latin American and Caribbean studies, something that this essay attempts to ameliorate.

Within this national context, Domínguez's *Lisístrata odia la política* uses comedy to subtly question stereotypes accepted in Caribbean society. This play is one of various works that allows us to understand why theatre practitioners return to the existing corpus of ancient Greek theatre and what this return means for Hispanic Caribbean theatre.[10] Through his use of an ancient canonical theatre text, Domínguez challenges the original from the margins and his audience from within, creating a new national and theatrical context that pushes boundaries and establishes canons.

A Dominican Lysistrata

The title of the play, *Lysistrata Hates Politics: A Theatrical Work in Three Acts Inspired by a Topic by Aristophanes*, highlights the genre into which Domínguez inscribes his rewriting and informs the public of the source text from which the Dominican author draws. The setting is titled 'Sálvese-Quien-Pueda' ('Save Yourself if You Can'), the time is undefined ('Intemporal' ['Timeless']), but the costume is described as 'moderno pero con reminiscencias griegas' ('modern but reminiscently Greek').[11] The first act begins with Lisístrata onstage, preparing a microphone and talking about the need to save the country and, in the process, their husbands, by declaring war on politics. Her husband Pompeyo, as chief of police, interrupts her, and she begs him to stay out of politics and keep the police neutral, a request that Pompeyo says he cannot carry out, maintaining that he is an intermediary.

The opening of the play suggests an interesting blending of antiquities: although Lisístrata retains her Greek name, Domínguez uses a Roman name for her husband. To the informed classical reader–spectator, this name choice carries political and gender connotations. The Roman 'Alexander the Great,' Pompey was an immensely successful Roman general since he was young – he was even nicknamed *adulescentulus carnifex* ('the teenage executioner', Val. Max. 6.2.8) – and formed the First Triumvirate with Julius Caesar and Crassus. As general, he gained *absolute* powers over the Eastern Mediterranean, a connection we can see with Domínguez's Pompeyo. However, he divorced his third wife for an alleged affair with Caesar.[12] This uneven dominance over external and domestic affairs is of importance since for the Romans control over one's own household indicated one's ability to rule outside of it. Domínguez's choice of this Roman name for his rewriting of a Greek comedy is significant. It underlines the connections between domestic and political control. While this blending of ancient traditions that the reader–spectator sees in these chosen names is present for the classical audience, it is equally important that Pompeyo also recalls Latin America, not being unheard of as a name in the Caribbean and Mexico.

Following this initial exchange, Lisístrata calls a meeting of women, capturing their attention by saying that the country is in danger. She admits that her husband is too busy to pay attention to her, even to have sex with her and, one by one, all the women concede that the same is happening with them.[13] Lisístrata urges them to unite into 'a sex struggle against politicians' ('una lucha del sexo contra los políticos'), to which she finally convinces them to pledge.[14]

The second act begins with an air of war, where the women talk about taking control of the public treasury while more and more women arrive to join their cause. This continues with control vacillating between the genders. The act ends with an encounter between Lisístrata and Pompeyo where he tries to seduce her; the women react by sending him back outside, dressed as a woman. The third act, however, opens with a change of atmosphere, as the women are fed up and want to return to their homes. Lisístrata tries to issue a declaration of resistance to the women, hoping to buy time in what Eugenia calls a 'curtain of smoke' ('cortina de humos').[15] An envoy from the men arrives to insultingly offer the women the chance to retract. Their delivery allows Lisístrata to refuse, saying 'what we want is husbands, not politicians' ('lo que deseamos son maridos, no políticos') and urges Pompeyo to come to negotiate.[16] While the women's alliance continues to disintegrate, word is sent that Pompeyo is waiting with a delegation. The two spouses discuss the situation, ultimately revealing that the men have surrendered, giving up politics to return to their women. During the celebration, a gay man enters with a message for Lisístrata. The stage directions read: 'Suddenly a homosexual man enters, a cautious and elegant figure' ('De pronto entra el homosexual, una figura circunspecta, elegante').[17] He says that after much deliberation the 'Association of Homosexuals' (Asociación de Homosexuales)[18] have decided to divide themselves in two groups and to align with the two sides. Lisístrata reveals that they have arrived too late and the celebration continues with the declaration that 'Men only know about war. We women know about love' ('Los hombres solo saben de Guerra. Las mujeres sabemos de amor'), a revelation that indicates that the women 'possess the secret to peace!!!' ('¡¡¡poseemos el secreto de la paz!!!').[19]

Besides the title, there are many connections between the Dominican play and the ancient Greek source text, which can be seen mainly in the play's plot, though the time and place are different. Despite this temporal and spatial difference, Domínguez's *Lisístrata* maintains the humorous connection with Aristophanes' original. Perhaps a central element to a comedy is its need to appeal to a wide audience and provoke laughter to make its point. As discussed earlier, comedy uses laughter to provoke reflection and criticism from the reader–spectator, and it is precisely this characteristic that allows the play to push boundaries.[20] This indirectness can afford it an effectiveness that is not seen in tragedy in that the sceptical or distrustful reader–spectator can be lured to the comedian's way of thinking through a laughter that breaks down the comic hero. As Ralph Rosen states, 'what is important about comic heroes is not *that* they are heroic, but that the author *says* they are.'[21] The comic hero is freed form the dictates of the tragic hero since there is more than one way to be a hero in a comedy.[22] The comic 'hero' or the main character may be belittled or spurned by the laughter provoked by his or her actions. In a comedy, no one is above laughter; all the characters' actions are meant to create opportunities to laugh through their shortcomings or failures, most notably. In this way, criticism is subtler. Comedy uses laughter to engage audiences and prompt them to pay close attention to the material. It is in this way that comedy is able to question its subject matter, a quality that lends itself well to Domínguez's *Lisístrata* since he is questioning not only the topic at hand, but the very canon into which his play is inserting itself.

Much of the comedy of both Aristophanes' and Dominguez's versions stems from the use of stereotypes common to the era in which the plays are written. This manipulation of stereotypes begins with the original version from Aristophanes where men engage in war and women worry about the home front.[23] It is through the exploitation of this very division that the play becomes funny and poignantly comments on the social situations in which it is written. For Aristophanes' play, this has been amply commented by experts in Classics.[24] For Domínguez, however, this exchange is exactly what makes the play a success in that during the play, the socially accepted stereotypes are turned upside down.

This use of stereotypes is not limited to stereotypes of gender, social class and sexuality, but also creeps into political divisions, such as the role of the police in Latin American society. Pompeyo, Lisístrata's husband, is the chief of police, a position that is sometimes tied to politics and politicians in Latin America, a fact that his wife dislikes and tries to change. She urges her husband to stop inserting the police into political affairs and to remain neutral. Pompeyo, on the other hand, sees his job as maintaining order and the political aspect of his position as essential to the peace and stability of the nation:

> No olvides que mi misión es hacer que se cumplan las leyes, mantener el orden y proteger al pueblo. Con mi actitud se cumplen las tres cosas. Si derrocan al Presidente, se cumple la ley del más fuerte; si estoy combinado con los golpistas e insubordinados, me mantengo en mi cargo y puedo controlar el orden y controlando el orden puedo proteger al pueblo fácilmente contra los desmanes y desatinos. ¡Mi actitud es lógica!

> Don't forget that my mission is to make sure that the laws are followed, maintain order, and to protect the people. With my attitude, all three are accomplished. If the President is overthrown, the law of the strongest is upheld; if I collaborate with the coup leaders and the insurgents, I keep my post and I can maintain order and by maintaining order, I can protect the people easily against excesses and nonsense. My attitude is logical![25]

For Pompeyo, keeping himself in the centre of political events is the way to maintain order, the very essence of his job. As he himself explains, by being involved in all the activities, Pompeyo can make sure nothing gets out of hand. Lisístrata, on the other hand, wants her husband to leave politics to the politicians and simply maintain law and order in the nation. Pompeyo's attitude is one that has been found in different Latin American nations where the police (or military) have been involved in *coup d'états*, particularly the Dominican Republic, given the close ties between these different branches and their involvement in politics.[26]

Domínguez presents one of the ways that the police chief can rationalize his behaviour when it so obviously steps outside the bounds of what is demanded. Contained in this rationalization, the reader–spectator finds a biting humour in the portrayal of the police, one that critiques, particularly in his final proclamation that views his opinion as 'logical', an obviously ironic interpretation. Stereotypes here, then, are used to provoke a critical gallows humour in the way that comedy does as opposed to tragedy. This laughter strips Pompeyo of the pomposity of his words and bares him as a ridiculous, power-hungry man, looking out for himself. Thus, in the process, Domínguez critiques the rule of order (or lack thereof) and attempts to turn the tables on the powerful, such as we see in the figure of the chief of police.

Challenging definitions in antiquity and modernity

The exploitation of stereotypes through reversal is nowhere more apparent than in the use of war and the martial aspect of the women's actions after they make their pact. As stated, the comedy of both plays emerges from the use of gender stereotypes: men wage war and politics, and women engage in love and the maintenance of the home. Nevertheless, in order to make the men listen to their demands, the women undertake actions that provoke a war, as seen in the stage directions that open the second act of *Lisístrata*: 'A fourth [woman] moves martially with a rifle on her shoulder and salutes another that comes from the other side also carrying a rifle' ('Una cuarta [mujer] se mueve marcialmente con fusil al hombro y se saluda con otra que entra por el lado contrario portando también un fusil').[27] The prominent placement of the rifles – as a protruding appendage – and the martial pacing of the women create a sensation of soldiers on watch, an identity traditionally occupied by men, which is underlined here in the phallic use of the rifle. The general atmosphere of the stage in this scene is of one side of a warring faction, one who has also gained control of government offices and is exercising political power, as the characters illustrate in their verbal exchange.[28] Engaging in the very activities that the women object to in their men, Lisístrata and her women take control of the political offices that are closely identified with government and physically defend them with guns and a war plan. The irony – that they engage in the activities that they protested – is not lost on the reader–spectator, who will find the laughter in these hypocritical actions, a laughter that belittles the women's struggle. However, Domínguez's use of stereotypes here does not question them or dismantle them, but simply turns them on their heads, suggesting that this binary of one or the other is inevitable unless carefully undone and will only perpetuate the problems it has created. In this way, comedy provides an outlet without offering a strong evaluation.

The use of stereotypes in *Lisístrata odia la política* is not limited to the ones that divide the two genders but is also found among the women. From the first meeting that Lisístrata calls, the women are divided into groups and one representative is sent to speak on the group's behalf. As is to be expected, difficulties arise between the women whose lives have led them in different directions despite their shared gender; the reader–spectator particularly sees this in the sniping between Eugenia and Lisandra, which Lisístrata tries to overcome. Eugenia represents the typical woman of means aspiring to more, as reflected in her name.[29] Lisandra, on the other hand, is a young woman with sharp, progressive ideals.[30] The names that are chosen for these two reflect their descriptions since Eugenia refers to noble (*eugenēs*) and Lisandra derives from *lysis* and *aner-andros* (man) to imply strength and manliness.[31] The clash between these two women can be seen in their verbal exchange, where they resort to stereotypical insults (of which part is quoted below):

Eugenia Si hubiera sabido que esta hija de ricos disfrazada de pueblo había de venir, no habría venido.

Lisístrata Un minuto, por favor ...

Lisandra Si hubiera sabido que esta hija de gente arruinada vividora de apellidos había de venir, no habría venido.

Eugenia If I had known that this daughter of rich people dressed up as one of the people was coming, I wouldn't have come.

Lisístrata One moment, please . . .

Lisandra If I had known that this daughter of broke people living off their last names was coming, I wouldn't have come.[32]

This quote shows that the women have been separated into different social groups, each with a representative who presents their issues. Lisandra, representing young women engaged in political activity on the left (even though they have come from privilege), clashes with Eugenia, an older woman of means speaking for the established women who have reached a certain status that they want to defend (although this may be a constructed fiction). Both see in the other a type of woman whom they believe they know and can characterize without trouble; they use this knowledge to trade insults, while Lisístrata endeavours to cut through the rhetoric and make the women engage with one another, one on one. The fact that the descriptions of both Lisandra and Eugenia as quoted above indicate that neither of these women is what they appear (or want to appear) to be exacerbates the tension between the exterior and the interior, the very issue at the heart of Domínguez's examination of stereotypes.

Nevertheless, we cannot be satisfied that Domínguez's goal is simply to debunk these social myths, since he presents one of these moments of social confusion later on in the same act in Eugenia's reading of Artemisa's actions. Artemisa is the representative of the prostitutes, although ironically her name is the Spanish name for the Greek goddess Artemis. She states that she has won and contemplates taking advantage of the economic opportunities of the moment by returning to work.[33] Eugenia and the other women see betrayal in Artemisa's actions and try to make her change her mind. During the discussion, Artemisa touches Eugenia, who reacts violently against this incursion:

Eugenia (retirando la mano de Artemisa que le ha tocado el hombro) . . . ¡Juntas, pero no revueltas! . . .

Artemisa Pues también somos mujeres de principios y conocemos mejor que ustedes lo que es un hombre. Yo hablé con todas ellas y les dije cuál era la situación. Les expliqué que todas ustedes eran viudas con maridos vivos. (Con lágrimas en sus ojos, vivamente emocionada) ¡Si las hubieran visto! ¡Parecían niños de teta! Tuve que darles a oler perfumes para calmarlas. ¡Juraron conmigo que se unirían a la causa!

Eugenia (Taking Artemisa's hand off her shoulder) . . . Together, but not scrambled! . . .

Artemisa Well, we are also women of principles and we know better than you what a man is. I spoke with them [the prostitutes] and I told them what the situation was. I explained to them that you all were widows with living husbands. (With tears in her eyes, visibly emotional) If you could have seen them! They looked like children! I had to use smelling salts to calm them down. They swore to me they would join the cause![34]

Initially, Eugenia, like many of the other women, believes the prostitutes that Artemisa represents are lacking in principles and will go back on their word as soon as the opportunity presents itself. Here is the commonplace assumption that a prostitute has no pride but is only looking for the greatest profit. However, Domínguez's Artemisa and her group prove themselves to be women of their words, doing what they pledged to do, and Eugenia feels ashamed of how she allowed her assumptions to rule her words and actions. *Lisístrata*, in this way, undoes the social patterns that it exploits in the play in such a way that we cannot state which way the play adheres. The use of these social patterns in this example is employed to poke fun and make an example of how they get us in trouble. In other examples, one of which we find at the very end of the play, they are exploited in a more traditional way.

In the final example of a social stereotype in the play, we have the introduction onstage of a group of gay men, entering in practically the last minute to profess their decision on where their loyalty lies. In the original *Lysistrata*, the sexual innuendos for the most part refer to relations between men and women, something that is replicated in the Dominican *Lisístrata* even though same-sex relationships were not unknown in either community. When considering the insertion of the gay man in *Lisístrata*, this idea of a homosexual identity that Domínguez includes was not found in Aristophanes and can be seen as an innovation that points to the identity politics that defined the late twentieth century in the Western world, which Domínguez is undoubtedly endeavouring to critique. However, neither text highlights a homosexual identity throughout the body of the action until the inclusion of the camp gay man at the very end of Domínguez's version. This is an interesting addition since up until this final point of the play, the stereotypes had been constructed along traditional gender lines – a tradition, however, that was slowly being challenged in the time period in which Domínguez is writing. In this way, highlighting a marginalized group that was not included in the above divisions allows the play to situate itself within the contemporary moment. Nevertheless, the way that Domínguez presents the group within the confines of the play does not allow for strong challenges to the social divisions of gender but instead confirms the established dichotomy:

Durante días hemos estado discutiendo de cuál lado debíamos colocarnos en esta lucha de los sexos. Por fin, anoche, después de una acalorada discusión, resolvimos dividirnos en dos grupos clásicos   uno que apoyaría a los masculinos y otro que apoyaría a las femeninas. Yo vengo en representación de este último grupo a ofrecer a ustedes nuestro más resuelto apoyo en la ardua lucha que libran contra el sexo feo.

For days we've been discussing on which side we should be in the fight between the sexes. Finally, last night, after a heated discussion, we decided to divide ourselves into two classic groups – one that would support the men and one that would support the women. I come to represent the latter group and to offer you our most resolute support in the arduous fight against the ugly sex.[35]

In the manifestation of stereotypes in *Lisístrata odia la política*, gay men do not easily fit into the division of gender that is supposed to account for all, and the modern adaptation of the Lysistrata story must take this into account. Domínguez's answer, then, is to divide the men into 'classic' groups – meaning one that will identify with the women and one that will go with the men, keeping the prevailing cultural normative from the time.[36]

Reconstructing Lysistrata through the Dominican lens

While the scene analysed above is a particularly comic moment that comes at the end of the light-hearted play and takes advantage of the camp gay man's stereotypical vivacity and casualness in his reaction to Lisístrata informing him he arrives too late,[37] it also points to a larger project of the play: Domínguez's challenge to the model. William García discusses how Domínguez deconstructs Sophocles' text in his *Antígona-Humor* (1961), a play that uses the myth of Antigone as a pretext for a comedy.[38] García's argument offers many insights to the analysis of Domínguez's *Lisístrata* – especially since he wrote *Lisístrata* after *Antígona-Humor*. In this essay, García proposes that the recreation of an ancient Greek myth in a Latin American theatre text is a subversion or a 'textual sabotage', in his own words, since it is a contestatory act from the margins, from a theatre that is not deemed important enough to be included in world analyses:

> La subversión del mito de Antígona en esta obra aparece como una respuesta metacrítica a un canon dramático/teatral elitista y etnocéntrica que, en el mejor de los casos, juzga la labor teatral latinoamericana como imperfecta e incapaz de producir un texto que se adhiera a las convenciones hegemónicas; y que en el peor de los casos, ignora o desconoce la producción teatral latinoamericana.

> The subversion of the myth of Antigone in this play appears as a metacritical response to a dramatic/elitist theatrical and ethnocentric canon that, in the best case, judges the Latin American theatrical labour as imperfect and incapable of producing a text that adheres to hegemonic conventions; and that in the worst case ignores or does not know Latin American theatrical production.[39]

This argument is also applicable to the Dominican *Lisístrata*, since García laments a fate common to all Latin American theatre. He argues that theatre written from a Latin American standpoint is subversive because it is written within a tradition that is not known and not taken into account in the construction of global theatre history. Therefore, to rewrite an ancient text, the playwright subverts the earlier one by inserting himself (in this case and the majority, *him*self is accurate) into a canon in which he has not been included. He is undoing the original as well as widening the definitions of canonical theatre.

As with Aristophanes' text, Domínguez takes advantage of traditional stereotypes to create the comedy in his play. The reader–spectator laughs or enjoys the story because she can see how the playwright is exploiting accepted notions on what women do and want and what men do and want. Nevertheless, because Domínguez is writing in a time when these gender divisions are being somewhat challenged (the play is written in 1981, after women's liberation and the gay men's movement had already initiated many cultural changes), these stereotypes can be seen to be slipping in their cultural stranglehold. Domínguez's spectators would be aware that these seemingly fixed identities were beginning to shift and were not as concrete as they had been. In this way, his comedy exploits the gender divisions of the play for laughs while simultaneously problematizing the dichotomies that result from these divisions. The play confirms that it is no more 'natural' that women be interested in love and the home than that they excel at war and politics. Domínguez's audience – in print and performance – would be aware of the challenges that identity politics was presenting in the 1970s and 1980s and would comprehend the comic effect of his use of gender stereotypes in that the reader–spectator in the Dominican Republic would be aware of both the social innovations found elsewhere and the more traditional views that competed with these. In this way, Domínguez's adaptation of Lysistrata is a subversion of the original at the same time as it is a homage to the ancient Greek story. It honours the original because they both attempt to interrogate the culture in which they are writing through comedy. The characters and the institutions they represent are ridiculed and mocked in the plays. On the other hand, Domínguez undermines the original by revealing the gender divisions used in the play to be elastic and social constructions that can be easily undone, thus both revering and challenging the theatrical canon within which they are writing.

Greek theatre has been a source of inspiration for Western theatre, and Hispanic theatre is no different. For this reason, it is necessary to understand why playwrights and the theatre community return to these tragedies and comedies again and again. For some, the canon of ancient Greece offers an opportunity to elevate national theatre given its rich history, while for others it is a way to explore plot and characters in a way that an original story may not allow. In other instances, ancient myth affords the space to criticize events and immortalize heroes while the use of comedy can provoke laughter that subtly breaks down barriers. Because of its vast repertoire, ancient Greek theatre encompasses all these examples. What is more important for the purposes of this essay is to understand why they return to such a 'far away' moment to make their points. By returning to the origins of Western theatre, Domínguez instantly legitimizes his own theatre by inserting himself into the traditional definitions. He contributes to a wider movement found within the Dominican Republic to strengthen the theatre community, using ancient Greece to argue that his nation and culture are part of this tradition. At the same time, his appropriation of ancient Greek comedy challenges the original since its use inserts the Dominican and Hispanic Caribbean tradition into a Western practice that does not recognize it. Despite the universal appeal of the myths from ancient Greece, the stories change when they are transported to the Hispanic Caribbean. They not only become modern and accessible to a new audience, they create a hybrid world where the old and the modern mix to bring a new light to the contemporary moment.

CHAPTER 12
AESCHYLUS AND THE CUBAN COUNTER-REVOLUTION
Jacques A. Bromberg

As the literature on Cuban adaptations of ancient drama grows, one is reminded that the Revolution in Cuba was also a theatrical revolution.[1] The fall of President Fulgencio Batista's government in 1958 marked a new beginning for Cuban theatre, featuring new playwrights and dramaturges including Antón Arrufat, José Ramón Brene, Nicolás Dorr, Abelardo Estonino López, Héctor Quintero, Manuel Reguera Saumell, José Triana and others.[2] In 1959 alone, more Cuban plays premiered than during Batista's six-year presidency, and 400 more followed during the 1960s.[3] Of course, the island was no stranger to the classical theatre before the revolution: Cuban classical scholars had been researching ancient dramas, hosting conferences, and staging performances since at least the 1920s.[4] Ludwig Schajowicz had directed *Antígona* and *Las coéforas* for the Teatro Universitario in 1941/2; and Luis Baralt had directed an *Agamemnon* in the summer of 1952.[5] In 1958, the year before Castro's revolution, an essay on Aeschylus' dramatic art appear in *El Gato*, a monthly general interest magazine, and the daily *El Mundo* published a brief history of the theatre, beginning with the Greeks.[6] Over the past decade, classical literary historians have become increasingly interested in Cuban receptions of Greek tragedy. These go back to the nineteenth century, beginning with the echoes of Aeschylus' *Persians* in *Abdala* by José Martí, published in 1869, and the adaptations of *Prometheus Bound* by Julián de Casal in *Las Oceánidas* (1880) and *Prometeo* (1891).[7] Among mid-century dramas, *Electra Garrigo* by Virgilio Piñera (1948) and *Medea en el Espejo* by José Triana (1960) have received extensive treatments in English;[8] and alongside Piñera and Triana, Antón Arrufat (b. 1936) has been recognized for his appropriations from classical literature, beginning with the lyric poem 'Antígone', one of his earliest publications.[9] Arrufat's award-winning 1968 adaptation of Aeschylus' *Seven against Thebes*, which is the subject of this essay, has been introduced to classical scholars in the Anglophone world in two essays by Isabelle Torrance, which unpack Arrufat's engagement with Aeschylus as an allegory of the revolution.[10]

Arrufat has never denied that *Los Siete* was inspired by the events of the Cuban Revolution, especially the Bay of Pigs invasion (April 1961). On the contrary, *Los Siete* was written in a flurry of creativity in May 1968 when 'historical realities' offered a unique perspective on Aeschylus' tragedy:

> Mi país atravesaba una situación de bloqueo, habíamos pasado la invasión de Playa Girón, es decir, todas esas realidades históricas permitían que yo hiciera una lectura de Esquilo como un texto de absoluta actualidad y de absoluta vitalidad.[11]

My country was undergoing a period of blockade, we had gone through the Bay of Pigs invasion, that is to say, all of these historical realities made it possible for me to read Aeschylus as an utterly current and utterly vital text.

The 'historical realities' of post-revolutionary Cuba offered Arrufat a clear and provocative parallel with Aeschylus' myth, as well as a unique opportunity to modernize the text. Nevertheless, the work was met with controversy. Although *Los Siete* won the prestigious 'José Antonio Ramos' prize from the Cuban writers' and artists' guild (*Unión de Escritores y Artistas Cubanos* = UNEAC), two of the five judges condemned *Los Siete* as counter-revolutionary; and when the play was published according to the rules for UNEAC winners, it was accompanied by a preface that rejected its ideology, lamenting how 'all the elements that Yankee imperialism would like to imagine as Cuban realities are present in this play' ('todos los elementos que el imperialismo yanqui quisiera que fuesen realidades cubanas, están en esta obra').[12] This controversy reveals the paradox of Arrufat's work: the play is a translation of Aeschylus (a faithful one, at times) and a comment on political life in Cuba following the Revolution. Despite (or, perhaps, because of) Arrufat's fidelity to his Aeschylean model, the dissenting UNEAC judges observed similarities between Arrufat's 'Polinice' and Cuban exiles living abroad (especially in the US) and cited passages that seemed inimical to the Revolution.[13] The play was banned from Cuba, and Arrufat was ostracized for fourteen years, neither writing nor producing another drama for over two decades. From 1968 until 1981, none of Arrufat's works was republished in Cuba. *Los Siete* was not performed until the Scottish premiere of Mike Gonzalez' English translation in November 2001, and only premiered in Cuba in 2007, nearly four decades after its initial publication.[14]

Beginning in the 1990s, scholars and critics prompted a re-evaluation of Arrufat's work, arguing that *Los Siete* represents some of his best writing.[15] Some pursued his version of the Theban myth, focusing on Polinice as a representative of the traditional value system that antedated Etéocles' rule;[16] others catalogued intertexts not only with the Aeschylean *Seven* but also with Euripides' *Phoenician Women*, an approach that I embrace in this chapter.[17] Like his ancient models, Arrufat concentrates on the fratricidal struggle between the sons of Oedipus; in many places, his language resembles Aeschylus' closely.[18] Etéocles' opening lines in Arrufat's play provide a useful example:

Ciudadanos, es menester que ahora
hable quien vele por la patria
sin rendir sus ojos al blanco sueño,
sin escuchar las voces enemigas
ni entregarse al recuerdo de su propia sangre.[19]

Citizens, it is necessary that he should now speak, [he] who safeguards our country without yielding his eyes to dreams, without heeding the enemy voices, and without surrendering to the memory of his own blood.

This beginning is strikingly similar to Aeschylus': 'Citizens of Cadmus [Κάδμου πολῖται], it is necessary that he speak the proper words [τὰ καίρια], who safeguards the affairs of state [ὅστις φυλάσσει πρᾶγος ἐν πρύμνῃ πόλεως], guiding its rudder, without his eyes being lulled to sleep [βλέφαρα μὴ κοιμῶν ὕπνῳ]' (1–3). So how could a play that seems often like a faithful translation of Aeschylus cause such controversy?

The answer lies in the play's post-revolutionary context.[20] Arrufat's *Los Siete* is not the faithful adaptation of Aeschylus that it sometimes appears to be, and while the play may at times adhere to its Aeschylean model, it makes emphatic points of its own as well.[21] By studying the text of Arrufat's *Siete* alongside Aeschylus' *Seven*, Torrance's essays have opened the door to further investigations of this complicated play. Even in its Aeschylean opening, cited above, Arrufat's Etéocles voices concerns of the Revolution: the dangers of foreign propaganda ('the enemy voices') and of nostalgia ('surrendering to the memory of one's own blood'). It is curious that UNEAC judges should reject the play for promulgating an imperialist ideology, when its opening lines appear to share their concern; but nostalgia is a product of Arrufat's imagination and a departure from Aeschylus, in whose drama Polyneices is characterized as a foreign invader. *Los Siete*, by contrast, focuses on the ambivalent nature of his homecoming, and by refusing to champion either brother reveals an important debt to Euripides' *Phoenician Women*. This paper adopts Torrance's model of direct comparison between the texts of Aeschylus and Arrufat by focusing on these issues and advancing the project of exploring Arrufat's debts to and departures from Aeschylus. I limit my discussion to four significant features, in four subsections: Arrufat's individuated Chorus, his introduction on stage of the six Theban champions as speaking characters, the confrontation between Etéocles and Polyneices, and the drama's unexpectedly optimistic conclusion. While these scenes have received individual attention elsewhere, taken together they illustrate more fully the complexity of Arrufat's engagement with Aeschylus and the originality of his dramatic vision. They also allow for a more complete treatment of Arrufat's debt to Euripides than is available in existing scholarship, echoing a theme of this volume that classical receptions are rarely direct derivatives of a single ancient *urtext*, but complex hybrids that combine source texts in diverse ways.

Arrufat's polyphonic chorus

Arrufat's *Los Siete* follows Aeschylus' choral architecture closely, staging an entry song, two extended odes and an exit.[22] The similarities are not only structural, as Arrufat constructs a female chorus that, like Aeschylus', embodies the city's 'deep-rooted social and religious institutions and its capacity for fear and suffering'.[23] Arrufat's most significant departures from the Aeschylean model are dramaturgical, in the individuation of the chorus into five distinct voices, and thematic, in its political ambivalence. This section presents a comparative analysis of Arrufat's text with its Greek model, seeking to show that a close reading of Arrufat's choruses allows us to observe this combination of reception and originality that characterizes Arrufat's adaptation of Aeschylus's play.

Etéocles' prologue is followed, as in Aeschylus, by the return of the two 'Spies' ('Espías') in Arrufat (compared to a single 'scout' (κατάσκοπος) in Aeschylus), who describe the enemy camp, the beginning of the sortition. Here, Etéocles includes a reference (absent from Aeschylus) to Polinice 'together with the foreign chiefs' (junto | a los jefes extranjeros').[24] Their entrance is announced by the Chorus of five Theban women who play an important role in Arrufat's play, as they do in that of Aeschylus.[25] They speak, as the stage direction indicates, one after another, 'like a long line of sentinels' ('como a lo largo de una fila de centinelas').[26] This manner of choral speech is characteristic of the play's individuated Chorus, who most often speak as independent actors, numbered 'I-V', and only occasionally as a group. By making their voices heard both individually and collectively, Arrufat emphasizes the price the whole community has paid for the brothers' fratricidal struggle.

Arrufat's first choral song contrasts the town's poverty with the wealth of the attacking Argives.[27] The ode develops the theme of 'dust' first introduced in Etéocles' reply to the spies' report. Here, Arrufat borrows some of his most striking imagery from Aeschylus. The 'air-borne dust [αἰθερία κόνις]', 81) that Aeschylus' Chorus calls, 'a clear messenger [ἄναυδος σαφής], silent but true [ἔτυμος ἄγγελος]' (82), is adopted by Arrufat when Etéocles expresses his hopes that the houses will not crumble to dust under the enemy's assault:

Que estos hogares no se derrumben
bajo el golpe enemigo. Que **el polvo**
de sus piedras no se disperse en el viento.[28]

May these homes not be demolished under the enemy's blow, and may **the dust** of their stones not be scattered in the wind.

In addition to the imagery, the sentiment is also Aeschylean, echoing Etéocles' prayer in *Seven*, 'do not let my capsized city [πόλιν γε πρυμνόθεν], utterly destroyed [πανώλεθρον], be ruined and taken captive' (71–2). But Arrufat replaces Aeschylus' nautical metaphor (cf. 62) with an image that reinforces the poverty of his Thebans. The word 'polvo' ('dust') appears five times in the ode.[29] The unsettling of everything is symbolized by the clouds of dust churned up by the hooves of the attackers' horses; and the 'shining weapons' ('armas lucientes'),[30] of the Argives reflect their wealth, which contrasts with the poverty of the local Thebans. Arrufat describes how the Chorus 'agitate themselves, terrified' ('se agitan aterradas'),[31] and the group trips over one another's words and 'approaches a hallucinatory state' ('alcanza un estado de alucinación'),[32] which also characterizes the Aeschylean ode: 'do you or do you not hear [ἀκούετ᾽ ἢ οὐκ ἀκούετ᾽] the smashing of shields [ἀσπίδων κτύπον]?' asks Aeschylus' chorus (100); as if in answer, Arrufat's Chorus member 'IV' cries, 'I hear the smashing of shields' ('Oigo el choque de los escudos').[33] While each woman articulates her terrified hallucination, 'others express with their bodies the images that the words provoke' ('otras expresan con el cuerpo las imagines que la palabra provoca'),[34] reinforcing the ode's intense visuality. This, too, is Aeschylean:

his Chorus is so terrified that they confuse sight and sound: 'I see the din [κτύπον δέδορκα]' (103). But whereas Aeschylus' Chorus turns to supplication (see appeals to individual gods at 87, 96, 105, 116, 130, 135, 145–8, 151 and *passim*), Arrufat's Chorus offers prophetic visions of the war: plains littered with slaughtered loved-ones, Etéocles' empty chariot and blood-stained gear.[35]

Despite these foreboding visions, Arrufat's Etéocles is far gentler to the Chorus than his Aeschylean counterpart. The reason is clear, for later in the play he will defend himself against Polinice by appealing to his populism; this is hardly a tenable position for someone who claims (as Aeschylus' Eteocles does), 'may I never share a home [ξύνοικος εἴην], either in bad times or in good, with the female race [τῷ γυναικείῳ γένει]' (187–8). This new dynamic is reflected in Arrufat's second ode,[36] where the Chorus' five distinct voices coalesce into a battle hymn that hardly resembles Aeschylus' anxious and tumultuous first *stasimon*. Though Arrufat's opening lines (given to Chorus member 'III') – 'Intento obedecerte, y sin embargo | la ansiedad no abandona mi pecho' ('I am keen to obey you [*sc.* Etéocles], and yet anxiety does not leave my chest')[37] – follow Aeschylus (e.g. 288), the similarities quickly vanish. Arrufat's ode begins with speakers 'III', 'IV' and 'V' echoing the anxiety of the *parodos*, while Chorus members 'I' and 'II' strike up a hymn to Ares.[38] III, IV and V are slow to join the song, singing instead the refrain, 'What crime did we commit? What freedom shall we lose?' ('¿Qué crimen cometimos? ¿Qué libertad perderemos?'),[39] and introducing the theme of *soberbia* (arrogance) that will play an important role in their later dealings with Etéocles. But by the end, II and IV have joined in the hymn, 'dragged along by [their] enthusiasm' ('arrastradas por el entusiasmo').[40] The dissonance of the ode's two contrasting parts is the first sign, as more chorus members join the battle song, that there may be some hope for victory, and the tone is a far cry from Aeschylus' first *stasimon*: in *Seven*, the Chorus laments, 'it is a pitiable thing for women to be led away, subdued – ah, ah! – both the young and the old, like horses [dragged] by their hair, with their clothes torn asunder' (326–9), but Arrufat's Chorus cries

> Mi pecho palpita,
> mi sangre se quema.
> ¡Oh cuánto yo diera
> por pelear también![41]

My heart pounds, my blood boils. What I wouldn't give to be able to fight too!

The veiled optimism of this ode is shared by the nervous machismo of the scene among the Theban champions.

After Etéocles exits to confront Polinice, the Chorus sings a long third ode, full of desperation and sadness, and echoing the tone (if not the content) of Aeschylus' second *stasimon*.[42] But whereas Aeschylus' ode (707–76) focuses on Oedipus' crimes and the curse upon his sons, Arrufat focuses on the emotions of the individual Chorus members. In contrast to the cautious optimism of the preceding scenes, the ode reiterates the desperate situation confronting the city and the helplessness of the Theban women. It focuses attention on the arbitrariness of the war, which the Chorus calls 'a game that has already been played' ('un juego que ya se ha jugado'),[43] and which depends on the haphazard fall of a sword: 'Cast your lot tonight, iron! Flash, blind arbiter of our future' ('¡Echa tu suerte, hierro, esta noche! | Fulgura, árbitro ciego de nuestro futuro').[44] Surprisingly, the Chorus does not seem to care which brother returns: 'Either Eteocles will enter or Polyneices. Choose, iron, we are poised upon your edge' ('O entra Etéocles o Polinice entra. | Escoge, hierro, pendemos de tu filo').[45] Their ambivalence is juxtaposed with stories of individual Chorus members, whose husbands and sons have gone to war and not returned. At first, the Chorus speaks with alternating voices, asking, 'What husband have we lost, what brother, what friend? Which of our sons will return?' ('¿Qué esposo perdimos, qué hermano, qué amigo? | ¿Cuál de nuestros hijos regresará?').[46] But the group dissolves into individuals, each with their own sad experience, while the others join individually to grieve for their lost sons.

The ambivalence of Arrufat's chorus toward the Theban war no doubt appeared to the dissenting UNEAC judges as ambivalence toward the Cuban revolution. To write a drama of this sort was a betrayal, supporting an imperialist 'Yankee' agenda, with the besieged Thebes echoing American representation of Cuba as an island of prisoners. The preface to the UNEAC publication observes that 'one can identify the "besieged city" in this version of Aeschylus with the "captive island" that John F. Kennedy used to speak of' ('se identifica a la "ciudad sitiada" de esta versión de Esquilo con la "isla cautiva" de que hablaba John F. Kennedy').[47] The reference is to the rhetoric of captivity exploited by Kennedy in his address on the Cuban Missile Crisis (October 1962), with its appeal 'to the captive people of Cuba'. By contrast, Arrufat's Chorus is strikingly apolitical. Their voices, and those of the six Theban champions, represent the anxieties of the Theban community and contrast with the flawed, monarchic worldviews of Etéocles and Polinice.

The shield scene

As the play's polyphonic choral odes encourage the audience to consider the war's toll on the community, the shield scene offers a fuller picture of the imperilled town.[48] In the Aeschylean *Seven*, the scene occupies over 300 verses. Eteocles' scout describes not only where each of the seven attacking Argive captains is stationed, but also what decorations their shields bear. The scene combines the stock mythic features of the epic catalogue (as in *Iliad* 2.494–759) with the 'viewing from the wall' (*teichoskopia*, as in *Iliad* 3.121–244), and signals Aeschylus' debts to Homeric mythmaking. As his scout describes each Argive's shield, Eteocles offers an interpretation of the decoration and assigns an auspicious Theban to confront each Argive in the city's defence. The scene allows Eteocles to take control of the siege rhetorically and symbolically, rewriting the boasts and claims of the Argives in favourable terms. This central scene of the play thus characterizes the Argives' motives and outlooks and goads Eteocles along the path to self-destruction. The episode is a highlight of Arrufat's drama as well, rewritten to echo the political climate of

1960s Cuba. In an important departure from the Aeschylean model, Arrufat's Theban champions interact on stage as speaking characters, and their words invoke the language of the Revolution and its programs. As a further departure from Aeschylus, while Etéocles remains offstage, a brief scene takes place (absent in *Seven*) among the Thebans defenders and the Chorus.[49] Their interactions are characterized by the anxious bravado of a departing army and the affectionate camaraderie of a tightly knit community. Unlike Etéocles, who asks the Chorus of Women, 'Can't you do anything but wail and groan?' ('¿No saben hacer otra cosa | que lamentarse y gemir?'),[50] Polionte (*sc.* Polyphontes) warmly reassures the women, 'it pleases us to hear you sing in the city' ('Nos alegra | oírlas cantar en la ciudad').[51] Like the other Theban defenders, he has left his peacetime duties in the city's time of crisis and comforts the Chorus that 'soon we will eat a lamb in your house' ('Pronto comeremos un cordero en tu casa').[52] When the bodies of the brothers are brought on stage at the drama's close, Polionte speaks the closing lines and appears poised to help rebuild the community.[53] Next, as Hiperbio (*sc.* Hyperbius) enters, the Chorus asks him, 'Son of Enopos, we have seen your schoolhouse, and it is lovely and simple. How long did it take you to build?' ('Hijo de Enopo, hemos visto tu escuela. Es hermosa y sencilla. ¿Que tiempo te llevo edificarla?').[54] Hyperbius responds, 'much longer than tonight, when I might lose it' ('Mucho mas tiempo que el de esta noche, en que puedo perderla'). His comrade, Megareo (*sc.* Megareus) comforts him, saying, 'we shall have a good fight, and tomorrow we shall reopen your school' ('Tendremos una buena batalla. Mañana abriremos tu escuela otra vez'). As others have suggested, Hiperbio's character recalls the 'Campaña de Alfabetización' (Cuban Literacy Campaign), which between 1959 and 1961 shrank Cuba's illiteracy rate from over 20 per cent to under 4 per cent, and increased the numbers of children in schools from 60 per cent to 80 per cent by bringing teachers to rural areas.[55] Arrufat's defenders are workers who are compelled to defend their community, in the way Castro (replying to Kennedy's October 1962 speech, cited above) argued that 'we have taken up arms against our wishes and our hopes because we have been compelled to fortify our military defence' ('Nos hemos armado en contra de nuestros deseos y de nuestras aspiraciones, porque hemos estados urgidos a fortalecer nuestra defensa militar').[56]

Like Hiperbio, Megareo is another Theban with close ties to the land. He draws wisdom from his 'work in the field' ('labores del campo'), contrasting the growth of an orange tree with the anxious and greedy hands of Polinice's men, 'impatient lovers of disaster' ('amantes impacientes del desastre').[57] As Hiperbio recalls Castro's Campaña de Alfabetización, Megareo evokes another early revolutionary program, the Agrarian Reform Institute (Instituto Nacional de Reforma Agraria or INRA), which Castro created to supervise the redistribution of land.[58] Finally, Háctor (*sc.* Aeschylus' Actor) is introduced and assigned by Eteocles to confront Partenópeo (*sc.* Parthenopaeus); he speaks only six verses, though they suffice to characterize him, like his comrades, as a man of simple decency:

Corazón, mi corazón, si te confunde el laberinto
de las armas, los alaridos, el golpe de los dardos,

levántate y resiste. Ofrece al adversario un pecho
firme. No te alegre el éxito demasiado si vences.
Regresa simple.[59]

Heart, oh my heart, if the labyrinth of weapons, battle cries, and spear-blows disorients you, stand up and resist. Offer your adversary a firm chest, and do not celebrate excessively in victory. Return simple.

By introducing the defenders as speaking characters, Arrufat shifts the focus of the shield scene away from Etéocles, and towards the Theban community. These figures – and not the arrogant and ambitious sons of Oedipus – will be responsible for shepherding the post-war community, and they usurp some of the Aeschylean Eteocles' most memorable and heroic lines: Melanipo, for instance, who, in preparing to face Tideo (*sc.* Tydeus), boasts, 'crests and jangling ornaments do not bite, and arrogant emblems cause no wounds' ('Los penachos no muerden ni los adornos sonoros. Los emblemas arrogantes no causan heridas'[60] = Aesch. *Seven* 399–400) – words that echo in over four decades of Castro's defiant rhetoric against North American 'arrogance'.

Unlike Arrufat's Thebans, who are humanized and made sympathetic during their brief appearances, his Argives are all figures of almost hyperbolic arrogance and do not appear on stage. Aeschylus characterizes Hippomedon's confrontation with Hyperbius (486–520) as the clash between the destroyer Typhon and the 'upright' (σταδαῖος, *Seven* 513) Zeus. Arrufat's Hipomedonte, on the other hand, is not a ravager of land, but a devourer. His greed emerges from the description of his 'landowner's hands' ('manos de dueño de tierras'),[61] recalling Megareo's description of the 'anxious hands' ('manos inquietas'),[62] of Polinice's men in general. Etéocles' spies take turns impersonating each Argive aggressor as the other describes him. Building on Barquet's analysis of the scene, Torrance has suggested that Hipomedonte is 'clearly a returning landowner intent on getting back his land', and recalls prominent, exiled landowners longing to regain lands nationalized by Castro's 1959 INRA legislation.[63] His selfishness is highlighted by the repetition of first-person pronouns in the singular and plural ('mí, mía, mís'), throughout the spy's account: 'The land before me, mine at last, as far as my powerful gaze can see' ('La tierra delante de mí, | mía al fin, hasta donde | mi vista poderosa abarca').[64] Appropriately, Arrufat's exiled landowner Hipomedonte confronts Hiperbio, who earlier in the play reflects on the school he has built. As Torrance puts it, 'Arrufat's Hippomedon is thus met by the very force which had deprived landowners like him of their land.'[65]

At the fifth gate is Amphiaraus, and again we see Arrufat adapting the Aeschylean scene. As in Aeschylus, Arrufat's Anfiarao bears no insignia; as the spy reports, 'he has guessed his own end, and he knows that he will fertilize this ground with his corpse' ('Adivinó de su propio fin, sabe que abonará este suelo con sus despojos').[66] Etéocles' reaction to Anfiarao differs from that of his Aeschylean counterpart: 'I do not admire this man,' says Arrufat's Etéocles. 'He is strange to me. He is too preoccupied with himself' ('No admiro a este hombre. Me es extraño. Se ocupa demasiado de si mismo').[67] For Etéocles, even in his frightening acceptance of his own failure and death, Anfiarao remains intrinsically selfish. Readers have recognized in this selfishness and egoism an articulation by Arrufat of a capitalist ideology, pitted against the concept of the common good. Arrufat's Argives are emblematic of the Chorus' advice to Etéocles (a sentiment alien in the monarchic universe of Aeschylus' play) that he should 'remember that there are other men in the world' ('Recuerda | que hay otros hombres en el mundo'),[68] but the scene is cut short by the unexpected entrance of Polinice, who asks to speak with his brother.

Etéocles and Polinice

Because Arrufat suppresses the family curse (which goes unmentioned in *Los Siete*), the plot revolves around the contrasting worldviews of the two brothers; and unlike the Aeschylean *Seven*, which does not name Polyneices for nearly 600 verses,[69] Arrufat's play fully exploits the drama of nostalgia. The climax is a confrontation between the brothers that is totally absent from Aeschylus' *Seven* and modelled instead on Euripides' *Phoenician Women*.[70] Etéocles has prepared the audience for this scene in his prologue, when he characterizes his brother as 'forgetting our days together, our brotherhood from the time we were infants, his paternal home, our language and our cause' ('olvidando | los días compartidos, la hermandad | de la infancia, el hogar paterno, | nuestra lengua y nuestra causa').[71] The similarities with Revolutionary Cuba are obvious. Polinice resembles the wealthy, land-owning Cuban exiles, who fled from Castro's communist policies, settled in America and supported the US in their invasion. He emerges as a figure of the nostalgic bourgeoisie – *un burgués* in the language of the Cuban Marxist-Leninist régime.[72] Etéocles is the defender of a new order of social justice, who seeks to eliminate the counter-revolutionary faction and retain power. This confrontation between the brothers is surprising given the play's focus on the Aeschylean myth, but even more surprising is the degree of sympathy which Arrufat allows Polinice.

In spite of Etéocles' initial characterization of his brother-antagonist as an exile, who has forgotten his family, his country and his language, Polinice appears on stage asking for a truce. This departure from the text of Aeschylus' *Seven* is a sign of the freedom which Euripides' *Phoenician Women* offers Arrufat – though in Euripides' drama it is Jocasta who arranges the meeting between her two sons (*Ph.* 81–2). Arrufat's omission of Jocasta from the drama reflects his desire to draw attention away from the family curse; his drama depends instead on the brothers' conflicting remembrances of their shared past. At times, their conversation borders on tenderness: 'You have handed yourself over to other people, Polinice, and you return with them to your native land. You are a stranger ... I do not recognize your voice, I have forgotten the light of your eyes' ('Te has entregado a otras gentes, Polinice, y con ellos vienes a tu tierra natal. Eres un extraño ... No reconozco tu voz, he olvidado el brillo de tus ojos').[73] But Polinice sees hypocrisy behind these words: 'the trembling of your voice betrays your lies, but it doesn't matter. I know that you must put on a show in front of these women. In this at least you are a good politician: you use the mask that the others expect and at the right moment' ('El temblor de tu voz te desmiente. | Pero no importa. Se que debes fingir | delante de estas mujeres. En eso eres | un buen gobernante. Usas la máscara | que los demás esperan y en el momento preciso').[74] Polinice's mockery of Etéocles' political theatre echoes the opening lines, in which Etéocles had expressed the need for a leader to say the right things at the right time.

As the two exchange accusations, each argues that his cause is just. Etéocles is quick to point out Polinice's crafty rhetoric, 'Your tongue is quick, and you argue with ease. What an orator you are!' ('Es pronta tu lengua, con facilidad argumentas. | ¡Eres un buen retórico!').[75] The line evokes *Phoenician Women* 494–6, where Polyneices assures Jocasta that he has expressed his thoughts plainly without sophisticated language: 'I have made these points, mother, without stringing together tangled words [περιπλοκὰς | λόγων], but justly, as it seems to me, in the eyes of the wise and the simple alike'; to which Euripides' Eteocles responds that 'if the same idea of honour and wisdom was inborn to all, there would be no strife to make men disagree [ἀμφίλεκτος ἀνθρώποις ἔρις]; but, as it is, fairness and equality have no existence in this world beyond names; there is really no such thing' (499–502). In Arrufat, Polinice's reply to Etéocles' accusation is to remind him that 'We both had the same teacher, don't you remember?' ('Tuvimos el mismo maestro. ¿No lo recuerdas?').[76]

As the conversation continues, it is in Etéocles' memories especially that Arrufat unleashes his imagination, describing moments of happy, youthful camaraderie, including a boar hunt in which Polinice saves Etéocles' life. In a span of fewer than fifty lines, first-person forms of the verb 'recordar' (to remember) appear twelve times, as both brothers painfully recall their individual experiences of their quarrel:

Recuerdo que vivíamos en la misma casa.
Recuerdo que comíamos juntos,
y juntos salíamos a cazar. **Recuerdo**
que un día, tu venablo más diestro,
me salvo de la muerte . . .
¿Qué otra cosa **recuerdo**?
Recuerdo que has armado un ejército enemigo
para destruir esa casa . . .[77]

I remember that we once shared the same home. **I remember** that we once ate together, and together we would go out hunting. **I remember** how one day, your more skilled spear saved my life. . . What else do **I remember**? **I remember** that you have armed an enemy force to destroy that house.

In turn, Polinice defends himself from this accusation with his own recollections: '**I too remember**. **I remember** the agreement that we made three years ago, and **I remember** how you broke it' ('también **recuerdo**. **Recuerdo** | el pacto que hicimos hace tres años, | y **recuerdo** que no lo cumpliste').[78] This narrative again reflects Euripides' myth, in which after having agreed to alternating rule, Eteocles exiled his brother from Thebes (*Ph.* 71–6;

cf. 318–19, 474–83). Arrufat's presentation of contrasting views depends on this creative fusion of Aeschylean and Euripidean elements, refusing to glorify or to demonize either side of the conflict. Their arguments are crowded with the language of the Revolution and demonstrate the ideological decontamination of past violence that makes state-sanctioned history possible. Each side blames the other, with Etéocles blaming Polinice for attempting to devastate his own home, and Polinice reminding Etéocles of the agreement they had made to govern one year each. Etéocles' refusal to share power is an emphatic portrayal of absolute rule, but Arrufat's critique resides in the flawed versions of the past offered by both brothers: while Etéocles rejects his history with Polinice in the face of his present betrayal, Polinice thinks only of an irretrievable past. He is furious at the loss of his patrimony and his wealth, and he suffers as much from nostalgia as from egoism: 'My arm is the same [which saved you that day], but you are not the same man. When someone forgets, he becomes another' ('Mi brazo es el mismo, | pero tú no eres la misma persona. | Quien olvida, se hace otro').[79] He is so consumed by nostalgia that he ignores the madness of his actions. He has, in Etéocles' words, 'surrendered to the memory of his blood'.

Meanwhile, Etéocles' memory is troublingly brief and imperfect. He greets his brother by claiming not even to recognize him.[80] A moment later, he claims paradoxically that 'we know you so well that we have already begun to forget you' ('Te conocemos tanto que hemos empezado a olvidarte').[81] He does remember the boar hunt, but all that matters to him is Polinice's armed assault. Etéocles rewrites even recent history in order to justify his revolutionary policies. When Polinice twice asks how he justified to the Thebans the decision to exile his own brother,[82] Etéocles replies that it was the Thebans' dissatisfaction with Polinice's government: 'I fixed the errors of your government, distributed bread, grew close to the poor' ('Rectifique los errores de tu gobierno, | repartí el pan, me acerqué a los pobres').[83] According to Etéocles, the Thebans only needed to be reminded of the evils that accompanied Polinice's rule: 'I reminded them of the unfulfilled promises, the disappointment of the last few months. You are incapable of ruling justly' ('Les recordé los males de tu gobierno. | Les recordé las promesas incumplidas, la desilusión | de los últimos meses. | Eres incapaz de reinar con justicia').[84] But Etéocles' allusions to Polinice's unjust government are completely at odds with Polinice's story (which Etéocles does not deny) that Etéocles had exiled him *before* he had had any opportunity to rule.

Etéocles ultimately acknowledges that he broke his oath, but he rejects Polinice's high-minded ethics: 'I work in the world among men. If necessary, I will get my hands dirty. To be just one must be unjust at moments' ('Yo obro en el mundo, entre los hombres. Si es necesario, sabré mancharme las manos. Para ser justos es necesario ser injusto un momento').[85] After Polinice exits, Etéocles' last words to the Chorus are to remind them that 'it's is a sad and bitter thing to establish justice, for it brings cruelty and violence. But it is necessary . . . You all remember this: it is necessary' ('Implantar la justicia es un hecho áspero | y triste, acarrea la crueldad y la violencia. | Pero es necesario . . . | Recuérdenlo: es necesario').[86] The price that Arrufat's Etéocles pays to establish his vision of justice is to accept that he, too, is a traitor.

An unexpected ending

Arrufat does not alter the fate of the sons of Oedipus: at six gates, the Theban champion wins out over his attacker, but at the seventh gate both brothers die at each other's hands. If Arrufat's Etéocles represents Castro, then the historical parallel ends here.[87] Thebes/Cuba is victorious, but Arrufat does not to praise or despise either of the two brothers. Instead, as the bodies of the two brothers are brought on stage, the Chorus promises that 'we will fulfil our duty, for you are no longer our enemy: you are a dead man' ('Cumpliremos nuestro deber. | Ya no eres nuestro enemigo: eres un hombre muerto').[88] Critics have noted that Arrufat omits the scene between Antigone, Ismene and Creon's Herald preserved in the manuscripts of the Aeschylean *Seven* beginning at verse 861. Some have read Arrufat's omission as acknowledging the controversy surrounding the scene's authenticity,[89] but surely the decision to end the play in this manner signals more than a desire for philological rigor. Without the contested closing scene, Arrufat's drama ends optimistically: the Chorus divides to receive the two brothers' bodies, remarking how 'both received their due' ('ambos recibieron su parte'), and observing the approach of springtime when 'new leaves will make their first appearance above the blood, friends' ('estrenarán hojas nuevas | sobre la sangre, amigas').[90] They then open the gates for the returning defenders who, representatives of the The(Cu)ban people, are the play's unmistakable champions. Their victory signals the end of monarchic Labdacid rule and the beginning of 'a new order' ('un orden nuevo'),[91] and Polionte's use of exclusively first-person plural verbs in his closing lines emphasizes their communal responsibility for the town's well-being:

> No te **perturbaremos** con lamentos y lágrimas.
> Adiós, Etéocles. No **podemos** censurarte:
> tu obra está en **nosotros**. **Sabremos** continuar
> esa justicia que no se arrepiente ni claudica.
> Por ti reinará un orden nuevo, mientras tu sueñas.
> Por eso **podremos** manana comer cordero.[92]

We will not trouble you with lamentations and tears. Farewell, Eteocles. We cannot condemn you: your deed is a part of us. We will know to continue that justice which neither backs down nor falters. For you a new order will reign, while you dream. For this reason, we will be able to eat lamb tomorrow.

The play ends with Polionte's instructions to the Chorus, 'You bury him [sc. Polinice]. We shall demonstrate for him the piety that he did not show towards Thebes' ('Ustedes, sepúltenlo. | Tendremos para él la piedad | que no supo tener para Tebas').[93] While the play seems to deny the possibility of a monarch ruling justly – Polinice accuses Etéocles of being the only free man in Thebes[94] – Arrufat does express hope that the The(Cu)ban people can chart a peaceful path for themselves. By adapting the Aeschylean myth in the ways we have examined, Arrufat shifts focus away from the fratricidal struggle and towards the community, for whom the brothers' deaths mark a fresh start.[95] The play's final message is hopeful, a far cry from the counter-revolutionary tract described by the preface, which admonishes Arrufat for his sympathy with Cuba's enemies and disregard for the revolution.[96] Nearly forty years would pass before the play premiered in Havana, for a Cuban audience, with a Cuban director.[97] Yet all three adaptations of the myth of Oedipus' sons share the same vision of power's corrupting influence and of the high price that entire communities often pay for the flawed political visions of their rulers.

As Torrance boldly suggests in her essays, a close reading of Arrufat's play offers clues to a fuller understanding of Aeschylus' *Seven*. One outcome of comparing the two dramas is a renewed appreciation for the moral complexity of Aeschylus' Eteocles and Polyneices, who share responsibility (as in Arrufat's retelling) for the tragic outcome.[98] Arrufat's adaptation of the myth to the political exigencies of his time encourages us to rethink the political context of Aeschylus' Theban tetralogy, including *Seven against Thebes*.[99] Attempting political interpretations of Greek tragedies is always speculative, but that has hardly restrained scholars' imaginations.[100] Aeschylus' play was produced in 467 BCE, approximately one year before Sicilian democrats in Syracuse overthrew the last of the Deimonemid tyrants, Thrasybulus, in 466/5 and founded a democracy. The roots of the political conflict were at least a generation deep, however, dating perhaps as far back as the 480s BCE, when Gelon established Syracuse as a major capital with himself as tyrant. Between 472 (when he produced *Persians*) and 467 (when he produced *Seven*), Aeschylus visited Syracuse at the invitation of Gelon's brother Hieron, who had seized power after Gelon's death by conspiring against their third brother, Polyzelos.[101] The story of the surviving brothers' rivalry is best chronicled by the Sicilian historian Diodorus, who explains that: 'upon observing how popular Polyzelos was becoming among the Syracusans and believing that he was sitting by in hopes of seizing the kingship, [Hieron] set about putting him out of the way' (11.48.3). After an unsuccessful attempt on his life by Hieron, Polyzelos fled Syracuse and took refuge with Theron of Acragas, whom Hieron prepared to attack (11.48.6). Although the brothers were reconciled by Theron before Aeschylus' production of *Seven* in 467 BCE – in fact, Hieron died that year – it nevertheless appears possible to me that the struggle for power in Syracuse between Hieron and Polyzelos, influenced his adaptation of the myth of Eteocles and Polyneices. In fact, scholars have noted certain similarities between Aeschylus' treatment of the myth and the fragmentary version by the Sicilian poet Stesichorus.[102] Just as the historical realities in Cuba made it possible for Arrufat to read Aeschylus as 'un texto de absoluta actualidad y de absoluta vitalidad',[103] the political situation in Syracuse in the 480s and 470s BCE may have offered Aeschylus himself a unique appreciation for the myth of Oedipus and his sons.[104] By dramatizing the processes behind popular revolutions – the destruction of communities, the shedding of kindred blood, the rewriting of history, the sanitization of past violence – both Aeschylus' *Seven* and Arrufat's *Los Siete* offer compelling examples of the potential for even the least obvious classical myths to address moments of cultural and political instability around the globe, from antiquity to today.

CHAPTER 13
THE CONTEST BETWEEN *CRÉOLITÉ* AND CLASSICS IN PATRICK CHAMOISEAU'S STAGE PLAYS

Justine McConnell

When Patrick Chamoiseau, together with his fellow Martiniquan writers Jean Bernabé and Raphaël Confiant, published *Éloge de la créolité* (*In Praise of Creoleness*) in 1989, it marked a decisive shift in the Francophone Caribbean literary and theoretical scene. Having been dominated for so long by the *négritude* developed by the trio of Aimé Césaire, Léopold Sédar Senghor and Léon Damas, which advocated pride in one's black identity and shared African heritage, the new manifesto marked an explicit break away from that earlier, Africa-centred philosophy towards a Caribbean-focused concept of identity. What the 'Creolists' (as Bernabé, Chamoiseau and Confiant came to be known) posited, echoing their compatriot Édouard Glissant,[1] was that 'Caribbean literature does not yet exist. We are still in a state of preliterature' ('La littérature antillaise n'existe pas encore. Nous sommes encore dans un état de prélittérature').[2]

This chapter explores two plays by Patrick Chamoiseau, both of which engage with classical literature and culture, and embed ancient Greek myth within Martinique. I argue that in these early works Chamoiseau's embryonic ideas about *créolité* can be seen to be taking shape. As dramatic works, the plays sit on the cusp between the spoken and the written word because performance is their primary mode of dissemination; particularly compelling is that the tension between orality and literacy is a central theme of the later play, explored by setting a written classical world against an oral Martiniquan one, even while this binary is seen not to hold.

Éloge de la Créolité, though a Martiniquan text, extends its boundaries far beyond that island. Alert to the differences between different nations,[3] *créolité* is nonetheless an effort to identify connections between peoples; the situation it describes and the solutions it offers are not limited to Martinique. Though their theory is developed from the Francophone Caribbean, and many of their examples are too, Bernabé, Chamoiseau, and Confiant make it clear that *créolité* is not geographically constrained: it is an experiential concept rather than a geographic one, created in response to the violence of colonial oppression in every place where that has occurred.[4]

The Creolists argued that the legacy of colonialism had left the Caribbean viewing itself through such Eurocentric eyes that there was none of the interaction between local authors and readers that is crucial to the development of a literature. So much so that the Creolists described as 'zombies' (*zombis*) the Caribbean poets who 'used to indulge in bucolic drifts, enraptured by Greek muses' ('s'enivraient en dérive bucolique, enchantés de muses grecques').[5] Yet Chamoiseau himself had earlier engaged with the 'Greek muses'.

Unlike those he criticizes, however, Chamoiseau sought a way to engage with classical literature without being 'enraptured' or in awe of it: instead, he incorporates the classical as one element among the many which combine to create *créolité*.

Not only had the European canon and gaze excessively infiltrated Caribbean writing – both in the Francophone sphere, and more widely – but a rupture had occurred that prevented the integration of local oral traditions into a written discourse.[6] The 'privileged mode' ('un mode privilégié') of *créolité*, the authors pronounced, is orality.[7] Caribbean literature must be developed out of the region's oral traditions and combined with the diverse and multiple roots of Caribbean culture. Rather than prioritizing Africa as the exponents of *négritude* had done,[8] or adopting Europe wholesale as earlier Caribbean writers had, the Creolists urged a 'kaleidoscopic totality' ('totalité kaléidoscopique'):[9]

> Nous sommes tout à la fois, l'Europe, l'Afrique, nourris d'apports asiatiques, levantins, indiens, et nous relevons aussi des survivances de l'Amérique précolombienne. La Créolité c'est *'le monde diffracté mais recomposé'*.

> We are at once Europe, Africa, and enriched by Asian contributions, we are also Levantine, Indians, as well as pre-Columbian Americans, in some respects. Creoleness is *'the world diffracted but recomposed'*.[10]

This ideology, characteristic of what Antonio Benítez-Rojo has termed the 'supersyncretism' of the Caribbean,[11] is negotiated in the two Chamoiseau plays on which this chapter focuses. The 1977 play, *Manman Dlo contre la fée Carabosse* (*Mami Wata Versus the Carabosse Fairy*),[12] will be examined as an embodiment of the issues later theorized in *Éloge de la créolité*, while his adaptation of Sophocles' *Antigone* from 1975, being more completely in thrall to a European vision from which it is making tentative steps to break free, has only glimpses of this *créolité*.

Long before publishing his treatise on *créolité*, Chamoiseau had been preoccupied by classical literature. Displaying evidence of his incipient *créolité*, his engagement with Greek myth embodies not only the 'kaleidoscopic totality' that is essential to *créolité*, but also the tussles between orality and literature which are a feature of both ancient Greek and modern Caribbean literature. Viewing these through the lenses of comparative oral poetics and Bakhtinian theory, the political intent of Chamoiseau's work and the complex ways in which this is interwoven with classical antiquity, come to the fore. Written for performance, these two early works offer fascinating examples of classical antiquity on the Martiniquan stage and the place that Greek literature held in the development of this Francophone Caribbean literary ideology in the last quarter of the twentieth century.

Une Manière d'Antigone

Chamoiseau's first play was written when he was just twenty-two. Announcing its engagement with its Sophoclean predecessor in the title, *Une Manière d'Antigone* (*A*

Kind of Antigone) simultaneously draws attention to the freeness of that adaptation with the prefix 'a kind of'.[13] In so doing, Chamoiseau is following in an illustrious line of Caribbean writers who have engaged with the classical canon, often to explore and express anti-colonial sentiments and to mobilize resistance towards imperial oppression. One of the first to do this was Aimé Césaire,[14] who was not only a Martiniquan compatriot of Chamoiseau but also considered a father figure by Chamoiseau and his fellow 'Creolists'. However, the Creolists went on to enact a kind of Oedipal complex on the father figure: having declared themselves forever Césaire's sons ('Nous sommes à jamais fils d'Aimé Césaire'),[15] they proceeded to castigate the *négritude* he founded, declaring it a betrayal of *créolité*, primarily on the grounds of *négritude*'s very strong identification with Africa at the cost of indigenous Caribbean culture and the other elements that comprise the culture of an island like Martinique. Or as they put it in their manifesto, 'Negritude replaced the illusion of Europe by an African illusion' ('la Négritude fit, à celle d'Europe, succéder l'illusion africaine').[16]

Chamoiseau's engagement with Sophocles is more overt than Césaire's was with Homer in his *Cahier d'un retour au pays natal*, and in that closeness it is more akin to Césaire's later engagement with Shakespeare in his 1969 play, *Une Tempête*. Despite having been performed a number of times in Martinique and Europe, Chamoiseau's *Antigone* remains unpublished.[17]

For Chamoiseau, Sophocles' play lent itself to the expression of his political concerns regarding the French rule of Martinique and the violent suppression of political demonstrations objecting to that rule. The death of a student, Gérard Nouvet, during one of these protests in 1971 was a catalyst for Chamoiseau's adaptation, which depicts Antigone's refusal to obey the command of a French state representative that the corpse of a young political opponent remain unburied.[18] She covers the corpse with the red, green and black Martiniquan flag, a symbol of independence from France,[19] and the young man, rather than being her brother, is no relation at all. Thus, the action is moved entirely away from the personal and the familial into the realm of the public and political.[20] Furthermore, in Chamoiseau's version, Antigone commits suicide on the first day of carnival. Somewhat like the ancient festivals of Kronia or the Saturnalia, carnival is a time when the usual roles are overturned, so Antigone's decision to die on this day symbolizes a reversal of the dominance of the colonial power: the French rulers can imprison her and take away her freedom, but they cannot deprive her of the autonomy to end her own life.

It is no coincidence that the most prominent literary critical analysis of carnival, Bakhtin's *Rabelais and his World* (1965), is also one in which the Russian theorist discusses orality. Bakhtin confronts the very same problem that Chamoiseau explores in his *Manman Dlo* play, as we will see: if orality is superior to literary expression, is it contradictory to express that in writing? Iurii Murashov thinks so, for while he identifies Bakhtin's conception of carnival as 'an attempt to simulate a retrogressive ancient orality', he sees written culture as democratizing, and thus its rejection makes Bakhtin's theory susceptible to appropriation by totalitarian powers.[21]

The two Chamoiseau dramas considered here explore the interplay of European French with Martiniquan Creole. Such an interaction is politically fraught, but the way it works in the Antigone play may surprise us. It is the guard, watching over the imprisoned Antigone, who speaks in Creole. We might have expected our sympathies to be steered in the direction of Antigone and for her to be given the role of a nationalistic hero, imbued with the language native to the island rather than that imported by the colonial French powers. But Chamoiseau's Antigone speaks in Metropolitan French throughout, while the guard – who likewise speaks primarily in that same colonial language – peppers his speech with Creole. This is part of what Stephanie Bérard has termed the 'Caribbeanization' of the Greek myth,[22] and goes hand in hand with the guard's tendency to tell stories, sing folk songs and impersonate the characters who are missing from Chamoiseau's version.[23]

In other words, the guard functions like a traditional Martiniquan storyteller, adopting the roles of everyone in his story. As he does so, he switches between Metropolitan French and Creole, and it is this – rather than the dramatic form per se[24] – which may act as the first prompt to view the play through a Bakhtinian lens. Bakhtin wrote of a 'hybridization' that resonates with the multiple roots of *créolité*:

> What is a hybridization? It is a mixture of two social languages within the limits of a single utterance, an encounter, within the arena of an utterance, between two different linguistic consciousnesses, separated from one another by an epoch, by social differentiation or by some other factor.[25]

This 'hybridity' is seen both within the guard's character, and between him and Antigone. As Bérard notes, 'the guard effectively embodies the popular and servile side of the Caribbean population, while Antigone embodies the thinking side, the resistance, and the rebellion.'[26] Chamoiseau's play, then, achieves the polyphony that Bakhtin associated most closely with the novel and breaks from the unitary language which he associated with drama, and with classical drama most of all.[27] Chamoiseau's adaptation of Sophocles introduces a dialogic that Bakhtin saw as absent from its ancient predecessor, and thus the Martiniquan writer achieves a polyphony of the sort Bakhtin considered crucial to the advancement of the '*artistic thinking* of humankind'.[28]

Over the course of the play, the guard comes to question the authority he represents and even tries to help Antigone escape. It is as if by embracing the dialogic, he comes to exemplify the 'unfinalizability' of the self which Bakhtin saw as innate to human nature. In this respect, Chamoiseau's engagement with Sophocles' tragedy is a more radical mode of 'reception' than it might at first have seemed: more than a mere transplantation of chronological and geographical context, Chamoiseau offers something closer to the dialogic where Sophocles offered (in Bakhtin's eyes) the monologic.[29]

With no Creon present within the play, and with Antigone incarnated not as a member of the ruling family, but as a peasant,[30] Chamoiseau's version of the myth moves all its focus to the people of Martinique. French colonial rule may be the force that gave rise to the events that precede the play, but Chamoiseau denies it any more attention. His interest lies firmly with the Martiniquan people and their struggle to thrive in the wake of French oppression. It is also striking to note that both here, and in *Manman Dlo*, the resistance by the people is led by female figures.

Despite the tragic nature of the play, it ends on a hopeful note: deeply affected by his encounter with Antigone, the guard is transformed. The play closes with both actors onstage proclaiming that though the future is uncertain nevertheless, 'the guard has changed! So from now on, we know that everything is possible' ('le Garde a changé! Alors désormais, nous le savons, tout est possible').[31] As Chamoiseau asks in the foreword: 'Will he become a maroon or will he continue leading a life of colonial repression, rum and music?' ('Deviendra-t-il un nègre marron ou poursuivra-t-il sa vie de répression colonial, de rhum et de musique?').[32]

Chamoiseau's engagement with the myth of Antigone highlights the link between his own theatrical practice and the oral tradition from which Sophocles' tragedy sprang. He plays with the Sophoclean source by ridding his drama of Creon, making Antigone and the young man unrelated, and disconnecting her from the royal family. This may recall other versions of Antigone's story which were known from the Theban Epic Cycle before Sophocles wrote his tragedy, but which now only exist in fragments. The connection is thereby made between the oral traditions of ancient Greece and the creole oral traditions of the contemporary Caribbean, which have remained flexible by not being 'fixed' into one, predominant written form.[33] By reverting to a time prior to Sophocles' canonization of the story of Antigone in his tragedy, Chamoiseau reaches back to an era before the myth had been set in stone, before it attained the shape and the concretization that made it part of the 'canon' which has been used so pervasively as part of the colonial apparatus of oppressive powers. The correspondence between the literariness (as opposed to orality) of a work and its deployment by repressive powers will be one theme of *Manman Dlo contre la fée Carabosse* written just two years later. In it, the literacy of the Graeco-Roman Carabosse fairy struggles with the orality of the creole Manman Dlo, as will be explored in the next section of this chapter.

The Creolists suggest that the non-integration of orality into literature in the Caribbean is a rift that has not occurred in other places.[34] Certainly, in antiquity that integration seems to have happened. Few now doubt that the Homeric poems were composed for performance: Milman Parry's ground-breaking work in the 1930s demonstrated the almost-irrefutable evidence that these were poems composed in the oral tradition.[35] Travelling around Yugoslavia, Parry and his assistant, Albert Lord, recorded local *guslari* (the Bosniak-Serbo-Croatian traditional epic storytellers), and from this research built a firm comparative foundation for their theory of oral-formulaic composition.

Having conceived and developed his ideas regarding Homeric formulae in his postgraduate theses, Parry's Yugoslavian fieldwork provided further comparative support to the theory.[36] The epic formulae which punctuate and structure so much of the Homeric epics were explicable, he discovered, not only as an *aide-mémoire*, but as an aid to improvisation. Recording the *guslari*, Parry and Lord learnt that even when poets claimed to be singing the same song over again, they would vary it according to the responses of their audience; the formulaic phrases enabled them to compose on the spot, so that they could riff on songs they had learnt from other poets. Such improvisation means that the work is, almost by definition, never finished or complete; each new audience contributes to its completion, which is enacted afresh each time it is performed, thereby ensuring that the performance is a collective enterprise. This, too, is important to Chamoiseau's view of the spoken word and to the articulation of what the Creolists termed the 'collective voice'; listening to and taking part in this 'collective voice' will lead to 'the crystallization of a common consciousness' which the colonizers had fragmented and repressed.[37]

Manman Dlo contre la fée Carabosse

The Bakhtinian polyphony which Chamoiseau brought to his version of the Antigone myth is a feature of *Manman Dlo contre la fée Carabosse* too, as are a number of other factors which have already arisen. Firstly, the contestation of the literate and the oral which the drama stages; secondly, Chamoiseau's deployment of classical myth to frame and illustrate his tale; and thirdly, the ways in which this Martiniquan staging casts light on ancient storytelling and the oral traditions that are fundamental to the founding epics of classical literature and the 'Western canon' as a whole. While still following the tenets of classical reception theory as articulated by Martindale and others, I am interested in moving away from a primary preoccupation with direct responses to a particular text towards considering the ways in which circumstances of composition and performance may be mutually illuminating.

Manman Dlo, known also as Mami Wata, is an aquatic divinity within African, Caribbean, and South American traditions, with roots in the Yoruba religion of Nigeria. Carabosse, perhaps more familiar as a 'wicked fairy godmother', is identified in the play as a witch of the forests and the snow, and as a 'Graeco-Roman culture-witch' ('culture-sorciere Greco-latine'). In Chamoiseau's play, her sidekick is named Balai ('Broom' in French), signifying the colonial notion that indigenous people and traditions could both be 'swept away' and 'cleaned up', as well as the traditional association of a witch and her broom. It is the European origins of these two figures, Carabosse and Balai, and their attempt to impose literature, and new, written laws on the island that so threatens its way of life.[38]

The preface of the play explains that colonization is not only of individuals or of peoples, but also of culture. Furthermore, Carabosse, 'in the name of brotherhood' ('au nom de sa confrérie'), 'imprisons' the country and 'enslaves' all the creatures of the 'Wondrous World' ('Le Monde de la Merveille'). Manman Dlo escapes, but in order to defeat Carabosse, she must undertake a quest that will lead her to examine her own sense of self. Carabosse *is* finally driven away, but nothing will be the same again thereafter: Manman Dlo will retain Carabosse's wand, but whether that will be a good or a bad thing, who can say?[39]

This, at least, is the question raised by the foreword, but the play itself resolves more adamantly on the side of 'hybridity' and the incorporation of elements from Carabosse into the island's *créolité*. Shakespeare's *Tempest* has already been evoked by Carabosse's silencing of the noises of the island ('la Sorcière des sapins et des neiges / installa le silence / un silence lourd / lourd / lourd'),[40] which calls to mind – by contrast – Caliban's famous contemplation that 'the isle is full of noises, / Sounds and sweet airs, that give delight, and hurt not' (*Tempest* III.ii.133–4). *The Tempest*, of course, contains within it both pro-imperial and anti-imperial voices and arguments, which have contributed to its centrality as a drama of empire and colonialism.[41] It is no coincidence, then, that it is this play that is evoked in Chamoiseau's anti-colonial drama, just as Césaire had done (even more directly) in *Une Tempête*. The other specific evocation of *The Tempest* comes at the end of Chamoiseau's play, when – contrary to Prospero's breaking of his wand and drowning of his books – Manman Dlo gives Carabosse's wand to her daughter Algoline and encourages her to incorporate its powers with their own creole strengths.[42]

The broader political point here is the retention and incorporation of European traditions into creole culture, without allowing them to overwhelm it. This exemplifies the mode of *créolité* that the Creolists will later articulate:

> Creoleness is the *interactional or transactional* aggregate of Caribbean, European, African, Asian, and Levantine cultural elements, unified on the same soil by the yoke of history.[43]

Within the play, what is remarkable in Manman Dlo's gift of the wand to her daughter is the change of heart it signifies: previously, she had advocated 'purity',[44] and indeed, she is not only indigenous to the island but also autochthonous.[45] Promisingly, and in keeping with the play's whimsical, allegorical tone and folkloric genre,[46] Manman Dlo's gift of the Graeco-Roman wand to her daughter signifies her acceptance of the need for creolization, which will incorporate all the influences that make up the Caribbean. She has, in one sense, embodied a form of *négritude* throughout the play,[47] but at the conclusion we see this *négritude* giving way to the more multi-faceted *créolité* of her daughter. What the play finally depicts – both in its story and its form – is a valorization of creole and its victory over European efforts to diminish and deride it.

Manman Dlo, then, does not respond to a classical myth as such, nor is it a rendition of a Martiniquan folktale. It does, however, engage with the issues underlying one of the most influential developments within classical studies during the twentieth century: that of the oral composition of the Homeric epics.[48] The distinctions between orality and literacy that have so exercised Homeric scholars are at the heart of Chamoiseau's play, though this time in the context of the contemporary Caribbean. With deliberate irony, the 'Graeco-Roman' Carabosse Fairy stands for literacy and the imposition of her own culture and written laws at the cost of the indigenous culture which she seeks to destroy. This marks Chamoiseau's firm identification of Classics as part of the colonial apparatus by which people of the Caribbean had been oppressed, both under imperialism and, in the case of Martinique, by the 'departmentalization' which even today means that Martinique is, technically, part of France.

Chamoiseau's very writing of a play that takes as its subject the tussle between the oral traditions of the Caribbean and the European traditions of writing and literacy makes the play an embodiment of the contest it depicts. Indeed, we learn that the Storyteller is being investigated for 'high treason' on the grounds that he has written his tales.[49] But theatre, occupying the intersection of the spoken and the written word, and Chamoiseau's use of creolized French embody possible ways of amalgamating the two. Yet Chamoiseau's own judgement on the success of his attempt to put orality into writing remains ambivalent. In his 1988 novel, *Solibo Magnifique*, which is preoccupied with similar themes of oral storytelling and literary narration, the eponymous protagonist Solibo chastises the author for his work in this very play:

> Solibo Magnifique me disait: '... Oiseau de Cham, tu écris. Bon. Moi, Solibo, je parle. Tu vois la distance? Dans ton livre sur Manman Dlo, tu veux capturer la parole à l'écriture, je vois le rythme que tu veux donner, comment tu veux serrer les mots pour qu'ils sonnent à la langue. Tu me dis: Est-ce que j'ai raison, Papa? Moi, je dis: On n'écrit jamais la parole, mais des mots, tu aurais dû parler. Écrire, c'est comme sortir le lambi de la mer pour dire: voici le lambi! La parole répond: où est la mer? Mais l'essentiel n'est pas là. Je pars, mais toi tu restes. Je parlais, mais toi tu écris en annonçant que tu viens de la parole. Tu me donnes la main par-dessus la distance. C'est bien, mais tu touches la distance ...'.[50]

> Solibo Magnificent used to tell me: 'Oiseau de Cham, you write. Very nice. I, Solibo, I speak. You see the distance? In your book on the water-mama, you want to capture the spoken word in your writing, I see the rhythm you try to put into it, how you want to grab words so they ring in the mouth. You say to me: Am I doing the right thing, Papa? Me, I say: One writes but words, not the spoken word, you should have spoken. To write is to take the conch out of the sea to shout: here's the conch! The voiced word replies: where's the sea? But that's not the most important thing. I'm going and you're staying. I spoke but you, you're writing, announcing that you come from the voiced word. You give me your hand over the distance. It's all very nice, but you just touch the distance ...'.[51]

Solibo's distrust of the written word recalls Lévi-Strauss' notion that 'the primary function of writing ... is to facilitate the enslavement of human beings';[52] at the same time, there is an echo of the relationship between Socrates and Plato, with the older man in each case refusing to write and the younger feeling compelled to. Nevertheless, *Manman Dlo*, particularly with the prominence of the Storyteller (*Le Conteur*) as a character in the play, does achieve the impression of being a written record of an oral performance, just as Plato's use of the dialogue form may be an attempt to 'recreate the atmosphere of oral discourse and debate', as Rosalind Thomas has discussed.[53]

The name 'Carabosse' was first given to the folkloric figure of the wicked fairy godmother by the seventeenth-century French writer Madame D'Aulnoy. It is striking, then, that it is 'Graeco-Roman' magic with which she is endowed. Why did Chamoiseau not cast his evil, colonizing character as French, given France's governance of Martinique to which he objects? The answer must lie in Chamoiseau's struggle against colonialism and oppression as a whole. Although he is specifically concerned with Martinique and its dominance by the French, his broader concern is with the inhumanity of colonialism in its entirety. One uniting element of European colonialism was the emphasis that many of these colonial powers put on the Graeco-Roman classics.[54] By choosing to make his witch learned in Graeco-Roman magic, she represents not just French imperial oppression, but all European imperialists, each of whom proclaimed Classics as their own and held it up as a pinnacle to which only the very brightest and best of the colonized people could aspire. Within the play itself, this prominence of classical antiquity within colonial missions is highlighted by Balai's analysis of Carabosse's real intentions underlying her proclaimed philanthropy:[55]

> Séparer l'indigène de sa peau
> De son Histoire, de sa Culture, lui ôter le chapeau
> Et remplir la place vide d'Héllénisme!
> Douce dépersonnalisation, exempte de traumatisme
> Hellène devant l'Idéal
> Il se glorifiera de nous être vassal

> To separate the native from his skin,
> history, and culture; to remove his hat
> and fill the empty space with Hellenic culture!
> A gentle, shock-free form of depersonalization
> With Greece as his Ideal
> he will celebrate being our slave.[56]

These lines recall a view of slavery familiar from antiquity as well as from the era of the Middle Passage. When the swineherd Eumaeus discusses slavery in the *Odyssey* (17.320–3), his argument likewise includes a 'depersonalization' and a sense that the enslaved need their masters:

> δμῶες δ', εὖτ' ἂν μηκέτ' ἐπικρατέωσιν ἄνακτες,
> οὐκέτ' ἔπειτ' ἐθέλουσιν ἐναίσιμα ἐργάζεσθαι·
> ἥμισυ γάρ τ' ἀρετῆς ἀποαίνυται εὐρύοπα Ζεὺς
> ἀνέρος, εὖτ' ἄν μιν κατὰ δούλιον ἦμαρ ἕλῃσιν.

> Slaves do not want to do their proper work
> when masters are not watching them. Zeus halves
> our value on the day that makes us slaves.[57]

Eumaeus's famous proclamation is undermined by a number of factors, not least his own virtuous example which does not follow this rule. Nevertheless, the overall supposition (that to enslave is to deprive a person not just of their freedom but also of their *arête*, their skin, their culture and their history) and the fact that both statements are voiced by those who are enslaved allows us to see an interesting echo.

What is clear from Chamoiseau's work is that his view of orality differs from that of the influential Toronto School of Communication, comprised of scholars such as Marshall McLuhan and Walter Ong. For these scholars, orality and literacy fall into a clear binary that not only opposes the two, but also suggests that orality is a less advanced form than literature. The latter is an argument uncomfortably reminiscent of so many colonial critiques, whereby the 'other' is denigrated because it is unfamiliar and not understood. But everywhere around us we see that the binary does not hold: Ong acknowledges this by his terminology of 'primary orality' (cultures entirely unfamiliar with writing) and 'secondary orality' (the orality of television, radio, the telephone, which he sees as dependent on writing in these cultures). However, he does not entertain the possibility of equality and mutuality between the two: for him, either orality exists in places where literacy does not, or it is subservient to it.

The other objection to Ong et al.'s notion is that already articulated in the words of Solibo, quoted earlier; that is, the assertion that orality is superior to literacy. The emergence of the European concern with literacy and orality can be located (as Derrida did) in Rousseau's *Essay on the Origin of Languages* (1754–62) in the middle of the eighteenth century.[58] Even if Rousseau did not identify it explicitly as such, Eric Havelock has argued that the 'natural' speech which Rousseau praises among peoples he sees as 'primitive' is oral.[59] Rousseau placed great value on orality and pre-literate discourse, and this attitude remained influential, as we see in Lévi-Strauss's work. Yet while the European philosophers may have valued orality, it is clear that this was often done with a sense of nostalgia: the written word had been dominant within Europe for so many centuries that to imagine a society without that was to hark back to a bygone era. Lévi-Strauss's identification of writing with oppressive wielding of power and colonization likewise contributed to this utopian vision of oral societies.[60]

If we think back to classical antiquity, however – and this is another reason why the comparison of ancient Greek and contemporary Caribbean poetics is so illuminating – it was orality that had the upper hand. We see this argument made most explicitly in the *Phaedrus*, as Socrates tells of the Egyptian god Theuth's invention of writing. Intending that it be used as an aid to memory, he presents his new invention to the king of Egypt, Thamus, who tells him that he is mistaken: far from helping one's memory, writing will create forgetfulness in people's souls.[61]

Yet despite the work of Plato, Rousseau and Lévi-Strauss, the equating of writing with the advancement of societies and the development of technology has been ingrained in European culture for a very long time. When Solibo chastises 'Oiseau de Cham' for writing, or Carabosse tries to impose her Graeco-Roman literacy on Manman Dlo's island, Chamoiseau echoes Lévi-Strauss's concerns regarding the colonizing use of writing, and his, Plato's, Rousseau's and the others' prioritizing of the spoken word; and he argues against Derrida's efforts to recalibrate the scale.

Adding complexity to the oral-literary binary in Chamoiseau's work is the Creole language. In *Une Manière d'Antigone*, it was only the guard that broke into Creole at times; but in *Manman Dlo*, all the characters except Carabosse and Balai use it to greater or lesser extents throughout the play. All the indigenous creatures speak in Creole for much of the time, and even the Storyteller, who – as narrator and 'author' of the piece, is a liminal figure, caught between two worlds – speaks in a Creole-inflected French. This is central to Chamoiseau's purpose to embrace a hybridity of Martiniquan influences that merge together; simultaneously, it once again recalls the 'hybridization' that Bakhtin lauded as a facet of polyphony.

Édouard Glissant has argued that because Martiniquan Creole was developed specifically as a form of resistance (its purpose was to subvert as much as it was to communicate),[62] and because it contains the French language within it, 'the oral tongue bears the secret, impossible and irreparable mark of writing.'[63] The binary is so intertwined that regarding it only as a duality is to disregard other crucial strands, and to simplify the picture in unhelpful ways. Just as the split between orality and literacy in the contemporary Caribbean is by no means entire, so it is important to consider the oral elements of the written works of authors like Patrick Chamoiseau, acknowledging the ways that they fuse literacy and orality. To do this is to abide by Glissant's 'poetics of Relation', which itself implies 'a dialectical relationship between writing and orality'.[64] Such a relationship was not envisioned by Parry and Lord, with the latter going so far as to argue that 'once the oral technique is lost, it is never regained. The written technique, on the other hand, is not compatible with the oral technique, and the two could not possibly combine, to form another, a third, a "transitional" technique.'[65] But as Richard Whitaker has argued of Xhosa poetry in South Africa, and as we see here in the Caribbean, this does not hold true.[66]

Glissant has remarked that his own literary activity 'takes shape at the edge of writing and speech ... I am referring to a synthesis, synthesis of written syntax and spoken rhythms, of "acquired" writing and oral "reflex", of the solitude of writing and the solidarity of the collective voice.'[67] This is why orality is such a fundamental consideration in the appreciation of Caribbean literature. Yet despite the boom in research on oral traditions, the Caribbean has been somewhat neglected so far.

The ways in which Classics has long since been used as a site on which to stage the struggle for political and cultural autonomy within Anglophone Caribbean literature has been analysed illuminatingly by Emily Greenwood.[68] A similar approach can be seen in both the plays considered here, but the analysis of the two side by side also reveals the progression of Chamoiseau as a writer and a theorist, even in this early stage of his career. While *Une Manière d'Antigone* transposes Antigone's story to contemporary Martinique and figures her struggle as that against French colonial oppression, a couple of years later the writer who will become a renowned advocate and theorist of *créolité* is moving further away from the Graeco-Roman classics. Yet they still inform his work, not least its exploration of orality and literacy. The very developments that are depicted in fairytale form in *Manman Dlo* can be seen to have also taken place within Chamoiseau's writing: just as Carabosse silenced the indigenous creatures of the island when she arrived, sweeping away orality and imposing the culture she brought over from Europe (marked humorously by the playing of Beethoven's Fifth Symphony whenever she laughs), so, in a sense, did the colonial education of Chamoiseau attempt to rid him of his Caribbean roots.[69] While Chamoiseau resisted this even as a boy, an early work such as his *Antigone* is, for the most part, traditionally 'European' in genre and structure as well as in language (being written in 'Metropolitan French'). Nonetheless, as we have seen, it radically introduces a Bakhtinian polyphony to the drama that signifies the diverse culture of the Caribbean.

Manman Dlo is a landmark in Chamoiseau's development as a writer: for this drama is not just a play, but is specifically labelled a '*théâtre conté*', a 'narrated piece of theatre', hence the inclusion and prominence of the storyteller himself,[70] and the Brechtian tendency to draw attention to the performative artistry of the piece. This highlights the amalgamation of two of the kinds of theatre which co-exist in the Caribbean: the theatrical tradition imported by the colonizers (which often included classical works), and the theatre of oral storytelling circles (as is depicted in *Solibo Magnifique*).[71] *Manman Dlo* also marks the start of what will become a Chamoiseau-ian trait: the inclusion of himself as a fictional storyteller figure within the narrative itself.[72] We see Chamoiseau gaining in confidence in this play: no longer keeping one hand on the renowned authors of the Western canon while reaching out towards the stories of Martinique (as he did in his *Antigone*), he has stepped ever further away from European literature, so that his 'reception' of Classics becomes ever more oblique, and subterranean, yet not peripheral.

Chamoiseau's relationship with Classics is complex and multifaceted. Despite rejecting the colonizing mission of Carabosse, he – in the manner of the most powerful anti- and postcolonial discourses – retains those elements of the colonizer's culture that will be of use, appropriating them for himself. This was exemplified in the ironic equating of the Graeco-Roman with writing and literature, when the fact that the founding texts of ancient Greek literature originally came from oral roots undermines Carabosse's mission to impose literacy on the island. This, in turn, underlines the ludicrousness of imperial assertions of the superiority of Classics over other literatures and oral traditions. We may recall Chamoiseau, Bernabé and Confiant's argument in *Éloge de la créolité* that 'Creoleness liberates us from the ancient world' ('La Créolité nous libère du monde ancien').[73] Liberates, but does not destroy: the ancient – whether that be West African or Graeco-Roman – can remain,[74] but will no longer dominate.

Patrick Chamoiseau, then, highlights the commonalities between classical literature and creole orality: that coming from the same roots of oral storytelling and identity-defining performance (what it means to be Greek, to be barbarian, to be creole or Martiniquan...), the two have far more in common than the European colonizers tended to admit. The plays suggest that the two could co-exist and interact in fruitful ways if the power dynamics of domination are excised.[75] This is at the heart of Chamoiseau's notions of *créolité*, which are being worked out in embryonic form in these plays, most especially *Manman Dlo contre la fée Carabosse*.

Finally, Chamoiseau's use of Classics in *Manman Dlo* and elsewhere, and his preoccupation with the process of *writing* an oral tradition, urges us to think again about that moment in antiquity when the bardic tales were first written down. To take on board what John Miles Foley termed the 'immanent art' (that oral-derived texts convey meaning differently to the way purely literary ones do), but also to consider what may have been lost in the move from the oral performance of the Homeric epics to their written incarnation; or as Chamoiseau's Solibo Magnifique might ask, how easily the conch can still sense the sea once the poems took the form in which we now have them. At the same time, considering the work of the Homeric oral poets alongside that of the Martiniquan Creolists points us towards another feature that they share: a kind of poetic genius, in both senses of the word. As exceptionally talented, yes, and also as fundamentally and inextricably tied to their own time and place. It is the combination of these two, the latter perhaps almost paradoxically, which makes them works that have (in the Homeric case) and will (in the Homeric and Caribbean cases) persist and flourish in diverse times and places throughout history.

CHAPTER 14
DISMANTLING THE ANTHROPOLOGICAL MACHINE: FELIKS MORISO-LEWA'S *ANTIGÒN* AND LUIS ALFARO'S *ELECTRICIDAD*
Tom Hawkins

Throughout most of Luis Alfaro's *Electricidad* (2003), his cholo adaptation of the myth of Electra set in the Boyle Heights neighbourhood of Los Angeles, Orestes is in exile in Las Vegas, where his mentor Nino trains him for gang life.[1] Eventually, affairs in LA demand Orestes' return, as Nino explains:

> In el mundo del cholo [the world of the cholo] the Four Directions are at war ...
> We're trapped between three freeways and a Pollo Loco. La Casa de Atridas [the House of Atridas] is vulnerable.[2]

Near the play's climax, Las Vecinas ('The Neighbors', a chorus of 'mujeres [women] from the hood', 66), share their foreboding that something bad is imminent. As with Nino's words, Las Vecinas express their dread in terms that blend narrative demands with a sense that the neighbourhood, despite being in the middle of LA, is a kind of prison:

> Don't go near the windows.
> Trapped in our casas [houses].
> Trapped in our yardas [yards].
> Trapped in our barrios [neighbourhoods].[3]

These passages typify the world of Alfaro's Graeco-cholo tragedies, both in terms of the urban confinement and his Anglo-friendly idiom of lightly inflected Spanglish.

This chapter centres in the intersection of verbal hybridity, socio-geographical marginalization, and the classical tradition. To access these issues more universally, I pair *Electricidad* with Feliks Moriso-Lewa's *Antigòn* (1953), the first major work of literature in Haitian Creole.[4] These examples are sufficiently separated in time, space, plot and cultural milieu that any direct influence is improbable. Instead, these two plays help us push beyond isolated case studies and work, together with many of the chapters in this volume, towards a more theoretical framework for approaching reception studies.

My impulse to pair these plays stems from the fact that both were composed in hybrid languages. Haitian Creole and Spanglish share certain similarities but also reveal, interestingly, different linguistic histories. Haitian Creole has long been the language used by the vast majority of Haitians, but French (and, increasingly English) continues to be the language of education, politics and upward mobility. Moriso, originally a Francophone writer, championed Creole and lobbied for its official recognition, which eventually happened in 1987. Prior to Moriso's efforts, Creole was an unofficial and almost exclusively oral language with no fixed orthography, and although his aspirations for the language have not been fully realized (most Haitian authors today publish in English or French), Creole thrives in Haiti and throughout the diaspora.[5]

Like Haitian Creole, Spanglish is a hybrid language, and Spanglish speakers have often been marginalized because of their language. The Mexican Nobel Laureate Octavio Paz, for example, said that Spanglish 'is neither good nor bad but abominable' ('ni es bueno, ni es malo sino abominable'), but the prevalence and even *gravitas* of Spanglish has been on the rise recently. Already in 2000, Ilan Stavans described it as 'a vital social code, whose sheer bravura is revolutionizing both Spanish and … English'.[6] Today, Spanglish exists in a host of localized forms, especially along the US–Mexico border, and in culturally heterogeneous cities, such as Miami and New York.[7] The work of musicians like Cardi B, Pitbull, Demi Lovato and Daddy Yankee have brought Spanglish to global audiences.[8]

Despite these similarities, the differences between Haitian Creole and Spanglish loom large. Creole coalesced around many languages mixed with French, whereas Spanglish variously blends two well-established languages. One implication is that Spanglish is more fluid than Creole both regionally (e.g. LA vs. Miami) and culturally (e.g. Dominican vs. Mexican). Furthermore, Creole primarily exists in Haiti and several diasporic centres, whereas Spanglish has no geographical centre except within each local manifestation. The variability of Spanglish reflects the ethnic heterogeneity of its speakers, who combine any number of Hispanophone cultures intersecting with Anglophone contexts.

In using hybrid languages, Moriso and Alfaro consciously chose not to work in more established literary languages. Both playwrights predicate their productions on a social mission to elevate communities that have been sidelined by their limited fluency in hegemonic languages. The disadvantages of this systemic oppression are addressed more directly by Alfaro, who often has characters speak of the urban topography's confinement, and this physical isolation parallels the social consequences of poverty in Spanglish and Creole communities.[9] In choosing not to compose in French, English or Spanish, Moriso and Alfaro resist social marginalization based on a hierarchy of languages. Their work problematizes notions that 'Latin America' refers geographically to anything south of the US–Mexico border or linguistically to any Hispanophone context.[10] Alfaro's focus on cholo communities within the US challenges such geographical delimitation, and Haitian Creole undermines the linguistic assumption.

To analyse this combination of linguistic marginalization and Greek tragedy's cultural centrality, I draw upon the biopolitical theory of Giorgio Agamben, who offers a useful framework for understanding the politics of these plays.[11] Biopolitics is the Foucauldian idea that with the advent of modernity, political regimes began to assume responsibility for the organization and management of human bodies and life processes.[12] Whereas traditional sovereign authority asserted the power to kill those who transgress the law, biopolitical authority uses scientific technologies to regulate the lives of its subjects to generate biopower. Foucault was particularly interested in institutions, such as prisons and hospitals, as mechanisms ('dispositifs') of controlling and regulating lives, but similar issues arise across the political spectrum, including policies about health care, pregnant women, foetuses, stem cells, immigrants, the mentally ill, the terminally ill, etc. The 1999 film *The Matrix* envisions a science-fiction biopolitical extreme, in which humans are farmed as living batteries to power the machines that control the world. Historically, the constant point of reference for biopolitical theory is the Holocaust, in which biopolitical control became so extreme that it morphed into a politics based on the production of death ('thanatopolitics') that claimed to purify the lives of those outside the camps.[13] Agamben's extension of Foucault's basic idea raises the possibility that by reworking classical narratives, typically reserved for elite educational programs, Moriso and Alfaro can resist the social stigmatization for communities regularly denied access to privileged educations. They can also respond to Agamben by broadening the scope of biopolitics to incorporate theatre as a force that can shape what I call *biopoetic* power.

In the following pages, I harness a biopolitical apparatus to the decisions to set Greek tragedy to hybrid languages. I first discuss each play, with an emphasis on language and religion. For both Moriso and Alfaro, the prestige of the classical (and, for Moriso, French neoclassical) model becomes the fulcrum against which the dynamism of Creole and Spanglish culture can be highlighted. I conclude by showing how Moriso and Alfaro similarly harness the classical tradition to demand more equitable systems of social organization. The staging of Haitian and cholo characters and concerns constitutes a decolonizing politics that forces the hegemonic cultural paradigm to listen with new ears to voices too often ignored.

Moriso's *Antigòn*

A seductive legend describes how Moriso (1912–98) conceived his plan for *Antigòn* as a friendly bet about Creole's (in)ability to accommodate Greek drama.[14] Classical and neoclassical drama was a staple of Haitian Francophone culture, but Moriso introduced such material to the wider Creole audience and couched it in a uniquely Haitian idiom.[15] Fradinger explores this theme insightfully in making the argument that Moriso's play amounts to a '*Haitian historical drama*'.[16] Given this goal, the idea of a wager inspiring Moriso's *Antigòn* sounds too bland, and Danticat is surely correct that composing in Creole represented a bold artistic statement in politically dangerous times.[17] Moriso himself outlined a history of Creole theatre extending back to the colonial era, suggesting that his task was not so much to stretch the powers of Creole but, rather, to instantiate them forcefully in public consciousness.[18] By adapting a classical story, he could wield the cultural prestige of that tradition against the Francophone minority who saw Creole as a defective language. Whereas Fradinger interprets *Antigòn* as a performance that works through many of the enduring cultural legacies of the Haitian Revolution, I follow Moriso's statements about his choice of language to show how he made Antigone a thoroughly Haitian tale.[19]

Lang has argued that 'a Creole literature does not just happen; it is willed into existence';[20] it is, therefore, essential to understand the general linguistic climate in which Moriso made his choice. Haitian Creole emerged in the colonization of the Caribbean when the Taíno population of Hispaniola was largely wiped out; in its place, French became the language of the educated class, while the rest learned to blend elements of European, African and Caribbean languages. The great rupture came in the Revolution of 1791–1804 when nearly all Europeans died or fled at the establishment of the first independent black nation. French, thus, had an ambivalent status as the language associated with colonial oppression but also the only established language of education, administration and social advancement. As McConnell argues in her chapter in this volume, this basic pattern holds true throughout the Francophone Caribbean. The case of Haiti is different in that the Revolution removed virtually all Europeans at the establishment of independence. This transformational moment inspired Aimé Césaire to describe Haiti in *Cahier d'un Retour au Pays Natal* (1939) as the place where *négritude* asserted itself for the first time.[21] Some Haitians wanted to see the entire nation embrace French, but this has always remained a minority perspective. English might seem like an alternative, especially since Moriso, like many Haitian intellectuals, completed his advanced education in the United States (MA, Columbia, 1943).[22] Yet he grew up under the shadow of the US occupation of Haiti (1915–34), which brought English, too, into the dynamics of colonial domination.[23] The 1920s and 1930s saw early debates about the value, potential, origins and status of Creole. Was it, for example, a language at all or merely a transitional step towards 'proper' French? In 1936, linguist Jules Fain and anthropologist Suzanne Comhaire-Sylvain published contrasting arguments that asserted Haitian Creole developed primarily from maritime French and Africa, respectively.[24]

In this cultural climate, Moriso decided to write in Creole after publishing his earliest works in French. This endorsement of a language with so few readers (albeit many speakers) represents a conscious two-part choice: first, *not* to write in an established literary language, and, second, to embrace a didactic role. As Moriso recalled, in composing his *Antigòn* he was obsessed with the status of Creole. He wanted the play to succeed not just for artistic reasons but also to prove that Creole could, as he put it, do more than 'just comedies and vaudeville'; he composed his *Antigòn* 'for the benefit of literature'.[25] This emphasis, contrasting the more political focus of his sequel to the story of Antigone, *Wa Kreyon* (*King Creon*), helps explain why his Creole adaptation of Anouilh's *Médée* from 1954 as well as Fouché's *Oedipe-roi* of 1953 never made it to print. Seeing Antigone not just to the stage but onto the page took particular focus and effort.

Antigòn's prologue juxtaposes the universalism of Antigone's story, as Moriso perceived it, with its own cultural specificity. The Haitian context of Moriso's play emerges most forcefully through his use of Creole and in his likening of Greek divinities to the spirits of Vodou. He introduces the latter point after relating the background of Antigòn's family:

Se yon kont yo te tire depi lontan, lontan.
Yo tire l deja nan tout peyi.

Yo mete l deja nan tout lang.
M di kite m wè si m pa ta mete l an kreyòl tou.
M pran tou sa m te kapab pran ladan l
jan yo te rakonte l lontan, lontan . . .
Epi, m mete ladan l solèy d Ayiti,
m mete ladan l yon jan yon mannyè,
pèp d Ayiti genyen pou l konprann lavi ak lanmò,
kouray ak lapenn,
chans ak devenn.
M mete ladan l
lèsen, lèmò, mistè,
lespri ki gade gran chimen,
simityè, baryè, pyebwa, jaden, lanmè, larivyè,
ki koumande lapli, van, loray, ann Ayiti,
e ki byen sanble ak sa mesye a yo rele
dye grèk la yo.
Antigòn pral antere Polinis
kou sa ta pase ann Ayiti.
Wa Kreyon pral touye Antigòn
kou yon gran nèg Ayisyen
konn regle yon zafè kon sa.
Epi, m ap kite Antigòn, Izmèn, Marenn,
Wa Kreyon, Tirezyas, Emon, Filo
di tout pawòl Ayisyen ta di
nan yon ka parèy.
M pa reskonsab sa yo fè . . .
M kou nou tout la a.
M prale rete gade yo.
M prale chita tande yo.
Men Antigòn nou an.[26]

This is a folktale they used to tell a long, long time ago.
They had already told it in every country.
They had already translated it into every language.
I said, let me see if I can translate it into Creole too.
I took everything I could take from it – the same as they told it long, long ago.
And I put into it the Haitian Sun,
I put into it a style and a manner
the Haitian people have of understanding life and death, courage and sorrow, chance and woe.
I put into it the saints, the dead, and the mysteries,
the spirits who give protection to the highway,
cemeteries, fences, trees, fields, seas, rivers,

the spirits who command the rain, wind, and thunder in Haiti,
which seem close to what the author called the Greek gods.

> Antigòn will bury Polinis, just as might happen in Haiti.
> King Kreyon will kill Antigòn, just as a rich man in Haiti might do in such a case.
> And I will let Antigòn, Izmèn, Marenn [the girls' godmother],
> King Kreyon, Tirezyas, Emon [Haemon], Filo [Kreyon's attendant]
> say everything a Haitian would say in a similar case.
> I am not responsible for what they do ...
> I am like all of you present here.
> I will stay and watch them.
> I am going to sit down and listen to them.
> Here is our Antigòn.[27]

Moriso opens a conduit through which Haiti takes over the story of Antigone. Like a theatrical alchemist, he adds Haitian culture into the story and then steps back to observe the results. He claims responsibility for bringing the two cultures together but not for what a Haitian Antigone or Creon might say or do. The characters and the cultural inputs take control, and the playwright joins the audience to watch the tale unfold.

In bringing Antigone into Creole, Moriso focuses on the similarity between the Haitian spirits (the Vodou *lwa*) and Greek gods. The parallel between divine beings actively engaged in human society in both cultures offers a superficial connection, but Moriso also uses Vodou as the mechanism for making his two most important plot innovations: Kreyon kills Antigòn directly (as opposed to the Sophoclean suicide) and Antigòn and Emon become happily married *lwa* after their deaths.

In the Greek play, Creon speaks with Haemon (635–780) before Antigone is led away (her last line is 943), after which Tiresias enters (987) and persuades the king to reconsider his judgement. Moriso reworks this sequence such that Kreyon sends Antigòn away, then speaks with Emon, and, before Tirezyas comes on stage, he flies into a rage and calls upon the spirits to help him kill Antigòn:

> [Emon] pral chèshe Antigòn? Se zonbi Antigòn l a kontre. Se kadav Antigòn l a kenbe men. Lò l ap konprann l ap pale ak Antigòn, se ak zonbi Antigòn la val fè kontwòlè sa a. (*Kreyon ... soti ak yon vè dlo, yon kouto.*) ... Sekle-Kite,[28] ou menm ki gade lèmò, gwo lwa mwen ... ou menm k ap veye Antigòn, ale chèche kote li ye, nanm Antigòn. Mennen l vini nan vè dlo sa a pou m pike l ... m ap pike nanm Antigòn ... M ap pran nanm Antigòn ... Ou wè m nan dwa mwen. M ap pike nanm Antigòn.[29]

> [Emon] will go and look for Antigòn? He will find her zombie. He will hold the hand of Antigòn's corpse. When he finds himself talking to Antigòn, he will be talking to Antigòn's zombie. (*Kreyon ... gets out a glass of water and a knife.*) ... Sekle-Kite, you who watch over the dead, my great *Lwa* ... you who protect

Antigòn, go and look for where it is, Antigòn's soul. Bring it into this glass of water, and I will stab it ... I stab Antigòn's soul ... I am taking Antigòn's soul ... You see that I am right. I stab Antigòn's soul.

Sophocles' Antigone can be understood as someone who has been reduced to a kind of living death, since her story emphasizes how much has been stripped away from her.[30] She is a daughter who has lost her parents amid the shocking revelation of her family's history, a sister who has lost her brothers, a fiancée who rejects her betrothed in favour of a dead brother, a member of the royal family who has been deemed a criminal and, most sweepingly, a living person who has committed herself to the demands of the dead.[31] Yet for all of Sophocles' efforts to present his Antigone as isolated and vulnerable, this aspect of her character emerges even more powerfully in the Haitian idea of the zombie (*zonbi* is a Creole word derived from African, most probably Bantu, rather than European language traditions).

Before becoming a staple of modern horror, the Haitian zombie was simply an animated corpse. Not a slathering monster eager to feed on the living, the Haitian zombie stands for the control that a *bokor*, or sorcerer, can exert over de-animated flesh. Fradinger sees Kreyon's fixation on Antigòn's zombie in terms of national trauma:

> [A zombie] is a haunting image in folk belief and an extreme metaphor for national consciousness: it represents the complete loss of will on the part of a slave; it is a body whose soul has been robbed with black magic and can be used to serve a *human* master, in contrast to the Vodou servitude to the spirits. Creon summons the most nightmarish image of the colonial past: Antigòn's 'No', in contrast, is everything that the Haitian rebellion stands for.[32]

The zombie – body without soul, human without humanity – offers an extreme manifestation of the typical Antigone motif of being reduced to a kind of living death. Stratton has already connected the thoroughly Hollywood-ized zombie that begins with Romero's film *Night of the Living Dead* (1968) with marginalized populations, such as *Muselmänner* of Nazi camps and displaced or immigrant populations.[33] Yet the zombie of the modern American imagination traces its roots back to Haitian contexts. William Seabrook's occultist novel *The Magic Island* (1929), the original zombie film *White Zombie* (1932) and Zora Neale Hurston's anthropological study *Tell my Horse* (1938) were all released against the backdrop of the US occupation of Haiti (1914–34). These popular works from Moriso's young adulthood all disseminated the connection between zombies and Haiti in the Anglophone imagination. *White Zombie*, in particular, because it presents zombies initially in the economic role of soulless workers in a sugar mill, uses zombies to comment on the oppressive tactics of capitalist overlords. Set (though not filmed) in Haiti but completely Americanized, the film parallels Fradinger's contextualization of Antigòn within Haiti's anti-colonial history. In both cases – the economic and the historical – zombies represent the extremity of human degradation. The Haitian cultural trauma that gave rise to the zombie, furthermore, suggests new dimensions for the Greek Antigone.

Moriso's second major plot innovation uses another aspect of Vodou culture to upend the pessimism of Kreyon's attempt to make Antigòn into a zombie. In Vodou, the *lwa* are not a fixed pantheon. Some, such as Papa Legba and Baron Samedi, endure across the country, while others represent the spirits of recently dead ancestors. That is to say that a *lwa* comes into existence when someone honours the spirit of a departed loved one. When that *lwa* no longer receives recognition, it passes away. When Kreyon kills Antigòn, he uses his sovereign power[34] to kill a rival, and he relies upon his human position to gain the support of the spirit world and seemingly assumes that Antigòn would not join the *lwa* upon her death. As he is completing the ceremony of killing Antigòn, Tirezyas arrives and convinces Kreyon of the error of his ways.

In Sophocles' play, Creon rushes to the cave in which Antigone had been imprisoned but arrives too late; in Moriso's version, the action splits between what happens on- and off-stage. After Tirezyas claims that the spirits (*lespri*) are abandoning the king, Kreyon asks him to contact Danbala, an extremely powerful *lwa*. Danbala does not respond. Instead, when Marenn, the godmother, comes on stage, she is immediately possessed by Èzili Freda, a female spirit of love who is married to Danbala. The voice of Èzili reveals that Emon is about to die. At this point, Kreyon leaves the stage in hopes of saving his son, while Tirezyas summons the voice of the dead Antigòn. While Kreyon is offstage, Moriso accomplishes what must have been an amazing and ethereal theatrical effect. We hear, but do not see, Antigòn lead Emon into a new realm of existence as *lwa*. The voices of the two lovers describe a spirit-marriage as their earthly concerns fade away. As Antigòn and Emon recede from this world, their bliss overwhelms their consciousness. Just then, Kreyon returns and announces that where he had expected to find Antigòn and Emon, he saw only two rainbows, the outward sign that they had become children of Danbala and become *lwa*. Moriso uses Vodou as a primary mechanism for making Antigone Haitian, and by showing that Antigòn and Emon can transcend the oppressive politics of Kreyon, he urges his audience to see that they can create their own *lwa*, their own gods and ultimately their own political destiny.[35]

Alfaro's *Electricidad*

As we jump half a century from Haitian Creole to Californian Spanglish, many of the same sociolinguistic issues surrounding Moriso's play persist. Powers has brought Luis Alfaro's adaptation of *Electra* by MacArthur fellow Luis Alfaro (b. 1963) into discussions of classical reception with an article that situates his play as 'a sort of therapy for the sociological problems' of the cholo community.[36] While she notes the importance of his use of Spanglish, especially as a tool for empowering the cholo youth with whom Alfaro regularly conducts workshops, I emphasize the impact of Spanglish among his wider, primarily Anglo audience. By bringing the often-insular world of the barrio to the consciousness of theatregoers, Alfaro addresses the social marginalization that hampers his characters' communities, and demands an end to that stigma by inviting American culture to hear a little Spanglish and witness the conflation of his Graeco-cholo adaptations.

A language that can rework the canon cannot be ignored, and communities that embody the ethos of tragic performance cannot be dehumanized. Whereas Moriso's primary achievement was to make Sophocles a Haitian writer,[37] Alfaro's success emerges from the invitation to his audiences to connect their biases and expectations about Greek tragedy and the cholo barrios of the Los Angeles basin.[38]

Alfaro has developed an iconic style of bringing together Spanglish and Greek tragedy. He is a professor at the University of Southern California's School of Dramatic Arts and a MacArthur Fellow, and his early plays and poetry have won many awards. But his adaptations of classical plays, beginning with *Electricidad*, which debuted at the Borderlands Theater in Tucson, Arizona (2003), present a provocative intersection of language and plot.[39] Since then he has staged *Oedipus el Rey* (San Francisco, 2010) and two adaptations of Euripides' *Medea*: *Bruja* (San Francisco, 2012) and *Mojada* (Los Angeles, 2015).

Asked in an interview to explain the mixture of English and Spanish that he developed for *Electricidad*, Alfaro responded: 'I consciously wanted to create a play in Spanglish that people who don't speak any Spanish could understand.'[40] This formulation does not go both ways: the verbal foundation of the play is English, since Alfaro's goal is to raise up one community, which is spread across monolithic language zones, to a new level of awareness among another that is primarily monoglot. Whereas Moriso had aimed to champion the ubiquitous Creole spoken throughout Haiti at a newly elevated social register, Alfaro uses a highly accessible version of Spanglish to suit his different theatrical agenda. Thus, one main difference between the languages of Moriso and Alfaro is that, while the former wanted to present his Creole Antigone in ways that seem natural, seamless and obvious to his primary audience, the latter emphasizes narrative and verbal hybridity as the characters navigate the cramped space of the barrio ('trapped between three freeways and a Pollo Loco') that squeezes the neighbourhood into a kind of bare life.

This hybridity shapes *Electricidad* on various levels, as Alfaro coaxes his primarily Anglo-audiences into a new experience of the theatrical and the verbal landscape of America.[41] Beyond the mixture of Spanish and English, the characters themselves sense the strangeness of their Graeco-cholo roles. Early in the play, Las Vecinas ask what sort of name Clemencia is, and one suggests, with a terse humour typical of Alfaro's plays, that it might be Texan (67); a few lines later, they note the strangeness of the name Agamenón and the nickname El Auggie (68).[42] Yet the most intriguing name is that of the title character, who evoked the Greek *a-lectros*, 'unmarried' for ancient readers.[43] Electricidad sounds like Electra, though Alfaro builds on this phonetic similarity to emphasize the energetic importance of Electra's new Spanish name (Electricity) by having Orestes marvel at the myriad lights of Las Vegas. The city of lights makes him long for the simplicity of the single bulb in the family's bathroom in LA and for his sister (75), whom he calls his 'little lightbulb' (82). For Orestes, who has a 'poet's corazón ['heart']' (71), Electricidad offers a guiding light.

Beyond this, Alfaro uses the name Electricidad to convey his interest in contrasting feminine roles. His title character, with her devotion to her father, represents 'the old ways, the indigenous ways', in contrast to whom Clemencia stands for progressive innovation; in Alfaro's own words: 'when [Electricidad] kills her mother, in some ways she kills off progress. To me, Clemencia is feminism.'[44] Electricidad is thus the electricity that drives the plot, but for all the modernity implicit in her name, it is Clemencia who wants the young cholas to take charge of their finances, start businesses, fight back when beaten and reject the sexual violence of men like El Auggie that engendered la casa de Atridas. (This aspect of Clemencia's relationship with her husband explains her coldness towards her children.) As Clemencia describes her sexual history (raped at thirteen in the back of El Auggie's car, rejected by her father as a dirty tramp, sold to El Auggie and forced into motherhood), she asks Electricidad to join her in a new vision for escaping the barrio (with the Spanglish fading into straight English):

> Did I get to escojer [sic]? No my stubborn daughter, I didn't get to choose. And neither will you. History just keeps repeating itself. Cholos don't move forward. They just keep going farther into the past ... And I want to change it. I want to take back every bruise your father gave me and turn it into a dollar. I want the memory of every one of his punches to be a kiss that could make me believe in myself.[45]

Homer had presented Clytemnestra in bluntly negative and largely passive terms;[46] in Athenian tragedy, she became a more complex character, though primarily in order to highlight the plight of Electra and the ethical challenge facing Orestes;[47] but the idea of a Clytemnestra-figure as admirably progressive had no place in the ancient world. Alfaro's Clemencia is hardly a likeable character, but her story, chafing against classicizing expectations, offers a compelling twist and broadens the ancient revenge-narrative to include the ethical demands of acknowledging and redressing sexual trauma.

Like Moriso, Alfaro also adapts the religious context of his play. The general atmosphere is one of disaffected Catholicism with moments that draw on Aztec mythology (including a gently mocking aetiology of the cholo), but Alfaro's Ifigenia uses religion to reshape the urban landscape. In Greek tragedy, Agamemnon kills Iphigenia before the Trojan War, so she is absent from stories about his doomed homecoming. Yet in *Iphigenia at Tauris*, Euripides has Artemis snatch the girl away from the knife and take her to Tauris. Alfaro plays up this aspect of his La Ifi, as she is known, being both dead and alive in his description of her as the meanest and most violent of them all, who is now born again. Both Abuela, Clemencia's mother, and Electricidad had assumed that Ifi died or was in jail, because she has been absent for so long, and they are surprised to see her return. Yet they are even more surprised to hear that she has been in a convent in Fresno.[48] Alfaro describes this religious rebirth as a socially viable way out of gang violence.[49] Ifi offers Electricidad an alternative to her obsessive, self-destructive devotion to her father and his violent legacy. Before running back to the convent, Ifi asks Electricidad to reconsider what killing their mother will accomplish (79). In contrast to the progressive vision of Clemencia, therefore, Ifi represents the possibility of side-stepping the cycles of violence demanded by the gang system.

La Ifi also draws attention to another type of language in Alfaro's play that reworks a classical motif: scars. Odysseus is recognized because of his famous scar, which he earned on a nearly deadly hunt (*Od.* 19.455–527). Euripides undermines the heroic *bona fides* of recognition-by-scar when his Orestes is discovered by the scar he got as a boy while playing with a pet deer (Eur. *El.* 573–4).[50] Far from ennobling, this scar suggests that Orestes was a typically accident-prone child, and it fits with Euripides' realism in drawing his characters. In all of Alfaro's Graeco-cholo plays, a different kind of bodily mark is always visible on stage, namely tattoos. His Orestes learns from Nino that tattoos tell your life's story, and that each one must be earned, since they preserve the achievements and sorrows of the community.[51] But Ifi, whose tattoos are not hidden by her Catholic school-girl attire,[52] connects these tattoos to the emotionally scarring experiences of their lives: 'Hermana [Sister], [El Auggie] gave us these tattoos. But these tattoos are also scars.'[53] At their reunion, Orestes brags to Electricidad that he has learned to read 'the map of our tattoos',[54] but only Ifi seems to realize the trauma that each recalls. Again, she offers a different perspective, one from outside the barrio, because Alfaro has constructed her in terms of the language of spiritual rebirth.

The language of Alfaro's tragedies encapsulates and reiterates his broader theatrical aims. The preponderance of English welcomes his primarily Anglo-audience into the storyline, but at every opportunity he insinuates material that allows viewers to see a little further into the cholo world. As if in a dialogue between audience and characters, everyone shares the burden of working through this strange fit. The Spanglish ought to disorient – though only slightly – anyone who knows no Spanish; but so too do the classical names strike the characters within the narrative as strange. Alfaro continually reminds us that Greek tragedy was never meant to take root in this cultural context, and that is precisely the perspective that makes his adaptations so compelling. Whereas Moriso had brought Greek tragedy into his Creole community to demonstrate the language's literary potential, Alfaro shares his Graeco-cholo tragedy with an audience that goes far beyond the Spanglish world in order to offer a glimpse into the barrio.

Conclusions: Agamben, bare life and the classical tradition

In *Homo Sacer*, published in Italian in 1995, Agamben develops Foucault's theories about biopolitics in two ways that are relevant to my reading of Moriso's *Antigòn* and Alfaro's *Electricidad*. First, Agamben sees biopolitics as a fundamental consequence of sovereignty rather than, as Foucault had suggested, its modern successor. He finds an Aristotelian distinction between *zoê*, biological life, and *bios*, a way of life within the polity, as proof that the assertion of sovereignty involves a biopolitical differentiation between these two categories. The foundational sovereign act delimits acceptable forms of *bios* from reduced forms of existence that Agamben calls bare life: 'The fundamental categorical pair of Western politics is not that of friend/enemy but that of bare life/political existence, *zoê/bios*, exclusion/inclusion.'[55] This bare life is exemplified in the Roman concept of the *homo sacer*, whose legal status initially seems contradictory: anyone may kill the *homo sacer* with impunity, but he cannot be killed as a sacrifice.[56] Agamben explains this idea in terms of a political ban, in which the *homo sacer* is included within the political order specifically by being excluded from it.[57] Much as the Church includes within its purview those who have been excommunicated from participating in its services, or the state maintains citizen-prisoners who are deprived of many forms of civic participation, the *homo sacer* is included by a logic of exclusion. The *homo sacer* exists outside normal civic life so that the rest of the population may define themselves in terms of their full inclusion; he represents the outer surface of the wall that separates civilized social space from its opposite.

Secondly, Agamben reformulates the modern situation as a shift from treating bare life as the excluded exception to a scenario in which it 'gradually begins to coincide with the political realm'.[58] Nazi concentration camps represent an ultimate example: 'The Jew living under Nazism is the privileged negative referent of the new biopolitical sovereignty and is, as such, a flagrant case of a *homo sacer* in the sense of a life that may be killed but not sacrificed.'[59] For Agamben, the isolated Roman *homo sacer* serves as the model for marginalized populations within modern states that permits the rest of society to see in themselves a naturally justified lifestyle in contrast to groups who are now reduced to bare life and excluded by a process of inclusion.

Having laid out the basic framework of his political theory in *Homo Sacer*, Agamben has refined his thinking in a series of subsequent works. In *The Open*, he develops a critical conceptual model of how a group identifies or creates the *homo sacer* in its midst. Based on a reading of Heidegger, Agamben asserts that 'the originary political conflict . . . [is] between the humanity and animality of man' and that 'humanity has been obtained only through a *suspension* of animality'.[60] Whereas many theories about what differentiates humans from non-human animals begin from the assumption that humans have something in excess (e.g. language, a soul, *vel sim.*), Agamben claims that humanity exists through the animalization of certain persons achieved via a mechanism that he calls 'the anthropological machine',[61] which marks the *homo sacer* as something other. This is the mechanism that has, at various points in history, deemed slaves, barbarians, women, Jews, Africans, homosexuals, epileptics, the impoverished, pagans, the homeless and immigrants to be less than human – an exclusion that creates the privileged category of human.

In applying this biopolitical model to Moriso's and Alfaro's contexts, we can recognize that the Creole population of Haiti and the Spanglish-speaking cholo populations of urban California have long suffered under an anthropological machine that has reduced them to something approaching Agamben's bare life.[62] This process results from a systemic racism within which non-hegemonic languages serve as one marker of marginalization. (We can contrast this to the English-only movement, which aspires to the institutionalization of language privilege in the United States.) The Creole and Spanglish stories may be less shocking than the carefully and proactively calculated genocidal plan of the Holocaust, but within their wider social contexts in Haiti and the US, speakers of these hybrid languages have been deemed less deserving, less valued, less visible and ultimately less human than their Francophone and Anglophone counterparts.

Yet whereas Agamben presents his biopolitical theories in markedly negative terms that make the idea of resistance seem all but impossible, I suggest that sovereign power does not have exclusive control of the anthropological machine.[63] Indeed sovereign power responds to and is shaped by cultural trends including literature and theatre, and Moriso and Alfaro, in using hybrid languages to retell ancient Greek tales, insist that bare life can be a space of contestation, that bare life can speak back to sovereign power from below and demand a new sociopolitical landscape.

A key biopolitical debate hinges on the origins of sovereignty, since the establishment of a political order does not have an obvious source of authority through which it brings itself into existence. As Antoni Negri puts it, the power to create a new order (*il potere constituente*) is 'an act of choice, the precise determination that opens a horizon, the radical apparatus of something that does yet exist, and whose conditions of existence imply that the creative act does not lose its characteristics in the act of creating'.[64] He contrasts this inchoate force with the normative and fixed parameters of sovereignty, which represents the 'termination' and 'exhaustion of the freedom that constituent power carries'.[65] By way of conclusion, I suggest that this model speaks to the adaptations of Moriso and Alfaro by seeing their plays as examples of constituent power that target the sovereign cultural authority of the classical tradition. Their plays represent revolutionary acts, examples of Danticat's injunction to 'create dangerously',[66] that can shape the biopolitical framework of respective cultures. Any specific form of biopolitical power, built upon the marginalization of a particular form of the Other, must arise from cultural inputs that frame and condition that system. Foucault emphasized the technologies that foster and inform biopolitical structures, but theatre and literature, too, can serve as such a Foucauldian *dispositifs* and can exert their own bio-*poetic* influence upon a system.[67] Biopolitical theory has tended to focus in negative terms on how such *dispositifs* are used to marginalize certain groups (as with the history of germ theory and eugenics underpinning the Nazi thanatopolitical regime), but Moriso and Alfaro make an implicit claim that biopoetics can work in the opposite direction as well. *Antigòn* and *Electricidad* work towards dismantling the anthropological machine that has kept Haitian Creoles and Spanglish Cholos in conditions of bare life. In both cases, bare life exists in large part due to a language segregation that connects to wider patterns of social marginalization (as Alfaro stresses through his comments about the organization of urban space).

Throughout the so-called Western tradition, especially since the Renaissance, classical learning has fuelled the anthropological machine in ways that legitimize the privileged status of elite white males. Richard Thomas, for example, has highlighted extreme cases of this in the attitude towards antiquity within Italian Fascism and German Nazism, and the Pharos website is now tracking the use of classical material by white supremacist groups.[68] Emily Greenwood has aptly described this process of identification between exclusive, privileged groups and the classical tradition in terms of a network of 'false genealogies and cultural traditions masked as historical continuities'.[69] These alleged historical continuities have traditionally contributed to mapping the globe in ways that mimic and reiterate patterns of Eurocentric sovereignty.

The infrastructure of that system reveals itself in the plays by Moriso and Alfaro, as I have outlined above. Most strikingly, Moriso uses the idea of Kreyon turning Antigòn into a zombie as a metaphor for the history of Francophone oppression of the Creole population of Haiti, and Alfaro continually returns to images that show the barrio in LA to be an island ('split by the freeway. / Border the river. / In the shadow of the skyscrapers')[70] around which the high-profile wealth, beauty and opportunity of Southern California speed. In many ways these playwrights, by speaking from within these communities that have been squeezed into the confines of bare life, articulate a demand for new considerations of the biopolitical landscape. By appropriating and speaking through the sovereign force of the classical tradition, they can lay bare and undo the 'false genealogies' Greenwood describes. Yet in other ways, one might wonder if the classical canon has simply expanded its purview. The genealogies may be false but the cultural capital of ancient Greece and Rome remains. Did Moriso and Alfaro have to participate in the legacy of that canon in order to achieve their theatrical and cultural aspirations? Such a question is impossible to answer succinctly. It may well be that even as Cholo and Creole adaptations of Athenian tragedy erode connections between the classical canon and structures of privilege, they may nevertheless reiterate the cultural centrality of that very canon – social and demographic progressivism counterbalanced by a conservative valorization of literary-aesthetic norms.[71]

CHAPTER 15
ANTIGONE UNDEAD: TRAGEDY AND BIOPOLITICS IN PERLA DE LA ROSA'S *ANTÍGONA: LAS VOCES QUE INCENDIAN EL DESIERTO*

Jesse Weiner

In Latin America, *Antigone* has been adapted to the stage more than any other ancient play.[1] This is in part because *Antigone* offers a 'source of inspiration' to 'give voice to the disappeared, defend those who died, and demand proper burial as an act of defiance, mourning, and remembrance'.[2] Many Latin American *Antigones* engage with other important social issues, such as 'female victims of drugs, prostitution, uprooting, and war'.[3] Antigone represents 'a symbol of resistance to civic oppression'[4] and frequently calls for a 'renegotiation of social boundaries and cultural values'.[5]

This chapter focuses on a Mexican rewriting of Sophocles' play by Perla de la Rosa, *Antígona: las voces que incendian el desierto* (*Antigone: The Voices that Set the Desert on Fire*). The play debuted in 2004, both set and staged in Juárez against a backdrop of extreme extrajudicial violence.[6] Between 1993 and 2004, Ciudad Juárez (on Mexico's northern border, opposite El Paso, Texas) was plagued by a series of rapes, murders and disappearances of hundreds of women – an epidemic that gained international notoriety as *el feminicidio* ('the femicide' or 'the feminicide').[7] What corpses were recovered were found discarded like trash in and around the city, and many bore signs of sexual assault, mutilation and torture. For example, in a now infamous 2001 incident, the bodies of eight female victims were discovered in a Juárez cottonfield (de la Rosa signals this episode with the setting of Scene 5 of her play). The majority of the victims came from socially marginalized populations; most were poor industrial workers, many of them immigrants, employed by one of the city's numerous factories, known as *maquilas* or *maquiladoras*.[8] These serial rapes and murders were dubbed *el feminicidio* not only because of the scale of the violence with which women have been targeted in Juárez but also because of the impunity with which these crimes have been committed; scandalously enough, since 2004 there has been only one conviction for one count of murder in connection with these cases.[9] While the femicide has to some extent tapered off in recent years, numerous subsequent incidents fit this pattern and the city remains immersed in a general culture of violence done with impunity.

As part of its inquiry into social boundaries and cultural values, de la Rosa's *Antígona* features a diverse cast of nameless characters, identified only by type (woman, mother, murderer, journalist). These characters perform choral functions, and this democratized cast offers a wider range of perspectives on the action than would, say, a Sophoclean chorus of town elders. This expanded cast has the effect of broadening the play's focus beyond Antígona herself to the community at large. Although the play is set in the mythic stage world of Tebas, de la Rosa's Tebas is manifestly a foil for Juárez and so connects with 'a "real" extra-textual referent'.[10] In this play, Polynices is reimagined as Polinice, Antígona's sister and a missing *maquiladora* worker presumed to be among the hundreds of murder victims. Antígona must therefore search for Polinice before burial can happen. Antígona never finds Polinice and, at the play's end, she continues to wander the desert in search of her sister.

While de la Rosa's *Antígona* is by no means the only play to address the femicide, nor unique in its use of Greek myth and tragedy to do so, it is remarkable in that it was staged in Juárez itself at the height of the femicide.[11] The play, as I have argued before, challenges its audience to re-evaluate its gender discourse and to indict its civic leadership with complicity in a disturbing normalization of violence.[12] As with Bárbara Colio's *Usted está aquí* (*You Are Here*; 2009) analysed by María Florencia Nelli, de la Rosa uses *Antigone* 'to help "denounce the standardization and trivialization of violence" by issuing "a crude wake-up call"' to her audience.[13] This audience was, at first, local to Juárez but became international with performances in Europe, and the play has since been revived in the United States.[14] *Antígona* thus spoke to a local audience while also garnering international attention.

I here offer a biopolitical reading of *Antígona* and its motif of symbolic or social death.[15] As is the case with many Latin American adaptations of Sophocles' play, de la Rosa's play participates in a long multinational and multicultural tradition, which reaches forward from Sophocles to include the *Antigone*s of Jean Anouilh and Bertolt Brecht,[16] as well as philosophical interpretations of the *Antigone* tradition by such modern thinkers as Jacques Lacan and Judith Butler. This tradition understands Antigone as a liminal figure who inhabits a space between two deaths, a symbolic and a real one. My analysis situates de la Rosa's play within this rich tradition of undead Antigones, seeking to establish points of continuity with and, more importantly, points of departure from the play's dramatic models and iconic interpretations of them. I read symbolic death in this rewriting through Giorgio Agamben's biopolitics, which offer a powerful framework for approaching not only the Antigone myth but also some of the most critical issues and humanitarian crises of modernity.[17] In this Mexican rewriting, symbolic death has more to do with extrajudicial violence, the threat of being killed without punishment, and reduction to 'bare life' (a term Agamben borrows from Walter Benjamin's *Critique of Violence*) than it does with the sheer will, desire or individuality of Antigone herself.

My reading builds upon and expands the scopes and arguments of my previous work. I have earlier used Agamben's work to offer a sustained reading of Sophocles' *Antigone* through its use of *bios* and *zoē*, two Greek words for 'life' at the core of Agamben's biopolitics.[18] Reading de la Rosa through Agamben thus places her play in conversation with previous *Antigone*s that have made distinctions between biological existence and life worth living – between political inclusion and exclusion – central elements of their drama. But this is more important than applying the same modern lens to yet another play related to Sophocles; de la Rosa's play restages the Antigone myth and symbolic death to address an actual, essential biopolitical crisis of modernity, and the stakes are far higher. Moreover, symbolic death may reach back to Sophocles' version of the myth, but, as I show, de la Rosa applies the trope in a new and radical way. I suggest that de la Rosa's *Antígona* goes beyond its predecessors to apply the space between the two deaths diffusely. De la Rosa overgoes both Sophocles and Brecht by amplifying her use of the space between the two deaths and applies the trope of symbolic death democratically, well beyond the figure of Antígona herself. In so doing, the play explores the femicide as egalitarian, shared trauma far more than it celebrates the death drive or Antigone's individuality. As a foil for Juárez, de la Rosa's Tebas comes to resemble Giorgio Agamben's conception of the camp. So long as hundreds of women remain missing, unidentified and unburied, and the spectre of violence looms over the city's women, the dead haunt the living and the entire community is condemned to the realm of the not-fully-alive.

Antigones undead: Symbolic death in Sophocles and the Sophoclean tradition

Borders and binary divisions permeate *Antígona* every bit as much as they do Sophocles' text, perhaps none more than those between the living and the dead. Many of de la Rosa's living characters inhabit the space between the two deaths, while Polinice, Antígona's sister, is but one of hundreds of unburied dead in this adaptation (*Antígona* retains Ismene as a character but does not include an Eteocles figure). As we will see, at least one corpse might even be said to be symbolically alive. De la Rosa thus reimagines and redeploys one of the most central motifs of the *Antigone* tradition.

Antígona remains alive at the play's end and, unlike Sophocles' heroine who is entombed in a cave, she walks the wide-open expanse of the desert. Nevertheless, as I will demonstrate, the Sophoclean motifs of symbolic death and the space between the two deaths pervade *Antígona*. However, de la Rosa uses them for a different effect than do her predecessors in the *Antigone* tradition.

Sophocles' Antigone suffers living entombment, and the paradox of being simultaneously alive and dead plays out verbally throughout the play.[19] Antigone tells Ismene, 'for you chose to live, but I to die' (σὺ μὲν γὰρ εἵλου ζῆν, ἐγὼ δὲ κατθανεῖν, 555) and that her 'soul has died long ago' (ἡ δ' ἐμὴ ψυχὴ πάλαι / τέθνηκεν, 559–60). Creon insists that, having been sentenced to death, the living Antigone 'no longer exists' (οὐ γὰρ ἔστ' ἔτι, 567). The motif is still more prevalent in the *kommos*, the lamentation song performed by the chorus and Antigone as she leaves the city for the cave. Antigone laments, 'Hades who lulls all to sleep is taking me, still living, to the shore of Acheron' (ἀλλά μ' ὁ παγ- / κοίτας Ἅιδας ζῶσαν ἄγει / τὰν Ἀχέροντος / ἀκτάν, 810–13). The chorus responds, 'but, self-willed, you alone of mortals descend to Hades while living' (ἀλλ' αὐτόνομος ζῶσα μόνη δὴ / θνητῶν Ἅιδην καταβήσῃ, 821–2). The repetition suggests thematic importance. Antigone and the chorus each make much of a living journey to

Hades and Acheron, while Creon re-emphasizes that Antigone will be entombed while living. Perhaps most poignantly, Antigone asserts her liminal status through an opposite articulation: she who is both alive and dead belongs with neither: 'Ah, wretched one, neither a resident alien among mortals nor a corpse among corpses, neither with the living nor with the dead' (ἰὼ δύστανος, βροτοῖς / οὔτε <νεκρὸς> νεκροῖσιν / μέτοικος, οὐ ζῶσιν, οὐ θανοῦσιν, 850–2). As Charles Segal observes of the repetition of μέτοικος at 852 and 868, the phrasing is 'almost a refrain' and 'evokes her emotional suffering as she recognizes, more and more fully, her isolation'.[20] Sophocles' imagery also develops a 'bride of Hades' motif, common to the tragic genre (and beyond), which enhances Antigone's murky state between life and death.[21]

Brecht's *Antigone*, also an important model for de la Rosa's *Antígona*, similarly makes vivid use of Sophocles' motif of symbolic death. Brecht, for instance, writes in his *Antigone Legend* that 'the cave shall receive her, living and dead'.[22] In Brecht's play proper, Antigone declares that she 'has a dead soul' (524), while Creon specifies that Antigone be put 'alive into the cave ... as though she were buried' and given 'the only meal that is fit for the dead' (713–17). The chorus tells Antigone that 'living your life, you go alive down to death' (759). Likewise, Brecht's Antigone marginalizes herself from the living, proclaiming, 'I mourn for you, survivors' (846). Antigone's liminal status in Brecht is amplified in its Anglophone traditions, since Judith Malina's script for her Living Theatre production of the play translates Brecht's '*Braut Des Acheron bin ich*' (I am the bride of Acheron; 765–6) as 'I am the *Bridge* of Acheron'. Whether this was a conscious decision or a marvellously poignant typo, Malina's emendation from 'bride' to 'bridge' creates vivid imagery of Antigone straddling the world of the living and the world of the dead while occupying the centre space between the two.

De la Rosa's *Antígona* fits this mould in several respects, collapsing the boundary between life and death. Early in the play, Ismene proclaims to Antígona, 'Finally, we are still here. Alive!' ('Finalmente nosotras seguimos aquí. ¡Vivas!'), to which Antígona responds, 'I am not' ('Yo no', Scene 4).[23] Antígona tells Ismene that if their sister Polinice is dead, 'we ought to live her death' ('deberemos vivir su muerte'). Similarly, Antígona echoes her models and proclaims to Creón, 'Since the day they killed my sister: I am dead!' ('Desde el día que mataron a mi hermana: ¡estoy muerta!', Scene 13).

Stemming from its Sophoclean source text, Antigone's liminal status between life and death has frequently been interpreted as a matter of choice. After all, Sophocles' Antigone insists, 'I chose to die', and the chorus interprets Antigone's fate as 'self-willed' or 'self-ruled' (αὐτόνομος, 821) and destruction by 'self-willed passion' (σὲ δ' αὐτόγνωτος ὤλεσ' ὀργά, 'your self-willed passion has ruined you', 875).[24] As Paul Allen Miller observes of lines 559–60, Antigone insists she had chosen death even before Creon's decree against the burial of Polynices.[25] Anouilh's Antigone proclaims: 'I don't want to understand ... I'm here for something else besides understanding. I am here to say "no" to you and to die' ('Je ne veux pas comprendre ... Moi je suis là pour autre chose que pour comprendre. Je suis là pour dire non et pour mourir').[26]

For this reason, Lacan uses Antigone not only to theorize his *l'espace de l'entre-deux-morts* but also to illustrate his conception of the death drive:

Antigone appears as αὐτόνομος ... She pushes to the limit the realization of something that might be called the pure and simple desire of death as such. She incarnates this desire.[27]

As Miller notes, Antigone is sublime in Lacan's reading, since the heroine becomes the incarnation of pure desire in a perfect moment between life and death. 'For Lacan, it is the beauty of Antigone's choice [death] of a Good beyond all recognized goods, beyond the pleasure principle, that gives her character its monumental status and makes her a model for an ethics of creation as opposed to conformity.'[28]

When Butler, in turn, writes of the heroine's social death in Sophocles, she notes that Antigone's 'fate will be an uncertain one, living within death, dying within life'.[29] This uncertainty pervades de la Rosa's play. However, I suggest that de la Rosa expands the motif of symbolic death well beyond the individuality of Antigone herself in ways that reach beyond her source texts. Absent in *Antígona* are causes for celebrating and fetishizing Antigone's desire for death (Lacan) as well as corruptions of kinship relations (Butler). Thus, even as *Antígona*'s motif of symbolic death participates within the traditions I have sketched above, these very traditions serve as points of departure for understanding de la Rosa's play.

Antigone reanimated: Symbolic death in de la Rosa's *Antígona*

De la Rosa's Antígona hardly represents pure desire and does not hurtle towards self-willed destruction, nor does she choose death as in Sophocles or Anouilh. Antígona does not die in de la Rosa's play; quite the opposite of living entombment, de la Rosa's protagonist wanders the expanse of the desert and continues her search for Polinice's body. Despite declaring to Creón that she is already dead, Antígona does not want to die. She explicitly supplicates the tyrant ('I beg/supplicate you', 'te lo suplico') and calls upon him to release her, shouting: 'Let me go!' ('¡Suéltame!', Scene 13).

In fact, to the extent that Antígona occupies the space between the two deaths, she is put there forcibly by others, not by her own will. This emerges powerfully when Antígona performs her social death by visiting the morgue (entering from below, no less).[30] On her first visit, Antígona witnesses an armed guard speaking to the corpse of a murdered girl as if it were both dead and alive: 'Wandering again? You will not escape the refuge of death' ('¿Otra vez vagando? No escapes del refugio de la muerte', Scene 9). The stage directions then specify that the guard lifts the corpse and dances with it, 'intimately', in a macabre '*danza fúnebre*' (funeral dance): 'He lifts her and when he feels her body, pulls it close to his, then initiates a brief funeral dance, a single beat, slow, intimate' ('La levanta y al sentir su cuerpo, la estrecha al suyo, luego inicia una breve danza fúnebre, un solo compás, lento, íntimo'). When Antígona sneaks into the morgue a second time, the guard catches her and, as per the stage directions, forcibly 'embraces her and dances with her in the exact same way he had with the dead girl':

¿No te da asco tocar cadáveres? ¿Qué tienes ahí? [mete la mano bajo su falda, la abraza y baila con ella al igual que lo hiciera con la muchacha muerta]. (Scene 11)

Touching corpses doesn't disgust you? What have you got here? [he puts his hand beneath her skirt, embraces her, and dances with her in the same way he had with the dead girl].

The scene sexualizes traditions that make Antigone a 'bride of death', and Antígona is violently treated as if she were already dead.[31] Moreover, Antígona shares this space between the two deaths, since the guard intimately dances with a corpse as if she were alive. The bodies of both the living and the dead are violently objectified by a uniformed representative of the state and they become virtually indistinguishable.

De la Rosa constructs a democratized and violent space between the two deaths, and applies it well beyond the figure of Antígona. Many characters in the play may be understood to undergo symbolic death and, while Antígona herself is heroic, the same cannot be said of each example. For instance, the only actions approaching funerary rites in the play are performed not on the corpse of a victim but rather on a living murderer. In a chilling scene in which a killer never utters a word, his mother washes blood from his body while reciting prayers (Scene 6; Figure 15.1). This murderer does not embody beauty in any sense.

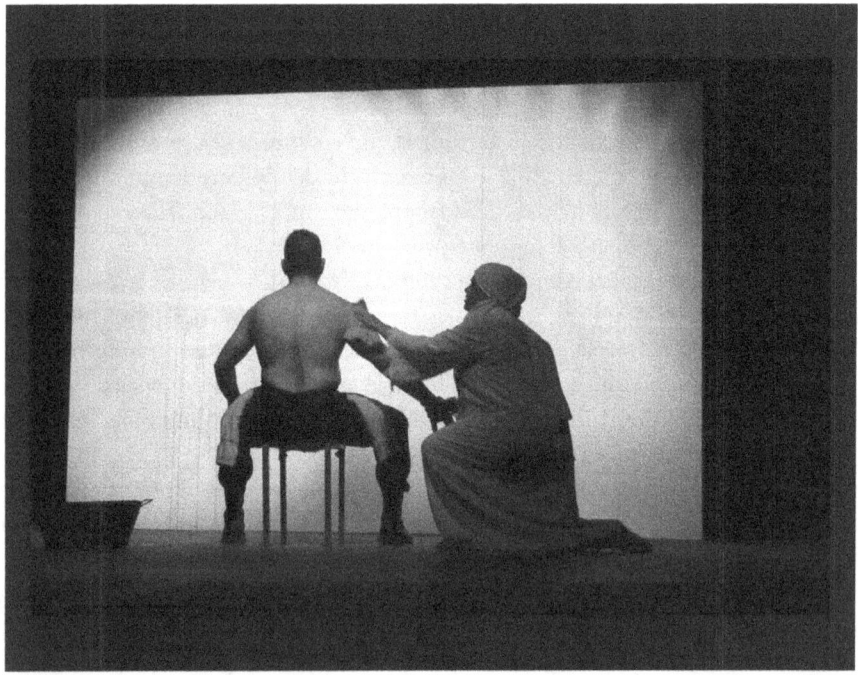

Figure 15.1 Perla de la Rosa's *Antígona: las voces que incendian el desierto*, Scene 6. Copyright. Guadalupe de la Mora.

Perhaps most significantly, the women of Tebas paradoxically live underground, not because they choose death but because they fear it. In a manner that recalls Antigone's burial of Polynices in Sophocles' play, these women cover themselves with sand 'in order to continue living' ('para continuar viviendo'). This information is used to introduce the play's action, and its structural primacy in the script indicates its importance. De la Rosa's play opens without Antígona on stage and, although she models her first full scene on Brecht's prologue, de la Rosa introduces her drama with her own original prologue. A nameless woman, waiting for the bus, informs the audience:

> Ser mujer aquí es estar en peligro. Por ello decidimos construir refugios bajo la arena. Cubrirnos de arena. Ampararnos bajo la arena para continuar viviendo. (Prologue)

> To be a woman here is to be in danger. Because of this, we decided to build shelters beneath the sand. To cover ourselves in sand. To shield ourselves under the sand in order to continue living.

Thus, with imagery recalling the manner in which Sophocles' Antigone buries Polynices, de la Rosa opens her play with the townswomen undergoing a symbolic death in order to escape violence and to stay alive. Later, when explaining her decision to enter an underground refuge, the woman insists that the stench of death besieges the city above: 'There is an overwhelming smell, up there, in the city. Could it be the plague?' ('Hay un olor insoportable, allá arriba, en la ciudad ¿Será la peste?', Scene 12).

At the play's midpoint, the woman from the prologue returns to give a brief monologue, entitled *La anécdota* (The Anecdote, Scene 10). The scene's stage directions specify that 'she now unravels the bandages from her fingers just as life unravels day by day' ('ahora deshace el vendaje de sus dedos, como se deshace día a día la vida'), suggesting that her life edges towards a life not worthy of being lived. The woman again speaks of life in Tebas in terms of mortal danger and liminality. She shares an anecdote in which she was nearly killed in a drive-by shooting while waiting for the bus, relating that 'In this city it is difficult to know you're alive' ('En esta ciudad es difícil saberse vivo'). While she describes hiding beneath a bus stop bench amidst several rounds of gunfire, the woman juxtaposes her fear and mortal danger ('They already killed someone, I thought', 'Ya mataron a uno, pensé') with vivid descriptions of feeling alive:

> Mi corazón se desbordaba, todo el pulso de la vida pendía de un hilo, después una tercera descarga ... por último el silencio ... por cierto aún estoy viva.

> My heart leapt out of my chest, the very pulse of life hung from a thread, then a third discharge of gunfire ... finally, silence ... by the way I'm still alive.

Caught in the wrong place at the wrong time, the woman's rapidly beating heart while her life hangs in the balance evokes a limit zone between life and death far different than that depicted in the *Antigone*s of Sophocles, Anouilh, and Brecht. Moreover, the scene's opening declaration of ontological uncertainty undermines the closing assurance of survival. The woman appears at best unsure of whether she is still alive. When she picks up her narrative again in Scene 12, she sees herself in the corpse of another woman.

Rather than portraying a fetishized death drive or using symbolic death to celebrate Antigone's individuality, de la Rosa stages an entire Thebes experiencing symbolic death before actual death, whereas the actual dead are not afforded burial or funerary rites. Žukauskaitė has observed 'an uncanny symmetry' in Sophocles' play between 'the unburied body of Polynices' and 'the body of Antigone, which is alive but enclosed in a tomb'.[32] In de la Rosa's rewriting, this symmetry is even more pronounced. However, the symmetry is not so much between the bodies of Polinice and Antígona as it is between the bodies of innumerable victims and the city's women en masse, who have undergone living entombment beneath the sand. Hundreds of dead, unburied and unidentified bodies litter the desert and morgue, while the city's women play dead as a defence mechanism for fear of being raped and murdered with absolute impunity.

Biopolitics

Giorgio Agamben's biopolitics provide a useful lens for approaching de la Rosa's *Antígona* and its use of symbolic death.[33] 'Biopolitics' is a term Agamben draws from Foucault to refer to social and political power over biological life. Biopolitics is, for Foucault, control over bodies, and biopower is the right to take (or make) life. While Agamben never mentions *Antigone* specifically in *Homo Sacer*, his discussion of sovereign power and bare life has been applied to Sophocles' source text (though often briefly) with some frequency over the two decades since *Homo Sacer*'s publication.[34] In these readings, the politics of exclusion reduce Antigone to 'bare life', a term borrowed from Walter Benjamin's *Critique of Violence*. 'Bare life' is a state, which, in an Aristotelian schema, exists between death and a politically realized life.[35]

Agamben begins *Homo Sacer* by reaching back to ancient Greek semantics and philosophy to draw a distinction between *bios* and *zoē*, two Greek words for life:

> The Greeks had no single word to express what we mean by the word 'life'. They used two terms that, although traceable to a common etymological root, are semantically and morphologically distinct: *zoē*, which expressed the simple fact of living common to all living beings (animals, men, or gods), and *bios*, which represented the form or way of living proper to an individual or a group.[36]

Applied to Sophocles, Antigone has *zoē*, the biological state of being common to all animals, but not *bios*, a proper way of life marked by political inclusion. She is, politically speaking, the living dead. As Andrew Norris writes of Creon's punishment of Antigone, her entombment results in 'a monstrous confusion of death and life'.[37]

María Florencia Nelli has brought Agamben's work to bear on Griselda Gambaro's *Antígona Furiosa* (1986), arguing that Antígona and the *desaparecidos* (disappeared persons) of Argentina's 'Dirty War' are, in effect, *homines sacri*. 'Deprived of all their rights and political status', they dwell 'in a no-man's land between life and death', where 'there is no longer *bios* but only *zoē*'.³⁸ In de la Rosa's version, whose focus is broadened beyond Antígona herself to the femicide's victims at large, a similar dynamic is at play.

The corpses of Polinice and the other victims of the femicide invoke the politics of exclusion. As Fradinger writes of Sophocles' Polynices, 'that the corpse in question is one of their own – not that of an outsider – is essential to the operation of inclusion/ expulsion ... Creon's carving out of an enemy is performed inside the community.'³⁹ At issue are questions over which members of the community enjoy political rights and the sovereignty of an individual or government over the bodies of its citizens. Following Sophoclean precedent, Creón redefines the political borders of his community by excluding femicide victims and critics from the body politic while simultaneously marking their bodies as subject to the most extreme violence.

Antígona's first line onstage identifies Tebas as a 'desolate city that has lost its voice' ('desolada ciudad ... la que perdió la voz', Scene 2). This loss of voice is political. Creón marginalizes both the femicide's victims and those who call for justice and government recognition of the violence.⁴⁰ Creón's first words distinguish those who speak of the femicide from the *ciudadanos* (citizens) and suggest that the former lack basic rights of citizenship when he calls them 'wretched women without a country' ('miserables mujeres sin patria') whom 'we cannot tolerate' ('no podemos tolerar', Scene 3).⁴¹ Both Creón and Eurídice impugn the characters of *desaparecidas* and their families, thereby devaluing their lives. Antígona speaks of 'the sacred right to life' ('el sagrado derecho a la vida', Scene 4). However, her life is sacred in the sense of Agamben: it is politically marginalized and can be taken away without the act being recognized as criminal or called murder.

Creón further excludes the city's women from *bios* in the Aristotelian sense, when he ridicules Antígona, asking, 'What do you know about politics? You are a woman' ('¿Qué sabes de política? Eres mujer', Scene 13). As Butler connects Agamben with Sophocles' Antigone, these women are denied entrance 'into the life of the legitimate community in which standards of recognition permit for an attainment of humanness'.⁴² This power to exclude is, for Agamben (who uses Carl Schmitt's definition of the sovereign), the very marker of sovereignty.⁴³ Sophocles' Antigone, too, places sovereign power at the root of human nature and forcefully connects it to political inclusion and exclusion. The chorus' iconic 'Ode to Man' makes this clear. At the ode's opening, the chorus names man 'the most powerful/awe-inspiring/terrible' (δεινότερον, 333) creature precisely because of the capacity to subjugate and subdue.⁴⁴ After listing several examples of mastery (sea-faring, agriculture, hunting and animal domestication), the argument climaxes with its ultimate example of man's power:

σοφόν τι τὸ μηχανόεν τέχνας ὑπὲρ ἐλπίδ' ἔχων
τοτὲ μὲν κακόν, ἄλλοτ' ἐπ' ἐσθλὸν ἕρπει.
νόμους παρείρων⁴⁵ χθονὸς
θεῶν τ' ἔνορκον δίκαν
ὑψίπολις· ἄπολις ὅτῳ τὸ μὴ καλὸν
ξύνεστι τόλμας χάριν.

μήτ' ἐμοὶ παρέστιος
γένοιτο μήτ' ἴσον φρονῶν
ὃς τάδ' ἔρδοι.⁴⁶

> Having such ingenuity of skill beyond hope, he proceeds sometimes to evil, other times to good. When he applies the laws of the earth and the justice sworn to the gods he is high in the city; the man with whom the ignoble consorts because of his recklessness is outcast from the city. Let he who does such things not share my hearth nor share my thoughts.⁴⁷

As Griffith notes, Sophocles' 'comprehensive list of human achievements' culminates with political life and, in striking juxtaposition, the political power to include other men high within the polis (ὑψίπολις) or to exclude from the polis (ἄπολις).⁴⁸

In both Sophocles and de la Rosa, the politics of exclusion extend to corpses. Creón claims that the women reported missing have been found on holiday far away in a Mediterranean spa, while a nameless woman accuses the government of dumping bodies far outside the city, complaining that 'They confine our daughters to oblivion. My daughter was buried so far from Thebes that I will never be able to visit her grave' ('Confinan a nuestras hijas al olvido. Mi hija quedó sepultada tan lejos de Tebas, que nunca podré visitar su tumba', Scene 8). This spatial marginalization maps onto Polynices' body and Antigone's tomb in Sophocles, both of which lie outside the city proper.

Creón's word is law, and the tyrant explicitly declares that the dead do not exist:

> Declaro, que no hay muertas. Que no existen cuerpos que identificar. Y esto es muy claro. No existen. (Scene 3)

> I declare that there are no dead women. That there exist no bodies to identify. And this is very clear. They do not exist.

Creón's decree places the *desaparecidas* in ontologically muddy waters. By sovereign decree, the dead are legally alive, and any actual violence done to them is deemed extrajudicial.

As for the living, Creón declares that anyone who asserts there are murdered women is an enemy of the state and subject to the full extent of the law, which is to say, his whim:

> Insisto: Serán considerados enemigos de la ciudad y recibirán, como enemigos, todo el peso de la ley. (Scene 3)

> I insist: they will be considered enemies of the state and they will receive, as enemies, the full weight of the law.

Creón's totalitarian edict crosses gender lines. After Hemón challenges Creón over the mounting bodies of evidence, his body, too, becomes forfeit. The tyrant authorizes his son's assassination through extrajudicial violence.

Thus, we might observe the paradox of Agamben's camp, that 'space that is opened when the state of exception begins to become the rule'. De la Rosa's Tebas/Juárez has become a 'zone of indistinction between outside and inside, exception and rule, licit and illicit, in which the very concepts of subjective right and juridical protection no longer ma[ke] any sense'.[49] The women of Juárez exist in a state of exception by sovereign decree, yet it is within the juridical space of the city that their bodies can be harmed with impunity. There are corpses aplenty in Tebas yet, legally, in this totalitarian state, they have not been killed.

De la Rosa's Antígona is indeed heroic and, in the final analysis, undead Antigone who is dead yet living demands inclusion in the political realm.[50] In her early exchange with Ismene, Antígona frames the dramatic conflict in such terms, challenging Creón's sovereign power over biological life and political inclusion/exclusion:

> ¿Y quién es Creón para decretar que mi muerta es menos muerta o menos ciudadana, que los muertos en paz de todos los días? (Scene 4)
>
> And who is Creón to declare that my dead woman is less dead or less of a citizen than the dead in peace from all time?

Antígona is the figure reduced to bare life who nevertheless struggles for a *bios politikos*. For instance, when Creón suggests she has no place in the political realm (quoted above), Antígona replies, 'I am queen' ('yo soy reina', Scene 13), demanding not only political inclusion but also political power.[51] As Butler writes of Sophocles' Antigone, Antígona subverts Creón's 'sovereign speech act by asserting her own sovereignty'.[52]

However, the use of symbolic death beyond Antígona herself constructs Juárez as a camp where its inhabitants find themselves in what Hannah Arendt might describe as a 'shadowy' realm.[53] To quote Agamben, although 'biologically alive', the women of Juárez come 'to be situated in a limit zone between life and death, inside and outside, in which they [are] no longer anything but bare life', and in which 'the human body is separated from its normal political status and abandoned, in a state of exception, to the most extreme misfortunes'.[54]

De la Rosa thus draws on *Antigone* and amplifies its traditions of symbolic death to address an actual biopolitical crisis of grave importance. As the play's subtitle suggests via its plural 'voices' (*voces*), both the crisis and its stakes are much bigger than Antígona herself. Taken together, these voices call attention to the harsh realities of 'life' under a biopolitical regime. Antígona's 'no' demands an end to the biopolitical order and, as Kirsten Nigro suggests, her survival perhaps offers a 'ray of hope', leaving open the possibility of 'another act and another conclusion'.[55]

Conclusions

As Fradinger reminds us, the 'indefatigable', 'undead' Antigone never seems to age.[56] More than a decade after the play's debut, de la Rosa's *Antígona* and its biopolitics remain poignant and timely to Mexico, Latin America and beyond.

In Juárez, the femicide has tapered off, yet overall violence without hope of legal recourse or protection has experienced periods of increase. Cartel violence escalated in 2010 and Amnesty International's 2011 annual report on Mexico alleges 15,000 gang related killings (mostly in the northern states, 3,000 of them in Juárez) and 'arbitrary detention, torture, excessive use of force and enforced disappearance by municipal, state, and federal police forces'.[57] On Juárez's women and accountability for violence, the report details:

> Despite the 2009 judgement by the Inter-American Court, the government failed to take effective measures to investigate and bring to justice those responsible for the abduction and killing of three women in Ciudad Juárez in 2001 (the Cotton Field case) or to combat the ongoing pattern of violence against women and discrimination in the city. More than 300 women were killed during the year. The bodies of at least 30 victims bore injuries suggesting that they had suffered sexual violence and torture. Few perpetrators were held to account. In December, Marisela Escobedo was shot and killed by a gunman outside the governor's palace in Chihuahua City during a protest to demand justice for her daughter who was murdered in Ciudad Juárez in 2008.

Outside of Mexico, patterns of femicide have emerged in Guatemala and elsewhere in Central America. David Carrey Jr. and M. Gabriela Torres argue that this 'gender-based violence morphed into femicide when peacetime governments became too weak to control extralegal and paramilitary powers'.[58] Their descriptions of femicide in Guatemala might easily depict Juárez and de la Rosa's Tebas: 'Since 2000, more than 5,000 women and girls have been brutally murdered in Guatemala. Their bodies litter city streets, urban ravines, and the imagination of the media.'[59]

Beyond Latin America, biopolitical crises surround us. These range from the plight of Syrian refugees to the experiences of Palestinians in the Gaza Strip and West Bank to police violence in the United States and the Black Lives Matter movement. For many of my North American students, the death of Michael Brown – whose body remained on the street for hours after he was shot to death by police in Ferguson, Missouri, USA on 9 August 2014 – has powerfully conjured Sophocles' Polynices.

De la Rosa's *Antígona* evokes Agamben's warning that 'if it is true that the figure proposed by our age is that of an unsacrificeable life that has nevertheless become capable of being killed to an unprecedented degree, then the bare life of *homo sacer* concerns us in a special way'.[60] The play's use of symbolic death participates in a long tradition of *Antigone*s, which make Antigone's liminal status between life and death an essential element of the tragedy. However, de la Rosa challenges her audience to look beyond Antigone's individual heroism and to understand the femicide as a collective trauma afflicting the entire community. So long as hundreds of women remain missing, unidentified and unburied, while state silence and the absence of judicial accountability nurture a culture of violent permissiveness, the spectre of violence looms over the city's inhabitants. The city persists in a permanent state of emergency, its residents reduced to bare existence. The dead haunt the living and the community at large is deprived of *bios*, the proper way of life. As Agamben cautions, 'if today there is no longer any one clear figure of the sacred man, it is perhaps because we are all virtually *homines sacri*'.[61]

NOTES

1 Staging the European Classical in 'Latin' America: An Introduction

1. E.g. Africa: Wetmore 2002; Goff and Simpson 2008; Van Weyenberg 2013; Europe: Gentili and Pretagostini 1986; Zimmermann 2000; Torlone, Munteanu, Dutsch 2017.
2. E.g. Zyl Smit 2003; Hardwick and Gillespie 2007; Goff and Simpson 2015.
3. The few studies in English penned by Classicists are chapters addressing examples typically from Argentina, Mexico, Brazil and Cuba. Notable exceptions are Hualde Pascual 2013 (adapted from Hualde Pascual 2012) and Bosher et al. 2015, which contains only eleven chapters (out of fifty-two) from these four countries plus Colombia. In Spanish and Portuguese, there are similarly few studies, either treating individual countries, or the entire 'Iberoamerican' tradition (but focusing on Spain and Portugal): Miranda Cancela 2005, 2006; López and Pociña 2009; Hualde Pascual 2012; Ribeiro Barbosa 2014; Fátima Sousa e Silva and Moraes Augusto 2015.
4. Hispanists and Latin Americanists typically examine Greek myth and tragedy as 'universal': e.g. Pianacci 2008; Duprey 2013; Ford 2017.
5. In referring to the 'European classical', the term 'classical' is open; i.e. we are not referring to a predetermined classical tradition.
6. Phelan 1968.
7. Ardao 1980; Rojas Mix 1986; Romero 1998; McGuinness 2003; Gobat 2013.
8. E.g. Briceño Pozo 1971 (on Simón Bolívar); Miranda Cancela 1990, 2018 (on José Martí); Cussen 1992 (on Andrés Bello and Simón Bolívar); Bocchetti 2010b (on Francisco de Miranda). For a broader consideration of nineteenth-century classicisms, see Bocchetti 2010a; Conn 2018. See n. 41 below.
9. Needell 1995; Bocchetti 2013; Meyer 2017.
10. Mazzotti 2015: 88. On Classics and nationalisms, see Stephens and Vasunia 2010.
11. Mora 2014. This is a limited category, since it excludes non-Spanish speakers, e.g. Brazilians and Haitians.
12. The sole exception is Andújar's contribution, given Puerto Rico's unique history.
13. Klor de Alva 1994: 241.
14. Mignolo 2000.
15. Hulme 2008.
16. Coronil 2008. See also Moraña et al. 2008.
17. E.g. Goff 2005; Goff and Simpson 2008; Hardwick and Gillespie 2007; Vasunia 2013.
18. A glance at the items listed in n. 2 above confirms this. To this list, Greenwood 2010 and McConnell 2013 must be added.

19. Goff and Simpson 2008: 1.
20. Rushdie 1982.
21. Hardwick 2011.
22. Lupher 2003.
23. Laird 2006; Arbo and Laird 2015; Feile Tomes 2015, 2017.
24. Laird 2015; Laird and Miller 2018. Notable exceptions from colonial Peru include e.g. Bernand 2006; MacCormack 2006; Valdivieso 2018.
25. Korenjak 2016: 93–4. See also Osorio Romero 1979; Tietz and Briesemeister 2001; Baldini and Brizzi 2010.
26. See e.g. Cullhed 2018: 183–5.
27. E.g. Conn 2018; Andújar 2018b.
28. Many examinations of 'Latin America' exclude Brazil; see Bethell 2010.
29. E.g. Augusto 2010; Hirata 2010; Cardoso 2014; Coelho 2015.
30. Schwartzman 1979.
31. García Guadilla 1996; Ribeiro 1971.
32. Greenwood 2010: 8–9.
33. McConnell 2013: 39.
34. James 1978: 45 notes that Frantz Fanon, one of Césaire's pupils, had similarly studied in France.
35. See e.g. Miranda Cancela 1990; Andújar 2018a: 103.
36. Benítez-Rojo 1996; Glissant 1999.
37. Cornejo Polar 1998: 7–8.
38. Our translation.
39. Santos 2014: 26. See also Klor de Alva 1994: 243.
40. Santos 2014: 48–69.
41. Santos 2014: 53. Simón Bolívar (1783–1830) was the revolutionary leader who helped achieve independence for Venezuela, Bolivia, Colombia, Ecuador, Peru and Panama. José Martí (1853–95) was also a revolutionary but also a dominant figure in both Cuban and early Latin American letters. See n. 8 above.
42. Santos 2014: 52.
43. In defining the term, Ortíz (1947: 102) speaks of the offspring who 'always has something of both parents but is always different from each of them'.
44. Bosher et al. 2015: 14.
45. Fradinger 2011a, 2011b, 2013.
46. Fradinger 2013: 63.
47. Butler 2016.
48. Jansen 2018: 25.
49. Fradinger 2013: 64.
50. Most of Mexico lies on the North American plate, hence its inclusion in standard definitions of North America (see e.g. the definition in the *Oxford English Dictionary*). However, Mexico is often grouped with Central America for geopolitical reasons.

51. On classical engagements in New Spain, see e.g. Rojas Silva 2018; Laird 2018; on the Youth Athenaeum, see Andújar 2018a. Happily, Francisco Barrenechea is working on a monograph addressing the long history of Greek drama in Mexico.
52. Jameson 2002: 23. On 'temporal continuity and disjunction' in classical reception, see also Brockliss et al. 2012: 5.
53. Laird 2007: 227.
54. López 2016: 208.
55. González Echevarría and Pupo-Walker 1996: 1. On classical reception in Brazil, see Nikoloutsos and Gonçalves 2018, as well as the various essays in the special issue of *Caletroscópio* 6.1 (2018).
56. Hardwick 2007a: 3.
57. Andújar 2019.
58. Barrenechea 2015: 254.
59. E.g. Itier 1999, 2010; Aracil Varón 2008: 121–4.
60. Luciani 1996: 411–12; Reverte Bernal 1999; Hualde Pascual 2009.
61. Barrenechea 2015: 253–6.
62. E.g. Zanelli 2008; Bosker 2012.
63. See further Greenwood 2004.
64. Hardwick 2003: 111.
65. Hardwick 2007b: 313.
66. Cf. Hardwick 2005: 109.
67. Macintosh et al. 2015: 9–10, developing the insights of Hall and Macintosh 2005.
68. Goff 2005: 13.
69. Dauster 1996: 11–15.
70. Taylor 1991: 39–45.
71. Dauster 1996: 14.
72. On this dialectical relationship, see further Nikoloutsos 2012b: 1.

2 From Epic to Tragedy: Theatre and Politics in Juan Cruz Varela's *Dido*

Research for this piece was made possible thanks to a Loeb Classical Library Fellowship from Harvard University, for which I am most grateful. Versions of the paper were read at various venues, including the Society for Classical Studies, University of Pennsylvania and Bryn Mawr College. I am indebted to the respective audiences for their feedback and criticism. All mistakes remain with me alone.

1. In addition to the three reviews in the Argentine press discussed below, the intertextual relation between *Dido* and the *Aeneid* is treated in Gutiérrez 1918: 56–74; Rojas 1915: 18–24; 1960: 646–50; Garelli 1996; Bernal Lavesa 2005: 93–112; Vilanova 2006; Zecchin de Fasano 2012: 411–17.
2. Meere 2016: 317.
3. Gutiérrez 1918: 11.

Notes to pp. 20–25

4. Davies et al. 2006. I wish to thank Heather Hennes for bringing this work to my attention.
5. Ibid.: esp. 3–75, 268–76.
6. *El Argos de Buenos Aires*, 30 July 1823, 61: 253. The release is excerpted in Corti 1934. All translations from Spanish are my own. Punctuation in all quotations as in the original text.
7. Shumway 1991: 93–6; Bernal Lavesa 2005: 84; Gallo 2006: 60–1; 2012: 107–8, 121–2.
8. The Literary Society was founded on 1 January 1822 under Rivadavia's patronage. Varela was admitted on 10 October as its fourteenth member. The group promoted Rivadavia's political agenda. They were Unitarians (advocates of a central government based in Buenos Aires) and committed to the dissemination of European culture. On the history of the Society, see Ibarguren 1937: 108–19; Shumway 1991: 87–90.
9. Rojas 1915: vi, 16; 1960: 645; Gutiérrez 1918: 272–3.
10. Woodyard 1995: 32.
11. Needell 1995: 519–21.
12. On Rivadavia's cultural reforms, see Shumway 1991: 81–111; Gallo 2006: 46–66; 2012: 104–29.
13. Coester 1916: 106.
14. Shumway 1991: 94. For additional titles pointing to the role of Varela as an 'aulic poet' and 'spokesman' of Rivadavia, see Arrieta 1948: 52.
15. *El Argos de Buenos Aires*, 30 July 1823, 61: 253.
16. Rojas 1915: 34.
17. Ugarteche 1929: 55.
18. *El Argos de Buenos Aires*, 23 August 1823, 68: 282.
19. Aisemberg 2005: 166.
20. Ibid.: 168. There is no record as to who played the various parts when *Dido* was produced. Gutiérrez (1918: 63) notes that the actress Trinidad Guevara read a monologue of Ana, but provides no additional information on the context of this recital.
21. Seibel 2002: 73; 2007: 21.
22. Rojas 1948: 526.
23. Arietta 1948: 54.
24. Aisemberg 2005: 167; Seibel: 2007: 22. A third, incomplete tragedy with a classical theme entitled *Idomeneo* has been attributed to Varela. See De Barsotti 1954.
25. In José Mármol's 1851 novel *Amalia*, the character doña Marcelina nostalgically recalls the splendid era of Varela and boasts: 'I knew *Argia* and *Dido* by heart, verse by verse, the day after they were performed for the first time' ('Sabía la *Argia* y la *Dido*, verso por verso, el otro día de representarse por primera vez'). For this and other quotations that could be read as testament to the popularity of Varela's plays, see Mármol 2001: 196–7, 568–9, 612. Many thanks to Aníbal Biglieri for drawing my attention to this source.
26. Gutiérrez 1918: 75. On the artistic context in which neoclassical tragedy rises in Buenos Aires, see López 2005.
27. Rojas 1915: 14. The view is repeated in Rojas 1960: 643–4 and echoed in Shumway 1991: 95; Bernal Lavesa 2005: 92.
28. Hardwick 2003: 111.
29. Varela 1872: 408 *apud* Dornheim 2000: 89.
30. Cova 1947: 138–9, 144, and 211 where San Martín is compared to Cato and Cincinnatus.

31. Myers 1999: 123–4 cited in Gallo 2006: 59; 2012: 121. See further Dávilo 2009: 399.
32. Bernal Lavesa 2005: 84–5.
33. Gutiérrez 1918: 50.
34. For a full list of neoclassical plays staged in Buenos Aires in 1810–23, see Pellettieri 2005: 47–53.
35. *El Centinela*, 14 September 1823, 60: 161.
36. Shumway 1991: 94–5. Scholars who are sceptical about *Dido*'s relation to its contemporary context include Rojas 1960: 653; Aisemberg and Lusnich 1997: 16.
37. Rojas 1915: 40.
38. Ibid.: 40.
39. Ibid.: 70.
40. Ibid.: 65.
41. *El Centinela*, 21 September 1823, 61: 167.
42. Rojas 1915: 70–1.
43. Goodkin 2005: 381.
44. Rojas 1915: 35.
45. Ibid.: 71.
46. Goodkin 2005: 377.
47. *El Argos de Buenos Aires*, 6 September 1823, 72: 298. For further criticism, see *El Centinela*, 14 September 1823, 60: 160–1.
48. *El Centinela*, 21 September 1823, 61: 170.
49. Marani (1977: 40 *apud* Zecchin de Fasano 2012: 415, n. 24) argues that in presenting Dido's suicide onstage, Varela adheres to conventions of Alfieri's dramaturgy.
50. Sedgwick 1985: 26. See further Kimmel 1994: 129. For an application of Sedgwick's theories to Dido's medieval reception, see Desmond 1994: 9, 100.
51. Lida de Malkiel 1974: 76–81. See also Kahn 2008: 60–2.
52. Hexter 1992: 340.
53. Lida de Malkiel 1974: 104–5.
54. Davies et al. 2006: 270.
55. Ibid.: 24.
56. The name *República Argentina* will be officially adopted in the 1853 Constitution.
57. Gallo 2006: 54; 2012: 116.
58. Virgil was born in a small village outside Mantua whose name is coincidentally identical to that of the main mountain range in South America: the Andes.

3 Leopoldo Marechal's *Antígona Vélez*: Rewriting Greek Tragedy as a Foundation Myth in Peronist Argentina

I am grateful to Rosa Andújar and Konstantinos Nikoloutsos for the revision of the English version of this paper and for helping me access recent bibliography on the play. I would also thank them and Carolina Brncić for their helpful comments.

1. Jauss 1970: 18–23.
2. Hardwick 2003: 4.
3. This phrase was frequently used by Perón throughout his regime.
4. Altamirano 2001: 19. All translations from Spanish are mine.
5. Rock 1987; Zanatta 1996.
6. See García and Cavallari 1995; Arlt 1997; Alonso and Houvenaghel 2009; Fradinger 2011a; Biglieri 2016; Fátima Silva 2017.
7. See Zanatta 2009: 92–9.
8. Zanatta 1996.
9. In an interview with Alfredo Andrés, published in *Words with Leopoldo Marechal*, the author tells that the rehearsals were delayed because Fanny Navarro, the actress who played Antígona, lost the only manuscript. This caused Eva Perón's indignation, who commanded Alejandro Apold, undersecretary of information and press, to speak to Marechal. After three denials from Marechal, who refused to write the play again and rehearse in such a short time, Eva Perón called him herself. I quote here Marechal's account (found in Andrés 1968: 50), which eloquently expresses his adherence to Peronism, his self-aggrandizement, and the influence of Eva Perón, herself an agent and product of Peronist propaganda: 'I heard immediately the voice of Eva Perón, who greeted me with the charm she manifested beyond her fights, and who appealing to my condition of "great poet" and "great Peronist", asked me to do the effort of reconstructing *Antígona Vélez*. Conquered by her charm, I got down to work during the whole next day and night . . .' ('Oí en seguida la voz de Eva Perón, que me saludaba con el encanto que traducía ella más allá de sus luchas, y que invocando mi condición de "gran poeta" y "gran peronista", me solicitaba el esfuerzo de reconstruir *Antígona Vélez*. Ganado por su encantamiento, me puse a la obra que me llevó todo ese día y su noche consiguiente').
10. Mogliani 1999: 263–4; Mogliani 2004: 245; Fiorucci 2007: 23.
11. Delaney 2002: 629.
12. Palti 1996: 68.
13. See, e.g. Buchrucker 1987; Rock 1987, 2002; Zanatta 1996, 2009; Altamirano 2001; Svampa 2006.
14. Zanatta 1999; Sigal and Verón 1986: 38–9.
15. Contrary to Zanatta (1999) who delves into a historic investigation, Sigal and Verón (1986) focus on a discursive analysis of Perón's speeches.
16. Palti 1996: 69.
17. Particularly expressive of this perception are the statements of Alberto Baldrich, a Catholic nationalist who became Minister of Culture during the military regime in 1944, when Marechal worked at the same office. Speaking to a group of students, Baldrich referred to his task as a 'redemptive crusade' whose aim was to rescue the 'spiritual Graeco-Latin heritage sublimated into the civilization of Catholic Christendom' ('el acervo espiritual grecolatino sublimado en la civilización de la cristiandad católica'); see Zanatta 1999: 180.
18. In the dramatic analysis, I use terms and concepts proposed by Pfister 1988.
19. For a detailed analysis of the connection between Marechal's works and Augustine, see López Saiz 2017: 45–98.
20. Marechal 1984: 167.
21. *Gen*, I: 26–28.

22. Marechal 1970: 10.
23. Ibid.: 3.
24. Ibid.: 10, 11.
25. Ibid.: 11.
26. Ibid.: 9.
27. Ibid.: 13.
28. Ibid.: 16.
29. Ibid.: 11.
30. The deceptive nature of the sensible world and the corruptibility of the matter is an important topic in the spiritual experience of *Adán Buenosayres*' protagonist, with which *Antígona Vélez* clearly connects.
31. Marechal 1970: 21.
32. Ibid.: 22.
33. Deane 1963: 42.
34. E.g. Marechal 1970: 22.
35. The so-called 'Liberal Republic' corresponds to the period 1880–1916. However, the development of a 'national project' with liberal orientation begins in 1861, during the presidency of Bartolomé Mitre who was succeeded by Domingo Faustino Sarmiento and Nicolás Avellaneda. Basic aspects of that project include: the political organization of Argentina as a Federal Republic; the importance of public education and European immigration conceived as a means of civilization and progress; and the defence of liberal values, such as freedom and citizenship, as the basis of the nation.
36. Palti 1996: 66.
37. Sigal and Verón 1986: 38.
38. Svampa 2006.
39. Perón, speech of 4 August 1944, quoted in Sigal and Verón 1986: 53.
40. In his analysis of the play, Biglieri (2016) focuses on the dichotomy barbarism vs. civilization, but admits the difficulty of relating his analysis to the Peronist context (2016: 355). Fátima Silva (2017: 419) mentions Peronism and the 'conquest of the desert' as contextual elements, and assesses Marechal's rewriting as 'a new reading of the conflict between "human law" ... and "divine law"', without developing more specific connections between text and context.
41. Marechal 1997: 230: 'El poeta es un imitador del Verbo en el "orden de la Creación", pero no en el "orden de la Redención" ... ¡En ese orden, solo el santo es su imitador perfecto!'
42. Ibid.: 312–13.
43. Marechal 1970: 36–8.
44. In her interpretation, Arlt (1997) sees a connection between the play and its context in the figure of Facundo Galván (Creon), a 'caudillo' aiming at the legitimation of Perón's leadership. I agree with the connection, but as I illustrate, the significance of the play goes beyond this relationship.
45. Marechal 1970: 47.
46. Fradinger (2011) sees a relationship between Antígona and Eva Perón, for both women 'sacrifice' (themselves) for the unity of the nation. To Fradinger, this sacrifice is part of a 'national "tradition" (that) has appropriated *Antigone* at foundational moments in which violence sealed tragic and unstable pacts of national unification and women played key roles,

summoned to build or to sacrifice for the nation or moved to resist power' (2011: 2). As opposed to other critics, Fradinger emphasizes the conflicting dimension of the play's political context and notes the presence in the play of 'icons of the neo-Hispanist nationalism of Peronism's military wing' (2011: 6) – a central aspect of my interpretation – but she does not pursue the subject further.

47. Marechal 1970: 44.
48. Ibid.: 40.
49. Taking these symbolic elements into account, Alonso and Houvenaghel (2009) and García and Cavallari (1995) read *Antígona Vélez* as a ritual of foundation, relating it to the Peronist project of founding a 'New Argentina'. Although I agree with their reading of archetypical and cosmogenic images in the play, I argue that these images are subordinated to a religious Catholic perspective and the conservative aspects of Peronism, which these scholars do not consider.
50. Marechal 1970: 58.
51. Expressions of this kind are frequent in Peron's speeches, like this example: 'Only love achieves unity' ('El amor es lo único que une'), from a speech delivered on 4 August 1944, quoted in Sigal and Verón 1986: 53.

4 Juan Radrigán's *Medea Mapuche*: Recreating Euripides' Revenge Tragedy in an Indigenous Chilean Context

I wish to express my profound gratitude to Rosa Andújar and Konstantinos Nikoloutsos for providing me with fundamental bibliography and also for their critical comments, corrections and patience.

1. Radrigán 2004a: 17. Unless otherwise indicated, translations of texts originally written in Spanish are my own.
2. Bengoa 2003: 21.
3. In the last six decades, around fifteen titles have been produced in Brazil, México, Cuba, Puerto Rico, Ecuador, Perú, Argentina and Chile. For an extensive bibliography, see Nikoloutsos 2015.
4. According to the last census (2017) 9.9 per cent of the Chilean inhabitants declared they belong to the Mapuche population: https://www.censo2017.cl (accessed 10 April 2019).
5. For a discussion of Euripides' revenge tragedy in the ancient context, see Burnett 1973; Mastronarde 2002: 8–15.
6. For a periodization of Radrigán's dramatic production, see Albornoz Farías 2005.
7. Hurtado and Piña 1993.
8. For an overview of Radrigán's work, see Oyarzún 2008.
9. Albornoz Farías 2004: 7–15.
10. The play's subtitle is 'Based on Euripides' *Medea*' ('Basada en "Medea" de Eurípides').
11. Radrigán's text draws on the 1951 Spanish translation of Euripides' *Medea* by Eduardo Mier y Barbery. In it, at least twenty quotes or paraphrases are taken directly from the Spanish translation; in the English translation of these lines, many of the comparable elements are unavoidably lost.
12. Radrigán 2004b: 142.

13. Sometimes also spelled as *huinca*, this means foreigners, i.e. Spaniards and their *criollo* descendants.
14. Radrigán 2004b: 148.
15. For discussion of the ambiguous marital status of Medea, see Nikoloutsos 2012c: 28; 2015: 346.
16. Burnett 1973: 12.
17. Kovacs 2001: 280.
18. For discussion of infringement of oath and contract in *Medea* and Euripides in general, see e.g. Burnett 1973: 12–24; Foley 2001: 243–71.
19. Radrigán 2004b: 150.
20. The marital status of Kütral is quite different from Medea's situation in Euripides. As Guevara (1929: 313) states, there are different kinds of marriages among the Mapuche, one of which is by elopement, consented to by the woman, but not by her parents. Therefore, the condition we are discussing here is a Mapuche marriage.
21. 'Arauco' and 'Auraucano' are words used by the Spanish invaders to denominate the region and the Mapuche people who inhabited the lands between the Bío-Bío and Toltén rivers.
22. For historical background of the period between the sixteenth and eighteenth centuries, see Bengoa 2003; for the nineteenth and twentieth centuries, see Bengoa 2002; 2004; Cifuentes 2009.
23. Radrigán 2004b: 145.
24. Ibid.: 144.
25. A frequently practised execution under the governance of García Hurtado de Mendoza, successor of governor Pedro de Valdivia following his death at the hands of Mapuche warriors in 1553/1554.
26. Ercilla 1993.
27. Ibid.: prologue.
28. 'Letter to Emperor Charles V' (4 September 1545) in Medina 1953: 17.
29. Letter from Fray Gil González de San Nicolás, 26 April 1559, in Medina 1901: 279. See also Medina 1953: 204, Pedro de Valdivia's 'Letter to Emperor Charles V' (Concepción, 15 October 1550), in which he informs the Emperor about killing around 2000 Indians, lancing a great many, and cutting the hands and noses of 200. Bengoa (1992) offers a well-documented vision of the conquest and subjugation of the Mapuche people, supported by historical sources from the period (e.g. letters to the Spanish Crown, chronicles and documents) which outline the excesses and cruelties committed against them. It is likely Radrigán was familiar with this book, published on the 500th anniversary of the so-called 'discovery' of America, as it had a large impact upon Chilean intellectuals.
30. Radrigán 2004b: 149.
31. The Spanish translation paraphrased in Radrigán's play is 'más quisiera yo embrazar tres veces el escudo que parir una sola'.
32. Guevara 1925: 459. Cf. Ibid.: 391: 'In this order of women's war activities, we must include the case of that Araucanian of the tribes of Villarrica called Janequeo, who upon the death of her husband joined a brother of hers and with him undertook a series of raids against the Spaniards who guarded that area' ('En este orden de actividades bélicas de las mujeres hai que incluir el caso de aquella arauca de las tribus de Villarrica llamada Janequeo, que a la muerte de su marido se unió a un hermano i con él emprendió una serie de correrías contra

los españoles que resguardaban esa zona'). According to the legend, the Spanish never managed to defeat Janequeo.
33. Admittedly, in the source text, Medea's utterance is aligned with fifth-century BCE social values concerning Greek women, on which see e.g. Sourvinou-Inwood 1997: 253–62.
34. Aylwin 2013: 44.
35. According to historians, the Mapuche living south of the Bío-Bío River were, at the time they negotiated a border with the Spaniards, a prosperous people who enjoyed great riches from livestock and highly valued work in silver and woven handcraft.
36. For example, Radrigán 2004b: 151: 'a royal order demanding that the conquistadors of these lands act less cruelly' ('una orden real [que] demanda ser menos crueles a los conquistadores de estas tierras'), or ibid.: 148, the advantages of winter when 'the rivers grow and they [*winkas*] cannot manoeuvre' ('los rios estén crecidos y ellos [los winkas] no puedan maniobrar'), a Mapuche strategy documented in several chronicles, including *La Araucana* (Canto XII).
37. Radrigán 2004b: 145: MAITU: '¿Porqué hablas en lengua? El winka lo ha prohibido y el aire lleva todas las palabras a sus oidos' (MAITU: 'Why do you speak in tongue? The *winkas* prohibited it and the wind blows all words to their ears').
38. Meza Villalobos 1975: 794.
39. Bengoa 1992: 124.
40. Radrigán 2004b: 145.
41. Ibid.
42. Cifuentes 2009, Vol. 2: 32–3.
43. Cifuentes 2009, Vol. 3: 42–7.
44. Huenchumilla 2010.
45. My emphasis.
46. Radrigán 2004b: 146.
47. A city in the Chilean south.
48. Huenchumilla 2010.
49. Bengoa 2013: 10.
50. Radrigán 2004b: 153.
51. Ibid.: 147.
52. All these quotes are taken literally from the Spanish translation of Euripides' text (1951): e.g. 'índole cruel, y . . . [el] ímpetu terrible de sus pasiones' (252), which is a loose translation of lines 103–4 of the Greek text: ἄγριον ἦθος στυγερἀν τε φύσιν / φρενὸς αὐθάδους, and 'nadie se reirá de mis dolores' (259), which corresponds to line 398: χαίρων τις αὐτῶν τοὐμὸν ἀλγυνεῖ κέαρ.
53. Radrigán 2004b: 148.
54. For discussion of Euripides' monologue by Medea and the controversy in scholarship about her 'divided self', see Foley 2001: 243–71.
55. Radrigán 2004b: 154.
56. Lehmann 1991: 197.
57. Murray 1965: 82.

58. Vernant and Vidal-Naquet 1972: 21–40. For further discussion of this controversial issue concerning contemporary politics and society in relation to Attic tragedy, see e.g. Mastronarde 2013: 15ff.; Griffin 1998: 39–61.

59. Radrigán 2004b: 147. The Spanish translation of these lines (205–10) echoes Euripides' text, lines 358, 362–3: δύστανε γύναι ... ὡς εἰς ἄπορόν σε κλύδωνα θεός, / Μήδεια, κακῶν ἐπόρευσεν.

60. For discussion of the performance of the Chorus in *Medea*, see Mastronarde 2002: 166–8; 2013: 116–19, 134; Rehm 2005: 178–80; Walton 2005.

61. As Mastronarde (2002: 166) comments: 'the nurse and chorus agree with Medea that she is a victim of injustice on Jason's part: 26, 157, 165, 207, 267, 578. The opinion of such humble, nameless figures as the nurse and the chorus is often in tragedy a useful pointer to the viewpoint the drama is designed to shape and elicit in the audience.'

62. Burnett 1973: 12.

63. Bengoa 2003: 116 n. 32: '*ad mapu* o código ético de los mapuches. *Ad* ... quiere decir algo así como "mandato". Se podría traducir *ad mapu* como ley consuetudinaria, literalmente el mandato de la tierra o el "uso de la tierra" o simplemente el peso de la costumbre' ('*Ad mapu* or ethical code of Mapuche people. *Ad* ... means something like a "command" ... We can translate *ad mapu* as customary law, literally commandment of the earth ... or just the weight of custom').

64. Guevara 1929, Vol. II: 154.

65. Ibid.: 216–17.

66. Burnett 1973: 13.

67. Ibid.: 14.

68. Radrigán 2004a: 19.

69. Bengoa 2004.

70. Here meant in cultural terms, that is, of 'cultural legacy' and not exclusively with respect to a specific ethnic group. I owe this definition to my colleague, Prof. José Luis Martínez, who speaks of 'mestización'.

71. E.g. one of Lemunao's lines: 'Have you ever met them? You'll never convince them [*winkas*] to utter an apology or sign of regret. They have hidden greed and tyranny, claiming themselves the defenders of good. Any recognition of fault would be fatal for to them' ('¿Acaso no los conoces? Jamás lograrás de ellos [los winkas] un gesto de perdón o arrepentimiento. Han ocultado la codicia y la tiranía arrogándose la custodia del bien, cualquier reconocimiento de culpa sería mortal para ellos'), Radrigán 2004b: 151. This quote perfectly depicts the author's viewpoint about how the Mapuche problem has been treated throughout their history.

72. In 2015, Radrigán stated in a newspaper interview his reticence about rewriting literary works of another author: 'because you must be half asshole to rewrite another. To do it, you must lose respect for the original author, without fear of changing a work that seemed finished. In 2002 (sic) I made my own version of *Medea*, which was called *Medea Mapuche*, but it was because I felt that the text still had something to say' ('Porque hay que ser medio cabrón para reescribir a otro. Para hacerlo, hay que perderle el respeto al autor original, sin miedo de cambiar una obra que parecía terminada. En 2002 (*sic*) hice mi propia versión de *Medea*, que se llamó *Medea mapuche*, pero fue porque sentí que el texto aún tenía algo que decir'), cited in Bahamondes 2015: 96.

73. See n. 57 above.

74. Aylwin 2013: 43.

5 Philoctetes and Medea in Contemporary Chilean Theatre

I am grateful to Rosa Andújar and Konstantinos Nikoloutsos for their helpful comments and revisions of this chapter.

1. Boyle 1992.
2. Pinochet's dictatorship began with the coup d'état on 11 September 1973 and ended with the surrender of power on 11 March 1990 after the 1988 plebiscite and the 1989 presidential election. The political transition (1990–2006), with the governments of Patricio Aylwin (1990–4), Eduardo Frei (1994–2000) and Ricardo Lagos (2000–6), has been known as the 'democracy of agreements'. This period is governed by two basic principles, reconciliation and consensus, whereby these government sought to overcome the traumas of the past. In this context, there are two historical milestones that mark a turning point in the recognition of the dictatorship's crimes. The first is the 'Rettig Report' (1991), in which 2,279 deaths are recorded. In this report, President Aylwin declares his willingness to establish 'justice insofar as it is possible', synthesizing the will to clarify human rights violations and, at the same time, the spirit permanently threatened by the Armed Forces, with Pinochet still being Commander-in-chief of the Chilean Army. The second milestone is the publication of the Valech Report (2003) that identified the victims of imprisonment and pressure under the dictatorship. Based on this report, President Lagos declares at the outset of *No hay mañana sin ayer* (2003), a proposal to 'continue advancing in the delicate process of *healing the wounds* produced by the grave violations of human rights' ('seguir avanzando en el delicado proceso de *sanar las heridas* producidas por las graves violaciones a los derechos humanos', emphasis added).
3. Moulián 1997.
4. Ibid.: 31–45.
5. Ibid.: 97–114.
6. Jelin 2002: 6.
7. Ibid.: 28.
8. Rojas 2006: 177–88.
9. Hurtado 2009b: 150–4.
10. On metatheatre or metadrama, see e.g. Abel 1963; Hornby 1986; Ringer 1998; Dobrov 2001; Slater 2002; Dunn 2010.
11. For instance, Benjamín Galemiri's *Edipo asesor* (2000) and *Infamante Electra* (2005); Juan Radrigán's *Medea Mapuche* (2000), for which see König's chapter in this volume; Benito Escobar´s *Ulises o no* (2006); Ana López Montaner's *Medea o la desesperada conquista del fraude* (2006) and *El thriller de Antígona* (2006); Rolando Jara's *El clownplejo de Edipo* (2009); Lucía de la Maza's *Ismene* (2010).
12. Recent studies of Sophocles' reception (Schein 2013; Budelmann 2017; Dugdale 2017) do not treat Latin America. In her review of Greek tragedy in Ibero-America, Pascual (2012) does not list any rewritings of the *Philoctetes*. The reception of the play dates back to (at least) 1964, when Dominican Héctor Inchaustegui Cabral published a trilogy entitled *Miedo en un puñado de polvo* ('Fear in a Handful of Dust') of *Prometeo, Filoctetes* and *Hipólito*.
13. Marcelo Sánchez Delgado (b. 1966) is actually a historian. He studied theatrical performance (1989–93) and in the 1990s dedicated himself to acting and dramaturgy. His first works *Signos vitales* (1994) and *Antes del mar* (1995) were selected for inclusion at the First and Second National Dramaturgy Exhibitions. These plays were followed by *Extramuros, Residuos Berlín Valparaíso, Cadáver* and *Puro Chile*. On his attitude to the practice of theatrical writing, see Sánchez 1997; 2003.

14. Sánchez 2004, 'Nota explicativa acerca del nombre de la obra y del personaje'.
15. All translations from Spanish are my own.
16. Schein 2013: 53.
17. Hall 2012: 157.
18. This is also the focus in many contemporary treatments of the *Philoctetes*, on which see Dugdale 2017.
19. On the language in Sophocles' *Philoctetes*, see Goldhill 2012; Segal 1999: 328–61; Kyriakou 2012; Hall 2012. On the problem of language in rewritings of *Philoctetes*, see Budelmann 2007; Dugdale 2017.
20. Sánchez 2004, Vista 3.
21. Ibid.
22. Ibid.: Vista 14.
23. Cf. Sophocles' *Philoctetes* 6–10.
24. Sánchez 2004: Vista 2.
25. Ibid.: Vista 3.
26. Ibid.
27. Ibid.
28. Ibid.: Vista 7.
29. Other *dramatis personae* are also characterized by their smell. The Assistant smells of *Old Spice* aftershave, the Auditioning Actresses smells of air freshener and so on. Victoria is the only one who has a natural odour. She smells of freshly squeezed grapefruit and does not mask her smell with artificial scents; Sánchez 2004: *passim*.
30. The concealment of identity emphasizes the literary reference to Sophocles' text. In the tragedy, Odysseus hides his identity, taking diverse roles to persuading Philoctetes and manipulating Neoptolemus. See Schein (2003) *ad* 11–26, 54–85. For Odysseus' roles, see Ringer 1998: 101–26; Worman 1999.
31. Sánchez 2004: Vista 3.
32. Ibid.: Vista 6.
33. Ibid.
34. Ibid.: Vista 10.
35. Ibid.: Vista 12.
36. Ibid.: Vista 14.
37. Ossa 2006: 73.
38. Sophocles 2003: lines 610–14.
39. Sánchez 2004: Vista 14.
40. José Palma Eskenazi is an actor, playwright and musician, known primarily for his roles as a supporting actor in television series. He has been part of the company Teatro La María, with whom he staged *Diarrea* the first time and for which he obtained a FONDART (National Fund for Cultural Development and the Arts).
41. See 'Ciclo de teatro reúne tres obras de dramaturgos chilenos contemporáneos', *La estrella*, 22 October 2003, http://www.estrellavalpo.cl/site/edic/20031022093436/pags/20031022101101.html (accessed 16 April 2019).
42. Palma 2002. In quoting from the play, I preserve the 'incorrectness' of the original text.

43. Ibid.
44. Ibid.
45. Ibid.
46. Ibid.
47. Hurtado 2009a:15.
48. https://www.collinsdictionary.com/dictionary/english/diarrhoea (accessed 26 April 2019).
49. On *flaite*, see Rojas 2015. Reviews of *Diarrea* 'did not recommend the play for the family' on account of its strong content, language and transvestism. See http://www.bibliotecanacionaldigital.cl/bnd/628/w3-article-250246.html (accessed 25 April 2019).
50. Palma 2002.
51. The commercial is available at https://www.youtube.com/watch?v=BuLm_XMsi1g (accessed 25 April 2019).
52. Palma 2002.
53. Ibid.
54. Sánchez 1997.

6 *A God Slept Here* by Guilherme Figueiredo: A Radical Modernist *Amphitruo* from Brazil

1. The 1949 production was by the Teatro Brasileiro de Comédia (Brazilian Comedy Theatre) and directed by Silveira Sampaio, an important playwright and director in the 1950s and 1960s. Paulo Autran (1922–2007) played Anfitrião/Júpiter and Tonia Carrero (1922–2018) Alcmena. The play was staged again, most notably in 1956 by Companhia Tônia-Celi-Autran under the direction of Adolfo Celi.
2. Gonçalves 2017.
3. Lindberger (1956), Margotton and Huby-Gilson (2010), Ferry (2011) overlook Figueiredo. Despite the play's long performance history, this neglect may be attributed to the difficulty in obtaining scholarship outside national borders.
4. Bertini 2010a: 53. Unlike other scholars, Bertini is interested in lesser-known receptions of the *Amphitruo*, from Vital de Blois' *Geta et Birria* to twenty-first-century authors, such as Ignacio Padilla and André Arcellaschi. He also discusses other receptions of the play in Portuguese, such as Luiz de Camões' *Auto dos Enfatriões* (from the sixteenth century) and Antonio José da Silva's *Anfitrião ou Júpiter e Alcmena* (from the eighteenth century).
5. Bertini 2010a: 56. All translations are mine except otherwise indicated.
6. On Plautine metatheatre and translation, see Gonçalves 2015b.
7. Exceptions include Cardoso 1996; Gross 2010; Frambach 2010; Gomes 2012. These are all articles or chapters in conference proceedings.
8. See e.g. Cacciaglia 1986; Magaldi 2004.
9. Cf. George 1992: 27, 29. On Rodrigues, see also Bakogianni in this volume.
10. Figueiredo 1957b.
11. Figueiredo 1998: 21–2. During a campaign in the jungle, he heard the rustling leaves and shot at it blindly, heard a cry and never knew if he had actually killed an opponent.

Notes to pp. 76–81

12. E.g. Figueiredo 1998: 60–1: 'In the mental confusion of my ten-to-thirteen years, two disciplines took hold of me: Christian catechism and military discipline ... Chasing [sin] away, immersed in Greek mythology, I left for the Revolution of 1932' ('Na confusão mental dos meus dez a treze anos, duas disciplinas se apossaram de mim: o catecismo cristão e a disciplina militar ... Afugentando-o [ao pecado], mergulhando em mitologia grega, parti para a Revolução de 1932').
13. See Ragno in this volume.
14. For productions outside Brazil, see the preface of Figueiredo (1970), the back cover of the 1964 edition of the play, and the flaps of both editions, though these are mentioned without specificities, such as dates and venues. For *A God Slept Here* cities and countries include Paris, New York, Lisbon, Antwerp, Buenos Aires, Israel and 'wherever they steal my copyright', on which see Figueiredo 1970: X. *The Fox and the Grapes* won the Artur Azevedo Award (Brazilian Academy of Letters) and *A God Slept Here* won the gold medal of the Brazilian Association of Art Critics.
15. Frambach 2010.
16. Figueiredo (1970) mentions Giraudoux in the preface: 'How to go further than Giraudoux, whose *Amphitryon* 38 counts thirty-seven predecessors – among which he probably did not include Camões and António José, the Jew?' ('Como ir ... mais longe do que Giraudoux, cujo *Anfitrião 38* conta trinta e sete antepassados – entre os quais provavelmente não incluiu os de Camões e Antônio José, o Judeu?'). Luiz Vaz de Camões, the Portuguese epic poet, published a version of the *Amphitruo* in 1587, a humanist comedy written in rhymed stanzas with many intertextual relations with Provençal and Portuguese lyric poetry. In the first half of the eighteenth century, Brazilian-born Portuguese playwright António José da Silva staged several popular puppet operas, including an *Amphitryon*, a *Medea* and a *Life of Aesop*. He was later deported to Portugal with his family, imprisoned, tortured and finally burned in an *auto da fé* by the 1739 Inquisition. On Camões, see Pascal 2010; Bertini 2010a; on António José da Silva, see Bertini 2010a; Gonçalves 2015a.
17. Figueiredo 1957b: 78; 1970: IX.
18. See also Figueiredo 1957b: 78, 93.
19. Ibid.: 66–7.
20. For *ludificatio* in Plautus, see e.g. Dupont 2007; Dupont and Letessier 2012.
21. Figueiredo 1964: 20.
22. Figueiredo 1957a: 36. My emendations to the English translation of George quoted from this point on will be included in square brackets.
23. In *Xanthias*, Figueiredo (1957b: 85) comments on the efficacy of this kind of joke, when Dionysus instructs Xanthias never to use a joke that the public will not understand.
24. Figueiredo 1964: 26.
25. Figueiredo 1957a: 46.
26. Figueiredo 1964: 26.
27. Figueiredo 1957a: 47–8.
28. Figueiredo 1975b: 20–1.
29. Moore 1998: *passim*; Marshall 2006: 73–82.
30. Gonçalves 2015b: mostly chapter 1.
31. Although not clear from the stills of the 1950s performances, the relationship between such carnivalization and the Rio carnival are evident in the stage and costumes, which roughly imitated a Greco-Roman setting, whereas the actors would speak their lines in the distinctive carioca dialect of Rio de Janeiro, at the time the universal Brazilian language of

radio, theatre, and later television and cinema. At every performance, the actors would update their Rio accent and slang. This is not found in stage directions, but was shared by the playwright in his discussions about his practice. See Figueiredo 1957b: 111.

32. Figueiredo 1957a: 51–2.
33. Figueiredo 1964: 32.
34. Translation my own, omitted without explanation from Figueiredo 1957a: 32.
35. Figueiredo 1964: 33–4.
36. Figueiredo 1957a: 61–2.
37. In this play, he mentions dithyrambs, Pindar, tragic contests, comedies, sophistry and especially the Milesian tale of the Widow of Ephesus (Petr. *Satyr.* 110.6–113.1). Not all of the references, allusions and intertextual connections mentioned here can be found in the citations, especially because Lloyd George's translation is at times very liberal. The interested reader is encouraged to read the original.
38. Figueiredo 1964: 9.
39. Figueiredo 1957a: 13.
40. See Bertini 2010a: 52; Jezewski 2010.
41. Regarding the previous versions mentioned by Figueiredo in n. 16 above, Camões and Antônio José portray Amphitryon as an almost tragic figure – following Plautus – incapable of understanding what takes place and threatening to destroy everything and everyone. In Antônio José's version, for instance, Amphitryon and Jupiter actually have a comic fence confrontation.
42. In Brazil, women were granted the right to vote in the Elections Code of 1932 (sanctioned by the Constitution of 1946).
43. Figueiredo 1964: 43.
44. Figueiredo 1970: 182–3.
45. Figueiredo 1957a: 89–90.
46. Slater 2000: 183.
47. Figueiredo 1957a: 64–5.
48. Figueiredo 1957b: 69.
49. Figueiredo 1957b: 80–1, 87.
50. Figueiredo 1957b: 83: 'Ao usar os mitos dessas figuras, será compreendido: modificando-os, surpreenderá a plateia que os identifique. Como no jogo de xadrez, suas peças são conhecidas, como o movimento delas' ('By using the [ancient] myths ... you will be understood: modifying them, you will surprise the audience that identifies them. Just as in a game of chess, your pieces are known, as is their movement').
51. Figueiredo 1970: XII.
52. This was the title proposed by French translator Gérard Caillet. See Figueiredo 1970: X.

7 Guilherme Figueiredo, Amphitryon and the Widow of Ephesus: Linking Plautus and Petronius

1. Maupoint 1733: 200.

Notes to pp. 89–91

2. Recent commentaries include Vannini 2010: 21–38, 234–63; Schmeling 2011: 427–35; Vannini 2013. For Petronius' text, I use Müller 2003. For the translation, I draw from Heseltine (= Warmington 1987).
3. E.g. J. Cocteau, *L'École des veuves* (1936); P. Morand, *La Matrone d'Éphèse* (1942); G. Sion, *La Matrone d'Éphèse* (1943); C. Fry, *A Phoenix Too Frequent* (1946).
4. For the theatricality of Petronius' version and certain theatrical adaptations, see Ragno 2009; Karakasis 2016. For its twentieth-century reception, see Gelzer 2003.
5. Figueiredo (Campinas, 1915 – Rio de Janeiro, 1997) began as a theatrical and literary critic in *O Jornal* and *Diário de Notícias* newspapers, respectively. He started his career as a playwright in 1948 with the comedy *Lady Godiva*. He published translations of Molière, Shakespeare and Bernard Shaw's texts. For his life and work, see Figueiredo 1984; 1998; Andrade 1989.
6. The Grupo Giz-en-Scène was set up in 1987 by professors and students at the Faculdade de Ciências e Letras of the Universidade Estadual Paulista Júlio de Mesquita Filho in Araraquara (São Paulo, Brasil). I thank Fernando Brandão dos Santos for granting me the opportunity of watching the video of the performance held in 1998.
7. This definition is employed here to mean a certain aspect of the twentieth-century Brazilian theatrical *renovaçao*: inspired by an intention for social action and pre-empted by the renowned strand of novelists known as 'Geração de 30', this movement had Jorge Andrade as one of its principal representatives.
8. For this discrepancy, see Jacobbi 1961: 92. For a general history of Brazilian theatre, see also Cacciaglia 1986; Prado 2001; Cortés and Barrea-Marlys 2003: 54–79; Magaldi 2004. For the connections with the classical tradition, see Cardoso 1998-9.
9. Figueiredo (1998: 123, 397) mentions this drama only few times in his own autobiography, referring to some negative reviews.
10. On this play, see Cardoso 1996; Gross 2010; Gomes 2012; Gonçalves 2017; Gonçalves in this volume. For Bertini's contributions, cf. n. 17 below.
11. Figueiredo 1973: 47. See also Figueiredo 1998: 492–518.
12. All English translations are mine.
13. Stegagno Picchio 2004: 13.
14. The first edition of this work is Figueiredo 1957b. I quote from Figueiredo 1973.
15. Figueiredo 1973: 44.
16. Ibid.: 38, 97.
17. See e.g. Pasetti 2007; Piselli 2009; Margotton and Huby-Gilson 2010; Ferry 2011; Oniga 2016. See also Bertini 1981: 332–5; 2007: 160–1; 2010a: 53–6; 2010b: 25–8.
18. Figueiredo (1970: IX) refers to Giraudoux's *Amphitryon 38*. Moreover, he translated Molière; see n. 5 above, Figueiredo 1998: 234–6, 423–5.
19. Figueiredo 1964: 14.
20. For these aspects and, in particular, Euclides' political involvement (his confinement in the Casa de Correção and, then, Guilherme's direct engagement in defending him), see Figueiredo 1977; 1998: 113–14, 267–9, 288–90; Dulles 2002: 82.
21. Davis 2008. The relationship between Figueiredo and his brother was controversial; see Figueiredo 1998: 445–7, 469–74, 565–7.

22. Figueiredo 1964: 194: 'As instituições vivem graças a êsses crimes ... É preciso manter uma certa dose de crime na sociedade' ('The institutions survive thanks to their crimes ... A certain quantity of crime is necessary in society').

23. Petron. *Sat.* 112.3: 'whichever from the acquaintances or strangers might have come to the tomb' ('quisquis ex notis ignotisque ad monumentum venisset'); 112.8: 'and the people wondered the next day' ('posteroque die populus miratus est').

24. Figueiredo 1964: 211.

25. Ibid.: 217: 'O povo precisa de símbolos como tu: és a própria mística da pátria!' ('People need symbols like you: you are the rightful Mystique of Nation').

26. For Figueiredo's sarcasm against Vargas' regime, see Figueiredo 1998: 297–8; 1984: 9–10, 30–2.

27. For the Second World War and postwar period in Brazil, see Skidmore 2007; Ioris 2014.

28. Figueiredo 1964: 225.

29. Figueiredo 1970: XI–XII.

30. Figueiredo 1964: 194: 'Preciso do cadáver do teu parente, para server de **exemplo**! ... O **exemplo**, é isto o que quero!' ('I need to take the corpse of your relative as an **example** ... The **example**, this is what I want!'); 238: 'Êsses ladrões crucificados, sabes? Eram um **exemplo** para a cidade! Um **exemplo**! ... Como tu com a promessa de morreres!' ('These thieves have been crucified. They were made an **example** to the city! An **example**! ... Like you who are determined to die') (All text in boldface is my emphasis).

31. Ibid.: 196–7: ARCONTE: Esta cidade tem quem dar um **exemplo** ao mundo! ... CÍNTIA: Sempre temos procurado ... dar o **exemplo** (ARCHON: This city has to set an **example** to the world ... CYNTHIA: We have always tried ... to set an **example**); 208: ARCONTE: És o **exemplo** da cidade (ARCHON: You are the **example** to the city).

32. Ibid.: 224: CÍNZIA: Tôda a cidade sabe que quero morrer, e devo morrer, como um **exemplo**! SENTINELA: Como um quê? CÍNZIA: Um **exemplo**. SENTINELA: Para a cidade tôda seguir êsse **exemplo**? CÍNZIA: ... Os soldados mais valentes dão o **exemplo**, nas guerras (CYNTHIA: Everybody in town knows that I want to die and must die, as an **example** to everyone! GUARD: As what? CYNTHIA: An **example**. GUARD: Should everybody in town follow your **example**? CYNTHIA: ... The bravest soldiers act as an **example** to everyone in the battle fields).

33. Usually conceived as a *spectaculum pulchritudinis* (Charit. 1.1.2; Parth. *narr. amat.* 6.1; *Hist. Apoll.* 1; Apul. *Met.* 4.28.3), this pattern is readapted by Petronius into a *spectaculum virtutis* (*Sat.* 111.1). On this, see Castagna 2003: 34. For the theme of fame in Petronius' Widow of Ephesus, see Dickison 2013.

34. Ragno 2009: 288–316.

35. Figueiredo 1964: 209: ARCONTE: Êste é um momento de verdadeira tragédia nacional (ARCON: This is a time of true national tragedy).

36. E.g. Cic. *leg.* 2.23.59.

37. Figueiredo 1964: 225: SENTINELA *Meio declamando*: Crês que podem ter cura as cinzas e os espíritos dos sepulcros? CÍNTIA: Que disseste? SENTINELA: Nada. Um troço de Virgílio. Poeta romano. Vamos, não queres voltar à vida? Não queres abandonar o teu êrro feminino, e voltar a gozar a alegria da luz? Isto é o que escreverá Petrônio (GUARD (*somehow declaring*): Do you believe that ashes and spirits of the dead can actually be cured [*ter cura*]? CYNTHIA: What did you say? GUARD: Nothing. Virgil's stuff. A poet from Rome. Let's go: Will you not return to life? Will you not remove your feminine failings and enjoy the happiness of the light again? This is what Petronius will write.). Cf. Verg. *Aen.* 4.34: 'Do you think ashes and spirits of the departed *care* for such things?' ('id cinerem aut manis credis

curare sepultos?') ~ Petron. *Sat.* 111.12: 'Believest thou that the ashes or the spirit of the buried dead can *feel* thy woe? Will you not begin life afresh? Will you not shake off this womanish failing, and enjoy the blessings of the light so long as you are allowed?' ('id cinerem aut manes credis **sentire** sepultos? vis tu reviviscere? vis discusso muliebri errore, quam diu licuerit, lucis commodis frui?'). Moreover, Ibid.: 227: SENTINELA *declamando*: Podes gostar de lutar contra um amor que te agrada? Outro troço de Virgílio (GUARD (declaring): Would you like to struggle against a love that you care for? More of Virgil's stuff). Cf. Petron. *Sat.* 112.2 where Verg. *Aen.* 4.38 is quoted. In general, Virgil was one of Figueiredo's favourite Latin poets during his school days; Figueiredo 1998: 108.

38. Rimell 2002: 129–39; Eickmeyer 2006: 94–7.
39. Paratore 1933: II, 352, n. 1.
40. Pecere 1975: 95–100; Huber 1990: 43–4.
41. Serv. and Claud. Don. *ad* Verg. *Aen.* 4,31. Cf. Vannini 2010: 252–3; Schmeling 2011: 431.
42. Figueiredo adopts the same strategy to other 'classical' authors, e.g. Shakespeare, Goethe, Baudelaire, Keats; on the opening of Keats' *Endymion*, see Figueiredo 1998: 496.
43. Prado 2001: 79.
44. Figueiredo 1964: 215.
45. Ibid.: 25.
46. On the theme of war, as developed in Plautus' text and its rewritings, see Piselli 2009: 84–7.
47. Figueiredo 1970: XII, quoted in Gonçalves (this volume) p. 87.
48. For the text of Plautus' *Amphitryon* and its translation, I use De Melo 2011.
49. E.g. Figueiredo 1964: 20–1: ALCMENA: êste homem vai morrer! ... Por que existem as guerras? Por quê? (This man is going to die! ... Why do wars exist? Why?); 22–3: 'Volta coberto de glória! ... "Ritorna vincitor"!' ('Come back covered in glory! ... "Ritorna vincitor"!')
50. Oniga 1991: 214.
51. In general, for a serious interpretation, see Sedgwick 1960: 103. For a grotesque reading, see Perelli 1983; Phillips 1984–5; Pérez Gómez 1991; Crampon 1993. See further Oniga 1998; Palmieri 2001: 145–8; Bianco 2007: 221–50.
52. On this etiquette ('la retorica del posto'), see Cipriani 1990: 116–20. For Sosia's *canticum*, its serious sources and parodic purposes, see Oniga 1985; Rivoltella 2008.
53. Figueiredo 1964: 18: 'Prefiro ser escravo vivo a ser herói morto' ('I prefer to be a living as a slave than a dead hero').
54. For this ritual (*res repetere*), see Petrone 2008–9.
55. For the expression 'imperio atque auspicio', which imitates the ritual formula engraved on the so-called *tabulae triumphales*, see Oniga 1991: 192; Christenson 2000: 176.
56. Figueiredo 1964: 12.
57. For the *spolia opima*, see Flower 2000.
58. Serv. *ad* Verg. *Aen.* 3.55.
59. Figueiredo 1964: 48–9, 52.
60. Ibid.: 10.
61. Ibid.: 54: 'Tens que escolher entres seres um covarde ou um marido enganado' ('You have to choose between being a coward or a cheated-on husband').
62. Figueiredo 1970: X.

63. Figueiredo 1964: 233–4.
64. Ibid.: 190.
65. Ibid.: 58.
66. For reversal as a Petronian narrative principle, see Fedeli 1986; Cicu 1986; McGlathery 2001.
67. See also vv. 839–43, 1086. For chastity as a quality of Alcmena already mentioned in Ps. Hes. *Scut.* 9–10, see Davidson 1998: 5.
68. Figueiredo 1964: 53–4.
69. For the test which Alcmena is put to, see Plaut. *Amph.* 688–9, 914. Furthermore, according to a version of the unfaithful widow subject, the husband is not truly dead, but merely pretends to be dead to test his wife's devotion. See Ragno 2012.
70. On the process of secularization achieved here by Figueiredo, see Cardoso 1998–9: 18.
71. Figueiredo 1964: 189.
72. Ibid.: 10.
73. Ibid.: I.
74. Apollod. *Bibl.* 2.4.8.
75. Figueiredo 1964: 204: DIANA: Podes mudar os destinos! JÚPITER: Posso apenas prever (DIANA: You can change destiny! JUPITER: I can just foresee it); 205: 'profeta não faz milagres ... Nós dizemos o futuro, mas não mudamos a lógica das coisas' ('a prophet can't do miracles ... We can say the future, but can't change the logic of things').
76. Ibid.: 204.
77. Ibid.: 'Não quero ter Cíntia nos meus braços como deus: quero que a sua virtude desmorone sem que eu a enfeitice! Nada de sobrenatural!' ('I don't want to hold Cynthia in my arms as a god: I want her virtue to collapse without bewitching her. Nothing supernatural!').
78. Molière, *Amphitryon*, I.3: 'En moi, belle, et charmante Alcmène, / vous voyez un mari, vous voyez un amant: / mais l'amant seul me touche, à parler franchement' ('Beautiful and charming Alcmene, you see a husband, you see a lover in me; but, to speak plainly, it is only the lover that I am interested in').
79. Giraudoux, *Amphitryon 38*, I.5: JUPITER: Un dieu aussi peut se plaire à être aimé pour lui-même ... Je remplirai d'abord l'office d'Amphitryon, de mon mieux, mais, bientôt ... serai ainsi aimé pour moi-même. (A god would also presumably enjoy to be loved as himself ... First, I will play Amphitryon's role as well as I can, but soon ... I will be loved as myself.).
80. Figueiredo 1964: 42–3: 'Oh, Alcmena, eu daria tudo para ser Anfitrião! ... Como um homem, Alcmena, quero amar-te como homem' ('Oh, Alcmene! I would give everything to be Amphitryon! ... As a man, Alcmene, I desire to love you as a man').
81. Plaut. *Amph.* 104–6, 134–5. For this typical trait of Jupiter, see De Martino 2000; Parisi 2013–14.
82. Figueiredo 1973: 66.

8 Electra's Turn to the Dark Side: Nelson Rodrigues' *Senhora dos Afogados*

1. Quoted in the programme of the 1954 production, directed by Bibi Ferrreira at the Municipal Theater of Rio de Janeiro. Author's own translation.

2. Bakogianni and Apostol 2018: 2.
3. On 'Deep Classics', see Butler 2016: 1–19.
4. Nikoloutsos (2012: 3) argues that this is representative of 'the syncretic, hybridized nature of Latin American rewritings of Greek and Roman drama'.
5. Bakogianni and Apostol 2018: 3–4.
6. http://www.academia.org.br/academicos/sabato-magaldi (accessed 13 August 2018). Scholarship on Rodrigues outside Brazil is limited and includes Spinu (1986); Yu Sun (2003). For a discussion of Brazilian theatre in the 1940s–1980s, and Rodrigues' role in it, see George (1992).
7. Magaldi 1998: 14–20.
8. Mythical echoes resurface in later work, e.g. in *All Nudity Shall Be Punished* (1965).
9. Magaldi 1998: 14.
10. Interview with João Valadares, director of the Cia da Farsa production of *Senhora dos Afogados*, on 15 June 2015. For a video recording of this production, see https://www.youtube.com/watch?v=b01hSLmfn3w (accessed 22 August 2018). My heartfelt thanks to the company and especially to João Valadares (Eduarda) and Sidneia Simões (Moema) for agreeing to be interviewed. This was the first time that the play was performed in the state of Minas Gerais.
11. For adaptation studies, see Bryant 2013: 47–67; Cartmell 2012: 1–12; Leitch 2012: 87–104. For comparative literature, see Ferris 2011: 28–45.
12. Drummond is a common surname in Brazil, arguably part of Rodrigues' strategy for appropriating the ancient play for his audience.
13. Bakogianni 2011.
14. On the appeal of antihero narratives, see Shafer and Raney 2012. Their analysis of how audiences in modern media can morally disengage while watching narratives featuring immoral characters (1028–31) is a useful tool with which to reflect on theatrical audiences of Rodrigues' anti-heroine.
15. The shade of Electra also haunts another Brazilian play, Francisco Pereira da Silva's *Lazzaro* (1948), modelled on Sophocles' and Euripides' dramas.
16. Rodrigues' surviving family does not grant access to his private papers, so any form of intentionality or biographical plausibility (for example, the extent of his knowledge and study of the Classics) is impossible to determine.
17. See Hardwick 2011: 56–7 on 'fuzzy' receptions.
18. For an analysis of O'Neil's reception of Greek tragedy, see Lambropoulos 2015: 221–9. On the reception of Electra in the first half of the twentieth century, see Bakogianni 2011; Scott 2005.
19. For Rodrigues' encounter with O'Neill's trilogy, see Magaldi 1981: 37–9; 1998: 15. For a comparison of Rodrigues and O'Neill's dramaturgy, see Rabelo 2004.
20. O'Neill 1988: 397.
21. For the impact of pop-psychology on O'Neill's *MBE*, see Pfister 1995: 53–104.
22. O'Neill 1992: 5.
23. Jung 1961: 154.
24. This crime takes place before the opening of Rodrigues' play.
25. Rodrigues 2012: 68. All Portuguese references are to the 1954 [2012] edition.
26. Rodrigues 1998: 256.

27. It is the sentence, she imposes on herself for inciting her brother Orin to kill Adam Brant, the Aegisthus character, and for her choice not to interfere when first her mother and then her brother commit suicide.
28. Bakogianni 2011: 195.
29. According to the stage directions (Rodrigues 1998: 201), Moema is dressed 'in strict mourning clothes'.
30. Magaldi 1981: 37–40; Campbell Britton 2008: 105.
31. For the position of the *Oresteia* in the Western canon, see Decreus 2004: 180.
32. Agamemnon also dies near the end of Piñera's *Electra Garrigo* (1948); see Andújar 2015: 363–4.
33. For Moema's 'mourning' clothes and her 'marvellous white dress' in the third act, see Rodrigues 1998: 201, 277.
34. The Cia da Farsa 2015 production ignored these stage directions; their Moema wears more colour, making her criminal behaviour all the more shocking because she hides it under 'normal' clothing.
35. http://www.wesleyan.edu/theater/productions/lady_of_the_drowned.html (accessed 19 May 2015); Origuela 2011: 134–47.
36. Nascimento 2008: 3.
37. In Greek tragedy, madness infects Orestes and not Electra; its effects are evident at the end of Aeschylus' *Choephori*, possibly also in the closing scene of Sophocles' *Electra* and during much of Euripides' *Orestes*. In Greek tragedy, however, madness is portrayed as an external God-given force (Harris 2013: 10), rather than an internal condition, as we understand it today. In the ancient tragic view, if Moema is mad, she is punished by the gods, which was not the case in the Cia da Farsa production.
38. For example, Kirstin Scott Thomas' 2014 portrayal of Sophocles' tragic heroine at London's Old Vic theatre: http://www.oldvictheatre.com/whats-on/2014/electra (accessed 14 July 2015). This Electra was deeply traumatized and thus more humane than Sophocles' uncompromising tragic heroine.
39. In the Cia da Farsa production, a red cloth was draped over Eduarda's hands to suggest their loss. In Rodrigues' dramatic text, the details of the punishment are revealed in a conversation between Misael, Paulo and the Comb Salesman who witnessed the amputation. See Rodrigues 1998: 279–81.
40. Eduarda complains that her husband possessed her without showing her physical affection. As a wife, she is not fulfilled and that is why, like Clytemnestra, she seeks affection elsewhere.
41. Rodrigues 1998: 282.
42. In the Cia da Farsa production, Valadares, who played Eduarda, drew the audience's attention to his hands throughout the performance. On the importance of hand gestures in Rodrigues' play, see Leite-Lopes 2007: 228–9; Meiches 2007: 95–6.
43. In the climax of the play, Rodrigues (1998: 286) makes explicit reference to this mirroring effect in his stage directions: 'Moema is in front of the mirror. We see Eduarda's image also ... Mother and daughter continue to make identical movements.'
44. Noivo: 'Reconhece a sua carne em mim?' (Fiancé: 'Don't you recognize your own flesh in me?', 247).
45. Magaldi (1998: 16) draws attention to the connection between Rodrigues' characters and the ancient story of Hippolytus and Phaedra, but does not discuss it extensively or specifically mention Euripides' source play.

46. Paulo: 'Podia ter matado o marido e não o amante ... Não podia? ... Podia ter matado nosso pai ... Tão culpado o marido quanto o amante; os dois a possuíram!' ('I could've killed the husband and not the lover ... Couldn't I? I could have killed our father ... The husband is as guilty as the lover, they both possessed her!', 279).

47. In the Wesleyan production, the ghosts of the Drummond dead appear on stage. In Rodrigues' dramatic text, their presence is implied. For example, in the stage directions for Act I, Scene: 'Ancestral portraits hang on the walls.' In Act II, Scene II: 'In this act, the size of ancestral portraits hanging on the walls has increased.' See Rodrigues 1998: 201 and 251, respectively.

48. Lavinia's decision to imprison herself at the end of O'Neill's trilogy offers the hope that she can find some peace and redemption.

49. This is the standard image of the city popularized in 1940s films, for example, those of singer and actress Carmen Miranda (http://www.imdb.com/name/nm0000544, accessed 29 May 2016). The Vargas regime (1930–54) promoted this uncomplicated view of its capital city.

50. As does O'Neill in *MBE* and Piñera in *Electra Garrigó*; Andújar 2015: 366.

51. The play demands a large cast of actors not usually feasible for smaller companies. The Cia da Farsa production featured only two or three chorus members played by the protagonists, when they were not required on stage for their main role. The play thus became more intimate, with the unintended result that the production de-emphasized Rodrigues' social criticism, a prominent feature of his drama.

52. Nunes 1986: 126; 130–1; Freire-Filho 2004: 21–3.

53. A Carioca is a resident of Rio de Janeiro. For Rodrigues' Carioca tragedies, see Magaldi 1998: 18–19; Campbell Britton 2008: 106.

54. Magaldi in Leite-Lopes 2007: 54.

55. Kwong Loke directed their 2006 production of *Senhora dos Afogados* at the Southwark Playhouse: http://stonecrabs.co.uk (accessed 19 May 2015).

56. StoneCrab's decision to add the pronoun 'Our' in front of their title for the play serves to strengthen its Catholic subtext, since 'our Lady' is shorthand for referring to the Virgin Mary. For a detailed discussion of the translation used in this production, see Origuela 2011: 123–33. On the key role played by the Catholic Church in Brazil, see Fausto and Fausto 2014: 23, 233, 259–60.

57. The Cia da Farsa production is a rare exception.

58. Pimental 1951: 101–3.

59. On Greek tragedy's performance reception in Brazil, see Motto 2011, especially his appendix that lists productions from 1990 to 2008.

60. Francisco Pereira da Silva's play *Lazzaro* (1948) is more closely modelled on Sophocles' and Euripides' texts than *Senhora dos Afogados*.

61. Leite-Lopes 2007: 222 and 225, respectively.

62. Martindale 2007: 309.

63. Bakogianni 2011: 197.

64. Rohter 2000: 2.

65. Magaldi 1998: 15.

9 Becoming Antigone: The Classics as a Model of Resistance in Jorge Andrade's *Pedreira das Almas*

1. Andrade 1978: 31. All translations, unless otherwise indicated, are my own.
2. Holanda 1963: 129–32. I owe special thanks to the Arquivo Multimeios at the Centro Cultural de São Paulo and to Prof. Elizabeth R. Azevedo of the Universidade de São Paulo for guidance with interviews and other archival material. Unless otherwise stated, all quotes are taken from the 1970 edition of *Pedreira das Almas* in *Marta, a Árvore, e o Relógio* and Lloyd-Jones' OCT of Sophocles.
3. Mazzara 1976: 205; Sant'Anna 1997: 12. In *Labirinto*, Andrade admits to being greatly influenced by the works of Holanda. Andrade 1978: 162–92, esp. 176.
4. Azevedo 2014: 88.
5. Rosenfeld connects the character of Mariana with Antigone and emphasizes Mariana's decision not to bury her brother's body, while Machado focuses on the similarity between Vasconcelos and Creon. Machado 1970: 621; Rosenfeld 1970: 607.
6. Azevedo 1998; Mazzara 1976, 1983; Moreno 1997; Mutran 2010.
7. Moreno 1997; Vilanova 1999; Júlio and Arantes 2010.
8. Garcia 1977.
9. Maddaluno 1991; Prado 2001; Barbosa and Mortoza 2017.
10. Azevedo 2014: 89; George 1992: 39.
11. Azevedo 2014: 88–90.
12. Andrade was not unique in his experimentation with classical forms of theatre during this time. Nélson Rodrigues drew on the myth of Electra in his 1947 play *Senhora dos Afogados* (see Bakogianni in this volume) and Vinícius de Moraes modernized the myth of Orpheus in his 1956 play *Orfeu da Conceição*, the inspiration for Camus' 1959 film *Orfeu Negro*. The film *Carnaval Atlântida* (1952) focuses on the myth of Helen of Troy and provides a parody of Hollywood-style epics set in classical antiquity. In 1962, two Brazilian plays used *Antigone* as an inspiration, Dias Gomes' *O Pagador de Promessas* (see Dixon 2015) and Carlos Henrique Escobar's *Antígona America*. In 1952, prior to the beginning of Andrade's career in the theatre, TBC produced Sophocles' *Antigone* as well as Anouilh's adaptation (see Magaldi and Vargas 2000; Prado 2001: 293–9). In the latter production, Antigone was played by Cacilda Becker, the actress who Andrade claims encouraged his career as a playwright.
13. Maddaluno 1991: 42.
14. Azevedo 2014: 87.
15. Andrade 1970b: 75. Both the real and the fictional town include underground systems of natural caves and mineshafts. The church that is depicted at centre-stage in *Pedreira* is a visual combination of the Igreja Matriz in the centre of São Tomé and the more rustic Igreja de Pedras, also in the city centre.
16. In the actual massacre, perpetrated by a group of renegade slaves on 13 May 1833, only one member of the family survived. In the play, Gabriel is this sole survivor of the massacre. Andrade 1970b: 86; Neto 2015.
17. Barman 1988: 191–216; Bieber 2000; 2001.
18. Barman 1988: 213.
19. Ibid.: 190–4.
20. Ibid.: 205.

21. Garcia 1977; Maddaluno 1991: 41. The dialogue between the two women was a change introduced in the 1960 edition. In the 1958 original, the opening dialogue is between Gabriel and Mariana. Azevedo 2014: 90.
22. Andrade 1970b: 78–9.
23. Ibid.: 81–4.
24. Andrade 1970b: 84. Maddaluno (1991: 41) points out that Urbana's very name, coming from the Latin *urbs* (city), aligns her with Creon, the staunch defender of the *polis* in *Antigone*.
25. Andrade 1970b: 84.
26. Urbana's actual inspiration is two-fold: 1) the *avó-onça* (jaguar grandmother), Andrade's term in *Labirinto* (Andrade 1978) for his powerful paternal grandmother, and 2) the mater dolorosa from Christian lore.
27. Andrade 1970b: 86.
28. Ibid.: 76.
29. Ibid.: 85.
30. Ibid.: 89.
31. Cf. the discussion between Creon and Haemon in *Ant.* 635–780.
32. Andrade 1970b: 80.
33. For multiplicity in post-colonial adaptations of classical literature, see Fradinger 2011a: 84–9; Van Weyenberg 2010.
34. Andrade 1970b: 89–90.
35. Ibid.: 91–2.
36. Ibid.: 95.
37. Ibid.: 96.
38. Dassin 1986: 25, 69.
39. Azevedo 1998: 170
40. Andrade 1970b: 97.
41. Andrade 1970b: 97.
42. Azevedo 2014: 90.
43. Andrade 1970b: 96.
44. Ibid.: 96–7.
45. Ibid.: 98–100.
46. Ibid.: 100–3.
47. Ibid.: 105–8.
48. Mariana hides Gabriel in a secret alcove in the grotto of São Tomé, not in the church. When she tells Vasconcelos he can find Gabriel by entering the church, she is technically correct, given the description of the tunnels and mineshafts that connect various parts of the city and that are used by members of the chorus to get out of doors without being spotted by the guards. See Andrade 1970b: 81, 90, 98.
49. Ibid.: 110.
50. Maddaluno 1991: 41. Cf. this to Lavinia's choice to stay behind in the house at the end of *Mourning Becomes Electra*. On O'Neill's influence on Andrade as a young playwright, see Azevedo 2014: 45–8.

51. The following is a full list of classical references in *Labirinto*, by character and page number: Actaeon – 135; Aeneas – 27, 30; Antigone and/or Polyneices – 35, 51–2, 67, 70, 105, 118, 157; Brutus – 191; Erinys – 159; Hecuba – 27; Io and/or Argus – 30–2, 79, 132, 135–7, 143, 146, 153, 158; Labyrinth and Minotaur – *passim*; Oedipus and Jocasta – 30, 31, 182, 185; Penelope – 68; Prometheus – 30, 142; satyrs – 161; Sparta and Leonidas – 118. Though not technically classical references, the following are recurring images that are also important to Andrade's oeuvre: mater dolorosa – 63, 101, 112, 223; *La Pietà* – 59, 61–3, 66, 79, 89, 106, 106, 117, 223.
52. Andrade 1970b: 34–5.
53. Ibid.
54. Andrade 1970b: 108.
55. This is Andrade's practice throughout *Labirinto* when he quotes his own writing.
56. Andrade 1978: 51, 118, 157.
57. Ibid.: 118; Andrade 1970b: 85.
58. The mother-son image also ties in with Andrade's recurring engagement with *La Pietá* in his writing. See Azevedo et al. 2012c; Andrade 1978: 58–66.
59. Maddaluno 1991: 41.
60. Azevedo 2014: 91.
61. Andrade 1978: 52.
62. Ibid.
63. Andrade 1970b: 109.
64. Or, as Maddaluno (1991: 42) says: 'Na peça de Jorge Andrade, pelo contrário, a morte está a serviço da vida' (in Jorge Andrade's play, on the contrary, death is in the service of life).
65. Arrabal 2012: 100.
66. Dassin 1986: 46–8.
67. Ibid.: 51–2.
68. Ibid.: 58–9.
69. Azevedo 2014: 89.
70. Andrade 1984: 20.
71. Arantes 2001: 48, n. 21; Vargas 1980: 26.
72. M. A. 1977.
73. M. A. 1977.
74. Garcia 1977.
75. Azevedo et al. 2012b: 112. Vargas 1980: 94.
76. Leite 2012: 107.
77. Ferreira 2008: 138–9; Néspoli 2010.
78. Arrabal 2012: 101.
79. Azevedo et al. 2012b: 117.
80. Andrade 1984: 20.
81. Leite 2012: 107.
82. Andrade 1978: 136.
83. Ibid.: 216.

84. Ibid.: 51–2, 219.
85. Azevedo 1998.
86. Andrade 1978: 148.
87. Andrade 1970b: 86.

10 Distorting the *Lysistrata* Paradigm in Puerto Rico: Francisco Arriví's *Club de Solteros*

I am indebted to Francis Mojica and Roberto Ramos-Perea for their assistance with accessing Arriví's papers in both the Centro de Estudios Avanzados de Puerto Rico y el Caribe and the Theatre Archive of the Ateneo Puertorriqueño. A British Academy Small Research Grant facilitated my research trip to Puerto Rico, for which I am grateful.

1. Miranda Cancela (2010: 40) lists Franklin Domínguez's *Lisístrata odia la política* as the only engagement with classical comedy in the Caribbean; see Ford in this volume. Anglophone accounts (e.g. Hall and Wrigley 2007; Olson 2014; Van Steen 2014) ignore Latin American receptions.
2. E.g. Dauster 1962; Morfi 1993: 421–54; Stevens 2004: 28–39. Montes Huidobro (1986: 599–606) provides the only existing detailed analysis.
3. This can be found throughout Arriví's unedited papers. Montes Huidobro (1986: 599) calls it a type of 'backwards *Lysistrata*' ('una especie de *Lisístrata* al revés').
4. See Kotzamani 1997 for a survey; Morales 2015 on *Chi-raq*. Cf. Klein 2014; Wetmore 2014.
5. Though this word has a variety of meanings across the Spanish-speaking world (for example, it is now associated with a popular drug), in a Puerto Rican context it invariably means 'mess' and 'confusion', hence my translation of 'A Big Ol' Mess'. See the entry in *El Tesoro lexicográfico del español de Puerto Rico*: https://tesoro.pr/lema/burundanga (accessed 12 April 2019).
6. Arriví 1953: 100–1.
7. All translations from *Club de Solteros* are my own.
8. Arriví 1953: 44.
9. Ibid.: 95.
10. Ibid.
11. Cf. Taaffe 1993: 62–6; Compton-Engle 2015: 52–3.
12. Cf. Foley 1982: 20.
13. Cf. Taaffe 1993: 79–87; Zeitlin 1996: 382–5.
14. Arriví 1953: 35–6: 'Entra Hipólito . . . Una barba y un bigote hirsutos le imparten un aspecto salvaje' ('Hipólito enters . . . A beard and a hirsute moustache give him a savage air').
15. E.g. Ibid.: 61.
16. See e.g. Ibid.: 80 (Don Juan and Orpheus), 104 (Zeus), 117 (Prometeo Segundo).
17. Ibid.: 80.
18. Montes Huidobro 1986: 600–1.
19. Arriví lists a six-credit Columbia Greek drama course on his general CV, several versions of which can be found among his unedited papers in the Library of the Centro de Estudios Avanzados de Puerto Rico y el Caribe in San Juan. Cf. Arriví n.d. b; n. d. c; n.d. d.

20. This theme can be traced to the misogynistic discourse of Hesiod and Semonides; Cf. Goff 1990: 10–11; Halleran 1995: 203.
21. Arriví 1953: 80.
22. Ibid.: 179: 'Cazar hombres no me arredra. Me euforiza.'
23. Ibid.: 183: Ello: Ahí verás al par de peces. (There you will see the pair of fish.)

    Lucila Los veo. No tardarán en llamarse pescados. (I see them. Soon they will be dead fish.)

    Ello El más grande es un tiburón guapísimo, interesante y difícil. (The largest is the most handsome shark, interesting and difficult.)

    Lucila Ya lo creo. Se ha cansado de atacar mujeres sin caer en el anzuelo. (I believe it. He's tired himself out attacking women without landing on the fishhook.)

24. Ibid.: 185.
25. Rosen 2014.
26. Cartledge 1990: 38.
27. Stuttard 2010b: 1.
28. Klein 2014: 108–26; Hardwick 2010: 82–3.
29. Revermann 2010: 71.
30. Morales 2013: 284.
31. Ibid.: 294.
32. Unfortunately, not much survives about the 1940 play, including its text, only that it involved puppets and featured a Don Osvaldo as protagonist rather than Dr Hipólito. Surviving accounts and anecdotes do not mention Aristophanes' *Lysistrata* and instead stress that this was a sketch staged by Arriví's high school students as part of a class on dramatic arts in the Escuela Superior de Ponce (Ponce High School). See Arriví 1953: 5; 1967: 153; Dauster 1977: 56; Montes Huidobro 1986: 599; Díaz Vélez 1993: iii.
33. Arriví 1953: 7; Díaz Vélez 1993: vii.
34. Arriví 1966b: 5; Montes Huidobro 1986: 599; Díaz Vélez 1993: vii.
35. Banham and Hill 1994: 222.
36. It is worth noting that Arriví re-edited other plays, e.g. *Sirena*, which has two versions, but he did not produce further sequels in the same manner as *Club de Solteros*.
37. Rosen 1997; Sommerstein 2010: 400–3; Nesselrath 2010: 443–5. One could argue that revision is a fundamental characteristic of ancient comedy: after all, Roman comedy is essentially a rebooting of Greek comic plots. Hunter (2017: 216) additionally points out that the genre 'provides the fullest circumstantial evidence for a whole range of "reperformance practices".
38. See Dover 1968: lxxx–xcviii; Revermann 2006: 326–32; Marshall 2012.
39. The text and translation (adapted) of both hypotheses are from Henderson 2007: 294–5.
40. It is noteworthy that the second version of *Clouds* was never performed, resulting in what Csapo and Slater (1995: 2) describe as 'the earliest drama whose survival is attributable to a purely literary transmission'; cf. Marshall 2012.
41. See also the discussion on this practice in Hunter 2017.
42. With the notable exception, of course, of Euripides' *Hippolytus*: see Barrett 1964: 10–44.
43. García del Toro 1988.

44. Cf. Díaz Quiñones 1996: 25.
45. Arriví 1966a.
46. Lyday and Woodyard 1976: xii.
47. Arriví 1967: 81–2.
48. See n. 2 above.
49. See Henderson 1987: xxvii who discusses the lack of female protagonists in Old Comedy.
50. Cf. Montes Huidobro 1986: 600.
51. This clipping (with no identifying date) from one of San Juan's English newspapers is found alongside material for the 1953 *Club de Solteros*, located in one of the two Arriví folders in the Theatre Archive of the Ateneo Puertorriqueño; Arriví n.d. a.
52. With seating for 2,000 spectators, cf. Cabrera 1986: 328.
53. Pilditch 1979: 7 states that between 1944 and 1956 not a single play by a Puerto Rican author was produced in the Teatro Universitario.
54. Johnson 1980: 36–9; Carr 1984: 167–8; Gallisá 2011: 74–8.
55. Gallisá 2011: 75.
56. Gallisá 2011: 76–7.
57. Arriví 1953: 7.
58. Ibid.: 76.
59. Ibid.: 100, quoted above.
60. Ibid.: 180.
61. Ibid.: 127.
62. For an overview, see Douglas Olson 2010.

11 Challenging the Canon in the Dominican Republic: *Lisístrata Odia la Política* by Franklin Domínguez

I would like to express my sincere thanks to Rosa Andújar and Konstantinos Nikoloutsos for their astute comments on this essay. I know without a doubt that their suggestions helped me to improve this chapter.

1. The theatre of the Dominican Republic warrants only a brief mention in contemporary scholarship. A notable exception is Aybar 1992, which includes an overview of the theatre from the Dominican Republic of the 1980s, recognizing that this was a pivotal decade where the theatre community endeavoured to make a concerted effort to understand Dominicanness through theatre. Other studies include Disla 1993; Martínez Tabares 2000; Quackenbush 2004a; 2004b; Stevens 2013.
2. All English translations of *Lisístrata odia la política* are mine. Throughout this essay, I will use the Spanish spelling (Lisístrata) to refer to Domínguez's text and the English spelling (Lysistrata) to speak about Aristophanes.
3. We can, of course, question whether comedy has a hero or not, on which see e.g. Rosen 2014.
4. This is an important point made about *Lysistrata* in e.g. Stuttard 2010a; Klein 2014: the play is not ground-breaking in terms of gender stereotypes since the women only temporarily upend the status quo.

5. Scholarship on the reception of ancient Greek theatre in the Hispanic Caribbean includes the papers in Nikoloutsos 2012a and Duprey 2013, and the chapters by Goff, Nikoloutsos, Andújar, Torrance and Billotte in Bosher et al. 2015.
6. On the challenges of adapting Greek drama in a colonial or 'postcolonial' setting, see Hardwick 2007 and Andújar and Nikoloutsos' introduction to this volume.
7. Andújar 2015: 362; Nikoloutsos 2015: 342.
8. Torrance 2015: 447.
9. See e.g. Matas 1971; Boal 1974; Smith 1984; Leal 2002; Taylor 2003; Meléndez 2006; Ford 2017.
10. Perhaps the most well-known example of a Hispanic Caribbean author drawing from ancient Greece is Virgilio Piñera's *Electra Garrigó* (1941), though there are others: Luis Rafael Sánchez's *La pasión según Antígona Pérez* (1968), José Triana's *Medea en el espejo* (1960), Antón Arrufat's *Los siete contra Tebas* (1968). On Piñera and Triana, see n. 8 above. On Arrufat, see Bromberg in this volume.
11. Domínguez 1981: 7.
12. Thanks to Konstantinos Nikoloutsos for the discussion of Pompey and its possible implications for this study.
13. Domínguez 1981: 37–8.
14. Ibid.: 43.
15. Ibid.: 95.
16. Ibid.: 109.
17. Ibid.:123.
18. Ibid.: 124.
19. Ibid.: 126.
20. While much of my discussion is on comedy in the ancient world, it is important to note that comedy and its role in resistance and performance is not limited to ancient Greece. For an analysis of comedy in the United States, see e.g. Gilbert 2016; Davies and Ilott 2018.
21. Rosen 2014: 231.
22. Ibid.: 230.
23. Stuttard 2010a contains excellent essays that explain the ancient context of this play. For this particular point, see Stuttard 2010b; also Hall 2010 and Hardwick 2010.
24. Henderson 1980; MacDowell 1995; Silk 2000; Reckford 1987; Stuttard 2010a.
25. Domínguez 1981: 13.
26. In his monumental study of Dominican history, Moya Pons (2010: esp. 357–8) confirms the importance of and the closeness between the police and the army when he discusses the administration of dictator Rafael Trujillo (1930–8). Though these events took place decades before Domínguez wrote *Lisístrata*, Trujillo and the legacy of his actions were never far from public consciousness in the 1980s. Joaquín Balaguer, who served in Trujillo's government, was president from 1966 to 1976 and again from 1986 to 1996.
27. Domínguez 1981: 50.
28. Ibid.
29. Ibid.: 22.
30. Ibid.: 24.

31. Thanks to Konstantinos Nikoloutsos for his insight in the etymology of these names.
32. Domínguez 1981: 28.
33. Ibid.: 52.
34. Ibid.: 56.
35. Ibid.: 124.
36. Nahm 2016 offers a fascinating discussion of subverting and reinscribing stereotypes within performance.
37. Bueno, me voy a casa. I'm sorry! (Sale con vivacidad casi dando saltitos) Carajo, ¡tan bien que me estaba yendo con esta maldita huelga. (Well, I'm going home. I'm sorry! (He exits in a lively way, almost jumping) Fuck, this damn strike was going so well for me.) Domínguez 1981: 125.
38. García 1997. See further Bátiz Zuk 2013.
39. García 1997: 16, with my translation.

12 Aeschylus and the Cuban Counter-Revolution

1. All translations from Spanish and Greek in this essay are mine, unless otherwise noted. The paper is affectionately dedicated to my son Simon, who became ill just before his six-month birthday and prevented me from presenting an early version of the argument in London. I am grateful to Rosa Andújar for reading the essay on my behalf on that occasion, and for sharing with me the audience's comments.
2. Reading 1980; Escarpanter 1986; 1990; Ford 2005; cf. Miranda Cancela 2006: 69–85.
3. Pérez Asensio 2009: 50.
4. E.g. the performances of *Edipo Rey* directed by Ludwig Schajowicz on 10 June 1945; and academic conferences in the University of Havana on 'The Character of Andromache across Literature' [*El character de Andrómaca a través de la literatura*] on 15 February 1919; 'The Ideals of Human Behavior and its Aesthetic Expression in the Theater of Sophocles' [*Los ideales de la conducta humana y su expression estética en el teatro de Sófocles*] on 10 March 1922; and 'History of a Tragedy: Greece' [*Historia de una tragedia*] focused on Aeschylean tragedy on 9 May 1923. See Vérez de Peraza 1959; Miranda Cancela 2006: 31–52.
5. Reviews by José Manuel Valdés Rodríguez in *Vida universitaria* 25 (1952): 16, and Rodolfo de Teatro Santovenia in *Germinal* 52 (1952): 18.
6. Vérez de Peraza 1959: 43, 50.
7. Miranda Cancela 2006: 25–6; Bromberg 2018: 498–500.
8. On Piñera, see Ford 2005: 101–6; Miranda Cancela 2006: 53–68; Andújar 2015; on Triana, see Escarpanter 1990; Ford 2005: 98–101; Miranda Cancela 2006: 87–105; Nikoloutsos 2012c; 2015.
9. Puig-Herz 2013.
10. Torrance 2007; 2015.
11. Bejel 1991: 5.
12. Arrufat 1968: 14.
13. Escarpanter 1990: 890; Ford 2005: 106.

14. Pérez Asensio 2010: 317; Torrance 2015: 446–7. The play ran from 9 to 15 November 2001 at the University of Strathclyde, in Glasgow, and premiered in Havana on 20 October 2007.
15. Escarpanter 1990: 889, and Martí de Cid and Wellington 1990: 37, respectively.
16. Bejel 1978.
17. Álvarez Morán and Iglesias Montiel 1999.
18. Arrufat explains to Barquet 2002: 137–49 that he consulted Spanish, French and English translations of Aeschylus as well as the Greek itself, alongside versions of the myth by Euripides, Seneca the Younger and Racine. Cf. Torrance 2007: 295 and n. 21 and 2015: 436 and n. 19. Cf. the prose adaptation, *Los Siete contra Tebas*, by César Miró (Peru, 1966), written only two years before Arrufat's version. This adaptation deserves a study of its own.
19. Arrufat 1968: 27.
20. Estévez 1992; Barquet 2002; Torrance 2007; 2015.
21. Barquet 1995: 78. Cf. Montes Huidobro 1973: 387–8; Estévez 1992: 863; Miranda Cancela 2006: 112–14 and *passim*.
22. Miranda Cancela 2006: 130–1.
23. Brown 1977: 305.
24. Arrufat 1968: 30.
25. Arrufat's chorus speaks 37 per cent (546/1475) of the play's verses. For comparison, approximately 49 per cent of Aeschylus' *Seven* is attributed to the Chorus. Without Arrufat's two non-Aeschylean scenes, however (among the Theban champions [205–9 = 118 verses; thirty-nine choral] and between the two brothers [222–30 = 255 verses; 0 choral]), *Los Siete* is 46 per cent choral (507/1102) and very near to the Aeschylean benchmark.
26. Arrufat 1968: 29.
27. Ibid.: 32–5.
28. Ibid.: 31.
29. Torrance 2007: 304.
30. Arrufat 1968: 33.
31. Ibid.: 32.
32. Ibid.: 34.
33. Ibid.: 33.
34. Ibid.: 34.
35. Ibid.: 35.
36. Ibid.: 41–4.
37. Ibid.: 41.
38. Ibid.: 42.
39. Ibid.
40. Ibid.: 41.
41. Ibid.: 43.
42. Ibid.: 84–93.
43. Ibid.: 86.
44. Ibid.: 87.
45. Ibid.

46. Ibid.: 89.
47. Ibid.: 14.
48. Torrance 2007: 296–302; 2015: 438–40.
49. Arrufat 1968: 44–50.
50. Ibid.: 35.
51. Ibid.: 44.
52. Ibid.: 48.
53. Ibid.: 102–5.
54. Ibid.: 45.
55. Barquet 1995: 82; Torrance 2007: 299.
56. Speech from 23 October 1962, p. 15: http://www.latinamericanstudies.org/fidel/FC-discurso-10-23-1962.pdf (accessed 24 April 2019).
57. Arrufat 1968: 46.
58. Barquet 1995: 81–2; 2002: 91–2; Torrance 2007: 299; 2015.
59. Arrufat 1968: 64–5. For the possible allusion to Archilochus (Fragment 211) in these lines, see Miranda Cancela 2006: 113 and n. 6.
60. Arrufat 1968: 52.
61. Ibid.: 53.
62. Ibid.: 46.
63. Barquet 1995: 82; Torrance 2007: 298; 2015: 439.
64. Arrufat 1968: 53.
65. Torrance 2007: 299; 2015: 439.
66. Arrufat 1968: 59.
67. Ibid.: 60.
68. Ibid.: 81.
69. His name appears for the first time in the messenger's report at line 577; Dauster 1976: 13–14.
70. Álvarez Morán and Iglesias Montiel 1999.
71. Arrufat 1968: 27.
72. Bejel 1991: 8.
73. Arrufat 1968: 69.
74. Ibid.
75. Ibid.: 72.
76. Ibid.
77. Ibid.: 72–3.
78. Ibid.: 74.
79. Ibid.: 73.
80. Ibid.: 69.
81. Ibid.: 70.
82. Ibid.: 75, 78.
83. Ibid.: 75.

84. Ibid.: 78.
85. Ibid.: 76.
86. Ibid.: 84.
87. For the contested opinion that the fratricidal struggle reflects the quarrel between Castro and Che Guevara, see Barquet 2002: 150; Torrance 2007: 310–11; 2015: 445–6.
88. Arrufat 1968: 102.
89. Torrance 2007: 295; cf. Reading 1980: 360.
90. Arrufat 1968: 104.
91. Ibid.: 105.
92. Ibid.
93. Ibid.
94. Ibid.: 78.
95. The play's final stage direction is 'the day breaks' ('amanece', ibid.: 105).
96. Dauster 1976: 16.
97. See above, n. 15.
98. Torrance 2007: 312–13; 2015: 447; cf. Podlecki 1964; Brown 1977; Hutchinson 1985: 142–3 (*ad* 631–52); Sommerstein 2013: 76–80.
99. On the tetralogy of 467 BCE, which included the lost tragedies *Laius* and *Oedipus* and the satyric *Sphinx*, see Hutchinson 1985: xvii–xxx. On the myth of the *Seven* before Aeschylus, see Thalmann 1978: 8 and 1982.
100. E.g. Tucker 1908: xliv; Post 1950; Podlecki 1966: 31–41.
101. On Aeschylus in Sicily, see Smith 2018 and Andújar 2019: 36–7.
102. Thalmann 1982; Hutchinson 1985: xviii–xxx; Smith 2018: 37 and n. 98.
103. Bejel 1991: 5.
104. The uncertain dating of Euripides' *Phoenician Women* (409–407 BCE seem to be the most likely years) makes it more difficult to align the play's themes with the complex political climate of the late fifth century BCE. Still, the characterization of Eteocles as a tyrant in love with power and willing to do anything to maintain it may have been influenced by the sentiments that produced the 'Decree of Demophantos', passed in 410 BCE, which incentivized individuals to kill prominent members of anti-democratic factions. On the decree, and the accompanying oath that Athenians recited before the Dionysia (when tragedies were also performed), see Andocides, *On the Mysteries* 96–8, and discussion in Teegarden 2013.

13 The Contest between *Créolité* and Classics in Patrick Chamoiseau's Stage Plays

1. Glissant, quoted in Degras and Magnier 1984: 15: 'Je ne crois pas qu'il existe encore une littérature antillaise' ('I don't think that an Antillean literature yet exists').
2. Bernabé, Chamoiseau and Confiant 1993: 76/14.
3. For the argument that the manifesto 'reduces the plural archipelago to a cultural and linguistic unity', see Tcheuyap 2001: 44.
4. Bernabé, Chamoiseau and Confiant 1993: 90/29.

5. Ibid.: 77/15.
6. Ibid.: 96/35: 'nonintegration of oral tradition was one of the forms and one of the dimensions of our alienation' ('Cette non-intégration de la tradition orale fut l'une des formes et l'une des dimensions de notre aliénation').
7. Ibid.: 95/33.
8. For an exemplification of the dominance of Africa within *négritude*, see Irele 1964 and the creative works of Césaire, Senghor and Damas.
9. Bernabé, Chamoiseau and Confiant 1993: 8/28.
10. Ibid.: 88/27 (italics in original).
11. Benítez-Rojo 1996: 12.
12. Chamoiseau 1982. This is the only one of Chamoiseau's plays (of which there have been seven so far) to have been published.
13. On the vast number of works inspired by Sophocles' play, see Steiner 1984; Mee and Foley 2011. It is likely that Chamoiseau – who is certainly aware of the work of the Haitian writer Feliks Moriso-Lewa by the time he writes *Éloge de la créolité* – knew of Moriso's 1953 *Antigone in Creole*. On Moriso-Lewa, see Hawkins in this volume.
14. See McConnell 2013: 39–69.
15. Bernabé, Chamoiseau and Confiant 1993: 80/18.
16. Ibid.: 82/20.
17. My analysis is indebted to the excellent article of Bérard (2008) on the play. In a turn of events made sweetly ironic by the problematic permanence of the written word which is explored in much of his work, Chamoiseau tells me that he no longer possesses a copy of *Une Manière d'Antigone* (email correspondence – 15 February 2019).
18. Bérard 2008: 41.
19. The official Martiniquan flag is the French flag.
20. Bérard 2008: 48.
21. Murashov 1997: 209. As Emerson (1997: 66–7) argues, Murashov's conclusion causes him to overlook Bakhtin's celebration of the literary in other works.
22. Bérard n.d.
23. Chamoiseau's play requires only two actors: Antigone and the guard – which in itself might remind us of Athol Fugard, John Kani and Winston Ntshona's famous South African 'reception' of *Antigone*, *The Island* devised just two years earlier.
24. Bakhtin 1981: 405: 'Pure drama strives towards a unitary language, one that is individualized merely through dramatic personae who speak it.'
25. Ibid.: 358.
26. Bérard: n.d.: 'Le garde incarne le côté populaire et servile de la population antillaise alors qu'Antigone est la réflexion, la résistance et la révolte' (translation my own).
27. Bakhtin 1981: 405.
28. Ibid.: 270 (italics in original).
29. Such a view of drama contravenes Bakhtin's own vision of the genre, since he believed that it was necessarily monologic: 'The whole concept of a dramatic action, as that which resolves all dialogic oppositions, is purely monologic' (1984: 17). However, this need not prevent the application of Bakhtin's theory to drama, particularly as Bakhtin can himself be seen as arguing a special case for Dostoevsky in this section, as he counters Leonid Grossman's

Notes to pp. 174–177

identification of a 'dramatic form' in Dostoevsky, by arguing that drama is monologic and 'for this reason, authentically dramatic dialogue can play only a very secondary role in Dostoevsky's polyphonic novel' (ibid.).

30. As Bérard (2008: 44) discusses, Chamoiseau's Antigone is not only a peasant, but she is a câpresse (the official definition of which is that she has two-thirds black blood and one-third white), which evokes her Creoleness, and 'the composite identity of the Antillean population of Martinique, born from the encounter of Africa and Europe'.
31. Quoted and translated in Bérard 2008: 48.
32. Ibid.
33. Bérard (2008: 49) mentions this connection, though without elaborating on the distinction between oral Greek myths and their literary counterparts.
34. Bernabé, Chamoiseau and Confiant 1993: 96/35.
35. Parry 1971. The details of this oral tradition and how the poems came to be written down continue to provoke debate. Meanwhile, the most prominent contemporary objector to the oralist school of thought is the prodigious Greek literary scholar, Martin West (2011).
36. Parry 1971: ix–x.
37. Bernabé, Chamoiseau and Confiant 1993: 100/39.
38. On the power and legitimacy that Carabosse feels are conferred on her by her writing of these laws, see Bérard 2009: 119.
39. Chamoiseau 1982: 6.
40. Ibid.: 26: 'the witch of the fir trees and the snow imposes silence, a heavy, heavy, heavy silence'. Carabosse literally silences the inhabitants of the island, who have been speaking in Martiniquan Creole, by paralysing their speech organs (26–7, 89). See Conteh-Morgan 2010: 98, 105.
41. See e.g. Brown 1994; Hulme and Sherman 2000; Willis 1989.
42. Chamoiseau 1982: 138–9.
43. Bernabé, Chamoiseau and Confiant 1993: 88/27.
44. Chamoiseau 1982: 33: 'Nous devons rester pure'. Despite her change of heart, her autochthonous roots remain important, as she counsels Algoline to be sure never to cut herself off from the Earth: 'mais jamais ho! Jamais ne te sépare de la Terre' (139). On this 'purity' standing in opposition to *métissage*, and Manman Dlo's change of heart, see Conteh-Morgan 2010: 100–1.
45. Dash 1998: 139.
46. On the play's tone, see Chamoiseau 1982: 21–3 where Carabosse, much to Balai's amusement, defines 'humans' as being exactly like herself (the same red hair, the same language, the same cults and rules of witchcraft, the same clothing). The ludicrous list becomes more ominous as she adds, as if as an afterthought, that they must also have the same nose, eyes and skin colour as she has. A multi-layered humour is also seen when the young Algoline wishes to be a blue cloud, but her mother, Manman Dlo, insists they will become black clouds. Her reasoning is that the rain they provide nourishes the plants and animals of the land, but as she adds that Algoline must keep herself as she is and remain pure ('Préserve-toi de tout / Ferme-toi tout / Reste pur'), there is a suggestion that her objection is also to the *métissage* that the blue suggests. See Chamoiseau 1982: 37–8.
47. Albeit a *négritude* that is less Césairian than Senghorian.

48. The oral roots of the Homeric epics had been asserted since the eighteenth century (not least by Friedrich August Wolf), but it was Parry and Lord's fieldwork in Yugoslavia in the 1930s that altered the scholarly landscape.
49. Chamoiseau 1982: 5. See also Conteh-Morgan 2010: 94.
50. Chamoiseau 1988: 52–3. It is ironic that, despite this recognition of the importance of the spoken word's ephemerality, Chamoiseau has claimed that some folktales have a monolithic form and that to adapt them is problematic. See Sahakian 2017: 116–17.
51. Chamoiseau 1997: 27–8. I have adapted Réjouis and Vinokurov's translation in order to note the important difference between 'parole' and 'mot' which is elided in their version.
52. Thomas 1992: 21.
53. Ibid.: 3–4.
54. Goff 2005. Cf. this volume's introduction for Spanish and Portuguese colonialism and the Classics.
55. See Chamoiseau (1982: 17, 25) for examples of Carabosse's disingenuous claims to be colonizing the island for its own sake: 'Mais c'est bien aux représentants de la brillante culture-sorcière gréco-latine que revient le fardeau de régenter ce monde'; 'Une oeuvre philanthropique / régenter ce chaos / charger ce monde sur nos épaules.'
56. Chamoiseau 1982: 78, translated and quoted in Conteh-Morgan 2010: 97.
57. Translation by Wilson (2017): 397.
58. Derrida 1967: 194 cited in Havelock 1986: 35–6.
59. Havelock 1986: 36.
60. Lévi-Strauss 1961: ch. 28.
61. Plato, *Phaedrus* 274c–275e.
62. Glissant, *Discours*, cited in Praeger 1992: 43.
63. Ibid.
64. Praeger 1992: 47.
65. Lord 1960: 129 cited in Whitaker 1996: 208.
66. Whitaker 1996.
67. Glissant 1999: 147.
68. Greenwood 2005: 67. This is explored at greater length in Greenwood 2010.
69. Chamoiseau (1994) depicts this attempt to deracinate Martiniquan children by compelling them to speak only in French at school, whipping them for speaking in creole and mocking any creole traditions they had.
70. On the storyteller's constant physical and vocal presence embodying the threatened Creole orality and resistance to Western culture, see Bérard 2009: 119–20.
71. Bérard 2005: 91.
72. Chamoiseau does this repeatedly in his fiction. See e.g. *Solibo Magnifique*.
73. Bernabé, Chamoiseau and Confiant 1993: 113/52.
74. Greenwood 2011: 365.
75. This resonates with Derek Walcott's theory, published just a few years earlier in 'The Muse of History' (1974), whereby temporal distance is replaced by simultaneity to undo the oppressive power of history.

14 Dismantling the Anthropological Machine: Feliks Moriso-Lewa's *Antigòn* and Luis Alfaro's *Electricidad*

1. Alfaro uses *cholo/a*, originally derogatory (López 2011: 224), in positive terms to refer to any Latinx from a barrio.
2. Alfaro 2006: 76. El Pollo Loco is a fast-food Mexican restaurant.
3. Ibid.: 80.
4. I use the Creole name Feliks Moriso-Lewa, rather than the Francophone Félix Morisseau-Leroy.
5. Spears and Joseph 2010 offers historical and contemporary studies of Haitian Creole.
6. Stavans 2000 on the rise of Spanglish and Paz's comment.
7. For the historical variability of Spanglish, see Stavans 2008; Rosa 2016; Zentella 2016.
8. See McFarland 2013 for such popularizations.
9. As discussed in Powers 2018: 51–88.
10. See this volume's introduction.
11. Weiner's chapter draws on Agamben and builds upon Weiner 2015a. On Agamben and classical models more broadly, see Hawkins 2018.
12. Developed particularly in Foucault 2003: 239–64.
13. Esposito (2004/2008: 41–2) demonstrates the ambivalent assessment of Foucault, for whom '[Nazism] was the old sovereign power that adopts biological racism for itself ... Or ... that it is the new biopolitical power that made use of the sovereign right of death in order to give life to a state racism.'
14. As recorded by Hoffman 1997: 567.
15. See Saint-Lot 2003: 31; Morisseau-Leroy 1992: 448–9.
16. Fradinger 2011b: 128, original emphasis.
17. Danticat 2010: 8–9.
18. Morisseau-Leroy 1992: 669–70; he states that some thought his *Antigòn* essentially predicted the Duvalier regime. His *Wa Kreyon* (*King Creon*) is an explicit commentary on Duvalier.
19. Fradinger (2011b: 128) resists reading *Antigòn* as 'a Haitian adaptation of a "Western classic" made palatable for local and international audiences'. 'Western' and 'classic' are both problematic terms, but however Antigone is phrased, Moriso made it meaningful for Haiti.
20. Lang 1997: 44.
21. Césaire 2017: 28.
22. Previously most Haitian intellectuals went to France for higher education, creating a colonial tension foregrounded in Césaire's career.
23. Morisseau-Leroy (1992: 667) describes shows called *Les cacos in caci* ['Soldiers in khaki'] that were popular during the occupation.
24. Lang 1997: 39–42.
25. Morisseau-Leroy 1992: 668–9. Reviews in Haiti were positive (Anonymous 1953a, 1953b), but negative in Paris (Kemp 1959).
26. Morisseau-Leroy 1987: 8–9.
27. Citations are from an unpublished translation created by Guilene Fiéfié and me based on Morisseau-Leroy 1987.

28. Fradinger (2011b: 140) discusses the name Sekle-Kite, an obscure Vodou *lwa*.
29. Morisseau-Leroy 1987: 31.
30. Weiner 2015a discusses this theme in detail from a biopolitical perspective.
31. Rehm (1994: 59–71) analyses the connection between Antigone's marriage and death. Although Antigone seems to be reduced to bare life, the choice to move in such a direction is her own. This bring her close to the model of Ziarek 2012, which shows that British suffragettes who resorted to hunger strikes simultaneously combined traits of both sovereign and bare life.
32. Fradinger 2011b: 141. Immediately after the prologue, Antigòn speaks the first line of dialogue in the play: 'I tell you, no!' (Mwen di w non!); Morisseau-Leroy 1987: 11. This 'no', already used to sum up Antigòn's character within the prologue, represents the totality of Antigòn's resilience in refusing what Kreyon represents. The final line of the play, by contrast, is the complicit and complacent 'Yes, King Kreon' ('Wi, Wa Kreyon') of Filo, Kreon's lackey; ibid.: 41. I am grateful to Jesse Weiner for his suggestion that the 'No' of Moriso's *Antigòn* may reveal an influence from Anouilh's version of her story.
33. Stratton 2011, including a discussion of Agamben's idea that werewolves are the quintessential monster of bare life.
34. Morisseau-Leroy (1992: 668) makes it explicit that his Kreyon 'was set up by the Haitian army and was an agent of political dictatorship in Haiti'.
35. Moriso's vision for Haiti has struggled amid decades of oppressive politics, economic disasters and environmental degradation, yet his more moderate goals of empowering Creole largely succeeded. As he put it in *New Testament* (1971): 'In 1954 I wrote my will. I said I don't want any priest to speak Latin over my head. I don't have that problem today because priests don't speak Latin anymore. Even God had to learn Creole like any white man coming here to do business with us.'
36. Powers 2011: 194.
37. Danticat 2010: 16: through Moriso's play, 'Sophocles . . . became a Haitian writer'.
38. Many of Alfaro's performances play to primarily affluent Anglos, such as the staging of *Mojada* I attended at the Oregon Shakespeare Festival in July 2017. Others, such as the 2011 performance of *Electricidad* at Seattle's eSe Teatro, draw a more mixed crowd.
39. In addition to the mixing of Greek with cholo, Spanish with English, Alfaro also draws upon Aztec mythology and Nahuatl language.
40. Alfaro 2006: 64.
41. I am grateful to Konstantinos Nikoloutsos for urging me to extend this contrast into the very titles of the two plays. Moriso presents Antigone herself in Creole guise, whereas Alfaro's Electricidad ('Electricity') is a hybrid from the start.
42. Interestingly, no character comments on the more unusual names Ifigenia and Orestes.
43. For this ancient etymology, see Aelian, *VH* 4.26.
44. Alfaro 2006: 64. Alfaro's point feels engaged with the Aeschylean Clytemnestra, but I have found no mention of Aeschylus in interviews with him. On the concept of *alektruos*, 'unmarried', in Aeschylus' *Oresteia*, see Ormand 1999: 69–70.
45. Alfaro 2006: 74.
46. Agamemnon presents Clytemnestra in the worst light at *Od.* 11.421–34; 24.199–204; other accounts of his death place the onus on Aegisthus (1.35–9, 3.304–10, 4.524–37).

47. Aeschylus (*Libation Bearers*, 876–8) has Clytemnestra nearly thwart Orestes' plan to kill her. In *Agamemnon* she dominates the stage throughout; she killed Agamemnon herself (1379–94) and defends her actions based on the execution of Iphigenia (1412–21), a point also made in Euripides' *Electra* (1000–3; 1011–50).
48. Alfaro 2006: 69, 72.
49. Ibid.: 65.
50. For both scars, see Goff 1991. Still valuable is Auerbach's meditation on Odysseus' scar (2003: 3–23). On Auerbach's reading, see Bakker 1999.
51. Alfaro 2006: 80.
52. Ibid.: 69.
53. Ibid.: 73.
54. Ibid.: 82.
55. Agamben 1998: 8.
56. This definition comes from Festus' *de Verborum Significatione*, s.v. *sacer mons*.
57. Agamben 1998: 28–9.
58. Ibid.: 9.
59. Ibid.: 114.
60. Agamben 2004: 73 (my emphasis).
61. Ibid.: 37.
62. Fischer 2007 uses Agamben's theories to analyse the objectification of Haitians in the photojournalism of Gilden 2002; and Whyte 2012 begins from Agamben's commentary on humanitarian organizations, thus prefiguring the events of 2018 in which President Trump described Haiti as a 'shithole', the Oxfam sex-scandal in Haiti was discovered and Mary Beard tweeted about the difficulty of remaining 'civilised' in a place like Haiti (@wmarybeard, 16 February 2018).
63. Thanks to Jesse Weiner for pointing me towards the discussion of Agamben in Butler and Spivak 2007, in which Butler comments on some of the limitations of Agamben's concept of bare life (42): 'We need more complex ways of understanding the multivalence and tactics of power to understand forms of resistance, agency, and countermobilization that elude or stall state power.'
64. Negri 1999: 21.
65. Ibid.
66. This is the title of Danticat 2010.
67. Agamben (2009: 14) makes this point, though he does not seem to have incorporated this idea into his biopolitical theory.
68. Thomas 2001: 222–59; pages.vassar.edu/pharos.
69. Greenwood 2010: xx.
70. Alfaro 2006: 67.
71. I composed this chapter amid the turmoil and anguish surrounding the death of Freddie Gray, an African-American man who lived in Baltimore and who died on 12 April 2015 due to spinal injuries sustained while in police custody on charges of possessing a switchblade. I pray that those inspired by the likes of Moriso and Alfaro continue to work towards dismantling the anthropological machines that divide us.

15 Antigone Undead: Tragedy and Biopolitics in Perla de la Rosa's *Antígona: Las Voces que Incendian el Desierto*

1. Hualde Pascual 2012: 199. Pianacci 2008 lists twenty-two adaptations. On *Antigone*'s Latin American history, see the essays in Nikoloutsos 2012a. Also, Steiner 1984; Avelar 1999; Fradinger 2011a, 2011b, 2013, 2015; Nelli and other essays in Wilmer and Žukauskaitė 2010; González González 2011; Mee and Foley 2011; Dixon 2015. I am grateful to Perla de la Rosa, who generously provided me with a filmed recording of the original production, which has enhanced my reading of the script. Thanks are also due to this volume's editors, as well as to Tom Hawkins and Tim W. Watson, who commented on drafts of this essay. I presented early versions of this chapter at University College London, Gettysburg College and Hamilton College, where I received constructive feedback on each occasion.
2. Poulson 2012: 48–9; Weiner 2015b: 280.
3. Pianacci 2009: 500.
4. Brunn 2012: 28.
5. Weiner 2015b: 280–1.
6. *Antígona* was produced by the Juárez theatre company Telón de Arena (Curtain of Sand). Telón de Arena remains active and its productions continue to address local and border issues. Perla de la Rosa continues to write and direct for the company, including the recent *King Tiger* (2019).
7. De la Rosa's *Antígona* is published as De la Rosa 2005. The play received scholarly treatment in Nigro 2008 and Pianacci 2009, as well as a brief mention in Fradinger 2011c. See also Guadalupe de la Mora's (2005) introduction to the published script of *Antígona*.
8. See Weiner 2015b: 278 on how Juárez's *maquilas* have attracted female labourers on the assumption that women will work for less pay and are more controllable. On *maquilas*, the demographics of their workers and labour issues surrounding them, see especially Livingston 2004; Cravey 1998.
9. Weiner 2015b: 279: 'Some statistics claim somewhat higher (though still appallingly low) conviction rates. However, these studies suggest that many, perhaps even the vast majority, of these convictions are illegitimate, and allege that authorities in Juárez have commonly tortured confessions out of innocent scapegoats.' See also Amnesty International 2003; Acosta Urquidi 2005; Wright 2006: 681.
10. Nigro 2008: 417.
11. See Staudt 2008 on the use of theatre and film to engage with the femicide and Weiner 2015b: 279. Caridad Svich's *Iphigenia Crash Land Falls on the Neon Shell That Was Once Her Heart (a rave fable)* (2004) features ghosts of the women of Juárez, and Mauricio Chernovetzky's short film *Cassandra* (2008) sets the *Trojan Women* in Chihuahua.
12. See Weiner 2015b, which offers a fuller treatment of the play's performance context.
13. Nelli 2012: 55; Weiner 2015b: 277.
14. Revivals include a 2015 production by Raíz Latinoamericana in Boston and a 2018 production at the University of Wisconsin-Madison.
15. See Foucault 2003: 240–7 for an overview of the term 'biopolitics'. While Foucault's definition of 'biopolitics' is Agamben's referent, the word itself appears in print well before Foucault.
16. Hualde Pascual 2012: 205. On Brecht's importance to Latin American theatre, see Brunn 2012: 39. On Anouilh's global influence on the *Antigone* tradition, see Mee and Foley 2011: 32–4, as well as the essays in Part VIII of that volume.

17. Agamben's biopolitics are also brought to bear on Latin American adaptations of Greek tragedy (including an *Antigone*) by Tom Hawkins' chapter in this volume.
18. Weiner 2015a and 2015b. Agamben (1998: 2) draws this distinction from Aristotle's *Politics*. As Hawkins (2018: 66) suggests in response to criticisms of Agamben's reading of Aristotle, 'the conceptual underpinnings of Agamben's system' exist from early Greek literature, and classical scholars 'ought to engage rigorously with his ideas' (50).
19. This paragraph adapts Weiner 2015a: 151–3.
20. Gibbons and Segal 2003: 150. Discussing Butler's (2000) reading of social and symbolic death in *Antigone*, Žižek (2004: 53–4) notes that Antigone lacks 'a full and definite socio-ontological status' and 'while still alive, she is already dead'. While Antigone's symbolic death and liminal space between the two deaths have been diversely interpreted, Lacan (1992) is instrumental in developing these readings of Sophocles. See also Harris 2017: 146; Hutchinson 1999: 68–9; Steiner 1984: 287.
21. See especially Rehm 1994 and Seaford 1987: 106–8. Seaford observes that wedding imagery in Attic culture commonly constructs bridal status as an ambiguous state of transition, often akin to death. As is the case with Antigone, death before marriage was 'often imagined, notably in epitaphs, as a kind of marriage, notably (for the girl) with Hades' (106). See also Honig 2013: 50; Ormand 1999: 90–8; Festic 2003: 86. Fradinger (2011a: 73) notes that Leopoldo Marechal's *Antígona Vélez*, first staged in Argentina in 1951, 'transforms Antígona into a mother-to-be'.
22. Brecht 1984: 4. All references to the main script of Brecht's *Antigone* (as opposed to the *Antigone Legend*) provide line numbers.
23. All subsequent references to De La Rosa's *Antígona* are from De La Rosa 2005.
24. On the ambivalence of *autonomos* in political contexts, see especially Goldhill 2012: 110–11 (with n. 5).
25. Miller 2007: 1.
26. Anouilh 1947: 88. Anouilh's contemporary Jean Paul Sartre understood Anouilh's Antigone similarly, arguing that she is 'not a character at all . . . She represents a naked will, a pure, free choice'. Sartre 1976: 34 (originally delivered as a lecture in 1946). On Antigone's 'no', see also Hawkins (this volume).
27. Lacan 1992: 282, also quoted in Miller 2007: 1.
28. Miller 2007: 1.
29. Butler 2000: 67. Also Žukauskaitė 2010: 68–9. On psychoanalytic readings and fetishizing of Antigone's 'desire for death', see Eagleton 2010; Griffith 2010. For a nuanced critique of Butler, see Honig 2013: 41–56.
30. While I do not wish to push this reading irresponsibly far, if we read significance into Antígona's entrance into the morgue from below, the same is true of Hemón. From the time Hemón enters the morgue with Antígona until his actual death onstage, his character undergoes a fundamental change and, like Antígona, he becomes an advocate for the dead.
31. See Rehm 1994: 59–71.
32. Žukauskaitė 2010: 77.
33. Weiner (2015b: 298) briefly connects Agamben with de la Rosa's *Antígona*, but does not develop the reading.
34. See Butler 2000: 81; Norris 2000: 50 n. 23; Fradinger 2010a: 59–60; Žukauskaitė 2010: 72–9; Chanter 2011; Honig 2013: 206 n. 8; Tripathy 2013; Gsoels-Lorensen 2014; Weiner 2015a. Aspects of Lacanian psychoanalysis point towards biopolitics. For example, Lacan argues that Antigone's life is 'not worth living'; see Lacan 1992: 263; Žukauskaitė 2010: 69.

35. In a critique of Agamben, Butler and Spivak (2007: 35–43) question the very possibility of 'bare life'.
36. Agamben 1998: 1. Agamben here draws on Plato's *Philebus* and especially Aristotle (*Nicomachean Ethics*, *Metaphysics*, *Politics*).
37. Norris 2000: 50 n. 23.
38. Nelli 2010: 359–60.
39. Fradinger 2010a: 59. See also Norris 2000: 50 n. 23: 'The action of the play [*Antigone*] revolves around a conflict over the city's duties toward a body that is placed neither inside the city nor outside it.'
40. On the marginalization of femicide victims and their advocates in Juárez, see Livingston 2004; Wright 2006.
41. In the play's original staging, its Juárez audience, presumably multi-gendered, occupies the position of '*ciudadanos*', since Creón speaks facing the audience without a cast of 'extras' onstage.
42. Butler 2000: 81.
43. Agamben 1998: 11. Also Norris 2000: 46.
44. Nussbaum 1986: 59.
45. παρείρων is corrupt. Griffith (1999) prefers γεραίρων.
46. Soph. *Ant.* 365–75.
47. Translation adapted from Lloyd-Jones (1994).
48. Griffith 1999: 181. Gsoels-Lorensen (2014) develops a reading of Antigone as ἄπολις to connect Sophocles' heroine with deportation and forcible removal from the polity.
49. Agamben 1998: 168–70. On the state of exception, see also Agamben 2005.
50. Antígona's biopolitical claim reaches beyond that of Sophocles' Antigone in its universality. De la Rosa's Antígona demands legal protections and political inclusion for all women, ostensibly including immigrants and those of low socio-economic status. As Chanter (2011: 132) notes, Sophocles' Antigone resists 'a polis that formally excludes her from political participation', yet she 'colludes with a system of chattel slavery'. Antigone justifies her actions to Creon with the qualification that 'it was not a slave, but my brother who died' (οὐ γάρ τι δοῦλος, ἀλλ' ἀδελφὸς ὤλετο, 517).
51. As Weiner (2015b: 303) notes, 'Antígona's words here recall Anouilh's Antigone, who tells Creon, "*moi je suis reine*"'; Anouilh 1947: 86.
52. Butler 2000: 11. See also Honig 2013: 45.
53. Arendt 1998: 38, 50. See also Butler 2000: 81.
54. Agamben 1998: 159.
55. Nigro 2008: 418. On *Antígona*'s lack of resolution, see Weiner 2015b: 303–6.
56. Fradinger 2010b: 15.
57. Amnesty International 2011.
58. Carey and Torres 2010: 142.
59. Ibid. See also the essays in Fregoso and Bejerano 2010.
60. Agamben 1998: 114.
61. Ibid.: 115.

BIBLIOGRAPHY

Abel, L. (1963), *Metatheatre: A New View of Dramatic Form*, New York: Hill and Wang.
Acosta Urquidi, M. (2005), 'The Women of Ciudad Juárez', *CLAS Policy Papers*, https://clas.berkeley.edu/sites/default/files/shared/docs/papers/AcostaBookwithtitleandcover.pdf (accessed 16 April 2019).
Agamben, G. (1998), *Homo Sacer: Sovereign Power and Bare Life*, trans. D. Heller-Roazen, Stanford: Stanford University Press.
Agamben, G. (2004), *The Open: Man and Animal*, Stanford: Stanford University Press.
Agamben, G. (2005), *State of Exception*, trans. K. Attell, Chicago: University of Chicago Press.
Agamben, G. (2009), 'What is an Apparatus?', in *What Is an Apparatus? And Other Essays*, 1–24, Stanford: Stanford University Press.
Aisemberg, A. (2005), 'Teatros, empresarios y actores', in Pellettieri, 159–73.
Aisemberg, A. and Lusnich, A. L. (1997), 'Dido y Argia: las primeras tragedias sudamericanas', in O. Pellettieri (ed.), *De Esquilo a Gambaro: teatro, mito y cultura griegos y teatro argentino*, 13–24, Buenos Aires: Editorial Galerna.
Albornoz Farías, A. (2004), 'Veinticinco afanosos años entre textos y escenas', in J. Radrigán, *Crónicas del amor furioso*, 7–15, Santiago de Chile: Ediciones Fronteras del Sur.
Albornoz Farías, A. (2005), 'Juan Radrigán, veinticinco años de teatro, 1978-2004', *Acta Literaria*, 31: 99–113.
Alfaro, L. (2006), '*Electricidad*: A Chicano take on the tragedy of *Electra*', *American Theatre* (February): 63–85.
Alonso, L. and Houvenhagel, E. (2009), 'Antígona Vélez: la tragedia clásica Antígona releída como rito fundacional de un espacio argentino', *Neophilologus* 93: 439–52.
Altamirano, C. (2001), *Bajo el signo de las masas (1943–1973)*, Buenos Aires: Ariel.
Álvarez Morán, M. C. and Iglesias Montiel, R. M. (1999), 'Fidelidad y libertad mitográficas en *Los siete contra Tebas* de Antón Arrufat', in id. (eds), *Contemporaneidad del los clásicos en el umbral del tercer milenio*, 261–70, Murcia: Universidad de Murcia, Servicio de Publicaciones.
Amnesty International (2003), *Mexico. Muertes intolerables: 10 años de desapariciones y asesinatos de mujeres en Ciudad Juárez y Chihuahua*, https://amnistiainternacional.org/publicaciones/30-mexico-muertes-intolerables-10-anos-de-desapariciones-y-asesinatos-de-mujeres-en-ciudad-juarez-y-chihuahua.html (accessed 17 April 2019).
Amnesty International (2011), 'Annual Report: Mexico 2011', https://www.amnestyusa.org/reports/annual-report-mexico-2011 (accessed 24 April 2019).
Andrade, J. (1970a), *Marta, a árvore e o relógio*; [dez peças], São Paulo: Perspectiva.
Andrade, J. (1970b), 'Pedreira Das Almas', in Andrade 1970a, 73–115.
Andrade, J. (1978), *Labirinto*, Rio de Janeiro: Paz e Terra.
Andrade, J. (1984), 'As Confissoes de Jorge Andrade (Pt.2)', *Boletim Informativo do Instituto Nacional de Artes Cenicas* April 30: 15–27.
Andrade, M. de (1989), *A lição do guru: cartas a Guilherme Figueiredo, 1937–1945*, Rio de Janeiro: Civilização Brasileira.
Andrés, A. (1968), *Palabras con Leopoldo Marechal*, Buenos Aires: Carlos Pérez.
Andújar, R. (2015), 'Revolutionizing Greek Tragedy in Cuba: Virgilio Piñera's *Electra Garrigó*', in Bosher, Macintosh, McConnell and Rankine, 361–79.

Bibliography

Andújar, R. (2018a), 'The Caribbean Socrates: Pedro Henríquez Ureña and the Mexican Ateneo de la Juventud', in E. Richardson (ed.), *Classics in Extremis: The Edges of Classical Reception*, 101–14, London: Bloomsbury.

Andújar, R. (2018b), 'Pedro Henríquez Ureña's Hellenism and the American Utopia', in Laird and Miller, 168–80.

Andújar, R. (2019), 'Sites of Performance and Circulation', in E. Wilson (ed.), *A Cultural History of Tragedy in Antiquity*, 35–48, London: Bloomsbury.

Anonymous (1953a), 'Antigone, adaptation créole de Félix Morisseau-Leroy', *Le Nouvelliste*, Port-au-Prince, 16 July.

Anonymous (1953b), 'Antigone en créole, de Félix Morisseau-Leroy', *Le National Magazine*, Port-au-Prince, 16 August.

Anouilh, J. (1947), *Antigone*, Paris: La Table Ronde.

Aracil Varón, B. (2008), 'Predicación y teatro en la América colonial (A propósito de Usca Paucar)', in I. Arellano and J. A. Rodríguez Garrido (eds), *El teatro en la Hispanoamérica colonial*, 119–43, Madrid/Frankfurt: Iberoamericana/Vervuert.

Arantes, L. H. M. (2001), *Teatro da memória: história e ficção na dramaturgia de Jorge Andrade*, São Paulo: Annablume/FAPESP.

Arbo, D. and Laird, A. (2015), 'Columbus, the Lily of Quito and the Black Legend: The Context of José Manuel Peramás' Epic on the Discovery of the New World, *De invento novo orbe inductoque illuc Christi Sacrificio* (1777)', *Dieciocho* 38 (1): 7–32.

Ardao, A. (1980), *Génesis de la idea y el nombre de América latina*, Caracas: Centro de Estudios Latinoamericanos Rómulo Gallegos.

Arendt, H. (1998), *The Human Condition*, 2nd edn, Chicago: University of Chicago Press.

Aristophanes (2003), *Lysistrata*, trans. S. Ruden, Indianapolis and Cambridge: Hackett.

Arlt, M. (1997), 'El mito griego: permanencia y relatividad en *Antígona Vélez* de Marechal', in O. Pelletieri (ed.), *De Esquilo a Gambaro: teatro, mito y cultura griegos y teatro argentino*, 49–57, Buenos Aires: Galerna.

Arrabal, J. (2012), 'Resistir é Preciso: Entrevista Com Jorge Andrade. Istoé, 15 Jun. 1977', in Azevedo, Martins, Neves and Viana 2012a, 100–5.

Arrieta, R. A. (1948), *La literatura argentina y sus vínculos con España*, Uruguay: Colección Argiropolis.

Arriví, F. (n.d. a), *Assorted Papers*, 2 Folders, San Juan, Puerto Rico: Archivo Nacional de Teatro y Cine del Ateneo Puertorriqueño.

Arriví, F. (n.d. b), *Patria y Teatro*, unpublished, bound papers, San Juan, Puerto Rico: Biblioteca del Centro de Estudios Avanzados de Puerto Rico y el Caribe.

Arriví, F. (n.d. c), *Teatro de muñecos y muñecas. Jáibol de serpientes*, unpublished, bound papers, San Juan, Puerto Rico: Biblioteca del Centro de Estudios Avanzados de Puerto Rico y el Caribe.

Arriví, F. (n.d. d), *Trayectoria Dramaturgica: Tres autoenfoques de mi teatro a fluir de conciencia*, unpublished, bound papers, San Juan, Puerto Rico: Biblioteca del Centro de Estudios Avanzados de Puerto Rico y el Caribe.

Arriví, F. (1953), *Club de Solteros: Una guiñolada en tres espantos*, Barcelona: Editorial Tinglado Puertorriqueño.

Arriví, F. (1958), 'Perspectiva de una generación teatral puertorriqueña (1938–1956)', *Revista del Instituto de Cultura Puertorriqueña* (October-December): 41–7.

Arriví, F. (1960), *La Generación del treinta: el teatro*, San Juan, Puerto Rico: Instituto de Cultura Puertorriqueña.

Arriví, F. (1964), *Entrada por las raíces. Entrañamiento en prosa*, San Juan, Puerto Rico: Instituto de Cultura Puertorriqueña.

Arriví, F. (1966a), *Areyto Mayor*, San Juan, Puerto Rico: Instituto de Cultura Puertorriqueña.

Bibliography

Arriví, F. (1966b), *Cóctel de Don Nadie*, Barcelona: Rumbos.
Arriví, F. (1967), *Conciencia puertorriqueña del teatro contemporáneo (1937–1956)*, San Juan, Puerto Rico: Instituto de Cultura Puertorriqueña.
Arrufat, A. (1955), 'Antígona', *Ciclón* 1: 37–45.
Arrufat, A. (1968), *Los siete contra Tebas*, Havana: UNEAC.
Artaud, A. (1958), *Theater and its Double*, trans. M. C. Richards, New York: Grove Press.
Auerbach, E. (2003), *Mimesis: The Representation of Reality in Western Thought*, Princeton: Princeton University Press.
Augusto, M. d. G. (2010), 'A tradição da retórica clássica no Brasil: entre a filosofia e a poesia', in T. R. Assunção, O. Flores-Junior and M. Martinho (eds), *Ensaios de Retórica Antiga*, 313–50, Belo Horizonte: Tessitura.
Avelar, I. (1999), *The Untimely Present: Postdictatorial Latin American Fiction and the Task of Mourning*, Durham, NC: Duke University Press.
Aybar, R. (1992), 'El teatro dominicano en la década del 80', *Latin American Theatre Review* 25 (2): 169–72.
Aylwin, J. (2013), 'La herida de Chile', in Le Monde Diplomatique (ed.), *Rebelión en Wallmapu. Resistencia del Pueblo-Nación Mapuche*, 43–8, Santiago, Chile: Editorial Aún Creemos en los Sueños.
Azevedo, E. R. (1998), 'Família e Resitência Política no Espelho do Teatro: Jorge Andrade e Oduvaldo Viana Filho', *Cultura Vozes* 92 (4): 157–74.
Azevedo, E. R. (2014), *Recursos Estilisticos na Dramaturgia de Jorge Andrade*, Literatura Brasileira edn, São Paulo: EDUSP.
Azevedo, E. R., Martins, F., Neves, L. de O. and Viana, F. (eds) (2012a), *Jorge Andrade 90 Anos Releituras, I: A Voz de Jorge*, São Paulo: Universidade de São Paulo.
Azevedo, E. R., Martins, F., Neves, L. de O. and Viana, F. (eds) (2012b), 'Teatro Não é Palanque: Entrevista Com Jorge Andrade. Istoé, 19 Abr. 1978', in Azevedo, Martins, Neves and Viana 2012a, 112–19.
Azevedo, E. R., Martins, F., Neves, L. de O. and Viana, F. (eds) (2012c), 'Depoimento de Jorge Andrade – Semana Do Escritor Brasileiro, Acervo Idart-CCSP', in Azevedo, Martins, Neves and Viana 2012a, 188–99.
Bahamondes, P. (2015), 'Los dramas que no mueren: los clásicos inspiran el teatro actual', *La Tercera* (Santiago, Chile), 28 February, 95–6.
Bakhtin, M. (1981), *The Dialogic Imagination: Four Essays*, trans. C. Emerson and M. Holquist, Austin: University of Texas Press.
Bakhtin, M. (1984), *Problems of Dostoevsky's Poetics*, ed. and trans. C. Emerson, Minneapolis: University of Minnesota Press.
Bakker, E. J. (1999), 'Mimesis as Performance: Reading Auerbach's First Chapter', *Poetics Today* 20: 11–26.
Bakogianni, A. (2011), *Electra Ancient & Modern: Aspects of the Reception of the Tragic Heroine*, London: ICS.
Bakogianni, A. and Apostol, R. (2018), 'Face to Face: Locating Classical Receptions on Screen', in R. Apostol and A. Bakogianni (eds), *Locating Classical Receptions on Screen: Masks, Echoes, Shadows*, 1–16, New York: Palgrave.
Baldini, U. and Brizzi, G. P. (eds), (2010), *La presenza in Italia dei gesuiti iberici espulsi: aspetti religiosi, politici, culturali*, Bologna: CLUEB.
Banham, M. and Hill, E. (1994), *The Cambridge Guide to African and Caribbean Theatre*, Cambridge: CUP.
Barbosa, T. V. R. and Mortoza, M. P. D. (2017), 'Jorge Andrade e os Clássicos Gregos: Miscelâneas em Pedreira Das Almas', *Caligrama* 22 (1): 5–27.
Barman, R. J. (1988), *Brazil: The Forging of a Nation, 1798–1852*, Palo Alto: Stanford University Press.

Bibliography

Barquet, J. J. (1995), 'Heteroglosia y subversión en *Los siete contra Tebas* de Antón Arrufat', *Anales literarios* 1: 74–87.

Barquet, J. J. (1999), 'Subversión desde el discurso no-verbal y verbal de *Los Siete Contra Tebas* de Antón Arrufat', *Latin American Theatre Review* 32: 19–33.

Barquet, J. J. (2001/2), 'Texto y Contexto en la Receptión y Génesis de *Los siete contra Tebas* de Antón Arrufat', *Number Five*, unpaginated.

Barquet, J. J. (2002), *Teatro y Revolución Cubana: subversión y utopía en Los siete contra Tebas de Antón Arrufat*, Lewiston, NY: E. Mellen Press.

Barreda, P. (1985), 'La tragedia griega y su historización en Cuba: *Electra Garrigó* de Virgilio Piñera', *Escritura* 10: 117–26.

Barrenechea, F. (2015), 'Greek Tragedy in Mexico', in Bosher, Macintosh, McConnell and Rankine, 252–70.

Barrett, W. S. (1964), *Euripides* Hippolytos, Oxford: OUP.

Bátiz Zuk, M. (2013), 'Social and Political Criticism: The Reformulation of the Myth of Antigone in Franklin Domínguez's *Antígona-Humor*', in Duprey, 114–29.

Beatriz, R. (2008), *Creación Colectiva: El legado de Enrique Buenaventura*, Biblioteca de Historia del Teatro Occidental, Siglo XX, Buenos Aires: Atuel.

Bejel, E. (1978), 'El mito de la casa de Layos en *Los siete contra Tebas* de Antón Arrufat', *Hispamérica* 7, 110–14.

Bejel, E. (1979), 'La Direccion del Conjuro en *Los Siete Contra Tebas* de Antón Arrufat', *La Palabra y el Hombre* 30: 10–16.

Bejel, E. (1991), *Escribir en Cuba: entrevistas con escritores cubanos 1979–1989*, Río Piedras: Editorial de la Universidad de Puerto Rico.

Bengoa, J. (1992), *Conquista y Barbarie*, Santiago, Chile: Ediciones Sur.

Bengoa, J. (2002), *Historia de un conflicto. El Estado y los Mapuches en el siglo XX*, Santiago, Chile: Grupo Editorial Planeta.

Bengoa, J. (2003), *Historia de los antiguos mapuches del Sur. Desde antes de la llegada de los españoles hasta las paces de Quilín*, Santiago, Chile: Catalonia.

Bengoa, J. (ed.) (2004), *La memoria olvidada. Historia de los Pueblos Indígenas de Chile*, Santiago, Chile: Publicaciones del Bicentenario.

Bengoa, J. (2013), 'El viento que agita los trigales', in Le Monde Diplomatique (ed.), *Rebelión en Wallmapu. Resistencia del Pueblo-Nación Mapuche*, 5–16, Santiago, Chile: Editorial Aún Creemos en los Sueños.

Benítez-Rojo, A. (1996), *The Repeating Island: The Caribbean and the Postmodern Perspective*, 2nd edn, trans. J. E. Maraniss, Durham, NC: Duke University Press.

Bérard, S. (2005), 'Patrick Chamoiseau, héritier du contour? Respect ou trahison de la tradition orale dans Manman Dlo contra la fée Carabosse', in M-C. Hazaël-Massieux and M. Bertrand (eds), *Langue et identité narrative dans les littératures de l'ailleurs: Antilles, Réunion, Québec*, 91–105, Provence: Publications de l'université de Provence.

Bérard, S. (2008), 'From the Greek Stage to the Martinican Shores: A Caribbean Antigone', *Theatre Research International* 33 (1): 40–51.

Bérard, S. (2009), *Théâtres des Antilles: Traditions et scènes contemporaines*, Paris: L'Harmattan.

Bérard, S. (n.d.), 'Fiche pièce: *Une manière d'Antigone*', http://www.afritheatre.com/fiche_titre.php?navig=fiche&no_spectacle=955 (accessed 15 April 2019).

Bernabé, J., Chamoiseau, P. and Confiant, R. (1993), *Éloge de la Créolité / In Praise of Creoleness*, trans. M. B. Taleb Khyar, Paris: Gallimard.

Bernal Lavesa, C. (2005), 'La tragedia *Dido* de Juan Cruz Varela', in J. V. Bañuls, F. De Martino and C. Morenilla Talens (eds), *El teatro greco-latino y su recepción en la tradición occidental*, 83–112, Bari: Levante.

Bernand, C. (2006), *Un Inca platonicien. Garcilaso de la Vega 1539–1616*, Paris: Fayard.

Bibliography

Bertini, F. (1981), 'Anfitrione e il suo doppio: da Plauto a Guilherme Figueiredo', in G. Ferroni (ed.), *La semiotica e il doppio teatrale*, 307–36, Napoli: Liguori.
Bertini, F. (2007), 'Luoghi comuni dell'Amphitruo plautino nei rifacimenti umanistici e contemporanei', in G. Petrone and M. M. Bianco (eds), *I luoghi comuni della commedia antica*, 151–64, Palermo: Flaccovio.
Bertini, F. (2010a), *Sosia e il doppio nel teatro moderno*, Genova: Il Melangolo.
Bertini, F. (2010b), 'Rifacimenti contemporanei dell'Amphitruo di Plauto', in P. Esposito (ed.), *Da classico a classico. Paradigmi letterari tra antico e moderno. Atti del Convegno della CUSL. Fisciano – Salerno, 8–10 novembre 2007*, 19–44, Pisa: ETS.
Bethell, L. (2010), 'Brazil and "Latin America"', *Journal of Latin American Studies* 42 (3): 457–85.
Bianco, M. M. (2007), *Interdum vocem comoedia tollit. Paratragedia 'al femminile' nella commedia plautina*, Bologna: Pàtron.
Bieber, J. (2000), 'When Liberalism Goes Local: Nativism and Partisan Identity in the Sertão Mineiro, Brazil, 1831–1850', *Luso-Brazilian Review* 37 (2): 75–93.
Bieber, J. (2001), 'A "Visão do Sertão": Party Identity and Political Honor in Late Imperial Minas Gerais, Brazil', *Hispanic American Historical Review* 81 (2): 309–42.
Biglieri, A. (2016), 'Antigone, Medea, and Civilization and Barbarism in Spanish American History', in B. v. Zylt Smit (ed.), *A Handbook to the Reception of Greek Drama*, 348–63, Chichester: Wiley & Blackwell.
Billotte, K. (2015), 'The Power of Medea's Sisterhood: Democracy on the Margins in Cherríe Moraga's *The Hungry Woman*: The Mexican Medea', in Bosher, Macintosh, McConnell and Rankine, 514–24.
Boal, A. (1974), *Teatro del oprimido y otras poéticas políticas*, Buenos Aires: Ediciones de la Flor.
Bocchetti, C. (ed.) (2010a), *La influencia clásica en América Latina*, Bogotá: Universidad Nacional de Colombia.
Bocchetti, C. (ed.) (2010b), 'El diário de viaje a Grecia de Francisco de Miranda: Grecia en el contexto de la independencia americana', in Bocchetti 2010a, 53–76.
Bocchetti, C. (2013), 'Neoclassical Pompai in Early Twentieth-century Cartagena de las Indias, Colombia', in P. Niell and S. G. Widdifield (eds), *Buen Gusto and Classicism in the Visual Cultures of Latin America, 1780–1910*, 72–91, New Mexico: University of New Mexico Press.
Bosher, K., Macintosh, F., McConnell, J. and Rankine, P. (eds) (2015), *The Oxford Handbook of Greek Drama in the Americas*, Oxford: OUP.
Bosker, J. A. (2012), 'Reading and Writing Sor Juana's Arch: Rhetorics of Belonging, Criollo Identity, and Feminist Histories', *Rhetoric Society Quarterly* 42 (2): 144–63.
Boyle, C. (1992), *Chilean Theater, 1973–1985: Marginality, Power, Selfhood*, New Jersey: Associated University Press.
Brecht, B. (1984), *Sophocles'* Antigone, trans. J. Malina, New York: Applause.
Briceño Pozo, M. (1971), *Reminiscencias griegas y latinas en las obras del Libertador*, Caracas: Academia Nacional de la Historia.
Brockliss, W., Chaudhuri, P., Haimson Lushkov, A. and Wasdin, K. (2012), 'Introduction', in W. Brockliss, P. Chaudhuri, A. Haimson Lushkov and K. Wasdin (eds), *Reception and the Classics: An Interdisciplinary Approach to the Classical Tradition*, 1–16, Cambridge: CUP.
Bromberg, J. A. (2018), 'In Search of Prometheus: Aeschylean Wanderings in Latin America', in R. F. Kennedy (ed.), *Brill's Companion to the Reception of Aeschylus*, 488–508, Leiden: Brill.
Brown, A. L. (1977), 'Eteocles and the Chorus in *Seven against Thebes*', *Phoenix* 31: 300–8.
Brown, P. (1994), '"This thing of darkness I acknowledge mine": *The Tempest* and the Discourse of Colonialism', in J. Dollimore and A. Sinfield (eds), *Political Shakespeare: Essays in Cultural Materialism*, 2nd edn, 48–71, Manchester: Manchester University Press.
Brunn, V. (2012), 'Revolutionizing *Antigone*: A Puerto Rican Adaptation of Sophocles' Tragedy', in Nikoloutsos 2012a, 36–47.

Bibliography

Bryant, J. (2013), 'Textual Identity and Adaptive Revision: Editing Adaptation as a Fluid Text', in J. Bruhn, A. Gjelsvik and E. Frisvold Hanssen (eds), *Adaptation Studies: New Challenges, New Directions*, 47–67, London: Bloomsbury.

Buchrucker, C. (1987), *Nacionalismo y peronismo: la Argentina en la crisis ideológica mundial (1927–1955)*, Buenos Aires: Sudamericana.

Budelmann, F. (2007), 'The Reception of Sophocles' Representation of Physical Pain', *American Journal of Philology* 128 (4): 443–67.

Burnett, A. (1973), 'Medea and the Tragedy of Revenge', *Classical Philology* 68 (1): 1–24.

Butler, J. (2000), *Antigone's Claim: Kinship Between Life and Death*, New York: Columbia University Press.

Butler, J. and Spivak, G. C. (2007), *Who Sings the Nation State? Language, Politics, Belonging*, Calcutta: Seagull Books.

Butler, S. (ed.) (2016), *Deep Classics: Rethinking Classical Reception*, London: Bloomsbury.

Cabrera, F. M. (1986), *Historia de la Literatura Puertorriqueña*, Río Piedras, Puerto Rico: Editorial Cultural.

Cacciaglia, M. (1986), *Pequena história do teatro no Brasil (quatro séculos de teatro no Brasil)*, São Paulo: Universidade de São Paulo.

Camões, L. de. (1980), *Teatro (Anfitriões, El-Rei Seleuco e Filodemo)*, ed. J. Cardoso and D. Guimarães de Sá, Braga, Lisbon: Edição da Câmara Municipal de Braga.

Campbell Britton, B. (2008), 'Antunes Filho's Prismatic Theatre: Staging Nelson Rodrigues and Brazilian Identities', PhD diss., University of Michigan Ann Arbor.

Cardoso, Z. de A. (1996), 'L'Amphitryon Tropical de Guilherme Figueiredo', *Cahiers du Gita* 9: 187–93.

Cardoso, Z. de A. (1998–9), 'El teatro brasileño y la tradición clásica', *Praesentia* 2–3: 15–27.

Cardoso, Z. (2014), 'O percurso dos Estudos Clássicos no Brasil', *Clássica* 27: 17–36.

Carey Jr, D. and Torres, M. G. (2010), 'Precursors to Femicide: Guatemalan Women in a Vortex of Violence', *Latin American Research Review* 45 (3): 142–64.

Carr, R. (1984), *Puerto Rico: A Colonial Experiment*, New York: Vintage.

Carrió, R. (1990), 'Estudio en blanco y negro: Teatro de Virgilio Piñera', *Revista Iberoamericana* 56: 871–80.

Cartledge, P. (1990), *Aristophanes and His Theatre of the Absurd*, Bristol: Bristol Classical Press.

Cartmell, D. (2012), '100+ Years of Adaptations, or, Adaptation as the Art Form of Democracy', in D. Cartmell (ed.), *A Companion to Literature, Film, and Adaptation*, 1–12, Malden, MA: Wiley-Blackwell.

Castagna, L. (2003), 'La novella della Matrona di Efeso: meccanismi del riso', in P. Senay (ed.), *La Matrone d'Éphèse, Histoire d'un conte mythique. Colloque international 25–26 janvier 2002*, 27–42, Trois-Rivières, Québec: Université du Québec à Trois-Rivières.

CEDOC Archive (Centro de Documentação e Informação da Funarte), Rio de Janeiro: http://www.funarte.gov.br.

Césaire, A. (2017), *The Complete Poetry of Aimé Césaire*, trans. A. J. Arnold and C. Eshleman, Middletown, CT: Wesleyan University Press.

Chamoiseau, P. (1975), *Une Manière d'Antigone* (unpublished).

Chamoiseau, P. (1982), *Manman Dlo contre la fée Carabosse*, Paris: Editions Caribéennes.

Chamoiseau, P. (1988), *Solibo Magnifique*, Paris: Gallimard.

Chamoiseau, P. (1994), *Chemin d'école*, Paris: Éditions Gallimard.

Chamoiseau, P. (1997), *Solibo Magnificent*, trans. R-M. Réjouis and V. Vinokurov, New York: Vintage.

Chang, D. (2011), '*Antigone* Interculturated in Tainan of Southern Taiwan', in Mee and Foley, 147–55.

Chanter, T. (2011), *Whose Antigone? The Tragic Marginalization of Slavery*, Albany: SUNY Press.

Christenson, D. M. (2000), *Plautus: Amphitruo*, Cambridge: CUP.

Cicu, L. (1986), 'La matrona di Efeso di Petronio', *Studi italiani di filologia classica* 79: 249–71.
Cifuentes O. (ed.) (2009), *La Historia de Arauco*, 4 vols., Santiago, Chile: Editorial Ercilla.
Cipriani, G. (1990), 'Il galateo del comandante: modelli comportamentali in Sallustio (Cat. 60–61) e Cesare (*civ*. 3,94–96)', *Aufidus* 11–12: 101–25.
Coelho, M. C. M. N. (2015), 'António Vieira between Greeks, Romans, and Brazilians: Comments on Rhetoric and the Jesuit Tradition in Brazil', *Rhetoric Society Quarterly* 45: 225–36.
Coester, A. (1916), *The Literary History of Spanish America*, New York: Macmillan.
Compton-Engle, G. (2015), *Costume in the Comedies of Aristophanes*, Cambridge: CUP.
Conn, R. (2018), 'Classicism in Modern Latin America from Simón Bolívar to Roberto Bolaño', in Laird and Miller, 132–43.
Conteh-Morgan, J. with Thomas, D. (2010), *New Francophone African and Caribbean Theatres*, Bloomington and Indianapolis: Indiana University Press.
Cooper Alarcón, D. (1997), *The Aztec Palimpsest: Mexico in the Modern Imagination*, Tuscon: University of Arizona Press.
Cornejo Polar, A. (1998), 'Mestizaje e hibridez: Los riesgos de las metaforas. Apuntes', *Revista de crítica literaria latinoamericana* 24 (47): 7–11.
Coronil, F. (2008), 'Elephants in the Americas? Latin American Postcolonial Studies and Global Decolonization', in Moraña, Dussel and Jáuregui, 396–416.
Cortés, E. and Barrea-Marlys, M. (2003), *Encyclopedia of Latin American Theater*, Westport and London: Greenwood Press.
Corti, D. (1934), 'La primera lectura de Dido', *Boletín de la Academia Argentina de Letras* 2: 274–5.
Cova, J. A. (1947), *San Martín, Aníbal de los Andes: Vida y obra del gran capitán*, Buenos Aires: Editorial Venezuela.
Crampon, M. (1993), 'La dérision de la femme et le double visage d'Alcmène dans l'Amphitryon de Plaute', in M. M. Mactoux and E. Geny (eds), *Mélanges Pierre Lévêque 7, Anthropologie et société*, 41–55, Paris: Les Belles Lettres.
Cravey, A. J. (1998), *Women and Work in Mexico's Maquiladoras*, Lanham, MD: Rowman and Littlefield.
Csapo, E. and Slater, W. J. (eds) (1994), *The Context of Ancient Drama*, Ann Arbor, MI: University of Michigan Press.
Cullhed, E. (2018), 'Born with the Wrinkles of Byzantium: Unclassical Traditions in Spanish America, 1815–1925', in Laird and Miller, 181–95.
Cussen, A. (1992), *Bello and Bolívar; Poetry and Politics in the Spanish American Revolution*, Cambridge Studies in Latin American and Iberian Literature 6, Cambridge: CUP.
Danticat, E. (2010), *Create Dangerously: The Immigrant Artist at Work*, Princeton: Princeton University Press.
Dash, J. M. (1998), *The Other America: Caribbean Literature in a New World Context*, Charlottesville: University Press of Virginia.
Dassin, J. (ed.) (1986), *Torture in Brazil: A Report by the Archdiocese of São Paulo*, trans. J. Wright, New York: Vintage Books.
Dauster, F. (1962), 'Francisco Arriví: The Mask and the Garden', *Hispania* 45 (4): 637–43.
Dauster, F. (1973), *Historia del Teatro Hispanoamericano Siglos IX y XX*, Mexico: Ediciones de Andrea.
Dauster, F. (1976), 'The Theatre of Antón Arrufat', in Lyday and Woodyard, 3–18.
Dauster, F. (1977), 'Francisco Arriví y la entrada por las raíces', *Revista del Instituto de Cultura Puertorriqueña* (July–December): 56–70.
Dauster, F. (1996), 'Introduction: Contemporary Spanish American Theatre', in *Perspectives on Contemporary Spanish American Theatre*, 11–15, Lewisburg, WA: Bucknell University Press.
Davidson, J. (1998), 'Portrait of an Archaic Lady', *Antichthon* 32: 1–11.
Davies, C., Brewster, C. and Owen, H. (2006), *South American Independence: Gender, Politics, Text*, Liverpool: Liverpool University Press.

Bibliography

Davies, H. and Ilott, S. (2018), 'Gender, Sexuality and the Body in Comedy: Performance, Reiteration, Resistance', *Comedy Studies* 9 (1): 2–5.

Dávilo, B. (2009), 'The Río de la Plata and Anglo-American Political and Social Models, 1810–1827', in B. Bailyn and P. L. Denault (eds), *Soundings in Atlantic History: Latent Structures and Intellectual Currents, 1500–1830*, 371–404, Cambridge, MA: Harvard University Press.

Davis, S. (2008), 'Figueiredo, João Baptista de Oliveira (1918–1999)', in J. Kinsbruner (ed.), *Encyclopedia of Latin American History and Culture*, III, 228, Detroit: Gale.

Deane, H. A. (1963), *The Political and Social Ideas of Saint Augustine*, New York: Columbia University Press.

De Barsotti, R. C. (1954), *Una tragedia inédita de Juan Cruz Varela*, Buenos Aires: El Ateneo.

Decreus, F. (2004), 'The Democratic Ideal and the *Oresteia* between "Back to Basics" and Cultural Studies, between Old and New Historicism', *Phasis: Greek and Roman Studies* 7: 179–95.

Degras, P. and Magnier, B. (1984), 'Édouard Glissant, préfacier d'une littérature future: Entretien avec Édouard Glissant', *Notre Librairie* 74: 14–20.

De la Mora, G. (2005), 'Las voces de Antígona en Ciudad Juárez', in V. H. R. Banda and G. de la Mora (eds), *Cinco Dramaturgos Chihuahuenses*, 169–83, Juárez: Gobierno Municipal.

De la Rosa, P. (2005), '*Antígona; las voces que incendian el desierto*', in V. H. R. Banda and G. de la Mora (eds), *Cinco Dramaturgos Chihuahuenses*, 185–228, Juárez: Gobierno Municipal.

Delaney, J. (2002), 'Imagining "El Ser Argentino": Cultural Nationalism and Romantic Concepts of Nationhood in Early Twentieth Century Argentina', *Journal of Latin American Studies*, 34 (3): 625–58.

De Martino, F. (2000), 'Il "trucco di Zeus" e il motivo dell' "uno in più"', in K. Andresen, J. V. Bañuls and F. De Martino (eds), *La dualitat en el teatre*, 317–70, Bari: Levante.

De Melo, W. (2011), *Plautus: Amphitryon; The Comedy of Asses; The Pot of Gold; Two Bacchises; The Captives*, Cambridge, MA: Harvard University Press.

Derrida, J. (1967), *De la Grammatologie*, Paris: Les Éditions de Minuit.

Derrida, J. (1995), *Archive Fever*, trans. E. Prenowitz, Chicago: University of Chicago Press.

Desmond, M. (1994), *Reading Dido: Gender, Textuality, and the Medieval Aeneid*, Minneapolis: University of Minnesota Press.

Díaz Quiñones, A. (1996), *La Memoria Rota*, San Juan, Puerto Rico: Huracán.

Díaz Vélez, F. (1993), 'Sacrificios del hombre maravilloso por un cuento de Hadas', in F. Arriví, *Tres obras de teatro Puertorriqueno*, i–xv, San Juan, Puerto Rico: Instituto de Cultura Puertorriqueña.

Dickison, S. (2013), 'A Note on Fame and the "Widow of Ephesus"', in D. Lateiner, B. K. Gold and J. Perkins (eds), *Roman Literature, Gender and Reception: domina illustris. Essays in honor of Judith Peller Hallett*, 85–9, London: Routledge.

Disla, R. (1993), 'Teatro dominicano en cuatro tiempos', *Conjunto* 94: 104–6.

Dixon, P. B. (2015), 'A Brazilian Echo of Antigone's "Collision": Tragedy, Clean and Filthy', in Bosher, Macintosh, McConnell and Rankine, 380–99.

Dobrov, G. W. (2001), *Figures of Play: Greek Drama and Metafictional Poetics*, Oxford: OUP.

Dobrov, G. W. (ed.) (2010), *Brill's Companion to the Study of Greek Comedy*, Leiden: Brill.

Domínguez, F. (1981), *Lisístrata odia la política: obra teatral en tres actos inspirada en un tema de Aristófanes*, Santo Domingo: Feria Nacional del Libro.

Dornheim, N. J. (2000), 'The Relation between System and Literary Translation in 19th Century Argentina', in L. D'Hulst and J. Milton (eds), *Reconstructing Cultural Memory: Translation, Scripts, Literacy. Volume 7 of the Proceedings of the XVth Congress of the International Comparative Literature Association 'Literature as Cultural Memory'*, Leiden, 16–22 August 1997, 85–96, Amsterdam and Atlanta, GA: Rodopi.

Douglas Olson, S. (2010), 'Comedy, Politics, and Society', in Dobrov, 35–70.

Dover, K. J. (1968), *Aristophanes* Clouds, Oxford: OUP.

Dugdale, E. (2017), 'Philoctetes', in R. Lauriola and K. Demetrios (eds), *Brill's Companion to the Reception of Sophocles*, 77–148, Leiden: Brill.
Dulles, J. W. F. (2002), *Sobral Pinto, the Conscience of Brazil: Leading the Attack against Vargas (1930–1945)*, Austin: University of Texas Press.
Dunn, F. (2010), 'Metatheatre and Metaphysics in Two Late Greek Tragedies', in K. Gounaridou (ed.), *Text & Presentation: The Comparative Drama Series* 7, 5–18, North Carolina: McFarland & Company.
Dupont, F. (2007), *Aristote ou le vampire du théâtre occidental*, Paris: Aubier.
Dupont, F. and Letessier, P. (2012), *Le théâtre romain*, Paris: Armand Colin.
Duprey, J. (ed.) (2013), 'Whose Voice is This? Iberian and Latin American Antigones', *Hispanic Issues* On Line 13 (Fall).
Eagleton, T. (2010), 'Lacan's Antigone', in Wilmer and Žukauskaitė, 102–9.
Eickmeyer, J. (2006), 'Eumolpus' fast cuts. Formen und Funktionen der Lesersteuerung in der "Witwe von Ephesus"-Episode (Satyrica 110,6–113,5), mit einem Ausblick auf Petrons Poetik des Blicks', *Göttinger Forum für Altertumswissenschaft* 9: 73–104.
Emerson, C. (1997), *The First Hundred Years of Mikhail Bakhtin*, Princeton: Princeton University Press.
Ercilla, Alonso de, (1993), *La Araucana*, ed. I. Lerner, Madrid: Cátedra.
Escarpanter, J. A. (1986), 'Veniticinco años de teatro cubano en le exilio', *Latin American Theatre Review* 19: 57–66.
Escarpanter, J. A. (1990), 'Tres dramaturgos del inicio revolucionario: Abelardo, Estorino, Antón Arrufat, y José Triana', *Revista Iberoamericana* 56: 881–96.
Esposito, R. (2004/2008), *Bios: Politics and Philosophy*, Minneapolis: University of Minnesota Press.
Estévez, A. (1992), 'El golpe de dados de Arrufat', in Centro de Documentación Teatral (ed.), *Teatro Cubano contemporáneo*, 861–7, Madrid: Fondo de Cultura Económica.
Eurípides (1951), *Medea*, in *Obras Dramáticas*, trans. Eduardo Mier y Barbery, Buenos Aires: El Ateneo.
Euripides (2006), *Medea*, trans. M. Collier and G. Machemer, Oxford: OUP.
Fátima Silva, M. de (2017), 'Antigone', in R. Lauriola and K. Demetriou (eds), *Brill's Companion to the Reception of Sophocles*, 391–474, Leiden: Brill.
Fátima Sousa e Silva, M. de and Moraes Augusto de, M. d. G., (eds). (2015), *A recepção dos Clássicos em Portugal e no Brasil*, Coimbra: Coimbra University Press.
Fausto, B. and Fausto, S. (2014), *A Concise History of Brazil*, 2nd edn, Cambridge: CUP.
Fedeli, P. (1986), 'La matrona di Efeso. Strutture narrative e tecnica dell'inversione', in L. Pepe (ed.), *Semiotica della novella latina. Atti del seminario interdisciplinare "La novella latina"*, Perugia, 11–13 April 1985, 9–35, Roma: Herder.
Feile Tomes, M. (2015), 'News of a Hitherto Unknown Neo-Latin Columbus Epic, Part I: José Manuel Peramás's *De Invento Novo Orbe Inductoque Illuc Christi Sacrificio* (1777)', *International Journal of the Classical Tradition* 22 (1): 1–28.
Feile Tomes, M. (2017), 'Neo-Latin America: The Poetics of the New World in Early Modern Epic', PhD diss., Cambridge University.
Ferreira, C. O. (2008), 'Uma breve história do teatro brasileiro moderno', *Revista Nuestra America* 5: 131–42.
Ferris, D. (2011), 'Why Compare?', in A. Behdad and D. Thomas (eds), *A Companion to Comparative Literature*, 28–45, Malden, MA: Wiley-Blackwell.
Ferry, A. (2011), *Amphitryon, un mythe théâtral: Plaute, Rotrou, Molière, Dryden, Kleist*, Grenoble: Ellug.
Festic, F. (2003), 'Antigone in (post-)modern Palestine', *Hecate* 29 (2), 86–98.
Figueiredo, G. (1957a), *A God Slept Here. A Play by Guilherme Figueiredo*, trans. L. F. George, Rio de Janeiro: MEC, Serviço de Documentação.

Bibliography

Figueiredo, G. (1957b), *Xântias. Oito diálogos sobre a criação dramática*, Rio de Janeiro: Editora Civilização Brasileira.
Figueiredo, G. (1964), *Um deus dormiu lá em casa (Quatro peças de assunto grego)*, Rio de Janeiro: Editora Civilização Brasileira.
Figueiredo, G. (1970), *A rapôsa e as uvas. Um deus dormiu lá em casa*, 2nd edn, Rio de Janeiro: Editora Civilização Brasileira.
Figueiredo, G. (1973), *Cartilhas de teatro, VI, Como escrever peças de teatro*, Rio de Janeiro: SNT.
Figueiredo, G. (1977), *Guilherme Figueiredo: depoimento, 1977*. Interviewers: Rosa Maria Barbosa de Araújo and Lucia Lahmeyer Lobo, Rio de Janeiro [FGV/CPDOC: História Oral].
Figueiredo, G. (1984), *Cobras & Lagartos (Rodapés de crítica literária, 1943 a 1945)*, Rio de Janeiro: Nova Fronteira.
Figueiredo, G. (1998), *A bala perdida. Memórias*, Rio de Janeiro: Topbooks.
Fiorucci, F. (2007), 'La administración cultural del peronismo: política, intelectuales y Estado', University of Maryland, Latin American Studies Center, Working Paper N°20, http://www.lasc.umd.edu/documents/working_papers/new_lasc_series/20_fiorucci.pdf (accessed 16 April 2019).
Fischer, S. (2007), 'Haiti: Fantasies of Bare Life', *Small Axe* 11: 1–15.
Flower, H. I. (2000), 'The Tradition of the Spolia Opima: M. Claudius Marcellus and Augustus', *Classical Antiquity* 19: 34–64.
Foley, H. P. (1982), 'The Female Intruder Reconsidered: Women in Aristophanes' *Lysistrata* and *Ecclesiazusae*', *Classical Philology* 77: 1–21.
Foley, H. P. (2001), *Female Acts in Greek Tragedy*, Princeton: Princeton University Press.
Foley, H. P. (2014), 'Performing Gender in Greek Old and New Comedy', in Revermann 2014a, 259–74.
Ford, K. (2005), 'El espectáculo revolucionario: El teatro cubano de la década de los sesenta', *Latin American Theatre Review* 39: 95–114.
Ford, K. (2010), *Politics and Violence in Cuban and Argentine Theater*, New York: Palgrave Macmillan.
Ford, K. (2017), *Theater of Revisions in the Hispanic Caribbean*, New York: Palgrave Macmillan.
Foucault, M. (2003), *Society Must Be Defended: Lectures at the Collège de France, 1975–76*, trans. D. Macey, New York: St. Martin's Press.
Fradinger, M. (2010a), *Binding Violence: Literary Visions of Political Origins*, Stanford: Stanford University Press.
Fradinger, M. (2010b), 'Nomadic Antigone', in F. Söderbäck (ed.), *Feminist Readings of Antigone*, 15–23, Albany, NY: SUNY Press.
Fradinger, M. (2011a), 'An Argentine Tradition', in Mee and Foley, 67–89.
Fradinger, M. (2011b), 'Danbala's Daughter: Félix Morisseau-Leroy's *Antigòn an Kreyòl*', in Mee and Foley, 127–46.
Fradinger, M. (2011c), 'Mexico', in Mee and Foley, 423–4.
Fradinger, M. (2013), 'Demanding the Political: *Widows*, or Ariel Dorfman's Antigones', in Duprey, 63–81.
Fradinger, M. (2015), 'Making Women Visible: Multiple Antigones on the Colombian Twenty-First-Century Stage', in Bosher, Macintosh, McConnell and Rankine, 556–74.
Fragoso, J. M. (2001), 'Feminicidio Sexual Serial en Ciudad Juárez', *Debate Feminista* 25: 279–308.
Frambach, L. B. (2010), 'Um Deus Dormiu lá em Casa: O Eu e seu duplo em Guilherme Figueiredo', *O Marrare* (12): 171–86.
Fregoso, M. L. and Bejarano, C. (eds) (2010), *Terrorizing Women: Feminicide in the Américas*, Durham, NC: Duke University Press.
Freire-Filho, A. (2004), 'Nelson Rodrigues, Primeiro e único', in *Nelson Rodrigues, Teatro Completo*, vol. 2: Peças Míticas, 2nd edn, Rio de Janeiro: Nova Fronteira.
Gallisá, C. (2011), *Desde Lares*, 4th edn, Humacao, Puerto Rico: CG Editores.

Gallo, K. (2006), *The Struggle for an Enlightened Republic: Buenos Aires and Rivadavia*, London: Institute for the Study of the Americas.
Gallo, K. (2012), *Bernardino Rivadavia: El primer presidente argentino*, Buenos Aires: Edhasa.
Garcia, C. (1977), 'Em Texto já Antigo a Presença do Real', *O Estado de São Paulo*, 12 June.
García, W. (1997), 'Sabotaje textual/teatral contra el modelo canónico: *Antígona-Humor* de Franklin Domínguez', *Latin American Theatre Review* 31 (1): 15–29.
García, G. and Cavallari, H. (1995), 'Antígona Vélez: justicialismo y estructura dramática', *Gestos* 10 (20): 75–89.
García del Toro, A. (1988), *24 Siglos Después: Comedia. Lisístrata y Guerra- Guerra = sexo*, San Juan, Puerto Rico: Editorial Edil.
García Guadilla, C. (1996), *Conocimiento, educación superior y sociedad en América Latina*, Caracas: CENDES-Nueva Sociedad.
Garelli, M. (1996), 'La tragedia Dido de Juan Cruz Varela (su relación de hipertextualidad con el Canto IV de la *Eneida*), *Praesentia: Revista Venezolana de Estudios Clásicos* 1: 137–48.
Gelzer, F. (2003), '"Man setze sich nur an die Stelle der Matrone! Man wird nichts Unnatürliches finden". Zur Rezeption der Witwe von Ephesus im 20. Jahrhundert', *Germanistik in der Schweiz* 2: 25–42.
Gentili, B. and Pretagostini, R. (eds) (1986), *Edipo: il teatro greco e la cultura europea. Atti del convegno internazionale (Urbino 15–19 novembre 1982)*, Rome: Edizioni dell'Ateneo.
George, D. (1992), *The Modern Brazilian Stage*, Austin: University of Texas Press.
Gibbons, R. and Segal, C. (2003), *Sophocles: Antigone*, Oxford: OUP.
Gilbert, J. (2016), 'Response Laughing at Others: The Rhetoric of Marginalized Comic Identity', in M. R. Meier and C. R. Schmitt (eds), *Standing Up, Speaking Out*, 89–100, London: Routledge.
Gilden, B. (2002), *Haiti*, Manchester: Dewi Lewis Publishing.
Giraudoux , J. and Giraudoux, J.-P. (1998), *Amphitryon 38 / Amphitryon 39*, Paris: Librairie Générale Française.
Glissant, É. (1999), *Caribbean Discourse: Selected Essays*, trans. J. M. Dash, Charlottesville: University of Virginia Press.
Gobat, M. (2013), 'The Invention of Latin America: A Transnational History of Anti-Imperialism, Democracy, and Race', *The American Historical Review* 118 (5): 1345–75.
Goff, B. (1990), *The Noose of Words: Readings of Desire, Violence and Language in Euripides' Hippolytos*, Cambridge: CUP.
Goff, B. (1991), 'The Sign of the Fall: The Scars of Orestes and Odysseus', *Classical Antiquity* 10: 259–67.
Goff, B. (ed.) (2005), *Classics and Colonialism*, London: Duckworth.
Goff, B. and Simpson, M. (2008), *Crossroads in the Black Aegean: Oedipus, Antigone, and Dramas of the African Diaspora*, Oxford: OUP.
Goff, B. and Simpson, M. (2015), 'New Worlds, Old Dreams? Postcolonial Theory and Reception of Greek Drama', in Bosher, Macintosh, McConnell and Rankine, 30–52.
Goldhill, S. (2012), *Sophocles and the Language of Tragedy*, Oxford: OUP.
Gomes, C. E. (2012), 'Um Anfitrião extemporâneo: ecos do texto plautino em Guilherme de Figueiredo', in A. López, A. Pociña and M. d. Fátima Silva (eds), *De ayer a hoy: influencias clásicas en la literatura*, 195–202, Coimbra: Classica Digitalia.
Gonçalves, D. (1970), 'Introdução', in Andrade 1970a, 10–15.
Gonçalves, R. T. (2015a), 'The Triumph of Juno in Antônio José da Silva's *Anfitrião, ou Júpiter e Alcmena*', in D. Dutsch, S. L. James, D. Konstan (eds), *Women in Roman Republican Drama* (Wisconsin Studies in Classics), 232–52, Madison: University of Wisconsin Press.
Gonçalves, R. T. (2015b), *Performative Plautus: Sophistics, Metatheater and Translation*, Newcastle: Cambridge Scholars Publishing.
Gonçalves, R. T. (2017), 'Guilherme Figueiredo e a reescrita radical do mito de Anfitrião', in R. T. Gonçalves (ed.), *A comédia e seus duplos: o Anfitrião de Plauto*, 335–68, Curitiba, Kotter Editorial; Cotia, Ateliê Editorial.

Bibliography

Gonçalves, R. T. (forthcoming), 'Reception Today: Theater, Movies and Television', in D. Dutsch and G. Franko (eds), *A companion to Plautus: Blackwell Companions to the Ancient World*, Malden, MA: Wiley-Blackwell.

González Echevarría, R. (1998), *Myth and Archive: A Theory of Latin American Narrative*, Durham, NC: Duke University Press.

González Echevarría, R. and Pupo-Walker, E. (eds) (1996), *The Cambridge History of Latin American Literature, Volume 3: Brazilian Literature*, Cambridge: CUP.

González González, M. (2011), 'La tumba de *Antígona* de María Zambrano. A propósito de la figura de Ana', *Nova Tellus* 29 (2): 257–68.

González Rodríguez, R. (1996), 'Teatro Escambray: Toward the Cuban's Inner Being', *The Drama Review* 40 (1): 98–111.

Goodkin, R. E. (2005), 'Neoclassical Dramatic Theory in Seventeenth-Century France', in R. Bushnell (ed.), *A Companion to Tragedy*, 373–91, Malden, MA: Blackwell.

Greenwood, E. (2004), 'Classics and the Atlantic Triangle: Caribbean Readings of Greece and Rome via Africa', *Forum of Modern Language Studies* 11 (4): 365–76.

Greenwood, E. (2005), '"We Speak Latin in Trinidad": Uses of Classics in Caribbean Literature', in Goff, 65–91.

Greenwood, E. (2010), *Afro-Greeks: Dialogues between Anglophone Caribbean Literature and Classics in the Twentieth Century*, Oxford: OUP.

Greenwood, E. (2011), 'Dislocating Black Classicism: Classics and the Black Diaspora in the Poetry of Aimé Césaire and Kamau Brathwaite', in D. Orrells, G. K. Bhambra and T. Roynon (eds), *African Athena: New Agendas*, 362–80, Oxford: OUP.

Griffin, J. (1998), 'The Social Function of Attic Tragedy', *Classical Quarterly* 48 (1): 39–61.

Griffith, M. (1999), *Sophocles: Antigone*, Cambridge: CUP.

Griffith, M. (2010), 'Psychoanalysing *Antigone*', in Wilmer and Žukauskaitė, 110–34.

Gross, I. (2010), 'O duplo em *Anfitrião*, de Plauto e *Um deus dormiu lá em casa*, de Guilherme Figueiredo', *Cadernos do CNLF* XIV (2.2): 1272–88.

Gsoels-Lorensen, J. (2014), 'Antigone, Deportee', *Arethusa* 47 (2): 111–44.

Guevara, T. (1925–9), *Historia de Chile Prehispánico*, 2 vols., Santiago, Chile: Balcells & Co.

Gutiérrez, J. M. (1918), *Juan Cruz Varela: Su vida – sus obras – su época*, Buenos Aires: Casa Vaccaro.

Hall, E. (2010), 'The Many Faces of Lysistrata', in Stuttard 2010a, 29–36.

Hall, E. (2012), 'Ancient Greek Responses to Suffering: Thinking with Philoctetes', in J. Malpas and N. Lickiss (eds), *Perspectives on Human Suffering*, 155–70, London: Springer.

Hall, E. and Macintosh, F. (eds) (2005), *Greek Tragedy and the British Theatre 1600–1914*, Oxford: OUP.

Hall, E. and Wrigley, A. (eds) (2007), *Aristophanes in Performance 421 BC – AD 2007*, London: Modern Humanities Research Association.

Halleran, M. R. (1995), *Euripides: Hippolytus*, Warminster: Aris & Phillips.

Hardwick, L. (2003), *Reception Studies, Greece & Rome, New Surveys in the Classics*, Oxford: OUP.

Hardwick, L. (2005), 'Refiguring Classical Texts: Aspects of the Postcolonial Condition', in Goff, 107–17.

Hardwick, L. (2007a), 'Introduction', in Hardwick and Gillespie, 1–11.

Hardwick, L. (2007b), 'Postcolonial Studies', in C. W. Kallendorf (ed.), *A Companion to the Classical Tradition*, 312–27, Malden, MA: Blackwell.

Hardwick, L. (2010), '*Lysistratas* on the Modern Stage', in Stuttard 2010a, 80–9.

Hardwick, L. (2011), 'Fuzzy Connections: Classical Texts and Modern Poetry in English', in J. Parker and T. Matthews (eds), *Tradition, Translation, Trauma: The Classic and the Modern*, 39–60, Oxford: OUP.

Hardwick, L. and Gillespie, C. (eds) (2007), *Classics in Post-colonial Worlds*, Oxford: OUP.

Harris, O. (2017), *Lacan's Return to Antiquity: Between Nature and the Gods*, London: Routledge.

Harris, W. V. (2013), 'Thinking about Mental Disorders in Classical Antiquity', in W. V. Harris (ed.), *Mental Disorders in the Classical World*, 1–23, Leiden: Brill.
Havelock, E. (1986), *The Muse Learns to Write: Reflections on Orality and Literacy from Antiquity to the Present*, New Haven: Yale University Press.
Hawkins, T. (2018), 'Agamben, "Bare Life" and Archaic Greek Poetry'. *Mouseion* 3 (15): 49–70.
Henderson, J. (1980), 'Lysistrata: The Play and its Themes', in *Aristophanes. Essays in Interpretation*, Yale Classical Studies 26, 153–218, Cambridge: CUP.
Henderson, J. (1987), *Aristophanes* Lysistrata, Oxford: OUP.
Henderson, J. (2007), *Aristophanes Fragments*, Loeb Classical Library 502, Cambridge, MA: Harvard University Press.
Hexter, R. (1992), 'Sidonian Dido', in R. Hexter and D. Selden (eds), *Innovations of Antiquity*, 332–84, New York: Routledge.
Hirata, F. Y. (2010), 'Uma visão sobre os avanços e desafios das publicações acadêmicas brasileiras em Letras Clássicas', in E. Miranda Cancela and G. Herrera Díaz (eds), *Actualidad de los clássicos: III Congreso de Filológia y Tradición Clásicas*, 280–90, Havana: UH Editorial, Grupo de Estudios Helénicos.
Hoffman, L.-F. (1997), 'Félix Morisseau-Leroy', in V. Smith (ed.), *Encyclopedia of Latin American Literature*, 567–8, Chicago: University of Chicago Press.
Holanda, S. B. de. (1963), *Raízes Do Brasil*, Brasilia: Editôra Universidade de Brasília.
Honig, B. (2013), *Antigone, Interrupted*, Cambridge: CUP.
Hornby, R. (1986), *Drama, Metadrama and Perception*, Lewisburg, USV: Bucknell University Press.
Hualde Pascual, P. (2009), 'Fuentes griegas y latinas de *Mitrídates, Rey del Ponto*, de Fray Francisco del Castillo, "El ciego de la Merced"', *Estudios griegos e indoeuropeos* 19: 183–16.
Hualde Pascual, P. (2012), 'Mito y tragedia griega en la literatura iberoamericana', *Cuadernos de Filología Clásica: Estudios griegos e indoeuropeos* 22: 185–222.
Hualde Pascual, P. (2013), 'Reception of Greek Tragedy in Latin American Literature', in H. M. Roisman (ed.), *The Encyclopedia of Greek Tragedy*, 1091–6, Malden, MA: Wiley-Blackwell.
Huber, G. (1990), *Das Motiv der 'Witwe von Ephesus' in lateinischen Texten der Antike und des Mittelalters*, Tübingen: Narr.
Huenchumilla, F. (2010), '¡EX ALCALDE ANALIZA EL CONFLICTO INDÍGENA!', *Tiroalblanco*, 5 October 2010, http://www.tiroalblanco.cl/index.php?not=6707&do=muestra (accessed 16 April 2019).
Hulme, P. (2008), 'Postcolonial Theory and the Representation of Culture in the Americas', in Moraña, Dussel and Jáuregui, 388–95.
Hulme, P. and Sherman, W. H. (eds) (2000), *'The Tempest' and Its Travels*, London: Reaktion.
Hunter, R. (2017), 'Comedy and Reperformance', in R. Hunter and A. Uhlig (eds), *Imagining Reperformance in Ancient Culture: Studies in the Traditions of Drama and Lyric*, 209–31, Cambridge: CUP.
Huntington, S. (1997), *The Clash of Civilizations and the Remaking of World Order*, New York: Simon & Schuster.
Hurtado, M. L. (2009a), *Antología. Dramaturgia chilena del 2000: nuevas escrituras*, Santiago: Cuarto Propio.
Hurtado, M. L. (2009b), 'Teatro chileno: historicidad y autorreflexión', *Revista Nuestra América* 7: 143–58.
Hurtado, M. L. and Piña, J. A. (1993), 'Los niveles de marginalidad en Juan Radrigán', in J. Radrigán, *Teatro de Juan Radrigán*, 5–37, Santiago, Chile: LOM Ediciones.
Hutchinson, G. O. (1985), *Aeschylus: Seven against Thebes*, Oxford: OUP.
Hutchinson, G. O. (1999), 'Sophocles and Time', in J. Griffin (ed.), *Sophocles Revisited: Essays Presented to Sir Hugh Lloyd Jones*, 47–72, Oxford: Clarendon Press.
Ibarguren, C. (1937), *Las sociedades literarias y la revolución argentina (1800–1825)*, Buenos Aires: Espasa-Calpe.

Bibliography

Ioris, R. R. (2014), *Transforming Brazil: A History of National Development in the Postwar Era*, New York: Routledge.
Irele, A. (1964), 'A Defence of Negritude', *Transition* 13 (March–April): 9–11.
Itier, C. (1999), 'Los problemas de datación, autoría y filiación de *El robo de Proserpina y sueño de Endimión*, auto sacramental colonial en quechua', in I. Arellano and J. A. Rodríguez Garrido (eds), *Edición y anotación de textos coloniales hispanoamericanos*, 213–31, Madrid/Frankfurt: Iberoamericana/Vervuert.
Itier, C. (2010), *Juan de Espinosa Medrano, El robo de Proserpina y sueño de Endimión. Auto sacramental en quechua edición, traducción y estudio preliminar*, Lima: Instituto Riva Agüero e Instituto Francés de Estudios Andinos.
Jacobbi, R. (1961), *Teatro in Brasile*, Bologna: Cappelli.
James, C. L. R. (1978), 'Fanon and the Caribbean', in *International Tribute to Frantz Fanon*, New York: UN Centre against Apartheid.
Jameson, F. (2002), *A Singular Modernity: Essay on the Ontology of the Present*, New York: Verso.
Jansen, L. (2018), *Borges' Classics: Global Encounters with the Graeco-Roman World*, Cambridge: CUP.
Jauss, H. R. (1970), 'Literary History as a Challenge to Literary Theory', *New Literary History* 2 (1): 7–37.
Jelin, E. (2002), *Los trabajos de la memoria*, Buenos Aires: Siglo XXI.
Jezewski, V. (2010), 'Georg Kaiser: *Zweimal Amphitryon* (1943), Dédoublement et reconnaissance de l'autre', in J.-C. Margotton, A.-C. Huby-Gilson (eds), *Amphitryon ou la question de l'Autre. Variations sur un thème de Plaute à Peter Hacks*, 133–52, Saint-Étienne: Publications de l'Université de Saint-Étienne.
Johnson, R. A. (1980), *Puerto Rico: Commonwealth or Colony?*, New York: Praeger.
Júlio, L. M. and Arantes, L. H. M. (2010), 'Dramaturgia e Teatro: Mito, História e Recriação', *OPSIS* 5 (1): 97–109.
Jung, C. G. (1961), *The Collected Works of C. G. Jung*, vol. 4, trans. R. F. C. Hull, H. Read, ed. M. Fordham and G. Adler, London: Routledge.
Kahn, A. M. (2008), *The Ambivalence of Imperial Discourse: Cervantes's La Numancia within the 'Lost Generation' of Spanish Drama (1570–90)*, Bern: Peter Lang.
Karakasis, E. (2016), 'Petronian Spectacles: The Widow of Ephesus Generically Revised', in S. Frangoulidis, S. J. Harrison and G. Manuwald (eds), *Roman Drama and its Contexts*, 505–32, Berlin: De Gruyter.
Kemp, R. (1959), 'Haïti au Théâtre des Nations', *Le Monde*, Paris, 13 Mai.
Kimmel, M. S. (1994), 'Masculinity as Homophobia: Fear, Shame, and Silence in the Construction of Gender Identity', in H. Brod and M. Kaufman (eds), *Theorizing Masculinities*, 119–41, London: Sage.
Klein, E. B. (2014), *Sex and War on the American Stage: Lysistrata in Performance 1930–2012*, London: Routledge.
Klor de Alva, J. (1994), 'The Postcolonization of the (Latin) American Experience: A Reconsideration of "Colonialism," "Postcolonialism," and "Mestizaje"', in G. Prakash (ed.), *After Colonialism: Imperial Histories and Postcolonial Displacements*, 241–76, Princeton: Princeton University Press.
Knepper, W. (2012), *Patrick Chamoiseau: A Critical Introduction*, Jackson: University Press of Mississippi.
Konstan, D. (2014), 'Defining the Genre', in Revermann 2014a, 27–42.
Korenjak, M. (2016), *Geschichte der neulateinischen Literatur: vom Humanismus bis zur Gegenwart*, Munich: C.H. Beck.
Kotzamani, M. (1997), 'Lysistrata, Playgirl of the Western World: Aristophanes on the Early Modern Stage', PhD diss., City University of NY.

Kovacs, D. (2001), 'Introduction' to Medea, in Euripides, *Cyclops, Alcestis, Medea*, 276–81, (ed. and trans. D. Kovacs), Cambridge, MA: Harvard University Press.

Kyriakou, P. (2012), 'Philoctetes', in A. Markantonatos (ed.), *Brill´s Companion to Sophocles*, 147–66, Leiden/Boston: Brill.

Lacan, J. (1992), *The Seminar of Jacques Lacan, Book VII: The Ethics of Psychoanalysis, 1959–60*, trans. D. Porter, New York: W. W. Norton.

Lagos, R. (2003), 'No hay mañana sin ayer', http://bibliotecadigital.indh.cl/bitstream/handle/123456789/183/no-hay-manana.pdf?sequence=1 (accessed 4 April 2019).

Laird, A. (2006), *The Epic of America: An Introduction to Rafael Landívar and the Rusticatio Mexicana*, Bristol: Bristol Classical Press.

Laird, A. (2007), 'Latin America', in C. W. Kallendorf, *A Companion to the Classical Tradition*, 222–36, Malden, MA: Blackwell.

Laird, A. (2015), 'Colonial Spanish America and Brazil', in S. Knight and S. Tilg (eds), *The Oxford Handbook of Neo-Latin*, 525–40, Oxford: OUP.

Laird, A. (2018), 'Universal History and New Spain's Indian Past: Classical Knowledge in Nahua Chronicles', in Laird and Miller, 86–103.

Laird, A. and Miller, N. (2018), *Antiquities and Classical Traditions in Latin America*, Bulletin of Latin American Research 37, S1.

Lambropoulos, V. (2015), 'Eugene O'Neill's Quest for Greek Tragedy', in Bosher, Macintosh, McConnell and Rankine, 221–9.

Lang, G. (1997), 'Islands, Enclaves, Continua: Notes toward a Comparative History of Creole Literature', in A. J. Arnold (ed.), *A History of Literature in the Caribbean*, vol. 3, 29–56, Amsterdam: J. Benjamins.

Leal, R. (1980), *Breve historia del teatro cubano*, Havana: Editorial Letras Cubanas.

Leal, R. (2002), 'Introducción', in V. Piñera, *Teatro Completo*, ed. R. Leal, v–xxxiii, Havana: Editorial Letras Cubanas.

Lefevere, A. (2007), *Tradução, Reescrita e Manipulação da Fama Literária*, trans. C. Matos Seligmann, Bauru, Brazil: Edusc.

Lehmann, H. T. (1991), *Theater und Mythos. Die Konstitution des Subjekts im Diskurs der antiken Tragödie*, Stuttgart: Metzler.

Leitch, T. (2012), 'Adaptation and Intertextuality, or, What isn't an Adaptation, and What Does it Matter?', in D. Cartmell (ed.), *A Companion to Literature, Film and Adaptation*, 87–104, Malden, MA, and Oxford: Wiley-Blackwell.

Leite, P. M. (2012), 'Milagre Na Cela Traz o Novo Jorge Andrade: Folha de São Paulo, 13 Jul. 1977', in Azevedo, Martins, Neves and Viana 2012a, 106–8.

Leite-Lopes, A. (2007), *Nelson Rodrigues: Trágico então Moderno*, rev. and expanded 2nd edn, Rio de Janeiro: Nova Fronteira.

Lévi-Strauss, C. (1961), *Tristes Tropiques*, trans. J. Russell, New York: Atheneum.

Lida de Malkiel, M. R. (1974), *Dido en la literatura española: su retrato y defensa*, London: Tamesis Books Limited.

Lindberger, Ö. (1956), *The Transformations of Amphitryon*, Stockholm, Almqvist & Wiksell.

Livingston, J. (2004), 'Murder in Juárez: Gender, Sexual Violence, and the Global Assembly Line', *Frontiers: A Journal of Women Studies* 25 (1): 59–76.

Lloyd-Jones, H. (ed.) (1994), *Sophocles Antigone, Women of Trachis, Philoctetes, Oedipus at Colonus*, Loeb Classical Library 21, Cambridge, MA: Harvard University Press.

Lloyd-Jones, H. and Wilson, N. G. (eds) (1990), *Sophoclis Fabulae*, Oxford: OUP.

López, A. M. (2016), 'Platón en la América colonial: la Atlántida y el origen de los nativos indios en José de Acosta y Gregorio García', in L Fernandez, B. Garí Barceló, A. Gómez Romero and C. Snoey (eds), *Clásicos para un nuevo mundo: estudios sobre la tradición clásica en la América de los siglos XVI y XVII*, 205–22, Bellaterra: Centro para la Edición de los Clásicos Españoles, Universidad Autónoma de Barcelona.

Bibliography

López, L. (2005), 'La tragedia', in Pellettieri, 207–15.
López, M. K. (2011), *Chicano Nations: The Hemispheric Origins of Mexican American Literature*, New York: NYU Press.
López, A. and Pociña, A. (eds) (2009), *En recuerdo de Beatriz Rabaza: Comedias, tragedias y legendas grecoromanas en el teatro del siglo XX*, Granada: Editorial Universidad de Granada.
López Saiz, B. (2017), *Nación católica y tradición clásica en obras de Leopoldo Marechal*, Buenos Aires: Corregidor.
Lord, A. B. (1960), *The Singer of Tales*, Cambridge, MA: Harvard University Press.
Luciani, F. (1996), 'Spanish American Theater of the Eighteenth Century', in R. González Echevarría and E. Pupo-Walker (eds), *The Cambridge History of Latin American Literature, Volume 1: Discovery to Modernism*, 401–16, Cambridge: CUP.
Lupher, D. (2003), *Romans in a New World: Classical Models in Sixteenth-century Spanish America*, Ann Arbor: University of Michigan Press.
Lyday, L. F. and Woodyard, G. W. (eds) (1976), *Dramatists in Revolt: The New Latin American Theater*, Austin: University of Texas Press.
M. A. (1977), '*Pedreira* no Momento Certo', *Folha São Paulo*, 8 June.
MacCormack, S. (2006), *On the Wings of Time: Rome, Spain, the Incas, and Peru*, Princeton: Princeton University Press.
MacDowell, D. M. (1995), *Aristophanes and Athens: An Introduction to the Plays*, Oxford: OUP.
Machado, L. G. (1970), 'Pedreira das Almas', in Andrade 1970a, 618–24.
Maciel Jr., S. and Bourscheid, M. (2017), 'Tradução e performatividade em *Los dioses y los cuernos*, de Alfonso Sastre', in R. T. Gonçalves (ed.), *A comédia e seus duplos: o Anfitrião de Plauto*, 409–30, Curitiba, Brazil: Kotter Editorial.
Macintosh, F., McConnell, J. and Rankine, P. (2015), 'Introduction', in Bosher, Macintosh, McConnell and Rankine, 3–16.
Maddaluno, F. B. M. (1991), *A intertextualidade no teatro e outros ensaios*, Niterói: EDUFF.
Magaldi, S. (1981), 'Introdução', in *Teatro Completo de Nelson Rodrigues*, vol. 2: Peças Míticas, 13–48, Rio de Janeiro: Nova Fronteira.
Magaldi, S. (1998), 'Angel of the Damned', in N. Rodrigues, *The Wedding Dress, All Nudity Shall be Punished, Lady of the Drowned, Waltz #6, The Deceased Woman*, trans. J. Rodrigues and T. Coe, 11–33, Rio de Janeiro: Funarte.
Magaldi, S. (2004), *Panorama do teatro brasileiro*, 6th edn, São Paulo: Global Editora.
Magaldi, S. and Vargas, M. T. (2000), *Cem anos de teatro em São Paulo, 1875–1974*, São Paulo: Senac.
Marani, A. N. (1977), 'Presencia de Alfieri en el teatro de Juan Cruz Varela', in A. N. Marani (ed.), *Tonos y motivos italianos en la literatura argentina*, 29–54, La Plata: UNPL.
Marechal, L. (1970), *Antígona Vélez. La otra cara de Venus*, Buenos Aires: Sudamericana.
Marechal, L. (1984), *Poesía 1924–1951*, ed. P. García Barcia, Buenos Aires: Ediciones del 80.
Marechal, L. (1997), *Adán Buenosayres*, ed. J. Lafforgue and F. Colla, Santiago, Chile: Universitaria/ALLCA XX.
Margotton, J.-C. and Huby-Gilson, A.-C. (eds) (2010), *Amphitryon ou la question de l'Autre*, Saint-Étienne: Publications de l'Université de Saint-Étienne.
Mármol, J. (2001), *Amalia*, trans. H. Lane, ed. D. Sommer, Oxford: OUP (Library of Latin America).
Marshall, C. W. (2006), *The Stagecraft and Performance of Roman Comedy*, Cambridge: CUP.
Marshall, H. (2012), '*Clouds*, Eupolis and Reperformance', in C. W. Marshall and G. Kovacs (eds), *No Laughing Matter. Studies in Athenian Comedy*, 63–76, London: Bristol Classical Press.
Martí de Cid, D. and Wellington, M. A. (1990), 'Antón Arrufat', in J. A. Martínez (ed.), *Dictionary of Twentieth-Century Cuban Literature*, 34–8, New York: Greenwood Press.
Martiatu Terry, I. M. (1998), 'Mythological and Ritual Theatre in Cuba', *Performance Research* 3: 54–60.

Martindale, C. (2007), 'Reception', in C. W. Kallendorf (ed.), *A Companion to the Classical Tradition*, 297–311, Oxford: OUP.
Martínez de Velasco, J. (1998), 'La recreación de mitos clásicos en el teatro del Caribe', PhD diss., University of Kansas.
Martínez Tabares, V. (2000), 'Quince voces en busca del teatro dominicano', *Conjunto* (116): 2–21.
Mastronarde, D. J. (2002), *Euripides* Medea, Cambridge: CUP.
Mastronarde, D. J. (2013), *The Art of Euripides: Dramatic Technique and Social Context*. Cambridge: CUP.
Matas, J. (1971), 'Theater and Cinematography', in C. Mesa-Lago, *Revolutionary Change in Cuba*, 427–46, Pittsburgh: University of Pittsburgh Press.
Maupoint (1733), *Bibliothèque des théâtres*, Paris: Prault.
Maurice, L. (2013), 'Contaminatio and Adaptation: The Modern Reception of Ancient Drama as an Aid to Understanding Roman Comedy', in A. Bakogianni (ed.), *Dialogues with the Past: Classical Reception Theory & Practice*, vol. 2, 445–65, London: Institute of Classical Studies.
Mazzara, R. A. (1976), 'The Theater of Jorge Andrade', in Lyday and Woodyard, 205–20.
Mazzara, R. A. (1983), 'Parallels between the Theater of Jorge Andrade and the Modern "Cycle" Novel of Brazil', *Hispania* 66 (2): 192–201.
Mazzotti, J. A. (2015), 'Criollismo, Creole, and Créolité', in Y. Martínez-San Miguel, B. Sifuentes-Jáuregui and M. Belausteguigoitia (eds), *Critical Terms in Caribbean and Latin American Thought: Historical and Institutional Trajectories*, 87–100, London: Palgrave.
McConnell, J. (2013), *Black Odysseys: The Homeric Odyssey in the African Diaspora since 1939*, Oxford: OUP.
McFarland, P. (2013), *The Chican@ Hip Hop Nation: Politics of a New Millennial Mestizaje*, East Lansing: Michigan State University Press.
McGlathery, D. B. (2001), 'The Tomb of Epic: Bakhtinian Parody and Petronius' Tale of the Widow of Ephesus', in P. I. Barta, P. Allen Miller, C. Platter and D. Shepherd (eds), *Carnivalizing Difference: Bakhtin and the Other*, 119–40, London: Routledge.
McGuinness, A. (2003), '"Searching for 'Latin America'": Race and Sovereignty in the Americas in the 1850s', in N. P. Appelbaum, A. S. Macpherson and K. A. Rosemblatt (eds), *Race and Nation in Modern Latin America*, 87–107, Chapel Hill: University of North Carolina Press.
Medina, J. T. (ed.) (1901), *Documentos inéditos para la Historia de Chile (1518–1818)*, Vol. XXVIII, Santiago, Chile: Imprenta Elzeviriana.
Medina, J.T. (ed.) (1953), *Cartas de Pedro de Valdivia que tratan del descubrimiento y conquista de Chile*, Santiago, Chile: Fondo Histórico y Bibliográfico J.T. Medina.
Mee, E. B. and Foley, H. P. (eds) (2011), *Antigone on the Contemporary World Stage*, Oxford: OUP.
Meere, M. (2016), 'The Politics of Transgenericity: Pierre Du Ryer's Dramatic Adaptations of John Barclay's Argenis,' *Studia Aurea* 10: 313–34.
Meiches, M. P. (2007), '*Senhora dos afogados* a encenação do obseno', in A. Labaki and A. Edson Cadengue (eds), *A esfinge Investigada Seminário Recife: Nelson Rodrigues 2006*, 91–101, Recife, Brazil: Fundaçao de Cultura.
Meléndez, P. (2006), *The Politics of Farce in Contemporary Spanish American Theatre*, Chapel Hill: University of North Carolina Press.
Meyer, E. da C. (2017), 'Neoclassical Architecture in Havana', Talk at *100 Years of Dialogue: Latin American Approaches to Hellenism*, Conference, held at the American School for Classical Studies: https://vimeo.com/221383602 (accessed 11 September 2018).
Meza Villalobos, N. (1975), *Historia de la Política Indígena del Estado Español en América*, Santiago, Chile: Ediciones de la Universidad de Chile.
Mignolo, W. (2000), *Local Histories/Global Designs: Coloniality, Subaltern Knowledges, and Border Thinking*, Princeton: Princeton University Press.
Miller, P. A. (2007), 'Lacan's Antigone: The Sublime Object and the Ethics of Interpretation', *Phoenix* 61: 1–14.

Bibliography

Milliares, S. (1997), 'La Subversion del Logos en el Teatro de Piñera', *Teatro: revista de estudios teatrales* 11: 235–45.
Minchin, E. (ed.) (2012), *Orality, Literacy, and Performance in the Ancient World*, Leiden: Brill.
Miranda Cancela, E. (1990), *José Martí y el mundo clásico*. Mexico: UNAM Press.
Miranda Cancela, E. (2005), 'Medea y la voz del otro en el teatro latinoamericano contemporáneo', *La Ventana* 22: 69–90.
Miranda Cancela, E. (2006), *Calzar el coturno americano: mito, tragedia griega y teatro cubano*, Havana: Alarcos.
Miranda Cancela, E. (2010), 'Mitos y cánones trágicos en el teatro actual del Caribe Insular hispánico', in C. Bocchetti (ed.), *La influencia clásica en América Latina*, 33–52, Bogotá: Universidad Nacional de Colombia.
Miranda Cancela, E. (2018), 'Greece and José Martí', in Laird and Miller, 157–67.
Mogliani, L. (1999), 'El resurgimiento del nativismo en el periodo 1940–1955 y su relación con la política cultural de la época', in O. Pelletieri (ed.), *Tradición, modernidad y posmodernidad*, 259–64, Buenos Aires: Facultad de Filosofía y Letras, UBA/ Fundación Roberto Arlt.
Mogliani, L. (2004), 'Teatro y poder durante el primer y segundo gobierno peronista', in O. Pelletieri (ed.), *Reflexiones sobre el teatro*, 35–50, Buenos Aires: Galerna.
Montes Huidobro, M. (1973), *Persona, vida y máscara en el teatro cubano*, Miami: Ediciones Universal.
Montes Huidobro, M. (1986), *Persona, vida y máscara en el teatro puertorriqueño*, San Juan, Puerto Rico: Centro de Estudios Avanzados de Puerto Rico y el Caribe.
Moore, T. J. (1998), *The Theater of Plautus: Playing to the Audience*, Austin: University of Texas Press.
Mora, G. C. (2014), *Making Hispanics: How Activists, Bureaucrats, and Media Constructed a New American*, Chicago: University of Chicago Press.
Morales, H. (2013), 'Aristophanes' *Lyistrata*, the Liberian "sex strike", and the Politics of Reception,' *Greece & Rome* 60: 281–95.
Morales, H. (2015), '(Sex) Striking Out: Spike Lee's *Chi-raq*', *Eidolon*, 17 December 2015, https://eidolon.pub/sex-striking-out-spike-lee-s-chi-raq-f18fe17dd86b#.tk7zzy8r3 (accessed 12 April 2019).
Moraña, M., Dussel, E. and Jáuregui, C. A. (eds) (2008), *Coloniality at Large: Latin America and the Postcolonial Debate*, Durham, NC: Duke University Press.
Moreno, I. del R. (1997), 'La recontextualización de Antígona en el teatro argentino y brasileño a partir de 1968', *Latin American Theatre Review* 30 (2): 11–29.
Morfi, A. (1993), *Historia crítica de un siglo de teatro puertorriqueño*, San Juan, Puerto Rico: Instituto de Cultura Puertorriqueña.
Morisseau-Leroy, F. (1953/1987), *Antigòn*. Port-au-Prince: Delmas.
Morisseau-Leroy, F. (1992), Untitled Interview, *Callaloo* 15: 667–70.
Motto, G. (2011), *O espaço da tragédia: na genografia Brasileira contemporânea*, São Paulo: Perspectiva.
Moulián, T. (1997), *Chile actual: Anatomía de un mito*, Santiago: Universidad Arcis/LOM.
Moya Pons, F. (2010), *The Dominican Republic: A National History*, Princeton: Markus Wiener Publishers.
Müller, K. (2003), *Petronii Arbitri Satyricon reliquiae*, Monachii et Lipsiae: Saur.
Murashov, I. (1997), 'Bakhtin's Carnival and Oral Culture', in C. Adlam, R. Falconer, V. Makhlin and A. Renfrew (eds), *Face to Face: Bakhtin in Russia and the West*, 203–13, Sheffield: Sheffield Academic Press.
Murray, G. (1965), *Euripides and his Age*, Oxford: OUP.
Mutran, M. H. (2010), 'Different Appropriations of Greek Tragedy in Contemporary Drama: Irish and Otherwise', *Ilha do Desterro* 58: 413–38.

Myers, J. (1999), 'Una revolución en las costumbres, las nuevas formas de sociabilidad de la elite porteña, 1800–1860', in F. Devote and M. Madero (eds), *Historia de la vida privada en la Argentina*, vol. 2, 107–37, Buenos Aires: Taurus.

Nahm, K. Y. (2016), 'Subvert/Reinscribe: Reading Self-consciously Employed Stereotypes Through Performativity', *Performance Research* 21 (3): 92–102.

Nascimento, T. C. (2008), 'Staging Nelson Rodrigues in the United States: Finding a Cross-Cultural Imagination', *Studia Dramatica* (Romania) 1: 33–45.

Needell, J. D. (1995), 'Rio de Janeiro and Buenos Aires: Public Space and Public Consciousness in Fin-de-Siècle Latin America', *Comparative Studies in Society and History* 37 (3): 519–40.

Negri, A. (1999), *Insurgencies: Constituent Power and the Modern State*, Minneapolis: University of Minnesota Press.

Nelli, M. F. (2010), '*Antígona Furiosa*: On Bodies and the State', in Wilmer and Žukauskaitė, 353–65.

Nelli, M. F. (2012), 'Usted está aquí: Antigone Against the Standardization of Violence in Contemporary Mexico', in Nikoloutsos 2012a, 55–65.

Néspoli, B. (2010), 'Anistia para Zé Celso', *O Estado de São Paulo*, 7 April, Cultura Sec.

Nesselrath, H-G. (2010), 'Comic Fragments: Transmission and Textual Criticism', in Dobrov 2010, 423–55.

Neto, P. J. F. (2015), *Revolta Escrava da Bela Cruz (1833)*, Joinville, Santa Catarina: Clube de Autores.

Nigro, K. F. (2008), 'Dangerous Spaces, Dangerous Liaisons: Performance Arts on and of the U.S./Mexico Border', *Theater and Performance in Nuestra América* 32 (2): 412–31.

Nikoloutsos, K. P. (ed.) (2012a), *Reception of Greek and Roman Drama in Latin America*, *Romance Quarterly* 59 (1).

Nikoloutsos, K. P. (2012b), 'Introduction', in Nikoloutsos 2012a, 1–5.

Nikoloutsos, K. P. (2012c), 'Seneca in Cuba: Gender, Race, and the Revolution in José Triana's *Medea en el espejo*', in Nikoloutsos 2012a, 19–35.

Nikoloutsos, K. P. (2015), 'Cubanizing Greek Drama: José Triana's *Medea in the Mirror* (1960)', in Bosher, Macintosh, McConnell and Rankine, 333–60.

Nikoloutsos, K. P. and Gonçalves, R. T. (2018), 'Classical Tradition in Brazil: Translation, Rewriting, and Reception', *Caletroscópio* 6.1: 11–20.

Norris, A. (2000), 'Giorgio Agamben and the Politics of the Living Dead', *Diacritics* 30 (4): 38–58.

Nunes, L. A. (1986), 'The Conflict between the Real and the Ideal: A Study of the Elements of Naturalism and Melodrama in the Dramatic Works of Nelson Rodrigues', PhD diss., The City University of New York.

Nussbaum, M. C. (1986), *The Fragility of Goodness: Luck and Ethics in Greek Tragedy and Philosophy*, Cambridge: CUP.

Olson, S. D. (ed.) (2014), *Ancient Comedy and Reception: Essays in Honor of Jeffrey Henderson*. Berlin and Boston: DeGruyter.

O'Neill, E. (1988), *The Unknown O'Neill: Unpublished or Unfamiliar Writings of Eugene O'Neill*, ed. T. Bogard, New Haven: Yale University Press.

O'Neill, E. (1992), *Mourning Becomes Electra: Homecoming, The Hunted, The Haunted*. London: Nick Hern Books.

Ong, W. J. (1982), *Orality and Literacy: The Technologizing of the Word*, London: Routledge.

Oniga, R. (1985), 'Il canticum di Sosia: forme stilistiche e modelli culturali', *Materiali e discussioni per l'analisi dei testi classici* 14: 113–208.

Oniga, R. (1991), *Tito Maccio Plauto. Anfitrione*, Venezia: Marsilio.

Oniga, R. (1998), 'Struttura e funzione dei cantica nell'Amphitruo', in R. Raffaelli and A. Tontini (eds), *Lecturae Plautinae Sarsinates. I. Amphitruo*, 31–48, Urbino: Quattroventi.

Bibliography

Oniga, R. (2016), 'Le riscritture dell'Anfitrione di Plauto dal Medioevo all'età contemporanea', in G. Cipriani and T. Ragno (eds), *TraPassato&Presente*, 179–204, Campobasso and Foggia: Il Castello.

Origuela, D. A. (2011), 'O teatro de Nelson Rodrigues: traduções e encenação em língua inglesa', MA diss., University of São Paulo.

Ormand, K. (1999), *Exchange and the Maiden: Marriage in Sophoclean Tragedy*, Austin: University of Texas Press.

Ortíz, F. (1947), *Cuban Counterpoint: Tobacco and Sugar*, trans. H. de Onís (trans.), New York: Knopf.

Osorio Romero, I. (1979), *Colegios y profesores jesuitas que enseñaron latín en Nueva España (1572-1767)*, México: UNAM.

Ossa, C. (2006), 'El jardín de las máscaras', in N. Richard (ed.), *Políticas y estéticas de la memoria*, 71–6, Santiago, Chile: Cuarto Propio.

Oyarzún, C. (ed.) (2008), *Radrigán*, Santiago, Chile: Ediciones Universidad Católica de Chile.

Palma, J. (2002), *Diarrea*: https://www.escenachilena.uchile.cl/CDA/dr_obra_contenido/0,1501,S CID%253D15658%26OBRASID=15018,00.html (accessed 6 April 2019).

Palmieri, N. (2001), 'Pour une lecture de l'*Amphitruo*: les souffrances d'Alcmène et la philosophie de Sosie', *Cahiers du GITA* 14: 139–65.

Palti, E. J. (1996), 'Imaginación histórica e identidad nacional en Brasil y Argentina: un estudio comparativo', *Revista Iberoamericana* LXII (174): 47–69.

Paratore, E. (1933), *Il Satyricon di Petronio*, 2 vols., Firenze: Le Monnier.

Parisi, S. (2013–14), '*Moechus* (e) *supremus*: gli epiteti di Giove nell'*Amphitruo* di Plauto', *Invigilata lucernis: rivista dell'Istituto di Latino* 35–6: 255–70.

Parry, M. (1971), *The Making of Homeric Verse: The Collected Papers of Milman Parry*, ed. A. Parry, Oxford: OUP.

Pascal, A-M. (2010), 'Luís de Camões: Les amphitryons (Auto chamado dos Enfatriões) (1587)', in J.-C. Margotton and A.-C. Huby-Gilson (eds) (2010), *Amphitryon ou la question de l'Autre. Variations sur un thème de Plaute à Peter Hacks*, 49–64, Saint-Étienne: Publications de l'Université de Saint-Étienne.

Pasetti, L. (ed.) (2007), *Anfitrione. Variazioni sul mito*, Venezia: Marsilio.

Pecere, O. (1975), *Petronio: la novella della matrona di Efeso*, Padova: Antenore.

Pellettieri, O. (ed.) (2005), *Historia del teatro argentino en Buenos Aires: el período del constitución (1700-1884)*, Vol. I, Buenos Aires: Editorial Galerna.

Perelli, L. (1983), 'L'Alcmena plautina: personaggio serio o parodico', *Civiltà classica e cristiana* 4: 383–94.

Pérez Asensio, M. (2009), 'El mito en el teatro cubano contemporáneo', PhD diss., University of Málaga.

Pérez Gómez, L. (1991), 'De la ambigüedad del texto dramatico: la Alcmena de Plauto', in A. R. Ramos Guerreira (ed.), *Mnemosynum. C. Codoñer a discipulis oblatum*, 233–44, Salamanca: Universidad de Salamanca.

Petrone, G. (2008–9), 'Si dixero mendacium... (Pl. *Amph*. 198): guerra e diplomazia nell'Amphitruo di Plauto', *Hormos* 1: 167–78.

Pfister, M. (1988), *The Theory and Analysis of Drama*, Cambridge: CUP.

Pfister, J. (1995), *Staging Depth: Eugene O'Neill and the Politics of Psychological Discourse*, Chapel Hill: University of North Carolina Press.

Phelan, J. L. (1968), 'Pan-Latinism, French Intervention in Mexico (1861–1867) and the Genesis of the Idea of Latin America', in J. A. Ortega y Medina (ed.), *Conciencia y autenticidad históricas: Escritos en homenaje a Edmundo O'Gorman*, 279–98, Mexico City: UNAM.

Phillips, J. E. (1984–5), 'Alcumena in the Amphitruo of Plautus: A Pregnant Lady Joke', *Classical Journal* 80: 121–6.

Pianacci, R. E. (2008), *Antígona: una tragedia latinoamericana*, Irvine, CA: Ediciones de Gestos.
Pianacci, R. E. (2009), 'Teatro, Mujer y Fronteras. *Antígona; las voces que incendian el desierto* de Perla de la Mora [sic]', in López and Pociña, 499–507.
Pilditch, C. (1979), 'Theater in Puerto Rico: A Brief History', *Revista/Review Interamericana* 9: 5–8.
Pimentel, A. F. (1951), *O Teatro de Nelson Rodrigues*, Rio de Janeiro: Margem.
Piñera, V. (1941), *Electra Garrigó*, in R. Leal (ed.), *Teatro Completo*, 3–38, Havana: Editorial Letras Cubanas.
Piñera, V. (1967), 'Notas sobre el teatro cubano', *Unión* 6: 130–43.
Piselli, B. (2009), *Metamorfosi dell'Amphitruo attraverso i secoli*, Genova: Tilgher.
Plautus (1904), *Comoediae* (Oxford Classical Texts), ed. W. M. Lindsay, Oxford: Clarendon Press.
Podlecki, A. J. (1964), 'The Character of Eteocles in Aeschylus' *Septem*', *Transactions of the American Philological Association* 95: 283–99.
Podlecki, A. J. (1966), *The Political Background of Aeschylean Tragedy*, Ann Arbor: University of Michigan Press.
Post, L. A. (1950), '*The Seven against Thebes* as Propaganda for Pericles', *Classical Weekly* 44: 49–52.
Poulson, M. K. (2012), 'In Defense of the Dead: *Antígona furiosa*, by Griselda Gambaro', in Nikoloutsos 2012a, 48–54.
Powers, M. (2011), 'Syncretic Sites in Luis Alfaro's *Electricidad*', *Helios* 38 (2): 193–206.
Powers, M. (2018), *Diversifying Greek Tragedy on the Contemporary US Stage*, Oxford: OUP.
Prado, D. de A. (2001), *Apresentação do Teatro Brasileiro Moderno*, São Paulo: Perspectiva.
Praeger, M. (1992), 'Edouard Glissant: Towards a Literature of Orality', *Callaloo* 15 (1): 41–8.
Prezotto, J. (2017), '*Anfitrião 38*, de Jean Giraudoux', in R. T. Gonçalves (ed.), *A comédia e seus duplos: o Anfitrião de Plauto*, 277–308, Curitiba, Kotter Editorial; Cotia, Ateliê Editorial.
Puig-Herz, A. (2013), 'Broken Treasures, Invincible Solitude: Silence, Absence, and Time in Antón Arrufat's "Antígona"', in Duprey, 99–113.
Quackenbush, L. H. (2004a), *Antología del teatro dominicano contemporáneo* Tomo 1, Brigham Young University: Ediciones Librería La Trinitaria.
Quackenbush, L. H. (2004b), *Antología del teatro dominicano contemporáneo* Tomo 2, Brigham Young University: Ediciones Librería La Trinitaria.
Quiroga, J. (2005), *Cuban Palimpsests*, Minneapolis: University of Minnesota Press.
Rabelo, A. (2004), 'Formas do trágico moderno nas obras teatrais de obras teatrais de Eugene O'Neill e Nelson Rodrigues', PhD. diss., University of São Paulo.
Radrigán, J. (2004a), 'Memorias del olvido', in *Crónicas del amor furioso*, 16–19, Santiago, Chile: Ediciones Fronteras del Sur.
Radrigán, J. (2004b), *Medea mapuche*, in *Crónicas del amor furioso*, 142–54, Santiago, Chile: Ediciones Fronteras del Sur.
Ragno, T. (2009), *Il teatro nel racconto. Studi sulla fabula scenica della matrona di Efeso*, Bari: Palomar.
Ragno, T. (2012), 'Les deux matrones. Qualche itinerario su Petronio, il dramma e il melodramma europeo. Con una nota su un inedito pugliese', in G. Cipriani and A. Tedeschi (eds), *Note sul mito, il mito in note. La musica e la* fabula *tra antichi e moderni*, 195–234, Irsina: Barile.
Reading, R. K. (1980), 'The Renewal of Traditional Myth and Form in the Work of Antón Arrufat', *Revista Interamericana* 10: 357–77.
Reckford, K. J. (1987), *Aristophanes' Old-and-New Comedy*, Chapel Hill: University of North Carolina Press.
Rehm, R. (1994), *Marriage to Death: The Conflation of Wedding and Funeral Rights in Greek Tragedy*, Princeton: Princeton University Press.
Rehm, R. (2005), 'Female Solidarity: Timely Resistance in Greek Tragedy', in J. Dillon and S. E. Wilmer (eds), *Rebel Women: Staging Ancient Greek Drama Today*, 177–92, London: Bloomsbury.

Bibliography

Revermann, M. (2006), *Comic Business: Theatricality, Dramatic Technique, and Performance Contexts of Aristophanic Comedy*, Oxford: OUP.
Revermann, M. (2010), 'On Misunderstanding the *Lysistrata*, Productively', in Stuttard 2010a, 70–9.
Revermann, M. (ed.) (2014a), *The Cambridge Companion to Greek Comedy*, Cambridge: CUP.
Revermann, M. (2014b), 'Introduction', in Revermann 2014a, 1–24.
Reverte Bernal, C. (1999), '*Mithridate*, de Jean Racine, e Hispanoamérica (Sobre las obras homónimas de Fr. Francisco del Castillo y Pablo de Olavide)', *Calíope* 4: 311–23.
Ribeiro, D. (1971), *La Universidad Latinoamericana*, Caracas: Ediciones de la Biblioteca de la Universidad Central de Venezuela.
Ribeiro Barbosa, T. V. (2014), 'A tragédia grega no brasil', *Phoînix* 20 (2): 75–90.
Rimell, V. (2002), *Petronius and the Anatomy of Fiction*, Cambridge: CUP.
Ringer, M. (1998), *Electra and the Empty Urn: Metatheater and Role Playing in Sophocles*, Chapel Hill: University of North Carolina Press.
Rivoltella, M. (2008), 'Parodia di un paradigma comportamentale eroico in Plaut. *Amph.* 252', in G. Aricò and M. Rivoltella (eds), *La riflessione sul teatro nella cultura romana*, 5–14, Milano: V&P.
Rock, D. (1987), 'Intellectual Precursors of Conservative Nationalism in Argentina, 1900–1927', *Hispanic American Historical Review* 67 (2): 271–300.
Rock, D. (2002), 'Argentina, 1930–1946', in L. Bethell (ed.), *Historia de América Latina. Vol. 15, El cono sur desde 1930*, 1–59, Barcelona: Crítica.
Rodrigues, N. (1998), *The Wedding Dress, All Nudity Shall be Punished, Lady of the Drowned, Waltz #6, The Deceased Woman*, trans. J. Rodrigues and T. Coe, Rio de Janeiro: Funarte.
Rodrigues, N. (2012), *Senhora dos Afogados*, 3rd edn, Rio de Janeiro: Nova Fronteira.
Rohter, L. (2000), 'Re-Awakening the Giant of Brazilian Theater'. http://www.nytimes.com/2000/12/17/theater/theater-reawakening-the-giant-of-brazilian-theater.html (accessed 14 April 2019).
Rojas, D. (2015), 'Flaite. Algunos apuntes epistemológicos', *Alpha* 40: 193–200.
Rojas, R. (1915), *Tragedias de J. C. Varela*, Buenos Aires: Librería la Facultad, de Juan Roldán.
Rojas, R. (1948), *Historia de la literatura argentina. Ensayo filosófico sobre la evolución de la cultura en el Plata*, Volumen 8, Los Modernos II, Buenos Aires: Editorial Losada.
Rojas, R. (1960), *Historia de la literatura argentina. Ensayo filosófico sobre la evolución de la cultura en el Plata*, Volumen 4, Los coloniales II, Buenos Aires: Editorial Guillermo Kraft Limitada.
Rojas, S. (2006), 'Cuerpo, lenguaje y desaparición', in N. Richard (ed.), *Políticas y estéticas de la memoria*, 177–88, Santiago: Cuarto Propio.
Rojas Mix, M. (1986), 'Bilbao y el hallazgo de América latina: Unión continental, socialista y libertaria', *Cahiers du Monde Hispanique et Luso-Brasilien-Caravelle* 46: 35–47.
Rojas Silva, A. (2018), 'Gardens of Origin and the Golden Age in the Mexican *Libellus de medicinalibus indorum herbis* (1552)', in Laird and Miller, 41–56.
Romero, V. (1998), 'Du nominal latin pour l'Autre Amérique. Notes sur la naissance et le sens du nom "Amérique latine" autour des années 1850', *Histoire et sociétés de l'Amérique latine* 7: 57–86.
Rosa, J. (2016), 'From Mock Spanish to Inverted Spanglish: Language Ideologies and Racialization of Mexican and Puerto Rican Youth in the United States', in H. S. Alim, J. R. Rickford and A. F. Ball (eds), *Raciolinguistics: How Language Shapes our Ideas about Race*, 65–80, Oxford: OUP.
Rosen, R. (1997), 'Performance and Textuality in Aristophanes' *Clouds*', *Yale Journal of Criticism* 2: 397–421.
Rosen, R. (2014), 'The Greek "Comic Hero"', in Revermann 2014a, 222–40.
Rosenfeld, A. (1970), 'Visão do Ciclo', in Andrade 1970a, 599–617.
Ruffell, I. (2014a), 'Character Types', in Revermann 2014a, 147–67.
Ruffell, I. (2014b), 'Utopianism', in Revermann 2014a, 206–21.

Bibliography

Rushdie, S. (1982), 'The Empire Writes Back with a Vengeance', *The Times* Newspaper (UK), 3 July 1982.
Sahakian, E. (2017), *Staging Creolization: Women's Theater and Performance from the French Caribbean*, Charlottesville: University of Virginia Press.
Saint-Lot, M-J. A. (2003), *Vodou, a Sacred Theatre: The African Heritage in Haiti*. Coconut Creek, FL: Educa Vision.
Sánchez, L. R. (1975), *La pasión según Antígona Pérez*, Río Piedras, Puerto Rico: Editorial Cultural.
Sánchez, M. (1997), 'Entrevista: Chile no es tan lindo', https://www.escenachilena.uchile.cl/CDA/dr_autores_entrevista/0,1510,SCID%253D15659%26OBRASID=17724,00.html (accessed 8 April 2019).
Sánchez, M. (2004), *Filoctetes (La herida y el arco)*, http://www.escenachilena.uchile.cl/CDA/dr_obra_contenido/0,1501,SCID%253D15659%26OBRASID=15585,00.html (accessed 6 April 2019).
Sant'Anna, C. (1997), *Metalinguagem e teatro: A obra de Jorge Andrade*, Cuiabá: EdUFMT.
Santos, B. d. S. (2014), *Epistemologies of the South: Justice Against Epistemicide*, London: Routledge.
Sartre, J. P. (1976), 'Forger des Mythes', trans. R. Gilder, in M. Contat and M. Rybalka (eds), *Sartre on Theater*, 33–43, New York: Pantheon.
Sastre, A. (1995), *Los dioses y los cuernos*, Hondarribia, Spain: Argitaletxe.
Schaeffer, J.-M. (2006), *¿Qué es un género literario?*, trans. J. Bravo Castillo and N. Campos Plaza, Madrid: Ediciones Akal.
Schein, S. (2013), *Sophocles: Philoctetes*, Cambridge: CUP.
Schmeling, G. (2011), *A Commentary on the* Satyrica *of Petronius*, Oxford: OUP.
Schwartzman, S. (1979), *Formaçao de Comunidade Científica no Brasil*, Rio de Janeiro: FINEP.
Scott, J. (2005), *Electra After Freud: Myth and Culture*, Ithaca: Cornell University Press.
Seaford, R. (1987), 'The Tragic Wedding', *Journal of Hellenic Studies* 107: 106–30.
Sedgwick, E. (1985), *Between Men: English Literature and Male Homosocial Desire*, New York: Columbia University Press.
Sedgwick, W. B. (1960), *Plautus: Amphitruo*, Manchester: Manchester University Press.
Segal, E. (1987), *Roman Laughter – The Comedy of Plautus*, Oxford: OUP.
Segal, C. (1999), *Tragedy and Civilization*, Norman: University of Oklahoma Press.
Seibel, B. (2002), *Historia del teatro argentino: Desde los rituales hasta 1930*, Buenos Aires: Ediciones Corregidor.
Seibel, B. (2007), 'Prólogo: El teatro en la época de la independencia', in Luis Ambrosio Morante et al. (eds), *Antología de obras de teatro argentino: desde sus orígenes a la actualidad. Tomo 2: Obras de la independencia (1818–1824)*, 5–24, Buenos Aires: Instituto Nacional del Teatro.
Shafer, D. M. and Raney, A. A. (2012), 'Exploring How We Enjoy Antihero Narratives', *Journal of Communication* 62: 1028–46.
Shumway, N. (1991), *The Invention of Argentina*, Berkeley and Los Angeles: University of California Press.
Sigal, S. and Verón, E. (1986), *Perón o muerte: los fundamentos discursivos del fenómeno peronista*, Buenos Aires: Legasa.
Silk, M. S. (2000), *Aristophanes and the Definition of Comedy*, Oxford: OUP.
Silva, A. J. da (2010), *A Critical Portuguese/English Edition of Anfitriao, Ou Jupiter E Alcmena / Amphitryon, or Jupiter and Alcmena (Portuguese Edition)*, trans. and ed. P. Krummrich. Lewiston, NY: Edwin Mellen Press.
Skidmore, Th. E. (2007), *Politics in Brazil, 1930–1964: An Experiment in Democracy*, 40th Anniversary edn, Oxford: OUP.
Slater, N. W. (2000), *Plautus in Performance: The Theatre of the Mind*. 2nd edn, Amsterdam, Harwood Academic Publishers.

Bibliography

Slater, N. W. (2002), *Spectator Politics. Metatheatre and Performance in Aristophanes*. Philadelphia: University of Pennsylvania Press.

Smith, D. G. (2018), 'The Reception of Aeschylus in Sicily', in R. F. Kennedy (ed.), *Brill's Companion to the Reception of Aeschylus*, 9–53, Leiden: Brill.

Smith, P. C. (1984), 'Theatre and Political Criteria in Cuba: Casa de las Américas Awards, 1960–1983', *Cuban Studies/Estudios cubanos* 14 (1): 43–7.

Sommerstein, A. (2010), 'The History of the Text of Aristophanes', in Dobrov 2010, 399–421.

Sommerstein, A. (2013), *Aeschlyean Tragedy*, London: Bloomsbury.

Sommerstein, A. (2014), 'The Politics of Greek Comedy', in Revermann 2014a, 291–305.

Sophocles (2003), *Philoctetes*, trans. C. Phillips, Oxford: OUP.

Sourvinou-Inwood, C. (1997), 'Medea at a Shifting Distance: Images and Euripidean Tragedy', in J. Clauss and S. Iles-Johnston (eds), *Medea: Essays on Medea in Myth, Literature, Philosophy and Art*, 253–95, Princeton: Princeton University Press.

Spears, A. K. and Joseph, C. M. B. (2010), *The Haitian Creole Language: History, Structure, Use and Education*, Lanham, MD: Lexington Books.

Spinu, M. (1986), *Das dramatische Werk des Brasilianers Nelson Rodrigues*, Frankfurt am Main and New York: Peter Lang.

Staudt, K. (2008), *Violence and Activism at the Border: Gender Fear, and Everyday Life in Ciudad Juárez*, Austin: University of Texas Press.

Staudt, K. and Campbell, H. (2008), 'The Other Side of the Ciudad Juárez Femicide Story', *ReVista: Harvard Review of Latin America*, https://revista.drclas.harvard.edu/book/other-side-ciudad-ju%C3%A1rez-femicide-story (accessed 19 April 2019).

Stavans, I. (2000), 'The Gravitas of Spanglish', *Chronicle of Higher Education*, 13 October.

Stavans, I. (ed.) (2008), *Spanglish*, Westport, CT: Greenwood Press.

Stegagno Picchio, L. (ed.) (2004), *Ruggero Jacobbi. Brasile in scena*, Roma: Bulzoni.

Steiner, G. (1984), *Antigones*, Oxford: Clarendon Press.

Stephens, S. and Vasunia, P. (eds) (2010), *Classics and National Cultures*, Oxford: OUP.

Stevens, C. (2004), *Family and Identity in Contemporary Cuban and Puerto Rican Drama*, Gainesville: University Press of Florida.

Stevens, C. (2013), '"Get Up, Stand Up, Stand Up for Your Rights": Transnational Belonging and Rights of Citizenship in Dominican Theater', in F. N. Becker, P. S. Hernández and B. Werth (eds), *Imagining Human Rights in Twenty-First-Century Theater: Global Perspectives*, 179–93, New York: Palgrave Macmillan.

Stratton, J. (2011), 'The Trouble with Zombies: Bare Life, *Muselmänner*, and Displaced People', *Somatechnics* 1: 188–208.

Stuttard, D. (2010a), *Looking at Lysistrata*, London: Bristol Classical Press.

Stuttard, D, (ed.) (2010b), 'An Introduction to *Lysistrata*', in Stuttard 2010a, 1–10.

Svampa, M. (2006), *El dilema argentino: civilización o barbarie*, Buenos Aires: Taurus.

Taaffe, L. K. (1993), *Aristophanes and Women*, London: Routledge.

Taylor, D. (1991), *Theatre of Crisis: Drama and Politics in Latin America*, Lexington: University Press of Kentucky.

Taylor, D. (1993), 'Negotiating Performance', *Latin American Theatre Review* 26: 49–57.

Taylor, D. (2003), *The Archive and the Repertoire: Performing Cultural Memory in the Americas*, Durham, NC: Duke University Press.

Tcheuyap, A. (2001), 'Creolist Mystification: Oral Writing in the Works of Patrick Chamoiseau and Simone Schwarz-Bart', *Research in African Literatures* 32.4 (Winter): 44–60.

Teatro Escambray, (1978), ed. R. Leal, Havana: Editorial Letras Cubanas.

Teegarden, D. A. (2013), 'Tyrant-Killing Legislation and the Political Foundation of Ancient Greek Democracy', *Cardozo Law Review* 34: 965–82.

Thalmann, W. D. (1978), *Dramatic Art in Aeschylus' Seven against Thebes*, New Haven: Yale University Press.

Thalmann, W. D. (1982), 'The Lille Stesichorus and "Seven against Thebes"', *Hermes* 110: 385–91.
Thomas, R. (1992), *Literacy and Orality in Ancient Greece*, Cambridge: CUP.
Thomas, R. F. (2001), *Virgil and the Augustan Reception*, Cambridge: CUP.
Tietz, M. and Briesemeister, D. (eds) (2001), *Los jesuitas españoles expulsos: su imagen y su contribución al saber sobre el mundo hispánico en la Europa del siglo XVIII*, Madrid/Frankfurt: Iberoamericana/Vervuert.
Torlone, Z. M., Munteanu, D. L. and Dutsch, D. (eds) (2017), *A Handbook to Classical Reception in Eastern and Central Europe*, Malden, MA: Wiley-Blackwell.
Torrance, I. (2007), 'Brothers at War: Aeschylus in Cuba', in J. Hilton and A. Gosling (eds), *Alma Parens Originalis? The Receptions of Classical Literature and Thought in Africa, Europe, the United States, and Cuba*, 291–315, Oxford: Peter Lang.
Torrance, I. (2015), 'Brothers at War: Aeschylus in Cuba, 1968 and 2007', in Bosher, Macintosh, McConnell and Rankine, 434–55.
Triana, J. (1991), *Medea en el espejo, La noche de los asesinos, Palabras communes*, Madrid: Editorial Verbum.
Tripathy, J. (2013), 'Biopolitics in Sophocles's *Antigone*', *The Explicator* 71 (1): 26–30.
Tucker, T. G. (1908), *The Seven Against Thebes of Aeschylus*, Cambridge: CUP.
Ugarteche, F. (1929), *La imprenta argentina: sus orígenes y desarrollo*, Buenos Aires: Talleres gráficos R. Canals.
Valdivieso, E. (2018), 'The Inca Garcilaso in Dialogue with Neoplatonism', in Laird and Miller, 74–85.
Vannini, G. (2010), *Petronii Arbitri Satyricon 100–115. Edizione critica e commento*, Berlin: De Gruyter.
Vannini, G. (2013), 'La Matrona di Efeso di Petronio e le altre versioni antiche dell'aneddoto', in M. Carmignani, L. Graverini and B. Todd Lee (eds), *Collected Studies on the Roman Novel. Ensayos sobre la novela romana*, 77–95, Córdoba: Editorial Brujas.
Van Steen, G. (2014), 'Snapshots of Aristophanes and Menander: From Spontaneous Reception to Belated Reception Study', in Revermann 2014a, 433–50.
Van Weyenberg, A. (2010), 'Revolutionary Muse: Femi Osofisan's Tegonni: An African Antigone', in Wilmer and Žukauskaitė, 366–78.
Van Weyenberg, A. (2013), *The Politics of Adaptation: Contemporary African Drama and Greek Tragedy*, Amsterdam: Rodopi.
Varela, J. C. (1872), 'Carta inédita de don Juan C. Varela al señor don Bernardino Rivadavia sobre la manera de traducir los poetas latinos y especialmente a Virgilio', *Revista del Río de la Plata* 7: 403–18.
Vargas, M. T. (1980), *Anuário Artes Cênicas 1977*, São Paulo: Idart.
Vasunia, P. (2013), *The Classics and Colonial India*. Oxford: OUP.
Vérez de Peraza, E. (1959), 'El Griego en Cuba', *Journal of Inter-American Studies* 1: 27–55.
Vernant, J. P. and Vidal-Naquet, P. (1972), *Mythe et tragédie en Grèce Ancienne*, Vol. I, Paris: Librairie François Maspero.
Versényi, A. (1993), *Theatre in Latin America: Religion, Politics, and Culture from Cortés to the 1980s*, Cambridge: CUP.
Vilanova, Á. (1999), 'Nuevas Aproximaciones a Las Antígonas Iberoamericanas', *Nueva Revista de Filología Hispánica* 47 (1): 137–50.
Vilanova, Á. (2006), 'La tradición clásica y el teatro rioplatense de las primeras décadas del siglo xix: la obra de Juan Cruz Varela,' *Praesentia: Revista Venezolana de Estudios Clásicos* 7 (online).
Walcott, D. (1998 [1974]), 'The Muse of History', in *What the Twilight Says: Essays*, New York: Faber and Faber.
Walton, J. M. (2005), 'Outside Looking in: Subversive Choruses in Greek Tragedy', in J. Dillon and S. E. Wilmer (eds), *Rebel Women: Staging Ancient Greek Drama Today*, 193–214, London: Bloomsbury.

Bibliography

Warmington, E. H. (1987), *Petronius*, trans. M. Heseltine; *Seneca Apocolocyntosis*, trans. W. H. D. Rouse, Cambridge, MA: Harvard University Press.

Weiner, J. (2015a), 'Between *bios* and *zoê*: Sophocles' *Antigone* and Agamben's Biopolitics', *Logeion* 5: 139-60.

Weiner, J. (2015b), 'Antigone in Juárez: Tragedy and Politics on Mexico's Northern Border', *Classical Receptions Journal* 7 (2): 276-309.

West, M. L. (2011), *The Making of the Iliad: Disquisition and Analytical Commentary*, Oxford: OUP.

Wetmore, K. J. (2002), *The Athenian Sun in an African Sky: Modern African Adaptations of Classical Greek Tragedy*, Jefferson, NC: McFarland.

Wetmore, K. J. (2014), 'She (Don't) Gotta Have It: African-American Reception of Lysistrata', in Olson 2014, 786-96.

Whitaker, R. (1996), 'Orality and Literacy in the Poetic Traditions of Archaic Greece and Southern Africa', in I. Worthington (ed.), *Voice into Text: Orality and Literacy in Ancient Greece*, 205-20, Leiden: Brill.

Whyte, J. (2012), 'The Work of Men is not Durable: History, Haiti and the Rights of Man', in M. Svirsky and S. Bignall (eds), *Agamben and Colonialism*, 239-60, Edinburgh: Edinburgh University Press.

Willis, D. (1989), 'Shakespeare's *Tempest* and the Discourse of Colonialism', *Studies in English Literature, 1500-1900* 29 (2): 277-89.

Wilmer, S. E. and Žukauskaitė, A. (eds) (2010), *Interrogating Antigone in Postmodern Philosophy and Criticism*, Oxford: OUP.

Wilson, E. (2017), *The Odyssey*, New York & London: W.W. Norton.

Woodyard, G. (1995), 'Argentina', in M. Banham (ed.), *The Cambridge Guide to Theatre*, 32-5, Cambridge: CUP.

Worman, N. (1999), 'Odysseus Panourgos: The Liar's Style in Tragedy and Oratory', *Helios* 26: 35-70.

Wright, M. W. (2004), 'From Protests to Politics: Sex Work, Women's Worth, and Ciudad Juárez Modernity', *Annals of the Association of American Geographers* 94: 369-86.

Wright, M. W. (2006), 'Public Women, Profit, and Femicide in Northern Mexico', *South Atlantic Quarterly* 105 (4): 681-98.

Yu Sun, L. (2003), *Nelson Rodrigues, The Great Rebel of Brazilian Theatre: The Man & His Plays*, Seattle, WA: YCP.

Zalacain, D. (1995), 'Entrevista a Franklin Domínguez', *Latin American Theatre Review* 29 (1): 107-11.

Zanatta, L. (1996), *Del estado liberal a la nación católica: Iglesia y ejército en los orígenes del peronismo*, Buenos Aires: Universidad Nacional de Quilmes.

Zanatta, L. (1999), *Perón y el mito de la nación católica: Iglesia y Ejército en los orígenes del peronismo 1943-1946*, Buenos Aires: Sudamericana.

Zanatta, L. (2009), *Breve historia del peronismo clásico*, Buenos Aires: Sudamericana.

Zanelli, C. (2008), 'De palestras, disputas y travestismos: La representación de América en el teatro de Sor Juana Inés de la Cruz', in I. Arellano and J. A. Rodríguez Garrido (eds), *El teatro en la Hispanoamérica colonial*, 201-24, Madrid/Frankfurt: Iberoamericana/Vervuert.

Zecchin de Fasano, G. C. (2012), 'Materia mítica grecolatina en el neoclasicismo rioplatense: Juan Cruz Varela', in M. Á. Montezanti and G. Matelo (eds), *El resto es silencio: Ensayos sobre literatura comparada*, 403-26, Buenos Aires: Editorial Biblos.

Zeitlin, F. I. (1996), 'Travesties of Gender and Genre in Aristophanes' *Thesmophoriazusae*', in *Playing the Other in Greek Literature*, 375-416, Princeton: Princeton University Press.

Zentella, A. C. (2016), '"Socials", "Poch@s", "Normals" *y los demás*: School Networks and Linguistic Capital of High School Students on the Tijuana-San Diego Border', in H. S. Alim, J. R. Rickford and A. F. Ball (eds), *Raciolinguistics: How Language Shapes our Ideas about Race*, 327-46, Oxford: OUP.

Ziarek, E. W. (2012), 'Bare Life', in H. Sussman (ed.), *Impasses of the Post-Global: Theory in the Era of Climate Change*, vol. 2, Ann Arbor: University of Michigan Press.

Zimmermann, B. (2000), *Europa und die griechische Tragödie: vom kultischen Spiel zum Theater der Gegenwart*, Frankfurt am Main: Fischer Taschenbuch Verlag.

Žižek, S. (2004), 'From Antigone to Joan of Arc', *Helios* 31: 51–62.

Žukauskaitė, A. (2010), 'Biopolitics: Antigone's Claim', in Wilmer and Žukauskaitė, 67–81.

Zyl Smit, B. van (2003), 'The Reception of Greek Tragedy in the "Old" and the "New" South Africa', *Akroterion* 48: 3–20.

INDEX

Note: Entries in italics indicate a page that includes an image.

Abdala (Martí, José) 157
Accords of Neuva Imperial 53
Acharnians (Aristophanes) 136
Ad Mupa, law of 56
Adán Buenosayres (*Adam Buenosayres*) (Marechal, Leopoldo) 34, 38–9, 42
Aeneas (character) 27, 28–32
Aeneid (Justin) 31
Aeneid (Virgil) 25, 93
    adaptations 31 *see also* Dido
Aeolosicon (Aristophanes) 139
Aeschylus 169
    Agamemnon 106
    Choephori 104
    Eumenides 109
    Oresteia 103, 104
    Persians 157
    Seven Against Thebes 157–65, 168, 169, 246 n.104 see also *Siete contra Tebas, Los*
AFDD (Agrupación de Familiares de Detenidos Desaparecidos) (Group of the Relatives of the Disappeared Detainees) 60
Afro-Greeks (Greenwood, Emily) 5
Afrodito (character) 134–5
Agamben, Giorgio 186, 187, 200, 206, 209, 211
    anthropological machine, the 196–7
    bare life 195, 196, 200, 206, 210
    Homo sacer 195–6, 206
    Open, The 196
    sovereign power 207
Agamemnon (Aeschylus) 106
Agrupación de Familiares de Detenidos Desaparecidos (AFDD) (Group of the Relatives of the Disappeared Detainees) 60
Al amor de madre no hay afecto que le iguale (There Is No Love Like a Mother's Love) (Silva y Sarmiento, Pedro de) 11
Alcmena (character) 77, 81–2, 83–4, 85, 94, 96, 97
Alfaro, Luis 185, 193
    Bruja 193
    Electricidad see Electricidad
    hybrid language 186
    Mojada 193
    Oedipus el Rey 193

sovereign power 197
Spanglish 186, 192–3
Alfieri, Vittorio
    Antigone 23
America *see also* USA
    mythical labels 9–10
Amphitrião (Silva, António José da) 97
Amphitruo (Plautus) 75
    comparison with *Deus Dormiu lá em Casa, Um* 94–8
    desertion 94–5
    female protagonists 96–7
    gods 77, 98
    metatheatre 85
    rewritings 75–6, 82 see also *Deus Dormiu lá em Casa, Um*
Amphitryon (character) 77, 79–80, 81–3, 84–5, 91, 94, 95
ancient drama 8–15, 61, 138–40, 146–7, 155–6
    Cuba 157
    Greek comedy 146
    Greek mythology 90
    Greek tragedy 61, 86–7, 101, 140, 169, 234 n.37
    political 143
    rewriting 138–40, 146–7, 154
    Roman mythology 90
Andrade, Jorge 115, 121, 125–6
    as Antigone 126–7
    Confrarias, As 127
    Labirinto 119, 121–2, 127
    Marta, a Árvore e o Relógio 115, 116, 123–4
    Milagre na Cela 119, 125
    Pedreira das Almas (Quarry of Souls) see *Pedreira das Almas*
    torture theme 119, 126
Andrade, Oswald de 6, 7
Anouil, Jean
    Antigone 200, 202
    Médée 188
anthropological machine, the 196–7
anthropophagy 6, 7
Antigón (Moriso-Lewa, Feliks) 185, 187–92
    anthropological machine, the 197
    comparison with *Antigone* (Sophocles) 190–2
    Creole 188–90

Index

Kreyon (character) 190–1, 192
  as metaphor for oppression 198
  Vodou 188–90, 192
Antígona (character) 200, 201–6, 209
Antígona Furiosa (Gambaro, Griselda) 206–7
Antígona: las voces que incendian el desierto (Antigone: The Voices that Set the Desert on Fire) (de la Rosa, Perla) 199, *204*
  Antígona (character) 200, 201–6, 209
  biopolitics 206–9
  Creón (character) 207, 208
  exclusion 207–8
  femicide 200, 201, 207, 208–9, 210
  Polinice (character) 200
  production history 199
  reception 200
  sovereign power 209
  symbolic death 200, 201–6, 209, 210
Antígona Vélez (Marechal, Leopoldo) 33, 38
  barbarism/civilization 40–1
  Catholic Nationalism
  context 33–4, 40–1
  divinity 39–40, 42–6
  good/evil 40–1, 44–6
  Lisandro (character) 44–5
  loss of manuscript 218 n.9
  national myth 36, 38, 41, 46
  pampa 38–9
  Peronism 34
  as propaganda 35–6
  Vélez, Antígona (character) 41–6, 219 n.46
  Vélez, Ignacio (character) 39–40
  Vélez, Martín (character) 39
Antigone (Alfieri, Vittorio) 23
Antigone (Anouil, Jean) 200, 202
'Antigone' (Arrufat, Antón) 157
Antigone (Brecht, Bertolt) 200, 202
Antigone (character in *Antigone*) 119–20, 126, 191, 200
  Fradinger, Moira 7
  symbolic death 201–2, 206
Antigone (character in *Une Manière d'Antigone*) 173, 174
Antigone (Sophocles) 33, 115, 116, 118
  Antigone (character) 7, 119–20, 126, 191, 200, 201–2, 206
  Creon (character) 117–18, 190, 207
  rewritings 23, 157, 172–6 see also *Antigón* and *Antígona: las voces que incendian el desierto* and *Antígona Vélez*
  sovereign power 206, 207–8
  symbolic death 201–3, 210
Antigone Legend (Brecht, Bertolt) 202
Antigone tradition 200
appropriation 11
  from myth 11

Araucana, La (Ercilla, Alonso de) 51
Arauco War 50–1
Argentina 32
  barbarism/civilization 40–1
  Buenos Aires 21–2
  Catholic Nationalism 34, 35, 36–7
  conquest of the desert 38, 40–1
  Dirty War 206–7
  drama in 24, 25–6
  European influence 20–1
  gender 20
  independence 19–20, 24, 25, 31
  Liberal Republic 219 n.35
  national myth 36, 38, 41, 46
  nationalism 34, 35, 36–7
  pampa 38–9
  Peronism 33–5, 37, 41
Argia (Varela, Juan Cruz) 23–4
Argos de Buenos Aires, El (newspaper) 20
Aristophanes 143
  Acharnians 136
  Aeolosicon 139
  Assemblywomen 132, 135
  Birds 136
  Clouds 138–9
  Lysistrata see *Lysistrata*
  Peace 136, 139
  Wealth 139
  Women at the Thesmophoria 135, 139
Arriví, Francisco 131
  Club de Solteros (Bachelor's Club) see *Club de Solteros*
  Cóctel de Don Nadie (Cocktail of Mr. Nobody) 132, 138
  comic rewriting 132, 138–40
  education 136
  rewriting 131–2, 138–40
  Sirena (Mermaid) 141
  social theatre 141
  Solteros 72 (Bachelors 72) 132, 138
  Vejigantes (Masks) 131, 141
Arrufat, Antón 157, 158
  'Antigone' 157
  Siete contra Tebas, Los (Seven Against Thebes) see *Siete contra Tebas, Los*
Arte nuevo de hacer comedias en este tiempo (New Art of Making Comedies in this Age) (Vega, Lope de) 25
Artemisa (character) 152–3
Assemblywomen (Aristophanes) 132
Autolycus (Eupolis) 139
Aylwin, Patricio (president) 53

Bacchae (Euripides) 136
Bakhtin, Mikhail 174, 180
  Rabelias and his World 173

Index

Baldrich, Alberto 218 n.17
Baralt, Luis 157
bare life 195, 196, 200, 206, 210
Belaval, Emilio
 'What a Puerto Rican Theatre Might Be'
  ('Lo que podría ser un teatro
  puertorriqueño') 140, 141
Belgrano, General Manuel 19
Belgrano, Manuel (playwright) 23
 Molina 23–4
Benjamin, Walter
 Critique of Violence 206
Bertini, F. 75
bienséance 28
biopoetics 187, 197
biopolitics 186–7, 195–8, 200, 206–9, 210
biopower 186–7
Birds (Aristophanes) 136
Black or White (Jackson, Michael) 70
Bolívar, Simón 6
Brazil 4–5, 9–10
 censorship 113, 125, 126
 colonization 102
 coup d'états 76, 123
 Estado Novo 92
 history 92
 Liberalist Revolt (1842) 116, 125
 military dictatorship 123
 Minas Gerais 116
 Regresso 116
 Revolta dos Alfaiates (Revolt of the Tailors) 122
 São Tomé das Letras 116
 social order 115
 torture 119, 123, 125
 uprisings 116
Brecht, Bertolt
 Antigone 200, 202
 Antigone Legend 202
Brown, Michael 210
Bruja (Alfaro, Luis) 193
Buenos Aires 21–2, 32
Burnett, Anne 56
Butler, Judith 200, 203, 207, 209
Butler, Shane 7

Cahier d'un retour au pays natal (Césaire, Aimé) 5, 173, 188
California 196, 198
Campaña de Alfabetización (Cuban Literacy Campaign) 263
Cané, Miguel 19
cannibalism 6, 7
canon 145–7, 154–5, 172, 173, 198
Caramuru: Poema Épico do Descobrimento da Bahia (Durão, Frei José de Santa Rita) 102

Caribbean 5
 colonialism 171–2, 177, 188
 literacy/orality 172, 175, 181
 literature 171–2, 173
 theatre 182
carnival 173, 227 n.31
Casal, Julián de
 Oceánidas, Las 157
 Prometeo 157
case studies 9
Castillo, Francisco del 11
 Mitrídates, rey del Ponto (Mithridates, King of Pontus) 11
Castro, Fidel (president) 163
Catholic Church 4 *see also* Catholic Nationalism
Catholic Nationalism 34, 35, 36–7
Celso, José 125
censorship 113, 125, 126
Césaire, Aimé 5, 171, 173
 Cahier d'un retour au pays natal 5, 173, 188
 Tempête, Une 173
Chamoiseau, Patrick 171, 172
 classical drama 182
 créolité 171, 172, 182
 education 181–2
 hybridity 174, 181
 literacy/orality 180, 182
 Manière d'Antigone, Une (*A Kind of Antigone*) see *Manière d'Antigone, Une*
 Manman Dlo contre la fée Carabosse (*Mami Wata Versus the Carabosse Fairy*) see *Manman Dlo contre la fée Carabosse*
 Solibo Magnifique 178
 storyteller figure 182
Chamoiseau, Patrick, Jean Bernabé and Raphaël Confiant
 Éloge de la créolité (*In Praise of Creoleness*) 171, 182
Chi-Raq (Lee, Spike) 137
Chile 48, 58, 224 n.2
 Accords of Neuva Imperial 53
 dictatorship 59
 Mapuche, the 47, 49, 50–3, 56
 memory/oblivion 59, 60, 64
 parleys (Peace Accords) 52–3
 playwrights 50
 post-dictatorial period/transition to democracy 57–8, 59–60, 71–2
 race 70
 society 58, 59–60, 70
 theatre 59, 60–1
 torture 50–1
 war 50–1
Chile, Anatomía de un mito (*Chile, Anatomy of a myth*) (Moulián, Tomás) 59
Choephori (Aeschylus) 104

Index

cholo 196, 197
Ciudad Juárez, Mexico 199, 200, 201, 210
classical antiquity 12, 179
    drama *see* ancient drama
    expansion 10
    Greek mythology 90
    legitimizing privileged status 197
    literacy/orality 175, 180, 182-3
    Roman mythology 90
    scars 195
    sex strikes 137
    transmission 3
classical tradition 9
Classics 182 *see also* classical antiquity
    Brazil 4-5
    Caribbean 5
    Spanish Latin America 4
Clemencia (character) 194
Clouds (Aristophanes) 138-9
Club de Solteros (*Bachelor's Club*) (Arriví, Francisco) 131, 143
    Afrodito (character) 134-5
    agōn 132-3
    comparison with *Lysistrata* 132-8
    context 140-3
    emasculation theme 135
    Hipólito (character) 134, 135
    Lucila (character) 132-4, 135, 136
    misogyny 134, 135, 136
    politics 142, 143
    production history 138
    rewriting 136, 138, 140
    setting 142
    women 141-2
Clytemnestra (character) 194
Cóctel de Don Nadie (*Cocktail of Mr. Nobody*) (Arriví, Francisco) 132, 138
Colio, Bárbara
    Usted está aquí (*You Are Here*) 200
collective voice 176
colonialism 3-5, 11, 179
    Brazil 102
    Caribbean 171-2, 177, 188
    classical antiquity 10, 179
    classical tradition 9
    drama as indoctrination 10
    France 173, 176, 177, 178-9, 188
    Haiti 188
    Hispaniola 188
    literacy/orality 180
    Martinique 173, 176, 177, 178-9
    resistance 173, 175, 181
    Spain 47, 50-4
    Tempest, The 176-7
    Tempête, Une 177
    USA 188

comedy 146, 149
comic heroes 149
concentration camps 196 *see also* Holocaust, the
Confrarias, As (Andrade, Jorge) 127
Cornejo Polar, Antonio 6
Creole 173-4, 180-1, 196 *see also* Haitian Creole
Creole population and the anthropological machine 196
Creolists, the 171, 172, 173, 175, 176, 177
créolité 171, 172, 173, 177, 182
Creón (character in *Antígona: las voces que incendian el desierto*) 207, 208
Creon (character in Sophocles' *Antigone*) 117-18, 190, 207
Critique of Violence (Benjamin, Walter) 206
Cuba
    Bay of Pigs invasion 157-8
    Campaña de Alfabetización (Cuban Literacy Campaign) 163
    as captive island 162
    classical theatre 157
    education system 5
    Instituto Nacional de Reforma Agraria (INRA) (Agrarian Reform Institute) 163, 164
    Revolution 12, 157-8, 165
    theatre 157
culture, subterranean 12
Cureses, David
    Frontera, La 47
Cursos de Cultura Católica (Courses on Catholic Culture) 35
Cynthia, widow of Ephesus (character) 93, 96

de la Rosa, Perla
    Antígona: las voces que incendian el desierto (*Antigone: The Voices that Set the Desert on Fire*) see *Antígona: las voces que incendian el desierto*
death drive 202-3
Death War 50
'Deep Classics' model 7
Deus Dormiu lá em Casa, Um (*A God Slept Here*) (Figueiredo, Guilherme de Oliveira) 75, 89, 94
    Alcmena (character) 77, 81-2, 83-4, 85, 94, 96, 97
    Amphitryon (character) 77, 79-80, 81-3, 84-5, 91, 94, 95
    carnivalization 227 n.31
    comparison with source text 94-8
    comparison with *Widow of Ephesus* 96-7
    contaminatio 94-9
    desertion 94-6
    deux ex machina 78
    doubles 97
    female unfaithfulness 97

gods, absence of 77, 78, 79, 80–2, 86
gods, the 97, 99
jealousy 85
Jupiter (character) 79, 82, 90, 97, 99
metatheatre 76, 77, 78–82, 85–6
myth 78, 83, 85
production history 75
prophecy 97–8
roles, neogotiation of 82–5
Sosia (character) 80, 95
themes 90–1, 94–7
Tiresias (character) 97
Diana (character) 97–8
Diarrea (Palma, José) 59, 66–71
   abandonment 71, 72
   consumerism 69–71
   language 68–9
   marginalization 71
   Medea Marisol Cuevas (character) 67–8
   as parody 69–70
   production history 66
   reception 66
   self-consciousness 67–8
   self-reflexivity 69
Dido (character) 27–8, 30–1
   as imperial Spain 31
Dido (Varela, Juan Cruz) 19, 26–8
   bienséance 28
   characteristics 25
   departure from Virgil 28
   divine, the 29–30
   gender 27, 28, 30–1
   neoclassical unities 27
   plot 27–9
   political connotations 19–20, 31–2
   in print 22–3
   production history 20–1, 23
   reception 20–1, 22, 23–4, 26, 29
   vraisemblance 29
Diocles
   Thyestes 139
Dionysus (Magnes) 139
Discépolo, Enrique Santos 35
Domínguez, Franklin 145, 147
   Antígona-Humor 154
   Lisístrata odia la política: obra teatral en tres actos inspirada en un tema de Aristófanes (Lysistrata Hates Politics: A Theatrical Work in Three Acts Inspired by a Topic by Aristophanes) see *Lisístrata odia la política: obra teatral en tres actos inspirada en un tema de Aristófanes*
Dominican Republic 145
   education system 5
   government/police 150
   theatre 145–7, 155–6

Western canon 146–7, 154
Doroteia (Rodrigues, Nelson Falcão) 101
drama 8–15
   Cuban Revolution, effect of 12
   monologic 247 n.29
   neoclassical 11, 12
   politics 12
   reflexivity 60–1, 65–6
Divino Narciso, El (The Divine Narcissus) (Inés de la Cruz, Sister Juana) 11
Durão, José de Santa Rita
   Caramuru: Poema Épico do Descobrimento da Bahia 102

Eclogues (Virgil) 22
Eduarda (character) 105–6, 108
education 4, 5
Electra (character) 101, 102, 112 *see also* Moema (character) *and* Electricidad (character) 193–4
   portrayed by Aeschylus 104
   portrayed by Alfaro, Luis 193–4
   portrayed by Euripides 105, 108
   portrayed by O'Neill, Eugene 103–4
   portrayed by Sophocles 104, 105–6
Electra (Euripides) 105, 108, 109, 195
   Orestes (character) 195
Electra (Sophocles) 104, 105–6
Electra Garrigó (Piñera, Virgilio) 147, 157
Electricidad (Alfaro, Luis) 185, 192–5, 198
   anthropological machine, the 197
   character names 193
   Clemencia (character) 194
   Electricidad (character) 193–4
   La Ifi (character) 194–5
   Orestes (character) 185, 193, 195
   production history 193
   religion 194
   scars/tattoos 195
   Spanglish 193, 195, 197
Electricidad (character) 193–4
Éloge de la créolité (*In Praise of Creoleness*) (Patrick Chamoiseau, Jean Bernabé and Raphaël Confiant) 171, 182
Endymion (character) 98–9
English 188
Epistemologies of the South: Justice against Epistemicide (Santos, B. de S.) 6
Ercilla, Alonso de 51
   Araucana, La 51
Espinosa Medrano, Juan de 11
   El robo de Proserpina y sueño de Endimión (The Snatching of Proserpina and the Dream of Endymion) 11
Essay on the Origin of Languages (Rousseau, Jean-Jacques) 180

Index

Eteocles (character in *Seven against Thebes*) 162, 246 n.104
Etéocles (character in *Siete contra Tebas, Los*) 161, 165–7, 168
Eugenia (character) 151–2
Eumenides (Aeschylus) 109
Eupolis
    Autolycus 139
Euripides
    Bacchae 136
    Electra 105, 108, 109, 195
    Hippolytus 135, 136
    Iphigenia at Aulis 106
    Iphigenia at Tauris 194
    Medea 47–8
    Phoenician Women 158, 159, 165, 166, 246 n.104
European antiquity *see* classical antiquity

Family Album (Rodrigues, Nelson Falcão) 101
fantasmas, Os (The Ghosts) (Figueiredo, Guilherme de Oliveira) 77
feliz experiencia, la (The Happy Experience) 32
femicide, the (*feminicidio, el*) 199–200, 201, 210
Fernández de Oviedo, Gonzalo 9
Figueiredo, Euclides (general) 76, 91
Figueiredo, Guilherme de Oliveira 76, 86–7, 89–90
    biographical information 76–7, 91
    Brazilian themes 86
    Deus Dormiu lá em Casa, Um (*A God Slept Here*) *see Deus Dormiu lá em Casa, Um*
    fantasmas, Os (The Ghosts) 77
    Greekness 86–7
    Greve Geral (General Strike) 77
    raposa e as uvas, A (The Fox and the Grapes) 77
    as theatre historian/critic 78
    Very Curious Story of the Virtuous Widow of Ephesus, A (*A Muito Curiosa História de Virtuosa Matrona de Éfeso*) *see Very Curious Story of the Virtuous Widow of Ephesus, A*
    Xanthias: Dialogues on Dramatic Creation 76, 78–9, 86, 90
Figueiredo, João 76, 91
Filoctetes (character) 62–3, 64–5
Filoctetes, la herida y el arco (*Philoctetes, the Wound and the Bow*) (Sánchez, Marcelo) 59, 61–6
    abandonment 63, 71
    Filoctetes (character) 62–3, 64–5
    Ignacio (character) 63–4
    language 62, 64, 66
    memory 64, 71
    reflexivity 65–6
    smell 61–2, 63–4, 72
    suffering 62

Flower of Obsession (Rodrigues, Nelson Falcão) 113
Foucault, Michel 186–7, 197, 206
Fouché, Franck
    Oedipe-roi 188
Fradinger, Moira 7, 8, 187
France 21
    as colonizer 173, 176, 177, 178–9, 188
Frascatore, Girolamo 9
French 173–4, 181, 188
French literature 4
Frontera, La (Cureses, David) 47
Fry, Christopher
    Phoenix Too Frequent, A 90

Gambaro, Griselda
    Antígona Furiosa 206–7
García, William 154
García del Toro, Antonio
    Guerra menos Guerra igual a Sexo (*War minus War equals Sex*) 140
Gelon (of Syracuse) 169
gender *see also* women
    Argentina 20
    Dido 27, 28, 30–1
    liberation 31
    Lisístrata odia la política 151, 153–4, 155
    Mother Nation 31
    Sedgwick, Eve Kosofsky 30
Generation of the 30s (Generación de los 30) 141
Glissant, Édouard 181
God Slept Here, A (*Um Deus Dormiu lá em Casa*) (Figueiredo, Guilherme de Oliveira) *see Deus Dormiu lá em Casa, Um*
Goff, Barabra 12
González de San Nicolás, Gil 51
Greek comedy 146
Greek mythology 90
Greek tragedy 61, 86–7, 101
    madness 234 n.37
    rewriting 140
    political context 169
Greenwood, Emily 197
    Afro-Greeks 5
Greve Geral (General Strike) (Figueiredo, Guilherme de Oliveira) 77
Group of the Relatives of the Disappeared Detainees (Agrupación de Familiares de Detenidos Desaparecidos, AFDD) 60
Guatemala 210
Guerra menos Guerra igual a Sexo (*War minus War equals Sex*) (García del Toro, Antonio) 140
Guevara, Tomás 56
guslari 175
Gutiérrez, Juan María 23–4

Index

Haiti 188
    Creole population and the anthropological machine 196, 197
    Vodou 190, 192
    zombies 191
Haitian Creole 185–6, 187–8
Hardwick, Lorna 10, 11
Haunted, The (O'Neill, Eugene) 103
Havelock, Eric 180
Hernández de Velazco, Gregorio 25
Hieron (of Syracuse) 169
Hipólito (character) 134, 135
Hippolytus (Euripides) 135, 136
Hispanic category 2
Hispaniola 188
Hoffman, François-Benoît
    Lysistrate 137
Holanda, Sérgio Buarque de
    Raízes do Brasil (Roots of Brazil) 115
Holocaust, the 186, 196
Homecoming (O'Neill, Eugene) 103
Homer
    Odyssey 179, 194, 195
    orality 175, 177
    slavery 179
Homo sacer (Agamben, Giorgio) 195–6, 206
homosociality 30–1
humanity 196
Hunted, The (O'Neill, Eugene) 103
Hurston, Zora Neale
    Tell my Horse 191
hybridity 5–8, 174, 181
    languages 185–6, 196–7

identity politics 154
Ignacio (character) 63–4
improvisation 175–6
Inés de la Cruz, Juana 11
    Divino Narciso, El (The Divine Narcissus) 11
    'Neptuno alegórico' (Allegorical Neptune) 11
Instituto Nacional de Reforma Agraria (INRA) (Agrarian Reform Institute) 163, 164
Iphigenia (character) 194
Iphigenia at Aulis (Euripides) 106
Iphigenia at Tauris (Euripides) 194
Iphigénie (Racine, Jean) 30
Isabel I (queen) 31

Jackson, Michael 69
    Black or White 70
Janequeo 51
Jansen, Laura 7
Jason (character) 50
Jelin, Elizabeth
    trabajos de la memoria, Los 60
Jesuits 4

Juárez, Mexico 199, 200, 201, 210
Jupiter (character) 79, 82, 90, 97, 99
Justin
    Aeneid 31
juxtaposition 102

Kaiser, Georg
    Zweimal Amphitryon 83
Kennedy, John F. (president) 162
Klor de Alva, J. 3
Kreyon (character) 190–1, 192
Kütral (character) 49–50, 52–7

La Ifi (character) 194–5
Labirinto (Andrade, Jorge) 119, 121–2, 127
Lacan, Jacques 200, 202–3
Laird, Andrew 9
Latin America 2, 185
    ancient drama in 8–15
    hybridity 5–8
    identity 6
    postcolonialism 3–5, 11
    problematic nature of term 2
    theatre 141, 154–5
Lavardén, Manuel José de 23
    Siripo 23
Lee, Spike
    Chi-Raq 137
Leite-Lopes, Angela 112
Lévi-Strauss, Claude 178, 180
Licán (character) 49, 52, 53, 57
Lisandro (character) 44–5
Lisístrata (character) 148–9, 151–2
Lisístrata odia la política: obra teatral en tres actos inspirada en un tema de Aristófanes (Lysistrata Hates Politics: A Theatrical Work in Three Acts Inspired by a Topic by Aristophanes) (Domínguez, Franklin) 145
    Artemisa (character) 152–3
    character names 148, 151, 152
    as comedy 146, 147, 149, 150
    Eugenia (character) 151–2
    gender 151, 153–4, 155
    homosexuality 153–4
    Lisístrata (character) 148–9, 151–2
    Pompeyo (character) 148, 150
    social class 151–3
    stereotypes 149–54, 155
    as subversion 155
    war 151
    Western canon 145–6
literacy 175, 177–8, 179–81
Literary Society, Argentina 216 n.8
López de Gómara, Francisco 9
Lord, Edward 175, 181
Lucila (character) 132–4, 135, 136

Index

lwa 190, 192
Lysistrata (Aristophanes) 77, 131, 136–7
   rewritings 132–3, 137, 140 see also *Club de Solteros* and *Lisístrata odia la política*
   stereotypes 149, 151
   women 137–8, 141
Lysistrata (character) 131, 145
Lysistrata project 137
Lysistrate (Hoffman, François-Benoît) 137

McLaughlin, Ellen
   'Theatrical Act of Dissent' 137
Magaldi, Sábato 101
Magic Island, The (Seabrook, William) 191
Magnes
   Dionysus 139
Malina, Judith 202
Malitzin, Medea americana (Sotelo Inclán, Jesús) 47
Malkiel, Lida de 31
Manière d'Antigone, Une (*A Kind of Antigone*) (Chamoiseau, Patrick) 172–6, 181, 182
   Antigone (character) 173, 174
   comparison with *Antigone* 173–5
   Creole 180
   hybridity 174
   literacy/orality 175
   polyphony 174
   use of language 173–4, 180
Manman Dlo contre la fée Carabosse (*Mami Wata Versus the Carabosse Fairy*) (Chamoiseau, Patrick) 172, 176–83
   Creole 180–1
   hybridity 181
   literacy/orality 175, 176, 177–8
   polyphony 181
   storyteller figure 182
   as *théâtre conté* 182
Mapuche, the 47, 49, 50–3, 56
   customary law 50, 56
Mapudungun 52
Marechal, Leopoldo 35
   Adán Buenosayres (*Adam Buenosayres*) 34, 38–9, 42
   Antígona Vélez see *Antígona Vélez*
   national myth 36, 37
   pampa 38–9
   Poemas Australes (*Southern Poems*) 34, 36, 37, 38–9
Mariana (character) 116, 117, 118, 119, 120, 121, 127
Marqués, René 141
Marta, a Árvore e o Relógio (Andrade, Jorge) 115, 116
Martí, José 6
   Abdala 157
Martiniano (character) 116

Martiniano de Alencar, José 116
Martinique 171
   Creole 173–4, 180–1
   education system 5
   French colonization 173, 176, 177, 178–9
'masked' receptions 101–2
Matrix, The (film) 187
Medea (character)
   Euripides 47, 49, 50, 51, 54–6
   Palma, José 58
   Radrigán, Juan 47, 49, 50, 54, 55
Medea (Euripides) 47–8, 54
   betrayal 55–6
   Jason (character) 50
   Medea (character) 47, 49, 50
   oath-breaking 50, 55, 56
   oral culture 56
   revenge 55
   rewritings 47 see also *Medea Mapuche* and *Diarrea*
Medea en el Espejo (*Medea in the Mirror*) (Triana, José) 147, 157
Medea Mapuche (Radrigán, Juan) 47–8
   betrayal 55–6
   context 48–9, 50–3
   Kütral (character) 49–50, 52–7
   Licán (character) 49, 52, 53, 57
   Mapuche, the 47, 49, 50–3, 56, 58
   oath-breaking 50, 55, 56
   oral culture 48, 56
   parleying 52, 53, 55
   production history 48
   as revenge tragedy 48, 50, 54, 55, 58
   winkas 49–50
Medea Marisol Cuevas (character) 67–8
Médée (Anouil, Jean) 188
memory/oblivion 59, 60
Méndez Ballester, Manuel
mestizaje 6
Mexico 8
   Ciudad Juárez 199, 200, 201, 210
   femicide, the (*feminicidio, el*) 199–200, 210
   violence 210
Milagre na Cela (Andrade, Jorge) 119, 125
Miller, Paul Allen 202, 203
Minas Gerais 116
Mitrídates, rey del Ponto (*Mithridates, King of Pontus*) (Castillo, Father Francisco del) 11
Moema (character) 102, 103–8, 109
Mojada (Alfaro, Luis) 193
Molina (Belgrano, Manuel) 23–4
Morales, Helen 137
Moriso-Lewa, Feliks
   Antigón see *Antigón*
   Creole 186, 187, 188, 193, 251 n.35

education 188
hybrid language 185
sovereign power 197
Wa Kreyon (*King Creon*) 188
Mother Nation 31
Moulián, Tomás
Chile, Anatomía de un mito (*Chile, Anatomy of a myth*) 59
Mourning Becomes Electra (O'Neill, Eugene) 103–4, 109, 112
Muito Curiosa História de Virtuosa Matrona de Éfeso, A see *Very Curious Story of the Virtuous Widow of Ephesus, A*
Murashov, Iurii 173

Nascimento, Cláudia Tatinge 106
national identity 2, 6
nationhood 36–7
Nazism 196 *see also* Holocaust, the
Negri, Antoni 197
négritude 171, 172, 173, 177, 188
Nelli, María Florencia 200, 206–7
neoclassical drama 11, 12
   bienséance 28
   unities 27
   vraisemblance 29
neoclassical tragedy 27, 29
'Neptuno alegórico' (Allegorical Neptune) (Inés de la Cruz, Sister Juana) 11
Night of the Living Dead (film) 191
'Nuestra América' ('Our America') 6

oath-breaking 50
Oceánidas, Las (Casal, Julián de) 157
Odyssey (Homer) 179, 195
   Clytemnestra (character) 194
Oedipe-roi (Fouché, Franck) 188
Oedipus el Rey (Alfaro, Luis) 193
Oedipus King (Sophocles) 77
'Omni-American' 6, 7
O'Neill, Eugene
   Haunted, The 103
   Homecoming 103
   Hunted, The 103
   Mourning Becomes Electra 103–4, 109, 112
Ong, Walter 180
Open, The (Agamben, Giorgio) 196
oral culture 48
orality 172, 173, 175–6, 177–8, 179–81
Oresteia (Aeschylus) 103
Orestes (character) 108, 185, 193, 195
Ortíz, Fernando 6
Ossa, Carlos 66
Oxford Handbook of Greek Drama in the Americas 7, 12

Pacification of Araucanía 50
Palma, José 225 n.40
   Diarrea see *Diarrea*
Palti, Elías José 36
Parley of Quilin 53
Parleys (Peace Accords) 52–3
Parry, Milman 175, 181
Paulista theatrical movement 89
Paulo (character) 109
Peace (Aristophanes) 136, 139
Pedreira das Almas (*Quarry of Souls*) (Andrade, Jorge) 115, 124, 126
   burial of the dead 118–21, 122–3, 127
   comparison with *Antigone* 116, 117–19, 121–2
   historical setting 116
   Mariana (character) 116, 117, 118, 119, 120, 121, 127
   Martiniano (character) 116
   production history 115, 116, 124, 126
   reception 124–5, 126
   as resistance symbol 123–6, 127
   Urbana (character) 117–18, 119, 122
   Vasconcelos (character) 116, 119, 120, 121
Pereira de Vasconcelos, Bernardo 116
Perón, Eva 218 n.9
Perón, Juán Domingo 33–5
Peronism 33–5, 37, 41
Persians (Aeschylus) 157
Peru 11
Petronius
   Satyrica 77, 89, 90, 96–7
Phaedrus (Plato) 180
Philoctetes (character) 59, 62, 63
Philoctetes (Sophocles) 59, 61, 62, 63, 64
Phoenician Women (Euripides) 158, 159, 165, 166, 246 n.104
Phoenix Too Frequent, A (Fry, Christopher) 90
Piñera, Virgilio
   Electra Garrigó 147, 157
Plato 178
   Phaedrus 180
Plautus
   Amphitruo see *Amphitruo*
Poemas Australes (*Southern Poems*) (Marechal, Leopoldo) 34, 36, 37, 38–9
poetics of Relation 181
Polinice (character in *Antígona: las voces que incendian el desierto*) 200
Polinice (character in *Siete contra tebas, Los*) 158, 165–7
politics 12
   Dido 19
   identity politics 154
Polyzelos (of Syracuse) 169
Pompey (Roman consul) 148

293

Index

Pompeyo (character) 148–9, 150
postcolonialism 3–5, 11
Powers, Melinda 192
privilege 197
Profecía de la graneza de Buenos Aires (*Prophecy of the Grandeur of Buenos Aires*) (Varela, Juan Cruz) 22
Prometeo (Casal, Julián de) 157
Prometheus Bound 157
Puerto Rico 131
    commonwealth status 142
    education system 5
    Generation of the 30s (Generación de los 30) 141
    independence 142
    nationalism 142
    theatre in 140–1, 142
push-pull model 12

Rabelias and his World (Bakhtin, Mikhail) 173
race 70, 171, 196 see also *créolité*
Racine, Jean
    Iphigénie 30
Radrigán, Juan 38, 57
    Medea Mapuche see *Medea Mapuche*
Raízes do Brasil (*Roots of Brazil*) (Holanda, Sérgio Buarque de) 115
raposa e as uvas, A (*The Fox and the Grapes*) (Figueiredo, Guilherme de Oliveira) 77
reception 8, 10
    Dido 20–1
resistance 173, 175, 181
revenge tragedy 48, 50, 54–5
Revermann, Martin 137
Revolta dos Alfaiates (*Revolt of the Tailors*) 122
Rivadavia, Bernardino 20, 21–2, 32
    feliz experiencia, la (*The Happy Experience*) 32
    Varela, Juan Cruz 22
robo de Proserpina y sueño de Endimión, El (*The Snatching of Proserpina and the Dream of Endymion*) (Espinosa Medrano, Juan de) 11
Rock, David 34
Rodrigues, Nelson Falcão 111, 112
    Carioca tragedies 111
    categorization of plays 111
    Dorotéia 101
    dramatic techniques 105, 111
    Family Album 101
    Flower of Obsession 113
    productions 106–7, 108, 110, 111
    Senhora dos Afogados (*Our Lady of the Drowned*) see *Senhora dos Afogados*
Roman mythology 90
Rome 148

Rousseau, Jean-Jacques
    Essay on the Origin of Languages 180
rumination theory 7, 8

San Martin, José de 25
Sánchez, Marcelo 224 n.13
    Filoctetes, la herida y el arco (*Philoctetes, the Wound and the Bow*) see *Filoctetes, la herida y el arco*
Santos, Boaventura de Sousa
    Epistemologies of the South: Justice against Epistemicide 6
São Tomé das Letras 116
Satyrica (Petronius) 77, 89, 90–3, 96–7
scars 195
Schajowicz, Ludwig 157
Seabrook, William
    Magic Island, The 191
Sedgwick, Eve Kosofsky 30
self-reflexivity 60
Senhora dos Afogados (*Our Lady of the Drowned*) (Rodrigues, Nelson Falcão) 101–2
    audience response 111–12
    censorship 113
    chorus, use of 110
    comparison with ancient Greek plays 109, 112
    Eduarda (character) 105–6, 108
    hands in 108
    'masked' reception 101, 102, 112
    masks, use of *110*–11
    Moema (character) 102, 130–8, 109
    Paulo (character) 109
    production history 106–7, 108, 110, 111
    psychology 103, 112
Seven Against Thebes (Aeschylus) 157–65, 168, 169
    Eteocles (character) 162, 246 n.104
Shakespeare, William
    Tempest, The 176–7
Shumway, Nicolas 26
Sicily 169
Siete contra tebas, Los (*Seven against Thebes*) (Arrufat, Antón) 147, 157–8
    censorship 158
    Chorus 159–62
    comparison with *Seven Against Thebes* 158–65, 168, 169
    Cuban Revolution 162, 163, 168
    Etéocles (character) 161, 165–7, 168
    imperialism 159, 162
    nostalgia 165–7
    optimistic ending 168–9
    Polinice (character) 158, 165–7
    production history 169
    reception 158

Index

shield scene 162–5
speaking characters 163–5
UNEAC competition and publication 158, 159, 162
Sigal, Silvia and Verón, Eliseo 37
Silva, António José da
   Amphitrião 97
Silva y Sarmiento, Pedro de
   Al amor de madre no hay afecto que le iguale (There Is no Love Like a Mother's Love) 11
Simões, Sidneia *107*
Sirena (*Mermaid*) (Arriví, Francisco) 141
Siripo (Lavardén, Manuel José de) 23
slavery 179
Sociedad del Buen Gusto del Teatro (Society of Good Taste in the Theatre) 25–6
Socrates, trial of 67
Solibo Magnifique (Chamoiseau, Patrick) 178
Solteros 72 (*Bachelors 72*) (Arriví, Francisco) 132, 138
Sophocles 7
   Antigone 33, 115, 116, 118
   Electra 104, 105–6
   emasculation theme 135
   Oedipus King 77
   Philoctetes 59, 61, 62, 63, 64
Sosia (character) 80, 95
Sotelo Inclán, Jesús
   Malitzin, Medea americana 47
South American Independence: Gender, Politics, Text (Davies, C. et al.) 20
sovereign power 186, 195, 197, 207–8
Spain
   occupation of Chile 47, 50–4
Spanglish 185, 186, 192–3, 196
Spanish Latin America 4
Statius
   Thebaid 23
Stesichorus 169
syncretic cultures 6
Syracuse, Sicily 169

Tell my Horse (Hurston, Zora Neale) 191
Tempest, The (Shakespeare, William) 176–7
Tempête, Une (Césaire, Aimé) 173, 177
'Theatrical Act of Dissent' (McLaughlin, Ellen) 137
Thebaid (Statius) 23
Theron of Acragas 169
Thomas, Richard 197
Thyestes (Diocles) 139
Tiresias (character) 97
Toronto School of Communication 180
Torrance, Isabelle 157, 159
torture 50–1, 119, 123, 125
trabajos de la memoria, Los (Jelin, Elizabeth) 60

Triana, José
   Medea en el Espejo (*Medea in the Mirror*) 147, 157

Urbana (character) 116–17, 119, 122
USA *see also* America
   as coloniser 188
   interests 2, 7
Usted está aquí (*You Are Here*) (Colio, Bárbara) 200

Valadares, João *107*
Valdivia, Pedro de 51
Varela, Juan Cruz 19, 20–1
   Argia 23–4
   Dido see *Dido*
   family/education 24–5
   Greco-Roman corpus 24
   neoclassicism 24, 25
   Profecía de la graneza de Buenos Aires (*Prophecy of the Grandeur of Buenos Aires*) 22
   Rivadavia, Bernardino 22
   as translator of Virgil 25
Vargas, Getúlio 76
Vasconcelos (character) 116, 119, 120, 121
Vega, Lope de
   Arte nuevo de hacer comedias en este tiempo (*New Art of Making Comedies in this Age*) 25
Vejigantes (*Masks*) (Arriví, Francisco) 131, 141
Vélez, Antígona (character) 41–6, 219 n.46
Vélez, Ignacio (character) 39–40
Vélez, Martín (character) 39
Veríssimo, Érico 127
Very Curious Story of the Virtuous Widow of Ephesus, A (*A Muito Curiosa História de Virtuosa Matrona de Éfeso*) (Figueiredo, Guilherme de Oliveira) 77
   comparison with *Deus Dormiu lá em Casa, Um* (*A God Slept Here*) 96–7
   comparison with source text 91–3
   contaminatio 94–9
   Cynthia, widow of Ephesus (character) 93, 96
   desertion 96
   Diana (character) 97–8
   doubles 97, 98
   Endymion (character) 98–9
   female chastity/adultery 97, 98
   gods, the 97, 98, 99
   Jupiter (character) 90, 97, 99
   mourning 92
   political stance 91–3
   production history 89
   themes 90–1, 94–7
Virgil
   Aeneid see *Aeneid*
   Eclogues 22

Index

Vodou 192
vraisemblance 29

Wa Kreyon (*King Creon*) (Moriso-Lewa, Feliks) 188
Wealth (Aristophanes) 139
Western canon 145–7, 154–5, 172, 173
'What a Puerto Rican Theatre Might Be' ('Lo que podría ser un teatro puertorriqueño') (Belaval, Emilio) 140, 141
White Zombie (film) 191
winkas 49–50
women *see also* gender
    chastity/adultery 96–7, 98
    Club de Solteros 141–2
    femicide 199–200, 201, 210
    Lysistrata 137–8, 141
    misogyny 134, 135, 136
    Sedgwick, Eve Kosofsky 30
    as vice 20
    warrior 51
Women at the Thesmophoria (Aristophanes) 135, 139
writing 180

Xanthias: Dialogues on Dramatic Creation (Figueiredo, Guilherme de Oliveira) 76, 78–9, 86, 90

Yugoslavia 175

Zanatta, Loris 34
zombies 191
Zweimal Amphitryon (Kaiser, Georg) 83

www.ingramcontent.com/pod-product-compliance
Lightning Source LLC
Chambersburg PA
CBHW070017010526
44117CB00011B/1608